REAL WORLD
MACRO

THIRTY-EIGHTH EDITION

EDITED BY ED FORD, ELIZABETH T. HENDERSON, BRYAN SNYDER,

AND THE *DOLLARS & SENSE* COLLECTIVE

REAL WORLD MACRO, THIRTY-EIGHTH EDITION

Published by: Economic Affairs Bureau, Inc. d/b/a *Dollars & Sense*
Mailing address: P.O. Box 209, Portsmouth, NH 03802
617-447-2177; dollars@dollarsandsense.org.
For order information, contact Economic Affairs Bureau or visit: www.dollarsandsense.org.

Real World Macro is edited by the *Dollars & Sense* Collective, which also publishes *Dollars & Sense* magazine and the classroom books *Real World Micro, Current Economic Issues, Real World Globalization, Labor and the Global Economy, Real World Latin America, Real World Labor, Real World Banking and Finance, The Wealth Inequality Reader, The Economics of the Environment, Introduction to Political Economy, Unlevel Playing Fields: Understanding Wage Inequality and Discrimination, Our Economic Well-Being, The Costs of Empire*, and *The Coronavirus Crisis Reader*.

The 2021 *Dollars & Sense* Collective:

Betsy Aron, Will Beaman, Sarah Cannon, Ed Ford, Elizabeth T. Henderson, Peter Kolozi, Tom Louie, John Miller, Jawied Nawabi, Zoe Sherman, Bryan Snyder, Abhilasha Srivastava, Chris Sturr, and Jeanne Winner.

Co-editors of this volume: Ed Ford, Elizabeth T. Henderson, and Bryan Snyder

Design and layout: Elizabeth T. Henderson
Cover image: The Marriner S. Eccles Federal Reserve Board Building houses the main offices of the Board of Governors of the Federal Reserve System. February 26, 2013. Credit: LunchboxLarry, via Flickr, CC BY 2.0.

Printed in U.S.A.

CONTENTS

INTRODUCTION   *1*

CHAPTER 1 • PERSPECTIVES ON MACROECONOMIC THEORY
Introduction   *7*
1.1 Covid-19 and Catastrophe Capitalism   *John Bellamy Foster and Intan Suwandi*   *9*
1.2 The "Shock Doctrine," "Disaster Capitalism," and Covid-19   *Bryan Snyder*   *13*
1.3 What's Wrong with Neoliberalism?   *Robert Pollin*   *16*
1.4 Opening Pandora's Box: The Basics of Marxist Economics   *Alejandro Reuss*   *22*
1.5 Sharing the Wealth of the Commons   *Peter Barnes*   *27*

CHAPTER 2 • MACROECONOMIC MEASUREMENT
Introduction   *35*
2.1 What Does It Mean to Be "Better Off"?   *Zoe Sherman*   *37*
2.2 GDP and Its Discontents   *Alejandro Reuss*   *46*
2.3 Measuring Economic Development   *Alejandro Reuss*   *51*
2.4 The Care Theory of Value   *Nancy Folbre*   *56*
2.5 Undercounting the Poor   *Jeannette Wicks-Lim*   *58*
2.6 Traditional Measures of Unemployment Are Missing the Mark   *Mark Paul*   *64*

CHAPTER 3 • ECONOMIC GROWTH AND BUSINESS CYCLES
Introduction   *67*
3.1 Dating the Recession   *John Miller*   *69*
3.2 Growth, Growth, Growth: What Will Happen?   *Arthur MacEwan*   *71*
3.3 A Future for Growth—If We Choose It?   *Gerald Friedman*   *78*
3.4 Growing Together, Flying Apart   *Gerald Friedman*   *83*

CHAPTER 4 • UNEMPLOYMENT AND INFLATION
Introduction   *87*
4.1 How the Coronavirus Crisis Became an Economic Crisis   *Alejandro Reuss*   *89*
4.2 App Workers in the Covid-19 Economy   *Nicole Aschoff*   *97*
4.3 The Relationship of Unemployment and Inflation   *Ramaa Vasudevan*   *102*
4.4 The "Natural Rate" of Unemployment   *Robert Pollin*   *104*

4.5 Getting Up to Speed on the Minimum Wage   *John Miller   109*
4.6 The Actual Effects of Enhanced Unemployment Benefits
     John Miller   114
4.7 Keynes, Wage and Price "Stickiness," and Deflation   *Alejandro Reuss   118*

CHAPTER 5 • WEALTH, INEQUALITY, AND POVERTY
Introduction   *123*
5.1 Pundits Claim Fighting Inequality Is Bad for Low-Wage Workers
     John Miller   126
5.2 Geese, Golden Eggs, and Traps: Why Inequality Is Bad for the Economy
     Chris Tilly   130
5.3 Can the Decline of Unions be Reversed?   *Arthur MacEwan   136*
5.4 Fifty Years After the Kerner Commission
     Janelle Jones, John Schmitt, and Valerie Wilson   140
5.5 Undervaluation is a Certainty: Measuring Black Women's Wage Gap
     Interview with Michelle Holder   147
5.6 Inequality, Sunk Costs, and Climate Justice   *Frank Ackerman   153*
5.7 Are Taxes the Best Way of Dealing with Inequality?
     Arthur MacEwan   157

CHAPTER 6 • FISCAL POLICY, DEFICITS, AND AUSTERITY
Introduction   *161*
6.1 The Coronavirus Consensus: "Spend, Spend, Spend"
     Gerald Epstein   164
6.2 State and Local Austerity   *Amanda Page Hoongrajok   170*
6.3 The Ideological Attack on Job Creation   *Marty Wolfson   176*
6.4 Fiscal Policy and "Crowding Out"   *Alejandro Reuss   181*
6.5 The Green New Deal as an Anti-Neoliberalism Program
     Robert Pollin   185
6.6 Financial Transactions Taxes   *Dean Baker   188*
6.7 Reform of Global Taxation Cannot Wait   *Jayati Ghosh   191*

CHAPTER 7 • MONEY AND MONETARY POLICY
Introduction   *195*
7.1 The Fed and the Coronavirus Crisis   *Gerald Epstein   198*
7.2 It's Time to Ditch "Pay-For" Politics
     Yeva Nersisyan and L. Randall Wray   201
7.3 What Is Money?   *Doug Orr   208*
7.4 Should We Blame "Fractional Reserve" Banking?   *Arthur MacEwan   212*
7.5 Pushing on Strings   *Gerald Friedman   214*
7.6 Keynes and the Limits of Monetary Policy   *Alejandro Reuss   216*
7.7 Dollar Dominance   *Arthur MacEwan   220*

CHAPTER 8 • FINANCE, SAVINGS, AND INVESTMENT
Introduction   *225*
8.1 Financialization: A Primer   *Ramaa Vasudevan   228*

8.2 From "Boring" Banking to "Roaring" Banking
    An interview with Gerald Epstein   231
8.3 The Stock Market and the Coronavirus Crisis   *John Miller*   239
8.4 Stock Buybacks: Any Positive Outcome?   *Arthur MacEwan*   242
8.5 Is "Short Selling" Bad For the Economy?   *Arthur MacEwan*   245
8.6 Bubble, Bubble, Toil, and Trouble   *Alejandro Reuss*   248
8.7 We're All Minskyites Now   *Robert Pollin*   252
8.8 Why Is Student Debt Cancelation Such a Big Deal?
    Arthur MacEwan   255

CHAPTER 9 • THE GLOBAL ECONOMY

Introduction   *259*
9.1 The Pandemic and the Global Economy   *Jayati Ghosh*   262
9.2 Neoliberalism as Neocolonialism   *Jayati Ghosh*   269
9.3 The Gospel of Free Trade: The New Evangelists   *Arthur MacEwan*   275
9.4 The Globalization Clock   *Thomas Palley*   285
9.5 Does U.S. Prosperity *Depend* on Exploitation?   *Arthur MacEwan*   288
9.6 Essential—and Expendable—Mexican Labor
    Mateo Crossa and James M. Cypher   292
9.7 Stringent, Stingy, and Severe: The Covid-19 Crisis in Modi's India
    Smriti Rao   301

CHAPTER 10 • RESISTANCE AND ALTERNATIVES

Introduction   *309*
10.1 Solidarity Beyond the Crisis   *Francisco Pérez and Luis Feliz Leon*   312
10.2 What Would Full Employment Cost?   *Arthur MacEwan*   319
10.3 In the Driver's Seat   *Luis Feliz Leon*   322
10.4 Police Violence Is Enabled by Massive Spending   *Sonali Kolhatkar*   331
10.5 International Labor Standards   *Arthur MacEwan*   334
10.6 Land Reform: A Precondition for Sustainable Economic Development
    Jawied Nawabi   336
10.7 India's Farmers' Protests   *Sirisha Naidu*   341
10.8 Bubble Breakthrough: The NBA Work Stoppage   *Abdul Malik*   350

Contributors   *355*

INTRODUCTION

"I survived 2020. Let's not do this again."
—Coffee mug slogan

As we slowly emerge from a year of lockdowns, social distancing, and Zoom teaching, we find ourselves a bit dazed but guardedly optimistic as we return to some form of "normalcy." Unfortunately, as the economy opens up, we find a changed landscape of unanticipated new macroeconomic problems as well as a host of old problems which have been aggravated by the pandemic. The Covid-19 pandemic was the single largest economic event in this country's history, as lockdowns throughout the country resulted in the abrupt idling of the more than 22 million workers—which comprised 6.7% of the labor force—who filed for unemployment benefits between March and April of 2020. As a point of reference, at the lowest point of the 2009 Great Recession, 2.6 million workers filed unemployment claims, constituting just 0.9% of the labor force. This is a massive shock. The pandemic was a "stress test" on our economic and social system which exposed the inadequacies of a health care system and social safety net that were not up to the task. The pandemic is also a wake-up call and a harbinger of things to come, unless we adapt accordingly.

In our study of macroeconomics, the Covid-19 pandemic is a game changer. Every aspect of macroeconomics as we know it has been affected by this global crisis. Every aspect. The 38th edition of *Real World Macro* contains the most up-to-date material and analysis covering the pandemic and its economic consequences.

As with the Great Financial Crisis of 2008, we find ourselves in another "teachable moment" in history in which we can test economic theories for the relative veracity of their claims. We can also begin to think about and evaluate policy and policy alternatives at the municipal, state, and federal level.

We have put together this 38th edition of *Real World Macro* to assist students in understanding what has happened in the wake of the Covid-19 pandemic and to help them transform this moment of crisis into a future that is safe and equitable for all.

THE TWO ECONOMIES

It sometimes seems that the United States has not one, but two economies. The first exists in economics textbooks and in the minds of many government policymakers. It is an economy in which no one is involuntarily unemployed for long, families are rewarded with an ever-improving standard of living, and anyone who works

1

hard can live the American Dream. In this economy, people are free and roughly equal, and individuals carefully look after themselves, making voluntary choices to advance their own economic interests. Government has some limited role in this world, but it is increasingly marginal, since the macroeconomy is a self-regulating system of wealth generation.

The second economy features vast disparities of income, wealth, and power. It is an economy where economic instability and downward mobility are facts of life. Jobs disappear, workers suffer long spells of unemployment, and new jobs seldom afford the same standard of living as those lost. As for the government, it sometimes adopts policies that ameliorate the abuses of capitalism, and other times does just the opposite, but it is always an active and essential participant in economic life.

If you are reading this introduction, you are probably a student in an introductory college course in macroeconomics. Your textbook will introduce you to the first economy, the harmonious world of self-regulating and stable markets. *Real World Macro* will introduce you to the second.

Why "Real World" Macro?

A standard economics textbook is full of powerful concepts. It is also, by its nature, a limited window into the economy. What is taught in most introductory macroeconomics courses today is a relatively narrow set of concepts. Inspired by neoclassical economic theory, most textbooks depict an inherently stable economy in little need of government intervention. Fifty years ago, textbooks were very different. Keynesian economic theory, which holds that government action can and must stabilize modern monetized economies, occupied a central place in introductory textbooks. Even Marxist economics, with its piercing analysis of class structure and the inherent instability of capitalism, appeared regularly on the pages of those textbooks. This contraction of economics education has turned some introductory courses into little more than celebrations of today's economy as "the best of all possible worlds."

Real World Macro, designed as a supplement to standard macroeconomics textbooks, is dedicated to widening the scope of economic inquiry. Its articles confront mainstream theory with a more complex reality—providing vivid, real-world illustrations of economic concepts. And where most texts uncritically present the key assumptions and propositions of traditional macroeconomic theory, *Real World Macro* asks provocative questions: What are alternative propositions about how the economy operates and who it serves? What difference do such propositions make? If this is not the best of all possible macroeconomic worlds, what might make the actual world better?

For instance, *Real World Macro*'s authors question the conventional wisdom that economic growth "lifts all boats," or benefits all of us. While mainstream textbooks readily allow that economic growth has not benefited all of us to the same degree, we go further and ask: Who benefits from economic growth and how much? Who has been left behind by the economic growth of the last few decades? The answers are quite disturbing. Today, economic growth, when it occurs, benefits far fewer of us than it did just a few decades ago. Economic growth during the last business-cycle expansion did more to boost profits and less to lift wages than during any economic upswing since World War II. This pattern continued during the long but slow recovery (which, with Covid-19, recently came to a halt) following the Great Recession. Spreading the benefits of economic growth more widely, through public policies intended to improve the lot of most people in the work-a-day world, would not only make our economy more equitable, but would also go a long way toward restoring more robust growth in the U.S. economy.

Thirteen years after the Great Recession, the worst effects of this financial crisis still linger—and they have now been compounded by the yet larger Covid-19 crisis. But you might not know that the day-to-day operation of the market economy—unregulated financial markets, the increasing concentration of power in the hands of business, and burgeoning inequality—caused the accumulation of debt that set the stage for the Great Recession, and also laid the groundwork for the current global health care and economic catastrophe. Explaining how and why these kinds of crises happen and what to do about it is every responsible economist's job.

During the start of the Covid-19 pandemic, we were told that we were all "in the same boat." But it has become increasingly obvious that some boats are significantly more buoyant and pleasant than others. As we are faced with persistently high levels of unemployment, the social safety net is wearing thin and low-income workers, in particular women, will bear the brunt of these ever-increasing burdens. On the other end of the wealth and income spectrum, the superrich will remain not only unscathed, but in most cases have realized obscene profits during the pandemic.

This lends credence to a more "visible hand" approach by government in order to ensure sustained full employment. Such a move would go a long way toward improving the lot of those who have fallen on hard times. Genuine and sustained full employment, with unemployment rates as low as 2%, would lead to "a major reduction in the incidence of poverty, homelessness, sickness, and crime," as William Vickery, the Nobel Prize–winning economist, once argued. We think that policies like these, and the alternative perspectives that lie behind them, are worth debating—and that requires hearing a range of views.

What's in This Book

Real World Macro is organized to follow the outline of a standard economics textbook. Each chapter leads off with a brief introduction, including study questions for the chapter, and then provides several articles, mostly drawn from *Dollars & Sense* magazine, that illustrate the chapter's key concepts. Here is a quick walk through the contents:

Chapter 1, Perspectives on Macroeconomic Theory, introduces alternatives to neoclassical-inspired macroeconomic theory. Right up front we have a piece by John Bellamy Foster and Intan Suwandi, which introduces the reader to the emergence of zoonotic diseases, such as Covid-19, and shows how they are linked to economic activities that bring people into close contact with the various species of animals that are natural carriers of these pathogens. The second explores the American response to the Covid-19 pandemic, and offers a primer on the "shock doctrine" and "disaster capitalism." The chapter then looks at what's wrong with neoliberal policies that would turn the operation of the domestic and international economy over to unregulated markets. Finally, the chapter moves beyond Keynesianism to include Marxist and environmentalist perspectives on the macroeconomy.

Chapter 2, Macroeconomic Measurement, takes a critical look at the standard measures of economic activity, such as gross domestic product (GDP), the unemployment rate, the Consumer Price Index (and other price indices), and the official poverty rate. What do these measures actually tell us about the quality of life in today's economy, and what crucial aspects of economic life do they leave uncounted? This chapter underscores that economic measurement issues are not just dry, technical questions for economists to answer—they play a critical role in defining the economic problems that face us and the economic goals we aspire to reach.

Chapter 3, Economic Growth and Business Cycles, covers two of the most important issues in macroeconomics: the causes of cyclical fluctuations in economic activity—the boom-and-bust patterns of capitalist economies—and the factors determining long-term economic growth and development. It also addresses the challenges facing the developing world, such as transitioning away from dependence on resource extraction and commodities booms, developing domestic demand-driven approaches to growth and development, and avoiding debt traps. Finally, this chapter explores the issue of environmental sustainability and the pairing of environmental goals and economic growth, as well as the widening gulf between the "real economy" and the "surreal economy."

Chapter 4, Unemployment and Inflation, looks at the relationships between these two macroeconomic variables and addresses the causes of unemployment and the impact of inflation, particularly in the wake of the Covid-19 pandemic. The first article explores the origins of the current economic crisis, and the second takes a look at the pandemic's impact on app workers. The chapter then continues with an article on the relationship between job loss and inflation, and a discussion of the "natural rate of unemployment," offering an interpretation that is very different from that intended by its originators. Then, we find two articles on the economic consequences of an increase in the minimum wage and the impact of unemployment benefits. Wrapping up the chapter is an article on the measurement of unemployment and the "stickiness" of wages, which have some rather deep and compelling roots in theory.

Chapter 5, Wealth, Inequality, and Poverty, examines these three outcomes of economic activity and growth. The articles in this chapter show who is accumulating wealth and who isn't, both in the United States and worldwide. They examine the reasons for increasing inequality in the United States over the last several decades and argue that inequality is not a prerequisite for economic growth, but rather a major contributor to today's economic problems. This chapter also includes a particularly timely article on the relationship between global inequality, climate change, and climate justice. Rounding out the chapter is an article that explores how to use taxes to address economic inequality.

Chapter 6, Fiscal Policy, Deficits, and Austerity, contests the orthodox view that short-term deficit reduction should be a high priority, arguing that fiscal stimulus is necessary to tackle stagnant growth and promote the prompt recovery of employment. The chapter begins with articles that examine the emergency policy decisions made to address the Covid-19 pandemic and the negative impacts of austerity at the state and local level. Next is a series of articles focusing on job creation, fiscal policy, and "crowding out," and an article that makes the case for the Green New Deal as an alternative to the prevailing neoclassical system. Finally, we close out this chapter with articles that assess some of the recent proposals for financial transactions and wealth taxes in the United States and call for global tax reforms and improved enforcement.

Chapter 7, Money and Monetary Policy, looks at what money is, how money is created, and how the Federal Reserve conducts monetary policy. The chapter starts off with coverage of the Fed's response to the coronavirus pandemic, followed by an article that highlights the positive role Modern Monetary Theory (MMT) can play in addressing the profound health and economic crises created by the pandemic. The next article takes us through the basics of money and the monetary system. We then present three articles on "fractional reserve" banking, the Fed, and the limits of monetary policy as a stimulus for weak economies. We end this chapter with a primer on the history and role of the U.S. dollar as the international currency of exchange.

Chapter 8, Savings, Investment, and Finance, peers inside the world of finance and comes up with some probing questions. What factors affect the pace of investment? What role did financial deregulation and exotic new financial instruments play in the economic crisis? Does the stock market reflect what's happening in the "real" economy? What are the sources of financial "bubbles"? And what alternative public policies can promote stable investment and functional financial markets? Primers on financialization, stock buybacks, and short selling, as well as Hyman Minsky's Financial Instability Hypothesis, all lend themselves to the analysis of both the financial crisis of 2007 and the current global health and financial crisis. The chapter concludes with an examination of the student debt crisis.

Chapter 9, The Global Economy, assesses the prevailing neoliberal policy prescriptions for the global economy and offers alternatives to them in light of the Covid-19 pandemic. This chapter opens with an article that examines the effect of the pandemic on the global economy, followed by an article that examines the impact of neoliberalism and neocolonialism on the Global South. The next two articles criticize globalization based on "free trade" and financial liberalization, looking closely at its effect on economic growth and development, as well as inequality, poverty, and labor conditions. They consider the changing place of the United States in the global economy and the impacts on businesses and households in the United States and worldwide. The next article in this chapter addresses underlying questions related to trade and inequality. Is trade truly fair and equal, with all parties benefitting equally? Next, we look at how the pandemic affected Mexican labor on both sides of the U.S. border. The article documents the abuses of Mexican workers found themselves both "essential" and sick. We conclude this chapter with a case study of India and its botched response to the Covid-19 pandemic.

Chapter 10, Resistance and Alternatives, returns to many of the issues covered in the course of the previous nine chapters, but with a special focus on challenges to prevailing economic policies and institutions. The chapter kicks off with an article that lays the groundwork for transformative changes in a whole host of areas that were affected by the pandemic; "building back better" is indeed the mantra for moving forward. Next is a short article on the cost and benefit of full employment. Then, we have an article about a ridesharing drivers' cooperative in New York City, followed by another article on why the United States needs to defund bloated and militarized police departments. Next, we cover why the right to form a union is a crucial step in improving workplace conditions, and how to achieve sustainable economic development, as well as the link between land reform and development. Then we have an article on the truly massive protests in India by farmers resisting neoliberal reforms. Finally, closing out this edition is an article about the remarkable work stoppage by NBA players during the peak of the Covid-19 pandemic. This article shows how people can step up, no matter how dire the circumstances, and offer safer and more equitable alternatives to the status quo.

Chapter 1

PERSPECTIVES ON MACROECONOMIC THEORY

INTRODUCTION

"... anyone who believes exponential growth can go on forever in a finite world is either a madman or an economist."
—Kenneth Boulding

Years ago, political economist Bob Sutcliffe developed a surefire economic indicator that he called the Marx/Keynes ratio—the ratio of references to Karl Marx to references to John Maynard Keynes in Paul Samuelson's *Economics*, the best-selling introductory economics textbook in the decades following World War II. During a recession or period of sluggish economic growth, the Marx/Keynes ratio would climb, as social commentators and even economists fretted over the future of capitalism. During economic booms, however, Marx's predictions of the collapse of capitalism disappeared from the pages of Samuelson's textbook, while the paeans to Keynesian demand-management policies multiplied.

Today, Sutcliffe's ratio wouldn't work very well. Marx has been pushed off the pages of most introductory macroeconomics textbooks altogether, and even Keynes has been left with only a minor role. Our authors don't agree that these important thinkers should be marginalized. In this chapter, they critically assess the classical-inspired mainstream models and reintroduce the dissident schools of thought that have been purged from economics textbooks in recent decades. And they offer a serious look at the forces that brought on the economic crisis and what to do about them.

We currently find ourselves in a unique and perilous situation, both globally and domestically, as what had been a fully globalized neoliberal world economy has suddenly been brought to a grinding halt. Every aspect of our analysis of the macroeconomy has now been brought into play as we attempt to sort out the wreckage of global neoliberalism with domestic attempts to deal with a profound economic and social crisis in the wake of the Covid-19 pandemic.

We begin this edition with the "800-pound gorilla in the room"—the Covid-19 pandemic. Article 1.1. by John Bellamy Foster and Intan Suwandi delves into the emergence of zoonotic diseases, such as Covid-19, and the economic forces that put people in contact with the fauna that are natural carriers of these pathogens. A cautionary tale of things to come.

Next, we have a brief primer by Bryan Snyder (Article 1.2) on a very timely concept, Naomi Klein's "shock doctrine." We find that the principles outlined in Klein's 2007 book, *The Shock Doctrine*, are being utilized by the current regime in order to provide ample opportunities for pandemic profiteering in a privatized system of disaster capitalism.

Then, economist Robert Pollin (Article 1.3) tackles the underpinnings of neoliberal policy prescriptions for the global economy. As he sees it, unfettered globalization will be unable to resolve three basic problems: an ever-larger "reserve army of the unemployed" that reduces the bargaining power of workers in all countries (the "Marx problem"); the inherent instability and volatility of investment and financial markets (the "Keynes problem"); and the erosion of "fairness" and a sense of "the common good" that lend legitimacy to the state (the "Polanyi problem").

Economist Alejandro Reuss contributes a primer on Marxist economics (Article 1.4). Marx rejected the idea of a self-equilibrating economy and argued that capitalism was inherently dynamic and unstable. Reuss describes some of Marx's key ideas, including the nature of capitalist exploitation, and what Marx saw as two ingredients of an eventual crisis of capitalism: overproduction and the falling rate of profit.

Finally, in Article 1.5, Peter Barnes focuses our attention on the oft-ignored forms of wealth that we do not own privately, but are held in "commons." He challenges the way that conventional economists view the environment and other goods that are shared by many people.

Discussion Questions

1. (Article 1.1) What is the "One Health Framework" perspective in assessing the origins and spread of pandemics? What is the "Structural One Health" perspective? What is the role of neoliberalism in driving the "Structural One Health" perspective?

2. (Article 1.2) What is the "shock doctrine?" What is "disaster capitalism?" Is such a system of public disaster relief "efficient?"

3. (Article 1.3) Summarize the Marx, Keynes, and Polanyi problems. Why does Pollin think that neoliberal globalization policies will be unable to resolve them?

4. (Article 1.4) What roles do a "falling rate of profit," a "reserve army of the unemployed," and "overproduction" play in Marx's theory of capitalist crisis? Do you think today's macroeconomy displays any of those tendencies?

5. (Article 1.5) What is a "commons"? According to Barnes, how has our common wealth been "given away"? What do you think of his plans on how to take it back?

Article 1.1

COVID-19 AND CATASTROPHE CAPITALISM

BY JOHN BELLAMY FOSTER AND INTAN SUWANDI
January/February 2021

This article was abridged and edited by the D&S Collective. The original version of this article appeared in the June 2020 issue of Monthly Review magazine.—Editors

The global pandemic that emerged with the sudden appearance of the coronavirus has shown how the current global system of capitalism has left the world vulnerable to catastrophe. Public services and the institutions of public health—eroded with decades of budget cuts—have been unable to cope with the pandemic. Like most of the corporate world, pharmaceutical companies were incentivized to reward shareholders through stock-buyback schemes instead of investing in research and development, which would have made a significant difference in their ability to quickly deliver a vaccine for the disease. However, what's often overlooked is the underlying structural reasons for why this global economic and health crisis is happening. It is true that, in our globalized economy, travel has increased exponentially in the past couple of decades both for business and pleasure, and that this can contribute to the global spread of communicable diseases. Yet that alone does not explain why we have seen a series of infectious disease outbreaks over the same time period, especially zoonotic diseases (or zoonoses), that is, diseases that are caused by pathogens transmitted to humans from wild or domesticated animals, such as SARS, MERS, Ebola, H1N1, and now, Covid-19. This article focuses on the role of the global economy in general, and agribusinesses in particular, in causing ecological degradation, emergent diseases, and potential global pandemics.

During the last decade, a holistic One Health-One World approach to the causes and origins of diseases arose in response to these outbreaks. The One Health model is a multidisciplinary approach that recognizes the connection between human and animal health and their shared environment. With the involvement of the World Bank, the World Health Organization (WHO), and the Centers for Disease Control and Prevention (CDC) in the United States, this approach makes it possible for people who are involved in protecting the health of humans, animals, and the environment—including public health providers, private medicine, agribusinesses, and pharmaceutical companies—to work together to develop a holistic approach to preventing the spread of zoonotic diseases. However, over time the original ecological framework that motivated the One Health approach has become dominated by agribusinesses, which have systemically downplayed the connections between epidemiological crises and the capitalist world economy.

While the One Health framework still dominates the national and international agencies' approach to public health issues, a critical perspective that comes out of the Marxist tradition, known as Structural One Health, has been proposed as an alternative way of understanding the causes and origins of disease. For proponents of Structural

One Health, the key is to ascertain how pandemics in the contemporary global economy are connected to the rapidly changing environmental conditions that are driven by the need of global capitalism for continuous growth. Instead of concentrating on certain locales in which novel viruses emerge as random events, this approach aims to understand local developments in the context of how these localities are connected to the global capitalist economy. Specifically, Structural One Health scientists explicitly recognize the role of global agribusiness in the destruction of natural ecosystems and focus on commodity chains as the global economic conduits of disease transmission.

In one of the most prominent works illustrating this approach, *Big Farms Make Big Flu*, Rob Wallace states that the breeding of monocultures of genetically similar animals, including massive hog feedlots and vast poultry farms, coupled with rapid deforestation and the chaotic mixing of wild birds and other wildlife with industrial animal production, have created the conditions for the spread of deadly diseases such as SARS, MERS, Ebola, H1N1, H5N1, and now Covid19. "Agribusinesses," Wallace writes, "are moving their companies into the Global South to take advantage of cheap labor and cheap land," and "spreading their entire production line across the world." As a result, increased interactions between birds, hogs, and humans produce more new diseases. "Influenzas," Wallace tells us, "now emerge by way of a globalized network of corporate feedlot production and trade, wherever specific strains first evolve. With flocks and herds whisked from region to region multiple strains of influenza are continually introduced into localities filled with populations of susceptible animals." Large-scale commercial poultry operations have been shown to have much higher odds of hosting these virulent zoonoses. Value-chain analysis has been used to trace the origin of new influenzas such as H5N1 along the poultry production commodity chain. The interconnected global commodity chains of agribusinesses, which provide the basis for the appearance of novel zoonoses, ensure that these pathogens move rapidly from one place to another, with human hosts moving in days, even hours, from one part of the globe to the other. Wallace and his colleagues write, "Some pathogens emerge right out of centers of production. ... But many like Covid-19 originate on the frontiers of capital production. Indeed, at least 60% of novel human pathogens emerge by spilling over from wild animals to local human communities (before the more successful ones spread to the rest of the world)."

Commodity Chains and Covid-19

Since the late 20th century, capitalist globalization has increasingly adopted the form of interlinked commodity chains controlled by multinational corporations, connecting various production zones, primarily in the Global South, with the center of world consumption, finance, and accumulation, primarily in the Global North. In this system, exorbitant profits are made not only from global labor arbitrage, through which multinational corporations overexploit industrial labor, but also increasingly through global land arbitrage, in which agribusiness multinationals expropriate cheap land in the Global South so as to produce export crops mainly for sale in the Global North. In the past decade, more than 81 million acres of land worldwide—an area the size of Portugal—have been sold off to foreign investors. Some of these deals are what's known as "land grabs": land deals that happen without the free, prior, and informed consent of communities. These conditions have been promoted by various development banks in the context of what is euphemistically known as "territorial restructuring," which involves removing subsistence farmers and small producers from the land at the behest of multinational corporations, primarily agribusinesses, as well as rapid deforestation and ecosystem destruction.

The 2008 spike in food prices—and the ensuing food shortages—triggered a rush in land deals in order to expand production. While these large-scale land deals were supposedly being struck to grow food, the crops grown on the land rarely feed local people. Instead, the land is used to grow profitable crops—like sugarcane, palm oil, and soy—often for export. In fact, more than 60% of crops grown on land bought by foreign investors in developing countries are intended for export, instead of for feeding local communities. Worse still, two-thirds of these agricultural land deals are in countries with serious hunger problems. The result is the mass migration of these communities, with people being thrown off the land. As subsistence farmers and small producers, and their practices, disappear, the agricultural ecology of whole regions is altered, replacing traditional agriculture with monocultures, and pushing rural populations into urban slums.

These urban slums contribute to the transmission of zoonotic diseases in multiple ways. The unequal distribution of health services, clean food and water, and sanitation lead to hotspots of diseases within cities. Cities also promote the increased movement of people, animals, and wildlife products between rural and urban locations—migrants may introduce zoonotic diseases to cities if they travel with animals or may also arrive in cities already infected with pathogens.

Buildings and impervious surfaces in urban areas, which prevent rainwater from soaking into the ground, may increase the prevalence of waterborne viruses and disease-carrying mosquitos. And as human settlements increasingly encroach on wild areas, human-wildlife interactions increase. As a result, humans and their domesticated animals (including livestock) are increasingly exposed to diseases that previously only impacted wild animals.

Covid-19, like other dangerous diseases that have emerged or reemerged in recent years, is closely related to a complex set of factors, including: 1) the focus of global agribusiness on breeding monocultures of genetically similar animals, which increases the likelihood of transmitting zoonotic diseases from wild to domestic animals and then to humans; 2) the destruction of wild habitats and disruption of the activities of wild species; and 3) the fact that human beings are living in closer proximity to wild areas. There is little doubt that global commodity chains and the kinds of connectivity that they have produced have become vectors for the rapid transmission of disease, throwing this whole globally exploitative pattern of development into question.

Nor are new viruses the only emerging global health problem. The overuse of antibiotics within agribusinesses, as well as modern medicine, has led to the dangerous growth of bacterial superbugs causing increasing numbers of deaths, which by midcentury could surpass annual cancer deaths, leading the WHO in 2018 to declare a "global health emergency." As the Structural One Health approach has suggested, the origin of the new pandemics can be traced to the overall problem of ecological destruction brought on by capitalism. Since communicable diseases, due to the unequal conditions created by capitalism, fall heaviest on the working class and the poor, the system that generates such diseases in the pursuit of wealth can be charged with social murder. The future of humanity in the 21st century lies not in the direction of increased economic and ecological exploitation and expropriation, imperialism, and war. Rather, attaining what Karl Marx called "freedom in general" and the preservation of a viable "planetary metabolism" are the most pressing necessities today in determining the human present and future, and even human survival. ❏

Sources: John Bellamy Foster, "Late Imperialism," *Monthly Review*, July-August 2019 (monthlyreview.org); Samir Amin, *Modern Imperialism, Monopoly Finance Capital, and Marx's Law of Value* (Monthly Review Press, 2018); Intan Suwandi, *Value Chains* (Monthly Review Press, 2019); Intan Suwandi, R. Jamil Jonna and John Bellamy Foster, "Global Commodity Chains and the New Imperialism," *Monthly Review*, March 2019 (monthlyreview.org); Holt-Giménez, *A Foodie's Guide to Capitalism* (Monthly Review Press, 2017); Evan Tarver, "Value Chain vs. Supply Chain," Investopedia, March 24, 2020 (Investopedia.com); Terence Hopkins and Immanuel Wallerstein, "Commodity Chains in the World Economy Prior to 1800," *Review*, Summer 1986; Karl Marx, *Capital, Vol. 1* (Penguin Classics, 1993); Robert G. Wallace, Luke Bergmann, Richard Kock, et al., "The Dawn of Structural One Health: A New Science Tracking Disease Emergence Along Circuits of Capital," *Social Science and Medicine*, March 2015; Rob [Robert G.] Wallace, "We Need a Structural One Health," *Farming Pathogens*, August 3, 2012; J. Zinsstag, "Convergence of EcoHealth and One Health," *Ecohealth*, Feb. 2013; Victor Galaz et al., "The Political Economy of One Health," STEPS Centre, Political Economy of Knowledge and Policy Working Paper Series, 2015 (steps-centre.org); Rodrick Wallace, Luis Fernando Chavez, Luke R. Bergmann, et al., *Clear-Cutting Disease Control: Capital-Led Deforestation, Public Health Austerity, and Vector-Borne Infection* (Springer, 2018); Rob Wallace et al., "COVID-19 and Circuits of Capital," *Monthly Review*, May 2020 (monthlyreview. org); István Mészáros, *Beyond Capital* (Monthly Review Press, 1995); Richard Levins and Richard Lewontin, *The Dialectical Biologist* (Harvard University Press, 1985); Rob Wallace, *Big Farms Make Big Flu* (Monthly Review Press, 2016); Rob Wallace, "Notes on a Novel Coronavirus," MR Online, Jan. 29, 2020 (mronline.org); John Bellamy Foster, Brett Clark, and Richard York, *The Ecological Rift* (Monthly Review Press, 2010); John Bellamy Foster, *The Return of Nature* (Monthly Review Press, 2020); Richard Levins, "Is Capitalism a Disease?," *Monthly Review*, September 2000 (monthlyreview. org); Howard Waitzkin, *The Second Sickness* (Free Press, 1983); Mathilde Paul et al., "Practices Associated with Highly Pathogenic Avian Influenza Spread in Traditional Poultry Marketing Chains," *Acta Tropica*, 2013; Philip McMichael, "Feeding the World," *Socialist Register 2007: Coming to Terms with Nature*, ed. Leo Panitch and Colin Leys (Monthly Review Press, 2007); Mike Davis, *Planet of Slums* (Verso, 2016); Mike Davis interviewed by Mada Masr, "Mike Davis on Pandemics, Super-Capitalism, and the Struggles of Tomorrow," Mada Masr, March 30, 2020 (madamasr. com); Walden Bello, "Coronavirus and the Death of 'Connectivity,'" *Foreign Policy in Focus*, March 22, 2010; Shannon K. O'Neil, "How to Pandemic Proof Globalization," *Foreign Affairs*, April 1, 2020 (foreignaffairs.com); Stefano Feltri, "Why Coronavirus Triggered the First Global Supply Chain Crisis," ProMarket, March 5, 2020 (promarket.org); Francisco Betti and Per Kristian Hong, "Coronavirus Is Disrupting Global Value Chains. Here's How Companies Can Respond," World Economic Forum, Feb. 27, 2020; Ahmed Mushfiq Mobarak and Zachary Barnett-Howell, "Poor Countries Need to Think Twice About Social Distancing," *Foreign Policy*, April 10, 2020; "Analysis: The Pandemic Is Ravaging the World's Poor Even If They Are Untouched by the Virus," *Washington Post*, April 15, 2020 (washingtonpost.com); Guy Standing, *Plunder of the Commons: A Manifesto for Sharing Public Health* (Pelican, 2019).

Article 1.2

THE "SHOCK DOCTRINE," "DISASTER CAPITALISM," AND COVID-19

BY BRYAN SNYDER
June 2020

Naomi Klein delivered a remarkable book in 2007—*The Shock Doctrine: The Rise of Disaster Capitalism*. The book documented the rise of neoliberal free-market policies delivered as "shock therapy" upon a traumatized populace reeling from the effects of natural or man-made disasters. As we make our way through the current Covid-19 pandemic, it's important to revisit

this concept of disaster capitalism to see if we can recognize some of the same policies that had been inflicted upon people in past disasters. And we find that, indeed, these policies are present today in the Trump administration's colossally incompetent response to the Covid-19 pandemic.

But first we must ask, what, exactly, is the "shock doctrine?"

The shock doctrine comes from Milton Friedman's policy weaponization of Machiavelli's *The Prince*, in which the sage proponent of Realpolitik suggests that with disasters come opportunities to both profit from crisis as well as to control the disaster in such a way as to remake the "facts on the ground" to one's ideological advantage. That is, to use the crisis in a transformative fashion to change the status quo to one's liking. For Friedman and other "free" market fetishists, this meant to privatize and defund the public sector under the cover of providing aid to a beleaguered community. This "shock" was provided by the rapid imposition of the new privatized order as the people traumatized by natural and/or man-made disaster could put up little resistance to the "new order." These new policies are orchestrated raids by crony capitalists on the public sector which then open up "exciting market opportunities" for the private sector.

As Naomi Klein wrote in *The Shock Doctrine*:

> ...[it is] crucial to act swiftly, to impose rapid and irreversible change before the crisis-racked society slipped back into the "tyranny of the status quo." [Friedman] estimated that "a new administration has some six to nine months in which to achieve major changes; if it does not seize the opportunity to act decisively during that period, it will not have another such opportunity." A variation on Machiavelli's advice that injuries should be inflicted "all at once," this proved to be one of Friedman's most lasting strategic legacies.

Once the public sector has been cracked open or displaced, the feeding frenzy of disaster capitalism then descends upon the beleaguered community with profiteering, price gouging, no-bid contracts, and other sorts of "pay-to-play" corruption which are now the norm. Disasters do offer great opportunities for making a great deal of money for those who are politically connected. This has historically been the case. The economist Joseph Schumpeter noted in his works that the rate of profit rises substantially when markets are disrupted. Schumpeter, of course, preferred this "disruption" to come through the introduction of game-changing new inventions and technologies which would then usher in a whole new era of prosperity and growth. But Schumpeter also acknowledged that natural disasters and/or calamities can also deliver rapid economic growth and above-average profit rates as well. Neoclassical economists know this sort of behavior as "rent-seeking" which explicitly takes advantage of an ill-performing market in rewarding noncompetitive returns to the well-positioned few. Wars, famines, floods, and now, disease, all offer profitable opportunities, which even the wealthiest and most powerful corporations swoop in to take advantage of.

What is particularly unnerving in the case of disaster capitalism is another one of Machiavelli's pearls of wisdom, and that is if a crisis does not currently exist, then an enterprising Prince should contrive to create one. Milton Friedman, Margaret Thatcher, and Ronald Reagan all have engaged in the active assault and sabotage of the public sector to give pretext to privatization as part of their greater ideological agenda. Unfortunately, the Trump administration has taken disaster capitalism to a whole new, stratospheric level.

Arrogant Greed

At first, the catastrophic delay in the Trump administration's response to the pandemic appears to be the product of gross incompetence, as they "fiddled while Rome burned." But members of the administration and extended political and corporate family were busy positioning themselves to make a killing in cornering the U.S. market in testing, protective gear, and treatments. Parceling out no-bid contracts to unqualified vendors, hawking unproven products, and suppressing existing testing and treatment options was the norm. The absurdity of this pandemic profiteering reached a pinnacle when the administration shamelessly promoted the drug Hydroxychloroquine—which proved lethal and ineffective in treating the Covid-19 virus— just because the president's family had bought into the company that manufactures it to make a quick buck.

We now know that the administration's refusal to distribute the World Health Organization's coronavirus test at the beginning of the first wave of the pandemic was due to Trump's family members scrambling to get a "piece of the action" with their own test. These were precious weeks squandered with next-to-no testing available as the pandemic crossed the Pacific Ocean and containment of Covid-19 was lost. Proactive measures were removed which meant that the United States would now be reactive in policy without having good information about where the disease was and where it would be heading.

The administration had also quietly dismantled the institutional system that the Obama Administration had set up to monitor such diseases in China in anticipation of another form of the coronavirus mutating and posing an imminent global threat. The Center for Disease Control was also effectively sidelined from operational control over all aspects of the pandemic in favor of direct control and parsimony from the Trump family. The Trump administration even went so far as seizing tests and PPE (Personal Protective Equipment) from desperate States. This situation got so far out of hand that governors of hard-hit states were forced to secretly arrange for their own shipments of materials from sources in China as well as hiding their existing stockpiles from the Feds, who had seized such materials by decree. In Massachusetts, the Governor Charlie Baker had to take up the New England Patriots owner's, Bob Kraft, offer to use the team's plane to fly to China to bring back much-needed supplies. Meanwhile, tens of thousands of people died from this sort of arrogant greed (as of early June, 120,000 Americans have perished from Covid-19).

As Milton Friedman was so fond of Machiavelli when creating or taking advantage of a crisis for ideological purposes or personal gain, we might also take solace from another luminary of antiquity, Saint Thomas Aquinas. In times of crisis, Aquinas saw such profiteering as "sinful," since it took unjust advantage of people who were in dire circumstances and led to social disharmony and strife. Is it really the role of the modern nation state to sell "indulgences" to cronies and steer contracts to family members whenever things go wrong? Engaging in this sort of behavior especially in times of famine, flood, or catastrophe is seen by Aquinas as sinful and socially destructive. It is only through the ideology of the likes of Friedman that we are told to embrace this individual and/or corporate greed and have faith in an abstract market mechanism which he proffers will deliver the goods in the form of disaster relief. ❑

Sources: Naomi Klein, *The Shock Doctrine* (Picador, 2008); Niccolo Machiavelli, *The Prince* (Hackett Publishing Company, Inc., 1995).

Article 1.3

WHAT'S WRONG WITH NEOLIBERALISM?
The Marx, Keynes, and Polanyi Problems

BY ROBERT POLLIN
May/June 2004

During the years of the Clinton administration, the term "Washington Consensus" began circulating to designate the common policy positions of the U.S. administration along with the International Monetary Fund (IMF) and World Bank. These positions, implemented in the United States and abroad, included free trade, a smaller government share of the economy, and the deregulation of financial markets. This policy approach has also become widely known as *neoliberalism*, a term which draws upon the classical meaning of the word *liberalism*.

Classical liberalism is the political philosophy that embraces the virtues of free-market capitalism and the corresponding minimal role for government interventions, especially as regards measures to promote economic equality within capitalist societies. Thus, a classical liberal would favor minimal levels of government spending and taxation, and minimal levels of government regulation over the economy, including financial and labor markets. According to the classical liberal view, businesses should be free to operate as they wish, and to succeed or fail as such in a competitive marketplace. Meanwhile, consumers rather than government should be responsible for deciding which businesses produce goods and services that are of sufficient quality as well as reasonably priced. Businesses that provide overly expensive or low-quality products will then be outcompeted in the marketplace regardless of the regulatory standards established by governments. Similarly, if businesses offer workers a wage below what the worker is worth, then a competitor firm will offer this worker a higher wage. The firm unwilling to offer fair wages would not survive over time in the competitive marketplace.

This same reasoning also carries over to the international level. Classical liberals favor free trade between countries rather than countries operating with tariffs or other barriers to the free flow of goods and services between countries. They argue that restrictions on the free movement of products and money between countries only protects uncompetitive firms from market competition, and thus holds back the economic development of countries that choose to erect such barriers.

Neoliberalism and the Washington Consensus are contemporary variants of this long-standing political and economic philosophy. The major difference between classical liberalism as a philosophy and contemporary neoliberalism as a set of policy measures is with implementation. Washington Consensus policymakers are committed to free-market policies when they support the interests of big business, as, for example, with lowering regulations at the workplace. But these same policymakers become far less insistent on free-market principles when invoking such principles might damage big business interests. Federal Reserve and IMF interventions to bail out wealthy asset holders during the frequent global financial crises in the 1990s are obvious violations of free-market precepts.

Broadly speaking, the effects of neoliberalism in the less developed countries over the 1990s reflected the experience of the Clinton years in the United States. A high proportion of less developed countries were successful, just in the manner of the United States under President Bill Clinton, in reducing inflation and government budget deficits, and creating a more welcoming climate for foreign trade, multinational corporations, and financial market investors. At the same time, most of Latin America, Africa, and Asia—with China being the one major exception—experienced deepening problems of poverty and inequality in the 1990s, along with slower growth and frequent financial market crises, which in turn produced still more poverty and inequality.

If free-market capitalism is a powerful mechanism for creating wealth, why does a neoliberal policy approach, whether pursued by Clinton, President George W. Bush, or the IMF, produce severe difficulties in terms of inequality and financial instability, which in turn diminish the market mechanism's ability to even promote economic growth? It will be helpful to consider this in terms of three fundamental problems that result from a free-market system, which I term "the Marx Problem," "the Keynes problem," and "the Polanyi problem." Let us take these up in turn.

The Marx Problem

Does someone in your family have a job and, if so, how much does it pay? For the majority of the world's population, how one answers these two questions determines, more than anything else, what one's standard of living will be. But how is it decided whether a person has a job and what their pay will be? Getting down to the most immediate level of decision-making, this occurs through various types of bargaining in labor markets between workers and employers. Karl Marx argued that, in a free-market economy generally, workers have less power than employers in this bargaining process because workers cannot fall back on other means of staying alive if they fail to get hired into a job. Capitalists gain higher profits through having this relatively stronger bargaining position. But Marx also stressed that workers' bargaining power diminishes further when unemployment and underemployment are high, since that means that employed workers can be more readily replaced by what Marx called "the reserve army" of the unemployed outside the office, mine, or factory gates.

Neoliberalism has brought increasing integration of the world's labor markets through reducing barriers to international trade and investment by multinationals. For workers in high-wage countries such as the United States, this effectively means that the reserve army of workers willing to accept jobs at lower pay than U.S. workers expands to include workers in less developed countries. It isn't the case that businesses will always move to less developed countries or that domestically produced goods will necessarily be supplanted by imports from low-wage countries. The point is that U.S. workers face an increased *credible* threat that they can be supplanted. If everything else were to remain the same in the U.S. labor market, this would then mean that global integration would erode the bargaining power of U.S. workers and thus tend to bring lower wages.

But even if this is true for workers in the United States and other rich countries, shouldn't it also mean that workers in poor countries have greater job opportunities and better bargaining positions? In fact, there are areas where workers in poor countries are gaining enhanced job opportunities through international trade and multinational investments. But these gains are generally quite limited. This is because a long-term transition out of agriculture in poor countries continues to expand the reserve army of unemployed and underemployed workers in these countries as well. Moreover, when neoliberal governments in poor countries reduce their support for agriculture—through cuts in both tariffs on imported food products and subsidies for domestic farmers—this makes it more difficult for poor farmers to compete with multinational agribusiness firms. This is especially so when the rich countries maintain or increase their own agricultural supports, as has been done in the United States under Bush. In addition, much of the growth in the recently developed export-oriented manufacturing sectors of poor countries has failed to significantly increase jobs even in this sector. This is because the new export-oriented production sites frequently do not represent net additions to the country's total supply of manufacturing firms. They rather replace older firms that were focused on supplying goods to domestic markets. The net result is that the number of people looking for jobs in the developing countries grows faster than the employers seeking new workers. Here again, workers' bargaining power diminishes.

This does not mean that global integration of labor markets must necessarily bring weakened bargaining power and lower wages for workers. But it does mean that unless some nonmarket forces in the economy, such as government regulations or effective labor unions, are able to counteract these market processes, workers will indeed continue to experience weakened bargaining strength and eroding living standards.

The Keynes Problem

In a free-market economy, investment spending by businesses is the main driving force that produces economic growth, innovation, and jobs. But as John Maynard Keynes stressed, private investment decisions are also unavoidably risky ventures. Businesses have to put up money without knowing whether they will produce any profits in the future. As such, investment spending by businesses is likely to fluctuate far more than, say, decisions by households as to how much they will spend per week on groceries.

But investment fluctuations will also affect overall spending in the economy, including that of households. When investment spending declines, this means that businesses will hire fewer workers. Unemployment rises as a result, and this in turn will lead to cuts in household spending. Declines in business investment spending can therefore set off a vicious cycle: the investment decline leads to employment declines, then to cuts in household spending and corresponding increases in household financial problems, which then brings still more cuts in business investment and financial difficulties for the business sector. This is how capitalist economies produce mass unemployment, financial crises, and recessions.

Keynes also described a second major source of instability associated with private investment activity. Precisely because private investments are highly risky propositions, financial markets have evolved to make this risk more manageable for any given investor. Through financial markets, investors can sell off their investments if they need or want to, converting their office buildings, factories, and stock of machinery into cash much more readily than they could if they always had to find buyers on their own. But Keynes warned that when financial markets convert long-term assets into short-term commitments for investors, this also fosters a speculative mentality in the markets. What becomes central for investors is not whether a company's products will produce profits over the long term, but rather whether the short-term financial market investors *think* a company's fortunes will be strong enough in the present and immediate future to drive the stock price up. Or, to be more precise, what really matters for a speculative investor is not what they think about a given company's prospects per se, but rather what they think *other investors are thinking*, since that will be what determines where the stock price goes in the short term.

Because of this, the financial markets are highly susceptible to rumors, fads, and all sorts of deceptive accounting practices, since all of these can help drive the stock price up in the present, regardless of what they accomplish in the longer term. Thus, if U.S. stock traders are convinced that Federal Reserve Chair Alan Greenspan is a *maestro*, and if there is news that he is about to intervene with some kind of policy shift, then the rumor of Greenspan's policy shift can itself drive prices up, as the more nimble speculators try to keep one step ahead of the herd of Greenspan-philes.

Still, as with the Marx problem, it does not follow that the inherent instability of private investment and speculation in financial markets are uncontrollable, leading inevitably to persistent problems of mass unemployment and recession. But these social pathologies will become increasingly common through a neoliberal policy approach committed to minimizing government interventions to stabilize investment.

The Polanyi Problem

Karl Polanyi wrote his classic book *The Great Transformation* in the context of the 1930s depression, World War II, and the developing worldwide competition with Communist governments. He was also reflecting on the 1920s, dominated, as with our current epoch, by a free-market ethos. Polanyi wrote of the 1920s that "economic liberalism made a supreme bid to restore the self-regulation of the system by eliminating all interventionist policies which interfered with the freedom of markets."

Considering all of these experiences, Polanyi argued that for market economies to function with some modicum of fairness, they must be embedded in social norms and institutions that effectively promote broadly accepted notions of the common good. Otherwise, acquisitiveness and competition—the two driving forces of market economies—achieve overwhelming dominance as cultural forces, rendering life under capitalism a Hobbesian "war of all against all." This same idea is also central for Adam Smith. Smith showed how the invisible hand of self-interest and competition will yield higher levels of individual effort that increases the wealth of nations, but that it will also produce the corruption of our moral sentiments unless the market is itself governed at a fundamental level by the norms of solidarity.

In the post-World War II period, various social democratic movements within the advanced capitalist economies adapted to the Polanyi perspective. They argued in favor of government interventions to achieve three basic ends: stabilizing overall demand in the economy at a level that will provide for full employment; creating a financial market environment that is stable and conducive to the effective allocation of investment funds; and distributing equitably the rewards from high employment and a stable investment process. There were two basic means of achieving equitable distribution: relatively rapid wage growth, promoted by labor laws that were supportive of unions, minimum wage standards, and similar interventions in labor markets; and welfare state policies, including progressive taxation and redistributive programs such as Social Security. The political ascendancy of these ideas was the basis for a dramatic increase in the role of government in the post-World War II capitalist economies. As one indicator of this, total government expenditures in the United States rose from 8% of GDP in 1913, to 21% in 1950, then to 38% by 1992. The IMF and World Bank were also formed in the mid-1940s to advance such policy ideas throughout the world—that is, to implement policies virtually the opposite of those they presently favor. John Maynard Keynes himself was a leading intellectual force contributing to the initial design of the IMF and World Bank.

From Social Democracy to Neoliberalism

But the implementation of a social democratic capitalism, guided by a commitment to full employment and the welfare state, did also face serious and persistent difficulties, and we need to recognize them as part of a consideration of the Marx, Keynes, and Polanyi problems. In particular, many sectors of business opposed efforts to sustain full employment because, following the logic of the Marx problem, full employment provides greater bargaining power for workers in labor markets, even if it also increases the economy's total production of goods and services. Greater worker bargaining power can also create inflationary pressures because businesses will try to absorb their higher wage costs by raising prices. In addition, market-inhibiting financial regulations limit the capacity of financial market players to diversify their risk and speculate.

Corporations in the United States and Western Europe were experiencing some combination of these problems associated with social democratic capitalism. In particular, they were faced with rising labor costs associated with low unemployment rates, which then led to either inflation, when corporations had the ability to pass on their higher labor costs to consumers, or to a squeeze on profits, when competitive pressures prevented corporations from raising their prices in response to the rising labor costs. These pressures were compounded by the two oil price "shocks" initiated by the Oil Producing Exporting Countries (OPEC)—an initial fourfold increase in the world price of oil in 1973, then a second fourfold price spike in 1979.

These were the conditions that by the end of the 1970s led to the decline of social democratic approaches to policymaking and the ascendancy of neo-liberalism. The two leading signposts of this historic transition were the election in 1979 of Margaret Thatcher as prime minister of the United Kingdom and in 1980 of Ronald Reagan as the president of the United States. Indeed, it was at this point that Thatcher made her famous pronouncement that "there is no alternative" to neoliberalism.

This brings us to the contemporary era of smaller government, fiscal stringency, and deregulation, i.e., to neoliberalism under Clinton and Bush, and throughout the less-developed world. The issue is not a simple juxtaposition between either regulating or deregulating markets. Rather it is that markets have become deregulated to support the interests of business and financial markets, even as these same groups still benefit greatly from many forms of government support, including investment subsidies, tax concessions, and rescue operations when financial crises get out of hand. At the same time, the deregulation of markets that favors business and finance is correspondingly the most powerful regulatory mechanism limiting the demands of workers, in that deregulation has been congruent with the worldwide expansion of the reserve army of labor and the declining capacity of national governments to implement full-employment and macroeconomic policies. In other words, deregulation has exacerbated both the Marx and Keynes problems.

Given the ways in which neoliberalism worsens the Marx, Keynes, and Polanyi problems, we should not be surprised by the wreckage that it has wrought since the late 1970s, when it became the ascendant policy model. Over the past generation, with neoliberals in the saddle almost everywhere in the world, the results have been straightforward: worsening inequality and poverty, along with slower economic growth and far more unstable financial markets. While Margaret Thatcher famously declared that "there is no alternative" to neoliberalism, there are in fact alternatives. The experience over the past generation demonstrates how important it is to develop them in the most workable and coherent ways possible. ❏

Article 1.4

OPENING PANDORA'S BOX
The Basics of Marxist Economics

BY ALEJANDRO REUSS
February 2000

In most universities, what is taught as "economics" is a particular brand of orthodox economic theory. The hallmark of this school is a belief in the optimal efficiency (and, it goes without saying, the equity) of "free markets."

The orthodox macroeconomists—who had denied the possibility of general economic slumps—were thrown for a loop by the Great Depression of the 1930s, and by the challenge to their system of thought by John Maynard Keynes and others. Even so, the orthodox system retains at its heart a view of capitalist society in which individuals, each roughly equal to all others, undertake mutually beneficial transactions tending to a socially optimal equilibrium. There is no power and no conflict. The model is a perfectly bloodless abstraction, without all the clash and clamor of real life.

Karl Marx and the Critique of Capitalist Society

One way to pry open and criticize the orthodox model of economics is by returning to the idiosyncracies of the real world. That's the approach of most of the articles in this book, which describe real-world phenomena that the orthodox model ignores or excludes. These efforts may explain particular facts better than the orthodoxy, while not necessarily offering an alternative general system of analysis. They punch holes in the orthodox lines but, ultimately, leave the orthodox model in possession of the field.

This suggests the need for a different conceptual system that can supplant orthodox economics as a whole. Starting in the 1850s and continuing until his death in 1883, the German philosopher and revolutionary Karl Marx dedicated himself to developing a conceptual system for explaining the workings of capitalism. The system that Marx developed and that bears his name emerged from his criticism of the classical political economy developed by Adam Smith and David Ricardo. While Marx admired Smith and Ricardo, and borrowed many of their concepts, he approached economics (or "political economy") from a very different standpoint. He had developed a powerful criticism of capitalist society before undertaking his study of the economy. This criticism was inspired by French socialist ideas and focused on the oppression of the working class. Marx argued that wage workers—those working for a paycheck—were "free" only in the sense that they were not beholden to a single lord or master, as serfs had been under feudalism. But they did not own property, nor were they craftspeople working for themselves, so they were compelled to sell themselves for a wage to one capitalist or another. Having surrendered their freedom to the employer's authority, they were forced to work in the way the employer told them while the latter pocketed the profit produced by their labor.

Marx believed, however, that by creating this oppressed and exploited class of workers, capitalism was creating the seeds of its own destruction. Conflict between the workers and the owners was an essential part of capitalism. But in Marx's view of history, the workers could eventually overthrow the capitalist class, just as the capitalist class, or "bourgeoisie," had grown strong under feudalism, only to supplant the feudal aristocracy. The workers, however, would not simply substitute a new form of private property and class exploitation, as the bourgeoisie had done. Rather, they would bring about the organization of production on a cooperative basis, and an end to the domination of one class over another.

Marx was strongly influenced by the ideas of the day in German philosophy, which held that any new order grows in the womb of the old, and eventually bursts forth to replace it. Marx believed that the creation of the working class, or "proletariat," in the heart of capitalism was one of the system's main contradictions. Marx studied capitalist economics in order to explain the conditions under which it would be possible for the proletariat to overthrow capitalism and create a classless society. The orthodox view depicts capitalism as tending toward equilibrium (without dynamism or crises), serving everyone's best interests, and lasting forever. Marx saw capitalism as crisis-ridden, full of conflict, operating to the advantage of some and detriment of others, and far from eternal.

Class and Exploitation

Looking at economic systems historically, Marx saw capitalism as only the latest in a succession of societies based on exploitation. When people are only able to produce the bare minimum needed to live, he wrote, there is no room for a class of people to take a portion of society's production without contributing to it. But as soon as productivity exceeds this subsistence level, it becomes possible for a class of people who do not contribute to production to live by appropriating the surplus for themselves. These are the masters in slave societies, the lords in feudal societies, and the property owners in capitalist society.

Marx believed that the owners of businesses and property—the capitalists— take part of the wealth produced by the workers, but that this appropriation is hidden by the appearance of an equal exchange, or "a fair day's work for a fair day's pay."

Those who live from the ownership of property—businesses, stocks, land, etc.—were then a small minority and now are less than 5% of the population in countries like the United States. (Marx wrote before the rise of massive corporations and bureaucracies, and did not classify managers and administrators who don't own their own businesses as part of the bourgeoisie.) The exploited class, meanwhile, is the vast majority who live by earning a wage or salary—not just "blue collar" or industrial workers but other workers as well.

Marx's view of how exploitation happened in capitalist society depended on an idea, which he borrowed from Smith and Ricardo, called the labor theory of value. The premise of this theory, which is neither easily proved nor easily rejected, is that labor alone creates the value that is embodied in commodities and that creates profit for owners who sell the goods. The workers do not receive the full value created by their labor and so they are exploited.

Students are likely to hear in economics classes that profits are a reward for the "abstinence" or "risk" of a businessperson—implying that profits are their just desserts. Marx would argue that profits are a reward obtained through the exercise of power—the power owners have over those who own little but their ability to work and so must sell this ability for a wage. That power, and the tribute it allows owners of capital to extract from workers, is no more legitimate in Marx's analysis than the power of a slaveowner over a slave. A slaveowner may exhibit thrift and take risks, after all, but is the wealth of the slaveowner the just reward for these virtues, or a pure and simple theft from the slave?

Joan Robinson, an important 20ᵗʰ-century critic and admirer of Marx, noted that mainstream economists, "by treating capital as productive, used to insinuate the suggestion that capitalists deserve well by society and are fully justified in drawing income from their property." In her view, however, "What is important is that *owning* capital is not a productive activity" [emphasis added].

The Falling Rate of Profit

Marx believed that his theory had major implications for the crises that engulf capitalist economies. In Marx's system, the raw materials and machinery used in the manufacture of a product do not create the extra value that allows the business owner to profit from its production. That additional value is created by labor alone.

Marx recognized that owners could directly extract more value out of workers in three ways: cutting their wages, lengthening their working day, or increasing the intensity of their labor. This need not be done by a direct assault on the workers. Capitalists can achieve the same goal by employing more easily exploited groups or by moving their operations where labor is not as powerful. Both of these trends can be seen in capitalism today, and can be understood as part of capital's intrinsic thirst for more value and increased exploitation.

With the mechanization of large-scale production under capitalism, machines and other inanimate elements of production form a larger and larger share of the inputs to production. Marx believed this would result in a long-term trend that would cause the rate of profit to fall, as the enriching contribution of human labor declined (relative to the inert contribution of these other inputs). This, he believed, would make capitalism increasingly vulnerable to economic crises.

This chain of reasoning depends, of course, on seeing workers as the source of the surplus value created in the production process, and can be avoided by rejecting this view outright. Orthodox economics has not only rejected the labor theory of value, but abandoned the issue of "value" altogether. Value analysis in the spirit of Ricardo and Marx was revived during the 1960s by a number of unorthodox economists, including the Italian economist Piero Sraffa. Marx did not get the last word on the subject.

Unemployment, Part I: The "Reserve Army of the Unemployed"

Marx is often raked over the coals for arguing that workers, under capitalism, were destined to be ground into ever-more-desperate poverty. That living standards improved in rich capitalist countries is offered as proof that his system is fatally flawed. While Marx was not optimistic about the prospect of workers raising their standard of living very far under capitalism, he was critical of proponents of the "iron law of wages," such as Malthus, who held that any increase in wages above the minimum necessary for survival would simply provoke population growth and a decline in wages back to subsistence level. Marx emphasized that political and historical factors influencing the relative power of the major social classes, rather than simple demographics, determined the distribution of income.

One economic factor to which Marx attributed great importance in the class struggle was the size of the "reserve army of the unemployed." Marx identified unemployment as the major factor pushing wages down—the larger the "reserve" of unemployed workers clamoring for jobs, the greater the downward pressure on wages. This was an influence, Marx believed, that the workers would never be able to fully escape under capitalism. If the workers' bargaining power rose enough to raise wages and eat into profits, he argued, capitalists would merely substitute labor-saving technology for living labor, recreating the "reserve army" and reasserting the downward pressure on wages.

Though this has not, perhaps, retarded long-term wage growth to the degree that Marx expected, his basic analysis was visionary at a time when the Malthusian (population) theory of wages was the prevailing view. Anyone reading the business press these days—which is constantly worrying that workers might gain some bargaining power in a "tight" (low unemployment) labor market, and that their wage demands will provoke inflation—will recognize its basic insight.

Unemployment, Part II: The Crisis of Overproduction

Marx never developed a single definitive version of his theory of economic crises (recessions) under capitalism. Nonetheless, his thinking on this issue is some of his most visionary. Marx was the first major economic thinker to break with the orthodoxy of "Say's Law." Named after the French philosopher Jean-Baptiste Say, this theory held that each industry generated income equal to the output it created. In other words, "supply creates its own demand." Say's conclusion, in which he was followed by orthodox economists up through the Great Depression, was that while a particular industry could overproduce, no generalized overproduction was possible. In this respect, orthodox economics flew in the face of all the evidence. In his analysis of overproduction, Marx focused on what he considered the basic contradiction of capitalism—and, in microcosm, of the commodity itself: the contradiction between "use value" and "exchange value." The idea is that a commodity both satisfies a specific need (it has "use value") and can be exchanged for other articles (it has "exchange value"). This distinction was not invented by Marx; it can be found in the work of Smith. Unlike Smith, however, Marx emphasized the way exchange value—what something is worth in the market—overwhelms the use value of a commodity. Unless a commodity can be sold, the useful labor embodied in it is wasted (and the product is useless to those in need). Vast real needs remain unsatisfied for the majority of people, doubly so when—during crises of overproduction—vast quantities of goods remain unsold because there is not enough "effective demand."

It is during these crises that capitalism's unlimited drive to develop society's productive capacity clashes most sharply with the constraints it places on the real incomes of the majority to buy the goods they need. Marx developed this notion of a demand crisis over 75 years before the so-called "Keynesian revolution" in economic thought (whose key insights were actually developed before Keynes by the Polish economist Michal Kalecki on the foundations of Marx's analysis).

Marx expected that these crises of overproduction and demand would worsen as capitalism developed, and that the crises would slow the development of society's productive capacities (what Marx called the "forces of production"). Ultimately, he believed, these crises would be capitalism's undoing. He also pointed to them as evidence of the basic depravity of capitalism. "In these crises," Marx writes in the *Communist Manifesto*:

> There breaks out an epidemic that, in all earlier epochs would have seemed an absurdity, the epidemic of overproduction. ... [I]t appears as if a famine, a universal war of devastation had cut off the supply of every means of subsistence; industry and commerce seem to be destroyed; and why? Because there is ... too much industry, too much commerce ...

This kind of crisis came so close to bringing down capitalism during the Great Depression that preventing them became a central aim of government policy. While government intervention has managed to smooth out the business cycle, especially in the wealthiest countries, capitalism has hardly become crisis-free.

Marx as Prophet

Marx got a great deal about capitalism just right—its incessant, shark-like forward movement; its internal chaos, bursting forth periodically in crisis; its concentration of economic power in ever fewer hands. Judged on these core insights, the Marxist system can easily stand toe-to-toe with the orthodox model. Which comes closer to reality? The capitalism that incessantly bursts forth over new horizons, or the one that constantly gravitates towards comfortable equilibrium? The one where crisis is impossible, or the one that lurches from boom to bust to boom again? The one where perfect competition reigns, or the one where a handful of giants tower over every industry? In all these respects, Marx's system captures the thundering dynamics of capitalism much better than the orthodox system does. As aesthetically appealing as the clockwork harmony of the orthodox model may be, this is precisely its failing. Capitalism is anything but harmonious.

There was also a lot that Marx, like any other complex thinker, predicted incorrectly, or did not foresee. In this respect, he was not a prophet. His work should be read critically, and not, as it has been by some, as divine revelation. Marx, rather, was the prophet of a radical approach to reality. In an age when the "free market" rides high, and its apologists claim smugly that "there is no alternative," Joan Robinson's praise of Marx is apt: "[T]he nightmare quality of Marx's thought gives it ... an air of greater reality than the gentle complacency of the orthodox academics. Yet he, at the same time, is more encouraging than they, for he releases hope as well as terror from Pandora's box, while they preach only the gloomy doctrine that all is for the best in the best of all *possible* worlds." ❑

Sources: Joan Robinson, *An Essay on Marxian Economics* (Macmillan, 1952); "Manifesto of the Community Party," and "Crisis Theory (from Theories of Surplus Value)," in Robert C. Tucker, ed., *The Marx-Engels Reader* (W.W. Norton, 1978); Roman Rosdolsky, *The Making of Marx's 'Capital'* (Pluto Press, 1989); Ernest Mandel, "Karl Heinrich Marx"; Luigi L. Pasinetti, "Joan Violet Robinson"; and John Eatwell and Carlo Panico, "Piero Sraffa"; in John Eatwell, Murray Milgate, and Peter Newman, eds., *The New Palgrave: A Dictionary of Economics* (Macmillan, 1987).

Article 1.5

SHARING THE WEALTH OF THE COMMONS

BY PETER BARNES
November/December 2004

We're all familiar with private wealth, even if we don't have much. Economists and the media celebrate it every day. But there's another trove of wealth we barely notice: our common wealth.

Each of us is the beneficiary of a vast inheritance. This common wealth includes our air and water, habitats and ecosystems, languages and cultures, science and technologies, political and monetary systems, and quite a bit more. To say we share this inheritance doesn't mean we can call a broker and sell our shares tomorrow. It does mean we're responsible for the commons and entitled to any income it generates. Both the responsibility and the entitlement are ours by birth. They're part of the obligation each generation owes to the next, and each living human owes to other beings.

At present, however, our economic system scarcely recognizes the commons. This omission causes two major tragedies: ceaseless destruction of nature and widening inequality among humans. Nature gets destroyed because no one's unequivocally responsible for protecting it. Inequality widens because private wealth concentrates while common wealth shrinks.

The great challenges for the 21st century are, first of all, to make the commons visible; second, to give it proper reverence; and third, to translate that reverence into property rights and legal institutions that are on a par with those supporting private property. If we do this, we can avert the twin tragedies currently built into our market-driven system.

Defining the Commons

What exactly is the commons? Here is a workable definition: The commons includes all the assets we inherit together and are morally obligated to pass on, undiminished, to future generations.

This definition is a practical one. It designates a set of assets that have three specific characteristics: they're inherited, shared, and worthy of long-term preservation. Usually it's obvious whether an asset has these characteristics or not.

At the same time, the definition is broad. It encompasses assets that are natural as well as social, intangible as well as tangible, small as well as large. It also introduces a moral factor that is absent from other economic definitions: it requires us to consider whether an asset is worthy of long-term preservation. At present, capitalism has no interest in this question. If an asset is likely to yield a competitive return to capital, it's kept alive; if not, it's destroyed or allowed to run down. Assets in the commons, by contrast, are meant to be preserved regardless of their return.

This definition sorts all economic assets into two baskets, the market and the commons. In the market basket are those assets we want to own privately and manage for profit. In the commons basket are the assets we want to hold in common and manage for long-term preservation. These baskets then are, or ought to be, the yin and yang of economic activity; each should enhance and contain the other. The role of the state should be to maintain a healthy balance between them.

The Value of the Commons

For most of human existence, the commons supplied everyone's food, water, fuel, and medicines. People hunted, fished, gathered fruits and herbs, collected firewood and building materials, and grazed their animals in common lands and waters. In other words, the commons was the source of basic sustenance. This is still true today in many parts of the world, and even in San Francisco, where I live, cash-poor people fish in the bay not for sport, but for food.

Though sustenance in the industrialized world now flows mostly through markets, the commons remains hugely valuable. It's the source of all natural resources and nature's many replenishing services. Water, air, DNA, seeds, topsoil, minerals, the protective ozone layer, the atmosphere's climate regulation, and much more are gifts of nature to us all.

Just as crucially, the commons is our ultimate waste sink. It recycles water, oxygen, carbon, and everything else we excrete, exhale, or throw away. It's the place we store, or try to store, the residues of our industrial system.

The commons also holds humanity's vast accumulation of knowledge, art, and thought. As Isaac Newton said, "If I have seen further it is by standing on the shoulders of giants." So, too, the legal, political, and economic institutions we inherit—even the market itself—were built by the efforts of millions. Without these gifts we'd be hugely poorer than we are today.

To be sure, thinking of these natural and social inheritances primarily as economic assets is a limited way of viewing them. I deeply believe they are much more than that. But if treating portions of the commons as economic assets can help us conserve them, it's surely worth doing so.

How much might the commons be worth in monetary terms? It's relatively easy to put a dollar value on private assets. Accountants and appraisers do it every day, aided by the fact that private assets are regularly traded for money.

This isn't the case with most shared assets. How much is clean air, an intact wetlands,

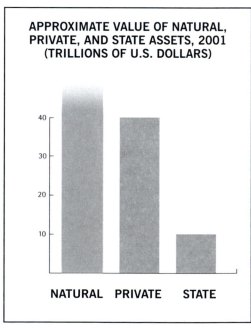

APPROXIMATE VALUE OF NATURAL, PRIVATE, AND STATE ASSETS, 2001 (TRILLIONS OF U.S. DOLLARS)

NATURAL   PRIVATE   STATE

or Darwin's theory of evolution worth in dollar terms? Clearly, many shared inheritances are simply priceless. Others are potentially quantifiable, but there's no current market for them. Fortunately, economists have developed methods to quantify the value of things that aren't traded, so it's possible to estimate the value of the "priceable" part of the commons within an order of magnitude. The surprising conclusion that emerges from numerous studies is that the wealth we share is worth more than the wealth we own privately.

This fact bears repeating. Even though much of the commons can't be valued in monetary terms, the parts that can be valued are worth more than all private assets combined.

It's worth noting that these estimates understate the gap between common and private assets because a significant portion of the value attributed to private wealth is in fact an appropriation of common wealth. If this mislabeled portion was subtracted from private wealth and added to common wealth, the gap between the two would widen further.

Two examples will make this point clear. Suppose you buy a house for $200,000 and, without improving it, sell it a few years later for $300,000. You pay off the mortgage and walk away with a pile of cash. But what caused the house to rise in value? It wasn't anything you did. Rather, it was the fact that your neighborhood became more popular, likely a result of the efforts of community members, improvements in public services, and similar factors.

Or consider another fount of private wealth, the social invention and public expansion of the stock market. Suppose you start a business that goes "public" through an offering of stock. Within a few years, you're able to sell your stock for a spectacular capital gain.

Much of this gain is a social creation, the result of centuries of monetary-system evolution, laws and regulations, and whole industries devoted to accounting, sharing information, and trading stocks. What's more, there's a direct correlation between the scale and quality of the stock market as an institution and the size of the private gain. You'll fetch a higher price if you sell into a market of millions than into a market of two. Similarly, you'll gain more if transaction costs are low and trust in public information is high. Thus, stock that's traded on a regulated exchange sells for a higher multiple of earnings than unlisted stock. This socially created premium can account for 30% of the stock's value. If you're the lucky seller, you'll reap that extra cash—in no way thanks to anything you did as an individual.

Real estate gains and the stock market's social premium are just two instances of common assets contributing to private gain. Still, most rich people would like us to think it's their extraordinary talent, hard work, and risk-taking that create their well-deserved wealth. That's like saying a flower's beauty is due solely to its own efforts, owing nothing to nutrients in the soil, energy from the sun, water from the aquifer, or the activity of bees.

The Great Commons Giveaway

That we inherit a trove of common wealth is the good news. The bad news, alas, is that our inheritance is being grossly mismanaged. As a recent report by the advocacy group Friends of the Commons concludes, "Maintenance of the commons is terrible, theft is rampant, and rents often aren't collected. To put it bluntly, our common wealth—and our children's—is being squandered. We are all poorer as a result."

Examples of the commons' mismanagement include the handout of the broadcast spectrum to media conglomerates, the giveaway of pollution rights to polluters, the extension of copyrights to entertainment companies, the patenting of seeds and genes, the privatization of water, and the relentless destruction of habitats, wildlife, and ecosystems.

This mismanagement, though currently extreme, is not new. For over 200 years, the market has been devouring the commons in two ways. With one hand, the market takes valuable stuff from the commons and privatizes it. This is called "enclosure." With the other hand, the market dumps bad stuff into the commons and says, "It's your problem." This is called "externalizing." Much that is called economic growth today is actually a form of cannibalization in which the market diminishes the commons that ultimately sustains it.

Enclosure—the taking of good stuff from the commons—at first meant privatization of land by the gentry. Today it means privatization of many common assets by corporations. Either way, it means that what once belonged to everyone now belongs to a few.

Enclosure is usually justified in the name of efficiency. And sometimes, though not always, it does result in efficiency gains. But what also results from enclosure is the impoverishment of those who lose access to the commons, and the enrichment of those who take title to it. In other words, enclosure widens the gap between those with income-producing property and those without.

Externalizing—the dumping of bad stuff into the commons—is an automatic behavior pattern of profit-maximizing corporations: if they can avoid any out-of-pocket costs, they will. If workers, taxpayers, anyone downwind, future generations, or nature have to absorb added costs, so be it.

For decades, economists have agreed we'd be better served if businesses "internalized" their externalities—that is, paid in real time the costs that they now shift to the commons. The reason this doesn't happen is that there's no one to set prices and collect them. Unlike private wealth, the commons lack property rights and institutions to represent it in the marketplace.

The seeds of such institutions, however, are starting to emerge. Consider one of the environmental protection tools the United States. currently uses, pollution trading. So-called cap-and-trade programs put a cap on total pollution, then grant portions of the total, via permits, to each polluting firm. Companies may buy other firms' permits if they want to pollute more than their allotment allows, or sell unused permits if they manage to pollute less. Such programs are generally supported by businesses because they allow polluters to find the cheapest ways to reduce pollution.

Public discussion of cap-and-trade programs has focused exclusively on their trading features. What's been overlooked is how they give away common wealth to polluters.

To date, all cap-and-trade programs have begun by giving pollution rights to existing polluters for free. This treats polluters as if they own our sky and rivers. It means that future polluters will have to pay old polluters for the scarce—hence valuable—right to dump waste into nature. Imagine that: Because a corporation polluted in the past, it gets free income forever! And, because ultimately we'll all pay for limited pollution via higher prices, this amounts to an enormous transfer of wealth—trillions of dollars—to shareholders of historically polluting corporations.

In theory, though, there is no reason that the initial pollution rights should not reside with the public. Clean air and the atmosphere's capacity to absorb pollutants are "wealth" that belongs to everyone. Hence, when polluters use up these parts of the commons, they should pay the public—not the other way around.

Taking the Commons Back

How can we correct the system omission that permits, and indeed promotes, destruction of nature and ever-widening inequality among humans? The answer lies in building a new sector of the economy that has a clear legal mission to preserve shared inheritances for everyone. Just as the market is populated by profit-maximizing corporations, so this new sector would be populated by asset-preserving trusts.

Here a brief description of trusts may be helpful. The trust is a private institution that's even older than the corporation. The essence of a trust is a fiduciary relationship. A trust holds and manages property for another person or for many other people. A simple example is a trust set up by a grandparent to pay for a grandchild's education. Other trusts include pension funds, charitable foundations, and university endowments. There are also hundreds of trusts in America, like the Nature Conservancy and the Trust for Public Land, that own land or conservation easements in perpetuity.

If we were to design an institution to protect pieces of the commons, we couldn't do much better than a trust. The goal of commons management, after all,

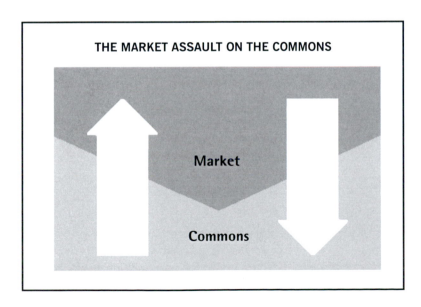

THE MARKET ASSAULT ON THE COMMONS

Market

Commons

is to preserve assets and deliver benefits to broad classes of beneficiaries. That's what trusts do, and it's not rocket science.

Over centuries, several principles of trust management have evolved. These include:

- Trustees have a fiduciary responsibility to beneficiaries. If a trustee fails in this obligation, he or she can be removed and penalized.
- Trustees must preserve the original asset. It's okay to spend income, but don't invade the principal.
- Trustees must assure transparency. Information about money flows should be readily available to beneficiaries.

Trusts in the new commons sector would be endowed with rights comparable to those of corporations. Their trustees would take binding oaths of office and, like judges, serve long terms. Though protecting common assets would be their primary job, they would also distribute income from those assets to beneficiaries. These beneficiaries would include all citizens within a jurisdiction, large classes of citizens (children, the elderly), and/or agencies serving common purposes such as public transit or ecological restoration. When distributing income to individuals, the allocation formula would be one person, one share. The right to receive commons income would be a nontransferable birthright, not a property right that could be traded.

Fortuitously, a working model of such a trust already exists: the Alaska Permanent Fund. When oil drilling on the North Slope began in the 1970s, Governor Jay Hammond, a Republican, proposed that 25% of the state's royalties be placed in a mutual fund to be invested on behalf of Alaska's citizens. Voters approved this proposal in a referendum. Since then, the Alaska Permanent Fund has grown to over $28 billion, and Alaskans have received roughly $22,000 apiece in dividends. In 2003 the per capita dividend was $1,107; a family of four received $4,428.

What Alaska did with its oil can be replicated for other gifts of nature. For example, we could create a nationwide Sky Trust to stabilize the climate for future generations. The trust would restrict emissions of heat-trapping gases and sell a declining number of emission permits to polluters. The income would be returned to U.S. residents in equal yearly dividends, thus reversing the wealth transfer built into current cap-and-trade programs. Instead of everyone paying historic polluters, polluters would pay all of us.

Just as a Sky Trust could represent our equity in the natural commons, a Public Stock Trust could embody our equity in the social commons. Such a trust would capture some of the socially created stock-market premiums that currently flow only to shareholders and their investment bankers. As noted earlier, this premium is sizeable—roughly 30% of the value of publicly traded stock. A simple way to share it would be to create a giant mutual fund—call it the American Permanent Fund—that would hold, say, 10% of the shares of publicly traded companies. This mutual fund, in turn, would be owned by all Americans on a one-share-per-person basis (perhaps linked to their Social Security accounts).

To build up the fund without precipitating a fall in share prices, companies would contribute shares at the rate of, say, 1% per year. The contributions would be the price companies pay for the benefits they derive from a commons asset, the large, trusted market for stocks—a small price, indeed, for the hefty benefits. Over time, the mutual fund would assure that when the economy grows, everyone benefits. The top 5% would still own more than the bottom 90%, but at least every American would have some property income, and a slightly larger slice of our economic pie.

Sharing the Wealth

The perpetuation of inequality is built into the current design of capitalism. Because of the skewed distribution of private wealth, a small self-perpetuating minority receives a disproportionate share of America's nonlabor income.

Thomas Paine had something to say about this. In his essay "Agrarian Justice," written in 1790, he argued that, because enclosure of the commons had separated so many people from their primary source of sustenance, it was necessary to create a functional equivalent of the commons in the form of a National Fund. Here is how he put it:

> There are two kinds of property. Firstly, natural property, or that which comes to us from the Creator of the universe—such as the Earth, air, water. Secondly, artificial or acquired property—the invention of men. In the latter, equality is impossible; for to distribute it equally, it would be necessary that all should have contributed in the same proportion, which can never be the case ... Equality of natural property is different. Every individual in the world is born with legitimate claims on this property, or its equivalent.

Enclosure of the commons, he went on, was necessary to improve the efficiency of cultivation. But:

> The landed monopoly that began with [enclosure] has produced the greatest evil. It has dispossessed more than half the inhabitants of every nation of their natural inheritance, without providing for them, as ought to have been done, an indemnification for that loss, and has thereby created a species of poverty and wretchedness that did not exist before.

The appropriate compensation for loss of the commons, Paine said, was a national fund financed by rents paid by land owners. Out of this fund, every person reaching age 21 would get 15 pounds a year, and every person over 50 would receive an additional 10 pounds. (Think of Social Security, financed by commons rents instead of payroll taxes.)

A Progressive Offensive

Paine's vision, allowing for inflation and new forms of enclosure, could not be more timely today. Surely from our vast common inheritance—not just the land, but the atmosphere, the broadcast spectrum, our mineral resources, our threatened habitats and water supplies—enough rent can be collected to pay every American over age 21 a modest annual dividend, and every person reaching 21 a small start-up inheritance.

Such a proposal may seem utopian. In today's political climate, perhaps it is. But consider this. About 20 years ago, right-wing think tanks laid out a bold agenda. They called for lowering taxes on private wealth, privatizing much of government, and deregulating industry. Amazingly, this radical agenda has largely been achieved.

It's time for progressives to mount an equally bold offensive. The old shibboleths—let's gin up the economy, create jobs, and expand government programs—no longer excite. We need to talk about fixing the economy, not just growing it; about income for everyone, not just jobs; about nurturing ecosystems, cultures, and communities, not just our individual selves. More broadly, we need to celebrate the commons as an essential counterpoise to the market.

Unfortunately, many progressives have viewed the state as the only possible counterpoise to the market. The trouble is, the state has been captured by corporations. This capture isn't accidental or temporary; it's structural and long term.

This doesn't mean progressives can't occasionally recapture the state. We've done so before and will do so again. It does mean that progressive control of the state is the exception, not the norm; in due course, corporate capture will resume. It follows that if we want lasting fixes to capitalism's tragic flaws, we must use our brief moments of political ascendancy to build institutions that endure.

Programs that rely on taxes, appropriations, or regulations are inherently transitory; they get weakened or repealed when political power shifts. By contrast, institutions that are self-perpetuating and have broad constituencies are likely to last. (It also helps if they mail out checks periodically.) This was the genius of Social Security, which has survived—indeed grown—through numerous Republican administrations.

If progressives are smart, we'll use our next New Deal to create common property trusts that include all Americans as beneficiaries. These trusts will then be to the 21st century what social insurance was to the 20th: sturdy pillars of shared responsibility and entitlement. Through them, the commons will be a source of sustenance for all, as it was before enclosure. Life-long income will be linked to generations-long ecological health. Isn't that a future most Americans would welcome? ❏

Chapter 2

MACROECONOMIC MEASUREMENT

INTRODUCTION

Most macroeconomics textbooks begin with a snapshot of today's economy as seen through the standard measures of economic performance. This chapter provides a different view of today's economy, one far more critical of current economic policy and performance, one that asks what the standard measures of economic performance really tell us and what they might be missing.

Increases in real gross domestic product (GDP) define economic growth and, for most economists, rising real GDP per capita shows that a nation's standard of living is improving. But our authors are not convinced. The first three articles in this chapter focus on critiques of GDP.

Zoe Sherman (Article 2.1) turns Ronald Reagan's famous 1980 presidential debate question—"Are you better off than you were four years ago?"—into a look at the changes in the quality of life in the United States in recent decades. She asks whether we're better off as a society than we were 45 years ago. Certainly, per capita income is higher (what mainstream economists would define as being "better off"), but we also have rising inequality, increased burdens of work, greater insecurity, and serious problems of environmental sustainability.

Next, Alejandro Reuss summarizes three key criticisms against the use of GDP to measure economic well-being, focusing on its failure to take into account income distribution, environmental quality, and non-market production (Article 2.2).

The following article focuses on an alternative way to measure economic performance, by viewing the economy as a means of achieving social goals rather than treating economic activity as an end in itself. Alejandro Reuss (Article 2.3) describes the ins and outs of the Human Development Index (HDI), the United Nations Development Programme's alternative to GDP as a single-number measurement of economic well-being.

Next, feminist economist Nancy Folbre (Article 2.4), using the context of the health care sector during the current pandemic, highlights the market's failure to correctly account for the value of activities in the care economy.

Economist Jeannette Wicks-Lim then tackles another measurement issue that directly addresses social well-being (Article 2.5). She analyzes an alternate way of calculating the official "poverty line"—the income threshold below which people are deemed "poor" for purposes of government statistics. The traditional poverty line, she argues, is both misdefined and too low, and the new one does not go far enough to correct these shortcomings.

Finally, Mark Paul (Article 2.6) explains the complicated unemployment situation in the early months of the Covid-19 recession, and why the official U-3 unemployment figure doesn't tell the whole story.

Discussion Questions

1. (Article 2.1) What are the main ways that Sherman argues that well-being in the United States has deteriorated over the last 45 years? In what ways does she argue it has improved?

2. (Article 2.2) How is GDP measured, and what does it represent? What are the three main criticisms of GDP described by Reuss? Do you find them convincing?

3. (Article 2.3) How does the HDI differ from GDP per capita? What problems of GDP as a measurement of well-being does the HDI attempt to overcome? How successful do you think the HDI is in overcoming these problems?

4. (Article 2.4) In Folbre's view, why, specifically, does the market fail to properly value activities in the care economy?

5. (Article 2.5) How is the federal poverty line calculated? How does the new Supplemental Poverty Measure differ, and why does Wicks-Lim consider these changes inadequate?

6. (Article 2.6) How do alternative measures of unemployment, like the "U-6" unemployment rate and the labor-force participation rate, help us better understand the unemployment situation in the current economic crisis?

Article 2.1

WHAT DOES IT MEAN TO BE "BETTER OFF"?

Taking stock of how U.S. society has progressed or faltered over the last 45 years.

BY ZOE SHERMAN
November/December 2014; updated June 2019

In 1980, Ronald Reagan, trying to defeat Jimmy Carter's bid for a second term as president, asked, "Are you better off than you were four years ago?" A conservative turn in American politics was already underway and, campaigning on that question, Reagan rode the wave into the presidency. Nearly forty years into the political epoch he symbolizes, and 45 years into this magazine's history, we might well echo Reagan's question: Are you better off than you were 45 years ago?

It is a deceptively simple question. What would it mean to be better off? Probably a lot of good things and a lot of bad things have happened to you in the last 45 years (or however many of those years you've been alive) and to decide whether you are better off you would have to do some weighing. For many of us the final answer would be, "well, yes and no…" For any one person many of the then-vs.-now differences are largely a matter of the life cycle—maybe you were a child decades ago and an adult now. It really makes more sense to ask whether we as a society are better off that we were 45 years ago.

The well-being of a society cannot be measured in a single dimension any more than a single person's well-being can. Assessments of our national well-being often begin—and too often end—with gross domestic product (GDP). Per capita GDP basically answers the question, "Are we collectively, on average, richer, as measured by the dollar value of the things we produce and sell to one another?" (This includes the government's provision of goods and services, even if they are not really "sold.")

Not only is GDP limited to measuring just one dimension of well-being—it doesn't even measure that dimension all that well. It fails to count the work we do for one another at home or in other non-monetized ways. It gives us only an aggregate with no information about how access to all those goods and services is distributed. And goods and bads get added together so long as they cost money and therefore generate income for someone—that is, $1,000 spent on cigarettes and treatments for emphysema add just as much to GDP as $1,000 spent on healthy foods and preventive medicine.

We'll certainly want to go beyond just GDP per capita, as we take a tour through various dimensions of well-being and take stock of how we have progressed or faltered over the last 45 years.

Income and Stuff

Though we know from the outset that we will not stop here, we may as well start in the traditional starting place: Changes in our national income, taking into account population growth and inflation. Real per capita GDP was $26,446 in 1974 (in 2012 U.S. dollars) and in 2018 it was more than double that at $56,702. A lot of that GDP growth represents more of the good stuff we already had in 1974 or cool, well-being-enhancing new stuff that we have now but didn't have then. I really like having a dishwasher and enough dishes that we don't have to wash the plates and forks after every meal (more of the already-invented good stuff). I am also awfully fond of my computer, the internet, DVDs, and streaming video services (cool new stuff).

But some of the higher production/higher income measured by GDP represents not-so-great things. Longer car commutes, for example, are costly and contribute to GDP through spending on gasoline, car repairs and replacement, and purchases of more cars per household. But long car commutes add nothing and likely subtract from the commuters' well-being. They also add pollutants to the air that affect us all.

Even if we subtract out the bads, the goods themselves can get to be too much of a good thing. Plenty of people know the experience of feeling that they are choking on stuff, crowded out of their living spaces by their belongings. Self storage ranks as the fastest growing segment of the commercial real estate industry since 1975. Self-storage businesses brought in revenues of $24 billion in 2013. Now, consider that the average size of a new single family home increased 57% from 1970 to the early 2000s. That means we spent $24 billion to store the things that we can't fit in our homes, even though many of our homes are bigger than ever!

Economic and Social Inequality

If the distribution of income had remained roughly the same over the last 45 years, then the fact that per capita GDP doubled would mean that everyone's income had doubled. That's not what happened. Instead, those at the top of the income distribution have vastly more income than 45 years ago while those at the bottom have less. The real income of a household at the 20th percentile (above 20% of all households in the income ranking) has scarcely budged since 1974—it was $22,000 and change then and is $24,000 and change now. The average income for the bottom 20% of households has gone from a meager $12,510 in 1974 to the scarcely-better $13,258 in 2017. The entire bottom 80% of households ranked by income now gets only 48.5% of the national pie, down from 56.5% in 1974. That means that the top 20% has gone from 43.5% to 51.5% of total income. Even within the top 20%, the distribution skews upward. Most of the income gains of the top 20% are concentrated in the top 5%; most of the gains of the top 5% are concentrated in the top 1%; most of the gains in the top 1% are concentrated in the top 0.1%.

By 1974, labor force participation rates were in the midst of a marked upward trend, driven largely by the entry of women into the paid labor force. Starting from a low of 59% in the early 1960s, the labor force participation rate passed 61% in 1974 and peaked at 67% in the late 1990s. Labor force participation has drifted back downward somewhat since then through a combination of baby boomer retirement and discouraged workers giving up on the labor force since the crisis that began in 2007, but it remains at 63%, still higher than in 1974. That means that even while more of us are participating in market work, the market is concentrating its rewards in a shrinking cabal of increasingly powerful hands.

More of us are working, but the share of national income that goes to ordinary workers is smaller. National income can be sorted into categories based on the route it takes to a person's pocket. One category of income—wages and salaries earned in return for work—is labor income. The other categories—profit, dividends, rent, interest—are all forms of income that result from owning. For many decades, the labor share of national income held fairly steady, but beginning in the mid-1970s it started falling. Economist James Heintz found that the share of the national income earned as private business sector wages (excluding executive compensation) fell from 58% in 1970 to 50% in 2010; the share that went to nonsupervisory workers fell from 45% to 31%.

Even as hourly pay for a broad swath of people in the middle—between the 20th and 80th percentiles—has just about kept pace with inflation, the traditional tickets to the middle class have become more of a reach. Rising costs of higher education and housing have consigned many to a near-permanent state of debt peonage to maintain a tenuous grasp on middle-class social status, while others are blocked from access entirely.

While more employers now require a college degree before letting a job applicant set foot on the bottom rung of the career ladder, college tuitions have risen more than three times as fast as inflation since 1974. The total volume of outstanding student debt has passed $1 trillion—greater than even the volume of outstanding credit card debt.

Housing, too, has become more unaffordable. For white people who bought houses in the mid-20th century with the benefit of supportive government policies, a home was a secure form of both savings and shelter. (Discriminatory neighborhood redlining prevented most nonwhites from enjoying these benefits.) Within recent decades, however, home prices have risen faster than median incomes and deceptive lending practices trapped many home buyers in unaffordable mortgages. For those who were lucky, and bought and sold at the right times, the housing bubble was a windfall. For many more, their home has become a millstone of debt, and the threat of foreclosure has rendered shelter uncertain.

The division of the national income pie may be more skewed, but do we all have an equal shot at finding our way into the charmed circle of plenty? The probability that a person who starts out in the bottom income quintile will make it into the top quintile has stayed remarkably constant since the mid 20th century. A child born in the bottom quintile in 1971 had an 8.4% chance of making it to the top quintile; for a child born in 1986, the probability is 9.0%. Our national mythology notwithstanding, mobility is lower in the United States than in other comparably developed economies.

Now for some good news: Although wealth and income disparities have worsened, we have made real strides in reducing disparities based on race and gender. Long-standing identity-based hierarchies have weakened, though they certainly have not disappeared. The narrowing of race and gender gaps in economic well-being owes everything to the social movements of the 20th century. The gaps' persistence can be attributed both to differential impacts of ostensibly race- or gender-neutral policies and to our low levels of social mobility. The war on drugs and other "tough on crime" polices really mean the mass incarceration of black men. "Welfare reform" withdrew much of whatever limited support there was for the intense labor—mostly women's—of raising children with minimal cash resources. Even as bigotry, in several forms, has lost explicit government sanction, the lack of social mobility casts the shadow of the more explicit inequities of the past longer and deeper.

Not only is income unequally distributed, it is also, for many, insecure. Having income is a good thing and helps to meet present needs. If there's some left over, present income might even help meet future needs. But confidence in future income matters to

Narrowing Race and Gender Gaps

The Civil Rights Movement, which achieved many of its judicial and legislative successes between 1954 (*Brown v. Board of Education*) and 1965 (Voting Rights Act), and the Women's Movement, whose judicial and legislative successes followed soon after (Title IX in 1972; *Roe v. Wade* in 1973) have reduced the role of outright, explicit discrimination. This is no small matter. Yet there are still wide gaps between white and nonwhite—especially black—Americans, in measures of economic well-being and also gaps between men and women of all races.

	White Men	White Women	Black Men	Black Women
1974 Median Income (in 2017 dollars)	39,804	14,013	24,663	12,651
2017 Median Income (in 2017 dollars)	41,578	25,793	29,962	23,499
1974 Unemployment rate	3.5%	5.1%	7.4%	8.8%
2019 1st Quarter Unemployment rate	3.5%	3.3%	7.8%	6.0%

Sources: Median income: Census Bureau, Current Population Survey, Table P02 (census.gov); Unemployment: Bureau of Labor Statistics (bls.gov).

The resources that would close the racial income gap are hard for individuals and families to come by. There is a strong correlation between educational attainment and future earnings, but black children on

us a lot. We worry about whether we will be able to meet our needs tomorrow—and we have more reasons to worry now than ever.

Employment is a sometime thing: Workers on short-term contracts—like the majority of undergraduate college instructors who work on an adjunct basis—and the self-employed, whose income is also unpredictable, add up to 30% of the U.S. work force with uncertain, episodic income. It is difficult to know exactly how the current level of job insecurity compares to 1974 because the Census Bureau only began systematic data collection on contingent labor in 1995. Median job tenure (years with one's current employer) has fallen for men over the past generation, though it has risen for women. Perhaps the feeling of greater insecurity is a result of men's paid work coming to resemble the precariousness of women's paid work, even while many families still think of a man's income as the mainstay.

The constant churn of a short-term-employment labor system means that for most who fall into poverty, poverty is not a permanent condition. By the mid-1970s, a decade into the War on Poverty, the poverty rate had fallen to 11%, but the reduction was not sustained. Since then, the poverty rate has fluctuated between 11% and 15% with no consistent long-term trend. After the Great Recession, the poverty rate remained stubbornly high, lingering around 15% until we finally saw three consecutive years of poverty rate decline from 2015 to 2017. While most spells of poverty last well under a year (6.6 months was the median according to a average get less from their public schools than white children get. The racial income gap has narrowed slightly between 1974 and now, but the median white household still has more than six times the wealth of the median nonwhite or Hispanic household. Low wealth reduces nonwhite families' ability to buy housing in better-funded public school districts or invest in college education—or in private K-12 substitutes if the public schools available to them are subpar.

People with criminal convictions, once released, face enormous barriers to employment. For the more than one-in-six black men who have been incarcerated (a rate six times that for white men), a criminal record consigns them to the margins of the labor market. In some states, moreover, a felony conviction results in a permanent loss of voting rights and therefore the loss of one of the most powerful tools for political change.

The story of the gender gap in economic well-being is mixed. Women earn lower average incomes and suffer higher poverty rates than men (despite now graduating from college in greater numbers than men). But the female unemployment rate is, on average, lower than it is for men, and it has become less volatile; in the

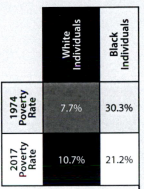

	White Individuals	Black Individuals
1974 Poverty Rate	7.7%	30.3%
2017 Poverty Rate	10.7%	21.2%

Source: Census Bureau, Historical Poverty Data, Table 2 (census.gov).

last few business-cycle downturns, men have been more at risk of job loss than women. Finally, the poverty rate in 2017 was 11% for men and 13.6% for women, 9.3% for married couple households, and 25.7% for female headed households with no husband present. Almost half of children under the age of six who live in households with a single female live in poverty.

Census report on the dynamics of economic well-being several years ago), a large minority of the population cycles in and out of poverty. From January 2009 to December 2011, 31.6% of the population spent at least two consecutive months below the poverty line.

Families can fall into poverty for a number of reasons. Loss of employment, certainly, is a major cause. Another common precipitating event is the birth of a child—without guaranteed paid family leave, childbirth often means a simultaneous increase in household size (and expenses) and decrease in income. Health problems are another trigger for economic distress. Medical bills are the number one cause of personal bankruptcy; even those who have health insurance may be unable to pay for their medical care. Insecurity is our constant companion.

What Money Can't Buy

Many measures of our well-being cannot be viewed through the lens of income and the consumer spending it enables. A full life is not just made of purchased goods. Some of the most important gains in well-being have to do with the political and social gains achieved by social movements countering sexism and racism. The Civil Rights and Women's Liberation movements helped achieve an increase in economic well-being, sure, but also an increase in dignity and political power.

In the mid-1970s, marriage was still a strikingly unequal contract that subordinated wives to husbands. (Same-sex marriage was not permitted anywhere in the United States. Though there were already legal cases on the issue in the early 1970s, the courts upheld same-sex marriage bans.) The criminal laws did not grant married women the right to sexual autonomy and did little to protect their physical or emotional safety; rape laws contained exemptions in the case of husbands, and domestic violence was largely hidden from view. But change was beginning. The Women's Movement brought attention to gender-based violence and built a network of support for survivors; the earliest rape crisis centers and emergency shelters are now marking their 45th anniversaries, taking stock of the considerable progress we've made, and pressing on with the work that still needs to be done. By 1993, all states had changed their rape laws, withdrawing a husband's unlimited sexual access to his wife's body. In 1994, President Bill Clinton signed into law the Violence Against Women Act, which devotes federal resources to the investigation and prosecution of violent crimes targeting women. Indeed, marriage contracts are now legally symmetrical (even if marriage is not yet symmetrical in practice)—and all states license marriages between any two unrelated adults, regardless of sex.

Not only are women safer at home than we were 45 years ago, we have also claimed larger roles outside of the home. Amendments made in 1972 to the Civil Rights Act expanded legal prohibitions on sex discrimination, including the Title IX provision prohibiting educational institutions receiving federal financial assistance from discriminating on the basis of sex. Protections against workplace discrimination are also stronger—the term "sexual harassment," unknown in 1974, is now recognized as describing a form of discrimination that can carry serious legal consequences. In the political arena, the number of women in Congress has more than tripled since the mid-seventies. The 116th Congress, with new representatives elected in 2018, has a record number of women, nearly a quarter of the body. Prior to 1974, only three women had ever served as state governors for a combined four terms. Since then, about 40 more women have held that office, six of whom were elected just in 2019.

Important work combating racial discrimination was also underway 45 years ago. The Equal Employment Opportunity Commission, responsible for enforcing the Civil Rights Act in the workplace, was not yet a decade old in 1974, still early in the process of setting legal precedent for documenting and opposing workplace discrimination, including the disguised discrimination of disparate impact (when a seemingly neutral rule disproportionately affects members of a protected group). The battle to make banks' mortgage lending data public was won in the mid-1970s, which then allowed organized (and ongoing) opposition to the "redlining" that the publicized data revealed. Twenty years after *Brown v. Board of Education* prohibited explicit, legally mandated school segregation, education activists in the mid-1970s pushed governments to take a more proactive role in school integration, albeit with mixed and in many places only temporary results.

A Time for Every Matter

The good life for most of us means not just money to buy the stuff we need, but also plenty of time off the job to participate in social and civic life and to rest. The inequities of the labor market have divided us into two categories—the overworked and the underemployed. For those with consistent employment, the work is often too much work. Even as output per worker hour rises—meaning that, as a society we could increase our material standard of living while holding leisure time steady, or hold our material standard of living steady while increasing leisure time, we have instead increased average work hours per year. Hours of paid labor per employee were about the same in 2000 as in 1973, but since more people were in the paid labor force, the average number of hours per working age person rose from 1,217 to 1,396, equivalent to a full extra month of 40-hour work weeks.

One consequence is that we have a leisure shortage. Chronic sleep deprivation has become the norm. According to a study by the National Academy of Sciences, Americans' average amount of sleep fell by 20% over the course of the 20th century. Meanwhile, the unemployed and underemployed have hours on their hands that they either spend job hunting, in the endless sequence of bureaucratic tasks necessary to access the meager benefits available through the threadbare social safety net, or idle, their unclaimed hours more a burden than a gift. The supposed benefit of unemployment—leisure time to mitigate the loss of income—is not in evidence in the subjective well-being of the unemployed, who are more likely to suffer depression and family stress.

The time crunch resulting from more hours of paid work also squeezes our ability to keep up with the necessary unpaid work at home. Sociologist Arlie Hochschild was already noting in her research during the 1980s that dual-income households were giving up leisure or letting the standards of housework and at-home caregiving slip—often a mix of both. When a stay-at-home mother goes out to work for pay and reduces her hours of home production, the household's increase in cash income gets added to the GDP but the household's loss of unpaid labor time is not subtracted. Or, if she hires a housecleaning service and a babysitter, the wages earned by the mother, the housecleaner, and the babysitter all get added to GDP, but the work done by the housecleaner and babysitter are substituting for unpaid work that was already being done. Correcting for the loss of home production that has accompanied the rise in female participation in the paid labor force requires us to revise downward the increase in output over the period of 1959–2004—the largest hit came between 1959 and 1972 with the withdrawal of about 500 hours of household labor per year, a reduction of almost 20%.

Common Resources and Public Goods

Just as mothers' labor is treated by official measures as a freely available resource, so are the gifts of nature. Nature is the source of the resources our lives depend on—trace back any production process and the Earth's resources are there at the origin. Nature is also the sink into which all the refuse and byproducts of our production get dumped. Environmental concerns were at the core of another one of the 1970s mass social movements. The first Earth Day was celebrated in 1970, and the Environmental Protection Agency (EPA) was created that same year. Concerns and activism around air pollution, water pollution, and the loss of biodiversity led, over the course of the 1970s, to the Clean Air, Clean Water, and Endangered Species Acts. Since the 1970s, the harms of an automotive culture have been lessened with emissions standards, fuel-efficiency standards, and the ban of leaded gasoline. Municipal recycling programs now divert tons of mate-

---

Private Wealth, Public Squalor

Just as we are depleting the gifts of nature, we are depleting or withdrawing many of the gifts we have collectively bestowed on ourselves, our publicly provided goods. We are consuming our public infrastructure—as seen dramatically in the 2004 failure of the levies in New Orleans, La. during Hurricane Katrina and in the 2007 collapse of a bridge in Minneapolis, Minn.

Public goods can only be sustained if we each contribute. If we don't trust one another to contribute, we each feel the need to hoard our resources privately. When we hoard our resources privately, we discourage others from contributing, and our public goods wither.

The hoarding is especially extreme at the top of the income distribution. The top marginal tax rate has fallen from 70% in the 1970s to less than 40% today. The money not put into the common kitty instead pays for private substitutes—private schools (instead of public), private clubs (instead of public parks), gated communities (instead of neighborhoods that welcome visitors), and private security to defend these private goods against the claims of those who are excluded.

---

rials back into the human production cycle, reducing the strains on the planet as both a source of materials and as a sink for waste products.

Over the past 45 years, we have made some important gains in how we make use of the gifts of nature, but our gains are nowhere near enough. Probably the most disastrous shortcoming of all is our collective failure to maintain the atmospheric balance. Since the middle of the 20th century, we have known that an increased concentration of carbon dioxide (CO_2) in the atmosphere will cause dangerous climate change. Despite that, we have continued to emit CO_2 at a staggering rate. Even if we were to stop tomorrow, the effects on the global climate would play out at an accelerating rate for centuries. Several of the destabilizing shifts—melting of the polar ice caps, thawing of the arctic permafrost—are only in the early stages of "positive feedback loops," in which the result of some warming triggers more warming. Rising sea levels threaten coastal cities around the world. Severe storms will continue to increase in frequency. Wider year-to-year variations in temperature and rainfall will disrupt food production.

Looking Backward, Looking Forward

When Reagan asked, "Are you better off than you were four years ago?" he predicted that many people would say "no" and that those who answered "no" would vote for change (not necessarily the kinds of change, as it turns out, that would solve their problems). We are still in the era that Reagan helped to usher in. How is it working for us? Are we better off now, or is it time for a change?

We have seen average income rise, though not as fast as it had in the post-World War II era. Many of the most important gains we have made, moreover, are not dependent on rising average income. The achievements of the Civil Rights and Women's Movements were about dismantling barriers to full participation in a society wealthy enough that it already could provide for all. Now rising income inequality is throwing up new barriers to inclusion.

There are enough ways in which we have lost ground that it must be time for a change. Not a change back—I would not trade the real gains we've made for a return to the so-called "Golden Age" of the 1940s–1970s—but a change that can carry us forward to a world we will still want to live in 45 years from now.

The environmental crisis means that continuing with business as usual would sink us soon. Salvation can only come with a turn away from the fetish of GDP growth. About 45 years ago, research began systematically documenting the failure of rising average income to keep delivering rising levels of happiness (a phenomenon known as the "Easterlin paradox," for researcher Richard Easterlin). Unorthodox economists re-thought the growth imperative: E.F. Schumacher wrote *Small is Beautiful* and Herman Daly penned *Steady-State Economics*. The kingdom of Bhutan famously rejected GDP and instituted instead the measurement of Gross National Happiness. All urged a turn away from defining well-being according to money incomes.

Once a society reaches a level of income that overcomes deprivation—when nobody need go hungry or homeless, nor suffer or die from preventable disease—more income has little affect on the dimensions of well-being that have intrinsic value.

Instead we must turn toward maximizing equality. In their book *The Spirit Level*, Richard Wilkinson and Kate Pickett demonstrate how consistently the empirical evidence shows that more equal societies have better social outcomes in many dimensions, including longer life expectancy, better educational outcomes, stronger environmental protection, and lower rates of incarceration, obesity, and teen pregnancy. Perhaps—after 45 more years of trying and failing to find our way to well-being through more and more market activity, in a quest for more and more income, which has been distributed more and more unequally—we are finally ready to set our priorities straight. It is equality and environmental sustainability that will allow for human flourishing. ❑

Sources: Self Storage Association (selfstorage.org); Margot Adler, "Behind the Ever-Expanding American Dream House," National Public Radio (npr.org); U.S. Census Bureau, Current Population Survey, Tables H-1 and H-2 (census.gov); Bureau of Labor Statistics, CPI Detailed Report, Data for August 2014 (bls.gov); Case-Shiller Home Price Index (us.spindices.com); Census Bureau, Table H-8 (census.gov); Jim Tankersley, "Economic mobility hasn't changed in a half-century in America, economists declare," *Washington Post*, Jan. 23, 2014 (washingtonpost.com); The Equality of Opportunity Project (equality-of-opportunity.org); U.S. Census 2012 Statistical Abstract, Table 721 (census.gov); NAACP, Criminal Justice Fact Sheet (naacp.org); Ibby Caputo, "Paying the Bills One Gig at a Time," WGBH, Feb. 1, 2012 (wgbh.org); Bureau of Labor Statistics, "Employee Tenure in 2014" (bls.gov); Ashley N. Edwards, "Dynamics of Economic Well-Being: Poverty, 2009-2011," Report Number: P70-137, January 2014 (census.gov); Moms Rising, Maternity/Paternity Leave (momsrising.org); Dan Mangan, "Medical Bills Are the Biggest Cause of US Bankruptcies: Study," CNBC, June 25, 2013 (cnbc.com); Christina LaMontagne, "NerdWallet Health finds Medical Bankruptcy accounts for majority of personal bankruptcies," March 26, 2014 (nerdwallet.com); Juliet Schor, "Sustainable Consumption and Worktime Reduction," *Journal of Industrial Ecology*, 2005; Edward Wolff, Ajit Zacharias, and Thomas Masterson, "Long-Term Trends in the Levy Institute Measure of Economic Well-Being (LIMEW), United States, 1959-2004," Levy Economics Institute of Bard College (levyinstitute.org); Nancy Folbre, *The Invisible Heart*, Chapter 3: "Measuring Success" (New Press, 2001); Environmental Protection Agency, "Earth Day and EPA History" (epa.gov); Environmental Protection Agency, Laws and Executive Orders (epa.gov).

Article 2.2

GDP AND ITS DISCONTENTS

BY ALEJANDRO REUSS
April 2013

Economists have been thinking for a long time about what it means for a country or its people to be rich or poor. That was one of the main questions Adam Smith, the British philosopher often described as the "father of modern economics," took on in his most famous book *The Wealth of Nations* (1776). At the very outset, Smith made a point of defining the "real wealth" of a country as consisting in the "annual produce of the land and labour of the society." (Note that Smith was using the word "wealth" in a way that is closer to the colloquial meaning of the word than to its current technical meaning in economics. He was actually defining a country's income rather than its wealth.) That definition might seem uncontroversial now. Many economists would certainly respond that *of course* it's the production of goods and services that makes a country wealthy. But Smith had an important axe to grind. He was arguing against the view, widespread in his day, that a country's wealth consisted in the accumulation of gold and silver—an aim that led to a set of policies (especially promoting exports and suppressing imports) known as "mercantilism." In his own time, Smith was a maverick.

The kind of approach that Smith advocated, of counting up the total quantities of goods and services produced in a country in a year, is now a central part of macroeconomic measurement. When economists tabulate a country's gross domestic product (GDP), they're trying to measure the "annual produce ... of the society" more or less as Smith proposed. GDP attempts to add up the total value, counted in money units, of the goods and services produced within a country in the course of a year. This approach, while a big advance over the view that a country's wealth consisted primarily of its hoards of precious metals, however, is more problematic and controversial than it might appear at first glance. Economists and other social scientists have, in various ways, criticized the ways that GDP is counted and used as a measure of a country's "wealth" or "development." Here, we'll focus on three key critiques: 1) the distributional critique, 2) the feminist critique, and 3) the environmental critique. The first is really a criticism of the approach of looking at the total (or average) production of goods and services for a society as a whole, and ignoring the distribution of access among its members. The other two argue that GDP is misleading because it fails to count all goods and services (focusing narrowly on those that are easiest to put prices on).

What is GDP Per Capita?

Gross domestic product (GDP) per capita is the standard measure of average income used by mainstream economists, and it has become widely used as a measure of economic well-being. Gross domestic product is a measure of the total value of all the goods and services produced in a country in a year, which we can also think of as the total incomes of all the people in that country. A country's total GDP is a very poor measure of how "rich" or "poor" its people are. A country can have a very high total income, even if the average income is low, just because it has a very high population. China, for example, now has the highest total income of any country in the world, even the United States. Its average income, however, is about one-sixth of that of the United States, in terms of real purchasing power. China ranks so high in total income because it is the largest country (by population) in the world. By the same token, a country can have a very large average income, but have a low total income, because it has small population. Developed countries have relatively high levels of income per capita. The top 20 countries, by this measure, include 13 European countries, the United States and two other British offshoots (Australia and Canada), and Japan. Two of the remaining three members of this exclusive list, Qatar and United Arab Emirates, are small, oil-rich countries.

This problem, unlike those spotlighted in the three critiques we'll discuss below, is easy to solve. Instead of stopping at total GDP, we can calculate a country's GDP per capita. The phrase "per capita" simply means per person. ("Capita" comes from the Latin word meaning "head," so "per capita" means "per head.") To get GDP per capita, we just divide a country's GDP by its population. This gives us the average GDP for that country, or a measure of the average income. (Other measures of a country's total income, such as Gross National Product or Gross National Income are similar to GDP, so GNP per capita or GNI per capita are similar to GDP per capita.) Income per capita gives us a better picture of the standards of living in a country than total income.

What's Wrong with GDP Per Capita?

Mainstream economists and policymakers have treated increasing GDP per capita as virtually synonymous with development, so it's important to discuss GDP in more detail. Here, we will focus on three major criticisms of GDP per capita as a measure of well-being or "development":

The Distributional Critique
Average income can be misleading. Average (mean) income is one estimate of the "middle" of the distribution of income in a country. Most people, however, do not get the average income. Most get less than the average, some get more (and a few get much, much more). A relatively small number of people with very high incomes can pull the average up by a great deal, making the average less representative of most people's standard of living.

Figure 1, for example, shows the income distribution for Brazil in 2007. The population has been ranked by income, and then divided into five equal parts (or quintiles). Each bar represents the difference between the average income for one of these quintiles and the average income for the country as a whole. The bar furthest to the left represents the difference between the average income of the lowest-income quintile and the overall average. The next bar represents this difference for the next-lowest-income quintile, and so on, all the way up to the bar at the far right, which represents this difference for the highest-income quintile. (The lowest-income quintile is called the "first" quintile, the next-to-lowest is called the "second" quintile, and so on, up to the highest-income, or "fifth," quintile.) The GDP per capita for Brazil in 2007 was about $9,800. Notice that the average income for each of the bottom four quintiles is less than the GDP per capita

INCOME DISTRIBUTION, BRAZIL, 2007 (DIFFERENCE BETWEEN EACH QUINTILE'S AVERAGE INCOME AND OVERALL AVERAGE INCOME)

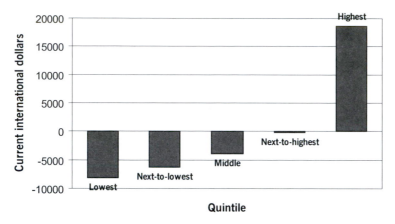

Source: World Bank, World Development Indicators: Income share held by lowest 20%, second 20%, third 20%, fourth 20%, highest 20%; GDP per capita, PPP (constant 2005 international $); GDP, PPP (constant 2005 international $) (data.worldbank.org/indicator).

(or average income) for the society as a whole, as indicated by the bars extending down. The average income for Brazil as a whole is more than six times as much as the average income for the first (lowest-income) quintile, almost three times as much as the average income for the second quintile, and more than one-and-a-half times as much as the average income for the third quintile. Even the average income for the fourth quintile is a little less than the average income for the whole country (so many people in the fourth quintile have incomes below the national average, though some have incomes above it.)

More than two-thirds of Brazil's population, then, have incomes below the country's per capita income—many of them, far below it. The reason GDP per capita for Brazil is so much higher than the incomes of most Brazilians is that the income distribution is so unequal. The average income for the fifth (highest-income) quintile is almost three times the average income for Brazil as a whole.

The Feminist Critique

GDP only counts part of the goods and services produced in a country. Earlier, we said that GDP was "a measure of the total value of goods and services" produced in a country. This is true, but it is a very flawed measure. GDP only includes the value of goods that are produced for sale in markets, ignoring goods and services that people produce for their own consumption, for the consumption of family members, and so on. In developed economies, most individuals or households have money incomes that allow them to buy most of the things they need to live. They also, however, produce goods and services for themselves, family members, and others. For example, people care for and educate their children, cook meals for themselves and other members of their family, clean their own homes, drive themselves and family members to work, school, and errands, and so on. These kinds of goods and services count as part of GDP when someone is paid to do them (for example, when we pay tuition to a school, the bill at a restaurant, the fee to a professional cleaning crew, or the fare to a taxi driver), but not when people do it for themselves, family members, or others free of charge. One could add many other examples, but the first lesson here is that GDP undercounts the total output of goods and services. Since so much of the labor that produces these uncounted goods and services is done by women, feminist economists, such as Marilyn Waring, the author of *If Women Counted: A New Feminist Economics*, have been in the forefront of this critique of GDP as a measure of economic development or well-being.

In some developing economies, the uncounted goods and services may form a larger part of the overall economy than in developed countries. Many people may have small farms and grow their own food. Some people weave their own cloth and make their own clothes. Some people build their own shelters. As economies "develop" economically, they may become more "monetized." This means that people produce fewer goods for their own consumption, for their families, or to trade for other goods (barter), relative to the total amount of goods and services. Instead, they start selling either goods they produce or selling their own labor for money, and buying the things they need. An increase in GDP over time may, in part, reflect an increasing output of goods and services. But it may also reflect, in part, that some goods went uncounted before (because they were not produced for sale in markets) and are now being counted. This means that GDP (or GDP per capita) may exaggerate the growth of economies over time.

The Environmental Critique

GDP does not account for changes in the natural environment. We can think of parts of the natural environment as providing people with valuable "natural services." Until recently, economic measurement has almost completely ignored natural services. Once we start thinking about the environment's services, it becomes obvious how critical they are for our well-being. A forest, for example, absorbs carbon dioxide from and provides oxygen to the atmosphere, provides flood control, reduces soil erosion, provides habitat for wildlife, offers natural beauty and outdoor recreation, provides some people with sources of food and fuel (especially in lower-income countries), and so on.

If GDP only counts human-produced goods and services, then, it is undercounting the total goods and services. If a forest is cut down for timber, and the wood is sold in a market, this adds to GDP. However, the value of the services that the forest provided are not deducted from GDP as conventionally measured, since these are not sold in markets and do not have prices. Cutting down a forest may both add something (harvested wood, which can be used, for example, to build houses or make furniture) and subtract something (natural services) from the well-being of society. There is no way to say, in general, whether what it gained is greater or less than what is lost. However, as long as we think that the services the forest provided were worth *something*, we can say for certain that what GDP measures as being gained is greater than what is really gained—since GDP only counts what is gained and ignores what is lost.

If Not GDP, then What?

Part of the power of GDP per capita is that it boils everything down to one easy-to-digest number. It is easy to create a table comparing the GDPs of many countries. (Obviously, it would be harder to compare many countries in more complex ways, including a bunch of descriptive numbers for each.) This is also at the core of the weaknesses of GDP per capita. When we calculate a total or average of anything, we are, in effect, throwing out the information we have about variation between different individuals. This problem is at the heart of the first critique: Calculating total GDP or GDP per capita means excluding information about income distribution. In addition, calculating the total output of goods and services, when a modern economy includes thousands and thousands of different kinds of goods, requires some unit in which we can measure the output of each one. (We can't add together pounds of potatoes and pounds of steel, much less goods and services that can't be measured in pounds at all, like electricity or haircuts.) GDP has accomplished this by measuring everything in terms of monetary units. This leads to the second and third critiques. Monetary measurement has led to a blind spot for goods and services that do not have market prices (household production, environmental services) and are not easy to measure in money terms.

There are three major possibilities. One is to go on calculating GDP per capita, but to do a better job at capturing what GDP misses. For example, some scholars have tried to put a dollar values on nonmarket production (like subsistence farming or household production) and add these to GDP to get a more accurate estimate.

Another is to come up with an alternative one-number measure to compete with GDP. Two important ones are the genuine progress indicator (GPI) and the human development index (HDI). The GPI incorporates, in addition to market production, measures of both nonmarket production and environmental destruction into a single summary figure (in money terms). It does not address the distributional critique. Calculated by the United Nations Development Programme (UNDP), the HDI combines GDP per capita, average educational attainment, and average life expectancy into a single numerical index. It addresses neither the feminist nor the environmental critique, and it does not explicitly address the distributional critique. However, more equal societies tend to rank better on HDI than on GDP per capita, because they tend to achieve higher average education and life expectancy. (The UNDP also calculates an inequality-adjusted HDI, which explicitly penalizes inequality.)

Finally, a third approach is to abandon the quest for a single summary measurement. Some environmental economists oppose attempts to incorporate environmental changes into GDP or other monetary measures, which requires reducing environmental services to money values. This implies, they argue, that some quantity of produced goods can substitute for any environmental good, which is not true. They propose instead "satellite accounts" that measure environmental changes alongside GDP. Widely used measures of income inequality also exist, and can enhance our picture of an economy. Measurements of median income, access to basic goods (like health and education), economic inequality, nonmarket production, environmental quality, and other factors all should figure, in some way, into our understanding of economic life. We may just have to accept that we need to take into account multiple measures, and that no single-number "bottom line" will do. ❏

Article 2.3

MEASURING ECONOMIC DEVELOPMENT
The "Human Development" Approach

BY ALEJANDRO REUSS
April 2012

Some development economists have proposed abandoning gross domestic product (GDP) per capita, the dominant single-number measure of economic development, in favor of the "human development" approach—which focuses less on changes in average income and more on widespread access to basic goods.

Advocates of this approach to the measurement of development, notably Nobel Prize-winning economist Amartya Sen, aim to focus attention directly on the *ends* (goals) of economic development. Higher incomes, Sen notes, are *means* people use to get the things that they want. The human development approach shifts the focus away from the means and toward ends like a long life, good health, freedom from hunger, the opportunity to get an education, and the ability to take part in community and civic life. Sen has argued that these basic "capabilities" or "freedoms"—the kinds of things almost everyone wants no matter what their goals in life may be—are the highest development priorities and should, therefore, be the primary focus of our development measures.

If a rising average income guaranteed that everyone, or almost everyone, in a society would be better able to reach these goals, we might as well use average income (GDP per capita) to measure development. Increases in GDP per capita, however, do not always deliver longer life, better health, more education, or other basic capabilities to most people. In particular, if these income increases go primarily to those who are already better-off (and already enjoy a long life expectancy, good health, access to education, and so on), they probably will not have much effect on people's access to basic capabilities.

Sen and others have shown that, in "developing" countries, increased average income by itself is not associated with higher life expectancy or better health. In countries where average income was increasing, but public spending on food security, healthcare, education, and similar programs did not increase along with it, they have found, the increase in average income did not appear to improve access to basic capabilities. If spending on these "public supports" increased, on the other hand, access to basic capabilities tended to improve, whether average income was increasing or not. Sen emphasizes two main lessons based on these observations: 1) A country cannot count on economic growth alone to improve access to basic capabilities. Increased average income appears to deliver "human development" largely by *increasing the wealth a society has available for public supports*, and not in other ways. 2) A country does not have to prioritize economic growth—*does not have to "wait" until it grows richer*—to make basic capabilities like long life, good health, and a decent education available to all.

The Human Development Index (HDI)

The "human development" approach has led to a series of annual reports from the United Nations Development Programme (UNDP) ranking countries according to a "human development index" (HDI). The HDI includes measures of three things: 1) health, measured by average life expectancy, 2) education, measured by average years of schooling and expected years of schooling, and 3) income, measured by GDP per capita. The three categories are then combined, each counting equally, into a single index. The HDI has become the most influential alternative to GDP per capita as a single-number development measure.

Looking at the HDI rankings, many of the results are not surprising. The HDI top 20 is dominated by very high-income countries, including 13 Western European countries, four "offshoots" of Great Britain (Australia, Canada, New Zealand, and the United States), and two high-income East Asian countries (Japan and South Korea). Most of the next 20 or so are Western or Eastern European, plus a few small oil-rich states in the Middle East. The next 50 or so include most of Latin America and the Caribbean, much of the Middle East, and a good deal of Eastern Europe (including Russia and several former Soviet republics). The next 50 or so are a mix of Latin American, Middle Eastern, South and Southeast Asian, and African countries. The world's poorest continent, Africa, accounts for almost all of the last 30, including the bottom 24.

TABLE 1: HDI RANKS COMPARED TO INCOME PER CAPITA RANKS (2010)

Highest HDI ranks compared to income per capita ranks (difference in parentheses)*	Lowest HDI ranks compared to income per capita ranks (difference in parentheses)
New Zealand (+30)	Equatorial Guinea (-78)
Georgia (+26)	Angola (-47)
Tonga (+23)	Kuwait (-42)
Tajikistan (+22)	Botswana (-38)
Madagascar (+22)	South Africa (-37)
Togo (+22)	Qatar (-35)
Fiji (+22)	Brunei (-30)
Ireland (+20)	Gabon (-29)
Iceland (+20)	United Arab Emirates (-28)
Ukraine (+20)	Turkey (-26)

* The numbers in parentheses represent a country's GDP-per-capita rank minus its HDI rank. Remember that in a ranking system, a "higher" (better) rank is indicated by a lower number. If a country is ranked, say, 50th in GDP per capita and 20th in HDI, its number would be 50 – 20 = +30. The positive number indicates that the country had a "higher" HDI rank than GDP per capita rank. If a country is ranked, say, 10th in GDP per capita and 35th in HDI, its number would be 10 – 35 = -25. The negative number indicates that the country had a "lower" HDI rank than GDP per capita rank.

Source: United Nations Development Programme, Indices, Getting and using data, 2010 Report—Table 1: Human Development Index and its components (hdr.undp.org/en/statistics/data/).

It is not surprising that higher GDP per capita is associated with a higher HDI score. After all, GDP per capita counts for one-third of the HDI score itself. The relationship between the two, however, is not perfect. Some countries have a higher HDI rank than GDP per capita rank. These countries are "overperforming," getting more human development from their incomes, compared to other countries. Meanwhile, some countries have a lower HDI rank than GDP per capita rank. These countries are "under-performing," not getting as much human development from their incomes, compared to other countries. The list of top "over-performing" countries includes three very high-income countries that had still higher HDI ranks (Iceland, Ireland, and New Zealand), three former Soviet republics (Georgia, Tajikistan, and Ukraine), two small South Pacific island nations (Fiji, Tonga), and two African countries (Madagascar, Togo). The list of top "under-performing" countries includes four small oil-rich countries (Brunei, Kuwait, Qatar, and the United Arab Emirates) and five African countries (Angola, Botswana, Equatorial Guinea, Gabon, and South Africa).

The UNDP also calculates an inequality-adjusted HDI. Note that, for all the measures included in the HDI, there is inequality within countries. The inequality-adjusted HDI is calculated so that, the greater the inequality for any measure included in the HDI (for health, education, or income), the lower the country's score. Since all countries have some inequality, the inequality-adjusted HDI for any country is always lower than the regular HDI. However, the scores for countries with greater inequality drop more than for those with less inequality. That pushes some countries up in the rankings, when inequality is penalized, and others down. Among the 13 countries moving up the most, five are former Soviet republics. Among the 10 moving down the

TABLE 1: INEQUALITY-ADJUSTED HDI RANKS
COMPARED UNADJUSTED HDI RANKS

Highest inequality-adjusted HDI ranks compared unadjusted HDI ranks (difference in parentheses)	Lowest inequality-adjusted HDI ranks compared unadjusted HDI ranks (difference in parentheses)
Uzbekistan (+17)	Peru (-26)
Mongolia (+16)	Panama (-20)
Moldova (+16)	Colombia (-18)
Kyrgystan (+15)	South Korea (-18)
Maldives (+14)	Bolivia (-17)
Ukraine (+14)	Belize (-16)
Philippines (+11)	Brazil (-15)
Sri Lanka (+11)	Namibia (-15)
Tanzania, Viet Nam, Indonesia, Jamaica, Belarus (+9)	El Salvador (-14)
	Turkmenistan (-12)

Source: United Nations Development Programme, 2010 Report, Table 3: Inequality-adjusted Human Development Index (hdr. undp.org/en/media/HDR_2010_EN_Table3_reprint.pdf).

most, seven are Latin American countries. The United States narrowly misses the list of those moving down the most, with its rank dropping by nine places when inequality is taken into account.

GDP Per Capita and HDI

The relationship between income per capita and the HDI is shown in the "scatterplot" graph below. (Instead of GDP per capita, the graph uses a closely related measure called Gross National Income (GNI) per capita.) Each point represents a country, with its income per capita represented on the horizontal scale and its HDI score represented on the vertical scale. The further to the right a point is, the higher the country's per capita income. The higher up a point is, the higher the country's HDI score. As we can see, the cloud of points forms a curve, rising up as income per capita increases from a very low level, and then flattening out. This means that a change in GDP per capita from a very low level to a moderate level of around $8,000 per year is associated with large gains in human development. Above that, we see,

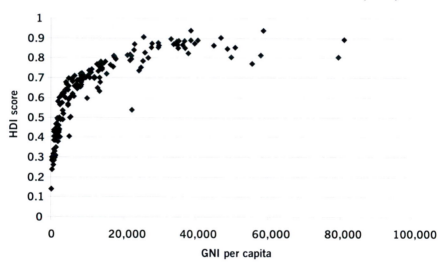

RELATIONSHIP BETWEEN HDI AND INCOME PER CAPITA (2010)

Source: United Nations Development Programme, Indices, 2010 Report - Table 1 Human Development Index and its components (hdr.undp.org/en/statistics/data/).

the curve flattens out dramatically. A change in income per capita from this moderate level to a high level of around $25,000 is associated with smaller gains in human development. Further increases in income per capita are associated with little or no gain in human development.

This relationship suggests two major conclusions, both related to greater economic equality.

First, achieving greater equality in incomes between countries, including by redistributing income from high-income countries to low-income countries, could result in increased human development. Over the highest per capita income range, from about $25,000 on up, increases in income are not associated with higher human development. Decreases in income above this threshold, by the same token, need not mean lower human development. On the other hand, over the lowest income range, below $8,000, increases in income are associated with dramatic gains in HDI (largely due to increased public supports). Therefore, the redistribution of incomes from high-income countries to low-income countries could increase human development in the latter a great deal, while not diminishing human development in the former by very much (if at all)—resulting in a net gain in human development.

Second, high-income countries might make greater gains in HDI, as their incomes continues to increase, if a larger share of income went to low-income people or to public supports. Part of the reason that the relationship between per capita income and HDI flattens out at high income levels may be that there are inherent limits to variables like life expectancy (perhaps 90–100 years) or educational attainment (perhaps 20 years). These "saturation" levels, however, have clearly not been reached by all individuals, even in very high-income countries. In the United States, as of 2008, the infant mortality rate for African Americans was more than double that for whites. The life expectancy at birth for white females was more than three years greater than that of African-American females; for white males, more than five years greater than for African-American males. As of 2010, over 40% of individuals over 25-years-old have no education above high school. Over 60% have no degree from a two- or four-year college. It is little wonder that higher income would not bring about greatly increased human development, considering that, over the last 30 years, many public supports have faced sustained attack and most income growth has gone to people already at the top. ❑

Sources: Amartya Sen, *Development as Freedom* (New York: Oxford University Press, 1999); United Nations Development Programme, Indices, Getting and using data, *2010 Report*, Table 1 Human Development Index and its components (hdr.undp.org/en/statistics/data/); United Nations Development Programme, *2010 Report*, Table 3: Inequality-adjusted Human Development Index (hdr.undp.org/en/media/HDR_2010_EN_Table3_reprint.pdf); U.S. Census Bureau, The 2012 Statistical Abstract, Births, Deaths, Marriages, & Divorces: Life Expectancy, Table 107: Expectation of Life and Expected Deaths by Race, Sex, and Age: 2008; Educational Attainment, Population 25 Years and Over, U.S. Census Bureau, Selected Social Characteristics in the United States, 2010 American Community Survey, 1-Year Estimates.

Article 2.4

THE CARE THEORY OF VALUE

BY NANCY FOLBRE
April 2020, Care Talk

As the Covid-19 pandemic rages through the United States, many hospitals are laying off or cutting the pay of doctors and nurses, even those working on the front lines. Unable to perform the elective surgeries (including face lifts and knee replacements) that are their best moneymakers, hospitals are taking huge losses on pandemic victims. By one estimate, their Covid-19 treatment costs will exceed reimbursements by about $1,800 per case.

You can take this as an indictment of market-driven health care, or a simple illustration of the maxim, "nice guys (and gals) finish last." It also illustrates why most jobs that involve care for other people pay less than other jobs, all else equal.

In conventional economic theory, prices (including wages) are determined by the intersection of supply and demand. In long-run equilibrium, prices should equal the cost of production. One of the important insights of Marxian theory (and this is not the labor theory of value) is that wages are influenced by the collective bargaining power of workers as a group.

One important indicator of collective bargaining power is the unemployment rate. The harder it is for you to find a job, the more important it becomes to do exactly what your employer says. Monopoly power also comes into play, because it allows employers the power to set wages at their favored level.

At least three other factors affect the collective bargaining power of different groups of workers:

1. Who they are (e.g., their gender, race/ethnicity, citizenship).
2. Who consumes the products of their labor (e.g., rich people, poor people, or the public sector).
3. How easy it is to measure and capture the value created by their labor (work that contributes to the public good cannot easily be monetized or even quantified).

The pervasive influence of market-centric logic makes point three the hardest to explain. The reason that we rely on public institutions, private families, and caring communities as well as markets is because our most important assets—natural assets, ecological services, and other people—do not have a market price. They are not bought and sold.

The limits of markets also help explain why we expect workers who provide care services—regardless of their level of education—to literally care, that is, to be motivated by concern for the well-being of others. This expectation, generally though not always fulfilled, makes it difficult for care workers to threaten to withdraw their services; it lowers their bargaining power.

This doesn't imply that care workers can't mobilize, unionize, or protest their wages and working conditions. It does imply that it is difficult for them to do so, particularly in a crisis like the one we face today.

Some doctors—those who provide easily measured and reimbursable specialty services—earn high salaries. Public health specialists and primary care doctors sit much lower on an earnings spectrum bracketed on the bottom by child care and elder care workers, with nurses and teachers in between. Most care workers pay a penalty relative to others with the same education and experience.

Workers in financial services, by contrast, earn a significant pay premium. And financial service firms vigorously resisted a "fiduciary rule" proposed by the Obama administration that would have imposed a legal "duty of care" on financial advisors, requiring them to act in the best interests of their clients—a costly responsibility. Altruism is apparently an expensive taste.

To bolster my care theory of value, I invoke the words of Warren Buffett, Sage of Omaha, referring to investment strategies: "Price is what you pay; value is what you get."

He just doesn't have the pronouns quite right for care workers on the front lines today: Value is what you get, but price is what they pay. ❏

Article 2.5

UNDERCOUNTING THE POOR

BY JEANNETTE WICKS-LIM
May/June 2013

In 1995, a blue-ribbon panel of poverty experts selected by the National Academy of the Sciences (NAS) told us that the "current U.S. measure of poverty is demonstrably flawed judged by today's knowledge; it needs to be replaced." Critics have long pointed out shortcomings, including the failure to adequately account for the effects of "safety net" programs and insensitivity to differences in the cost of living between different places.

The Census Bureau, the federal agency charged with publishing the official poverty numbers, has yet to replace the poverty line. However, in the last couple years it has published an alternative, the Supplemental Poverty Measure (SPM). The SPM is the product of over two decades of work to fix problems in the federal poverty line (FPL).

This new measure takes us one step forward, two steps back. On the one hand, it has some genuine improvements: The new measure makes clearer how the social safety net protects people from economic destitution. It adds basic living costs missing from the old measure. On the other hand, it does little to address the most important criticism of the poverty line: it is just too damned low. The fact that the poverty line has only now been subject to revision—50 years after the release of the first official poverty statistic—likely means that the SPM has effectively entrenched this major weakness of the official measure for another 50 years.

The 2011 official poverty rate was 15.1%. The new poverty measure presented—and missed by a wide margin—the opportunity to bring into public view how widespread the problem of poverty is for American families. If what we mean by poverty is the inability to meet one's basic needs a more reasonable poverty line would tell us that 34% of Americans—more than one in three—are poor.

What's in a Number?

The unemployment rate illustrates the power of official statistics. In the depths of the Great Recession, a new official statistic—the rate of underemployment, counting people working part time who want full-time work and those who have just given up on looking for work—became part of every conversation about the economy. One in six workers (17%) counted as underemployed in December 2009, a much higher number than the 9.6% unemployment rate. The public had not been confronted with an employment shortage that large in recent memory; it made political leaders stand up and pay attention.

The supplemental poverty measure had the potential to do the same: a more reasonable poverty line—the bottom-line level of income a household needs to avoid poverty—would uncover how endemic the problem of economic deprivation is here in the United States. That could shake up policymakers and get them to prioritize anti-poverty policies in their political agendas. Just as important, a more accurate count of the poor would acknowledge the experience of those struggling mightily to put food on the table or to keep the lights on. No one wants to be treated like "just a number," but not being counted at all is surely worse.

With a couple of years of data now available, the SPM has begun to enter into anti-poverty policy debates. Now is a good time to take a closer look at what this measure is all about. The supplemental measure makes three major improvements to the official poverty line. It accounts for differences in the cost of living between different regions. It changes the way it calculates the standard of living necessary to avoid poverty. And it accounts more fully for benefits from safety net programs.

Different Poverty Lines for Cost-of-Living Differences

Everyone knows that $10,000 in a small city like Utica, N.Y., can stretch a lot farther than in New York City. In Utica, the typical monthly cost of rent for a two-bedroom apartment, including utilities, was about $650 during 2008–2011. The figure for New York City? Nearly double that at $1,100. Despite this, the official poverty line has been the same regardless of geographic location.The supplemental poverty measure adjusts the poverty income threshold by differences in housing costs in metropolitan and rural areas in each state—a step entirely missing in the old measure.

We can see how these adjustments make a real difference by simply comparing the official poverty and SPM rates by region. In 2011, according to the official poverty line, the Northeast had the lowest poverty rate (13.2%), the South had the highest (16.1%), and the Midwest and the West fell in between (14.1% and 15.9%, respectively). With cost-of-living differences factored in, the regions shuffled ranks. The SPM poverty rates of the Northeast and South look a lot more alike (15.0% and 16.0%, respectively). The Midwest's cheaper living expenses pushed its SPM rate to the lowest among the four regions (12.8%). The West, on the other hand, had an SPM rate of 20.0%, making it the highest-poverty region.

Updating Today's Living Costs

Obviously, household expenses have changed a lot over the last half-century. The original formula used to construct the official poverty line used a straightforward rule-of-thumb calculation: minimal food expenses times three. It's been well-documented since then that food makes up a much smaller proportion of households' budgets, something closer to one-fifth, as new living expenses have been added (e.g., childcare, as women entered the paid workforce in droves) and the costs of other expenses ballooned (e.g., transportation and medical care).

The new poverty measure takes these other critical expenses into account by doing the following. First, the SPM income threshold tallies up necessary spending on food, clothing, shelter, and utilities. The other necessary expenses like work-related childcare and medical bills are deducted from a household's resources to meet the SPM income threshold. A household is then called poor if its resources fall below the threshold.

These nondiscretionary expenses clearly take a real bite out of family budgets. For example, the "costs of working" cause the SPM poverty rate to rise to nearly double that of the official poverty rate among full-time year-round workers from less than 3% to over 5%.

Bringing the Social Safety Net into Focus

Today's largest national anti-poverty programs operate in the blind spot of the official poverty line. These include programs like Supplemental Nutrition Assistance Program (SNAP) and the Earned Income Tax credit (EITC). The supplemental measure does us a major service by showing in no uncertain terms how our current social safety net protects people from economic destitution. The reason for this is that the official poverty measure only counts cash income and pre-tax cash benefits (e.g., Social Security, Unemployment Insurance, and Temporary Assistance to Needy Families (TANF)) towards a household's resources to get over the poverty line. The supplemental poverty measure, on the other hand, adds to a household's resources near-cash government subsidies—programs that help families cover their expenditures on food (e.g., SNAP and the National School Lunch program), shelter (housing assistance from the Department of Housing and Urban Development (HUD)) and utilities (Low Income Home Energy Assistance Program (LIHEAP))—as well as after-tax income subsidies (e.g., EITC). This update is long overdue since the 1996 Personal Responsibility and Work Opportunity Reconciliation Act (also known as the Welfare Reform Act) largely replaced the traditional cash assistance program AFDC with after-tax and in-kind assistance.

Social Security, refundable tax credits (largely EITC but also the Child Tax Credit (CTC)), and SNAP benefits do the most to reduce poverty. In the absence of Social Security, the supplemental poverty rate would be 8.3% higher, shooting up from 16.1% to over 23.8%. Without refundable tax credits, the supplemental poverty rate would rise 2.8%, up to nearly 19%, with much of the difference being in child poverty. Finally, SNAP benefits prevent poverty across households from rising by 1.5%. The SPM gives us the statistical ruler by which to measure the impact of the major anti-poverty programs of the day. This is crucial information for current political feuds about falling over fiscal cliffs and hitting debt ceilings.

A Meager Supplement

Unfortunately, the new poverty measure adds all these important details to a fundamentally flawed picture of poverty.

In November 2012, the Census Bureau published, for only the second time, a national poverty rate based on the SPM: it stood at 16.1% (for 2011), just 1% higher than the official poverty rate of 15.1%. Why such a small difference? The fundamental problem is that the supplementary poverty measure, in defining the poverty line, builds from basically the same level of extreme economic deprivation as the old measure.

In an apples-to-apples comparison (see sidebar), the new supplemental measure effectively represents a poverty line roughly 30% higher than the official poverty

---

Federal Poverty Line vs. Supplemental Poverty Measure

The new supplemental measure (SPM) modestly bumps up the federal poverty line (FPL). Let's start with the published measures of the two thresholds. When you compare these, for a family of four (two adults, two children) the SPM is only 11% more than the official poverty line: $22,800 versus $25,200. But this isn't an apples-to-apples comparison. The official income poverty threshold is supposed to represent the income a family needs to cover all the expenses they have to support a minimal standard of living. The SPM income threshold on the other hand represents only the income a family needs to cover necessary food, clothing, shelter, and utility expenses (FCSU). "Nondiscretionary spending"—money spent on things like work-related expenses (transportation, childcare, and taxes) don't get counted in the income threshold. Instead, the SPM deducts these from what they call the "economic resources" a household has to cover their FCSU expenses. This way of accounting for such work-related expenses has the effect of making the SPM threshold look lower than it is actually is relative to the official poverty line. In order to make an apples-to-apples comparison, we have to adjust the SPM income threshold upward so that it includes the income needed to cover "nondiscretionary spending" the way the official poverty line does. This adds about 20% to the SPM income threshold, so that the supplementary poverty measure actually stands about 30% higher than the FPL.

---

income threshold for a family of four. For 2011, the official four-person poverty line was $22,800, an adjusted SPM income threshold—one that can be directly compared to the FPL—is about $30,500. Unfortunately, the NAS panel of poverty experts appears to have taken an arbitrarily conservative approach to setting the poverty income threshold. Reasonably enough, the NAS panel uses as their starting point how much households spend on the four essential items: food, clothing, shelter, and utilities. In a self-proclaimed "judgment call," they chose what they call a "reasonable range" of expenditures to mark poverty. What's odd is that their judgment leans back toward the official poverty line—the measure they referred to as "demonstrably flawed."

To justify this amount they show how their spending levels fall within the range of two other "expert budgets" (i.e., poverty income thresholds) in the poverty research. What they do not explain is why, among the 10 alternative income thresholds they review in detail, they focus on two of the lower ones. In fact, one of these two income thresholds they describe as an "outlier at the low end." The range of the 10 thresholds actually spans between 9% and 53% more than the official poverty line; their recommended range for the threshold falls between 14% and 33% above the official poverty line.

Regardless of the NAS panel's intention, the Inter-agency Technical Working Group (ITWG) tasked with the job of producing the new poverty measure adopted the middle point of this "reasonable range" to establish the initial threshold for the revised poverty line. This conflicts with what we know about the level of economic deprivation that households experience in the range of the federal poverty line. In a 1999 book *Hardship in America*, researchers Heather Boushey, Chauna Brocht,

Bethney Gunderson, and Jared Bernstein examined the rates and levels of economic hardship among officially poor households (with incomes less than the poverty line), near-poor households (with incomes between the poverty line and twice the poverty line), and not-poor households (with incomes more than twice the poverty line).

As expected, they found high rates of economic distress among households classified as "officially poor." For example, in 1996, 29% of poor households experienced one or more "critical" hardships such as missing meals, not getting necessary medical care, and having their utilities disconnected. Near-poor households experienced these types of economic crises only a little less frequently (25%). Only when households achieved incomes above twice the poverty line did the frequency of these economic problems fall substantially—down to 11%. (Unfortunately, the survey data on which the study was based have been discontinued, so more up-to-date figures are unavailable.) This pattern repeats for "serious" hardships that include being worried about having enough food, using the Emergency Room for healthcare due to lack of alternatives, and falling behind on housing payments. So if what we mean by poverty is the inability to meet one's basic needs, then twice the poverty line—rather than the SPM's 1.3 times—appears to be an excellent marker.

Let's consider what the implied new poverty income threshold of $30,500 feels like for a family of four. (This, by the way, is about what a household would take in with two full-time minimum-wage jobs.)

This annual figure comes out to $585 per week. Consider a family living in a relatively low-cost area like rural Sandusky, Mich. Based on the basic family-budget details provided by the Economic Policy Institute, such a family typically needs to spend about $175 on food (this assumes they have a nearby grocery store, a stove at home, and the time to cook all their meals) and another $165 on rent for a two-bedroom apartment each week. This eats up 60% of their budget, leaving only about $245 to cover all other expenses. If they need childcare to work ($180), then this plus the taxes they have to pay on their earnings ($60) pretty much wipes out the rest. In other words, they have nothing left for such basic needs as telephone service, clothes, personal care products like soap and toilet paper, school supplies, out-of-pocket medical expenses, and transportation they may need to get to work. Would getting above this income threshold seem like escaping poverty to you?

For many federal subsidy programs this doesn't seem like escaping poverty either. That's why major anti-poverty programs like that National School Lunch program, LIHEAP, and the State Children's Health Insurance Program (SCHIP) step in to help families with incomes up to twice the poverty line.

If the supplementary poverty measure tackled the fundamental problem of a much-too-low poverty line then it would likely draw an income threshold closer to 200% of the official poverty line (or for an apples-to-apples comparison, about 150% of the SPM income threshold). This would shift the landscape of poverty statistics and produce a poverty rate of an astounding one in three Americans.

Now What?

The Census Bureau's supplemental measure doesn't do what the underemployment rate did for the unemployment rate—that is, fill in the gap between the headline number and how many of us are actually falling through the cracks.

The poverty line does a poor job of telling us how many Americans are struggling to meet their basic needs. For those of us who fall into the "not poor" category but get struck with panic from time to time that we may not be able to make ends meet—with one bad medical emergency, one unexpected car repair, one unforeseen cutback in work hours—it makes us wonder, if we're not poor or even near poor, why are we struggling so much? The official statistics betray this experience. The fact is that so many Americans are struggling because many more of us are poor or near-poor than the official statistics lead us to believe.

The official poverty line has only been changed—supplemented, that is—once since its establishment in 1963. What can we do to turn this potentially once-in-a-century reform into something more meaningful? One possibility: we should simply rename the supplemental poverty rates as the severe poverty rate. Households with economic resources below 150% of the new poverty line then can be counted as "poor." By doing so, politicians and government officials would start to recognize what Americans have been struggling with: One-third of us are poor. ❑

Sources: Kathleen Short, "The Research Supplemental Poverty Measure: 2011," *Current Population Report*, U.S. Bureau of the Census, November 2012 (census.gov); Constance F. Citro and Robert T. Michael (eds.), *Measuring Poverty: A New Approach* (National Academy Press, 1995); Trudi Renwick, "Geographic Adjustments of Supplemental Poverty Measure Thresholds: Using the American Community Survey Five-Year Data on Housing Costs," U.S. Bureau of the Census, January 2011 (census.gov).

Article 2.6

TRADITIONAL MEASURES OF UNEMPLOYMENT ARE MISSING THE MARK

BY MARK PAUL
May/June 2019

We've heard it countless times in recent media accounts: The economy is at "full employment." The most recent jobs numbers, out the first week in May, show the official unemployment rate and applications for unemployment benefits are at a 50-year low. The last time a recovery was able to push the unemployment rate to these levels was in 1969, when my mom was just entering elementary school and the United States was in the heyday of the "Golden Age" of capitalism.

But economists are puzzled. Despite low unemployment (the current rate is just 3.6%), significant wage increases remain elusive. In other words, workers aren't benefiting much. This is deeply troubling in an era of unprecedented inequality, driven in large part by decades of a falling wage share. The size of our economic pie may be getting bigger, but the wage share, or the share of the economic pie going to workers, has been contracting. Further, a lack of wage growth isn't allowing for the true recovery that Main Street so desperately needs.

There could be a number of things at work which may explain the fact that wages aren't rising much, despite a low unemployment rate. For one, perhaps the relationship between wages and unemployment isn't as clear as economists previously thought. Many have criticized the Phillips curve—a graph, or family of graphs, that supposedly shows an inverse relationship between the unemployment rate and the inflation rate—arguing that it may have been a good model at one point in history, but no longer describes our current economy.

But maybe the puzzle isn't a puzzle at all. In economics, mainstream theory claims that a tight labor market will lead to rising wages, with the largest benefits going to those at the poorly compensated end of the labor market. Rather than this relationship being broken, it's plausible that the labor market isn't actually that tight. Perhaps there's still a sizable reserve army of unemployed that would work if there were decent paying jobs actually available.

Official unemployment, measured by the U-3 rate from the Bureau of Labor Statistics (BLS), is the percentage of individuals who are not employed at all but are currently looking for and available for work, as a percentage of the civilian labor force—excluding individuals who are incarcerated, institutionalized, or in the armed services. To be counted as unemployed, the person must have applied for a job within a four-week period. Importantly, this leaves out large swaths of people that should be counted among the unemployed, including people who are marginally attached to the labor force and people who are only working part time despite wanting to work full time.

Calculating the U-6 Unemployment Rate

The BLS calculates the official unemployment rate, U-3, as the number of unemployed people as a percentage of the civilian labor force. The civilian labor force consists of employed workers plus the officially unemployed. According to the BLS, the unemployed includes those without jobs who are available to work and have looked for a job in the last four weeks. Using this definition yields an official unemployment rate of 11.2%, or a seasonally adjusted rate of 11.1%, for June 2020, or about 12.3% after correcting for the miscalculations in the BLS survey.

But these headline unemployment rates dramatically understate the true extent of unemployment. First, they exclude anyone without a job who is ready to work but has not actively looked for a job in the previous four weeks. The BLS classifies such workers as "marginally attached to the labor force" so long as they have looked for work within the last year. Marginally attached workers include so-called discouraged workers who have given up looking for work because they can't find a suitable job, plus others who have given up for reasons such as school and family responsibilities, ill health, or transportation problems.

Second, the official unemployment rate leaves out part-time workers looking for full-time work: Part-time workers are counted as "employed" even if they work as little as one hour a week. The vast majority of people involuntarily working part time have had their hours cut due to slack in the labor market or unfavorable business conditions. The rest are working part time because they could only find part-time work.

Accounting for the large number of marginally attached workers and those involuntarily working part time raises the count of unemployed workers to 29.9 million for June 2020. It also expands the labor force by the number of marginally attached workers. Those numbers together push up the U-6 unemployment rate to 18.3%, or a seasonally adjusted rate of 18.0.%, or about 19.2% after correcting for the miscalculations in the BLS survey. —*John Miller*

Source: "The Employment Situation—June 2020," Bureau of Labor Statistics, July 6, 2020.

TABLE 1: THE JUNE 2020 UNEMPLOYMENT PICTURE
(DATA IN MILLIONS, NOT SEASONALLY ADJUSTED)

Employed	142.811
Unemployed	18.072
Civilian Labor Force	160.883
Marginally Attached Workers	2.486
Discouraged Workers	.684
Other reasons	1.803
Part time for Economic Reasons	9.306
Slack work or business conditions	8.043
Could only find part-time work	.978

Source: Bureau of Labor Statistics, Table A-1, A-5, A-8, A-15, A-16. The data are not seasonally adjusted because seasonally adjusted data for marginally attached workers are not available.

These mainstream measurements create an artificially low unemployment number. Importantly, the unemployment number is a critical indicator that informs policies across the government, including at the Federal Reserve. A misleading unemployment rate can have profound implications for the economy. For instance, if the Fed thinks the economy is at or near full employment, they may start tapping the breaks, as we saw numerous times in 2018. But broader indicators of unemployment show us this is still premature.

Alternative measures of labor market tightness, such as the employment to population ratio for workers in their prime working age (25–54), still haven't recovered to prerecession levels. Other indicators, like the labor force participation rate, are more than 4% below the rate that was reached during the economic boom in the late 1990s. While some economists point to an aging population, this accounts for only about half of the decline. Yet another alternative measure is the U-6 unemployment rate, which accounts for workers marginally attached to the labor force and workers forced to work part time due to economic reasons. This indicator shows that there is still significant slack in the labor market, with the BLS' U-6 unemployment rate (which adds the underemployed and workers who have given up looking for work to the U-3 rate) hovering around 7.3%.

The failure of the official unemployment rate to function as an adequate indicator of labor market strength is even catching the attention of economists at the White House. In the recent 2019 Economic Report of the President, economists started to question how we have long defined what it means to be "out of the labor force." Traditionally, if someone is out of the labor force, they're not counted as unemployed—and therein lies the problem.

For decades, roughly 55%–65% of people who were starting new work came from outside of the labor force; today, that number is approaching 75%. That's telling us three out of four people who are just starting to work again weren't counted as unemployed before. With few new hires coming from the pool of the unemployed, it's clear that our traditional measure is not measuring true labor market slack.

Policymakers need credible indicators to inform their decisions as they attempt to fine-tune the valves which help govern the economy. Looking across a broad span of labor market data, it's clear that many people remain on the sidelines, ready and willing to work if a decent paying job were available. It seems clear that the relationship between unemployment and wages hasn't totally broken, but the same can't be said for our measure of unemployment. ❏

Sources: U.S. Bureau of Labor Statistics, "Employment Population Ratio: 25-54 years," Federal Reserve Bank of St. Louis, May 2019 (fred.stlouis.org); U.S. Bureau of Labor Statistics, "Civilian Labor Force Participation Rate," Federal Reserve Bank of St. Louis, May 2019 (fred.stlouis.org); Jason Furman, "Trends in Labor Force Participation," Council of Economic Advisers, August 2015; "Economic Report of the President," March 2019 (whitehouse.gov).

Chapter 3

ECONOMIC GROWTH AND BUSINESS CYCLES

INTRODUCTION

Economic growth and business cycles could hardly be a more pertinent topic than they are today. Twelve years after the world went through the Great Recession, we are now experiencing yet another financial crisis. The Covid-19 pandemic, which is the deepest economic crisis since the Great Depression, has profound consequences for economic growth both at home and abroad. In this transformative moment, we need to ask ourselves what kind of growth we can live with on a warming planet, and what forms of growth are to be pursued.

The coronavirus pandemic has delivered the fastest, deepest economic shock in history, and in Article 3.1 John Miller explains the role of the National Bureau of Economics Research (NEBR) in determining the start date of the current recession.

Next, Arthur MacEwan (Article 3.2) chimes in on a subject of vital importance in macroeconomics—growth. MacEwan considers the carrying capacity of the planet, as well as externalities and the sustainability of growth, as he grapples with the possibilities for growth on a planet with a rapidly growing global population. The article includes an addendum that discusses the specific impact of the Covid-19 pandemic on growth.

Gerald Friedman (Article 3.3.) then addresses long-running debates about the reasons for the slowdown in the growth of economic output and standards of living. He disputes the view that "supply-side" factors, like the exhaustion of technological innovation, are the root problem. Rather, he points to economic policies that have stifled the growth in demand, as well as the growing power imbalance between employers and workers (which has stuck workers with a shrinking share of the economic pie).

Wrapping up the chapter is a short but incredibly relevant article on regional inequality in the United States by Gerald Friedman (Article 3.4). Regional growth disparities have led to increasing political and social polarization.

Discussion Questions

1. (Article 3.1) What, specifically, does the Dating Committee of the NEBR look for when determining whether or not the economy has entered a recession? What is a business cycle?

2. (Article 3.2) Is growth, in and of itself, a good thing, according to MacEwan? What is an "externality"? What is "sustainable growth"?

3. (Article 3.3) Why does Friedman disagree with the view that stagnant growth in output and standards of living are due to the exhaustion of technological innovation? What alternate explanation does he offer?

4. (Article 3.4) Why does Friedman say that "Wall Street favors the urban coasts"? What economic policies over the past 30 years reflect Wall Street's interests and how has that affected regional disparities in growth?

Article 3.1

DATING THE RECESSION

BY JOHN MILLER
June 2020

My wife Ellen and I got married in 2013 after living together for 15 years. The Justice of the Peace who married us told our twelve-year-old son Sam that we had already been married, and all she was doing was helping us fill out the paperwork to make our marriage official.

On June 8 of this year, the National Bureau of Economics Research (NBER), the nation's official arbiter of the business cycle, finished its paperwork, and made what we already knew official: The Covid-19 economic collapse is a recession, and a damn bad one. After reviewing data on the calamitous drop in employment and consumer spending and the deterioration of other economic variables, the NBER declared that the recession began in February 2020.

The depth and diffusion across the economy of the downturn convinced the NBER to announce the onset of the recession far more quickly than it usually does. The Business Cycle Dating Committee waited a full year into the last recession to declare that the Great Recession had begun in December 2007. This time, the NBER declared the onset of the current recession just four months after it had begun. The downturn was so pronounced that the Dating Committee didn't even bother waiting for data to confirm that the economic contraction would meet the economist's shorthand definition of a recession, two consecutive quarters of negative real (corrected for inflation) GDP growth.

Identifying Business Cycles

To understand what economists call a "recession," we need to look more closely at the method used by the NBER dating committee to date a business cycle, and its two phases—economic expansions and economic contractions (also called "recessions").

The NBER tracks the waves of economic activity that economists call "business cycles." A business cycle runs its course from the trough of a recession to the peak of an expansion and back down into a trough. In the first phase of the cycle—the expansion—the economy grows as companies produce more goods and services and hire workers. When the economy begins contracting, its second phase, companies produce fewer goods and workers lose their jobs. The NBER has identified 10 complete business cycles in the U.S. economy since World War II. The current task of the NBER was to decide when the expansion of the business cycle that began in June 2009 ended and entered its recession phase.

The NBER's Dating Committee, a group of eight economists, has no rigid rules for determining the start or finish of a business cycle. For instance, the committee looks for "a significant decline in economic activity that is spread across the economy and lasts more than a few months" to identify a recession. The committee considers a broad array of macroeconomic indicators but pays particular attention to two broad monthly measures: personal income less transfer payments, in real terms, and payroll employment from the Bureau of Labor Statistics' household survey, just as they did in dating the onset of the current recession.

In short, the committee eyeballs the data and is guided by their malleable definition of an economic contraction to identify a recession. Dating a recession using the economists' shorthand definition of a recession as two consecutive quarters of negative real growth measured by GDP would assign similar starting and ending points to a recession, but not always—particularly when a downturn is interrupted by a quarter of slow but positive economic growth. In addition, GDP data are available only after a considerable lag and are often subject to revision.

End of the Expansion

The NBER announcement also closed the books on the economic expansion that began in June 2009 and lasted 128 months, making it the longest expansion on record. The expansion, which spanned the Obama and Trump presidencies, might have been historically long but it was also slow, and did little to improve the lot of most people by historical standards. "Long but limp growth" was the *Financial Times'* far from flattering description of U.S. economic performance during the decade-long expansion. Its 2.3% economic growth rate was the slowest of any U.S. economic expansions since 1949. It also failed to even match the 2.9% average posted by the sluggish economic expansion during the last decade that led up the Great Recession, and it was nowhere close to the 4.3% average growth of the 10 previous expansions since 1949.

The employment record of the expansion was also a mixed bag. The expansion created fewer jobs per month than any economic expansion in the last five decades, with the exception of the jobless expansion from 2002 through 2007. But 113 straight months of positive job growth was enough to push the unemployment rate down to 3.5%, the lowest rate since 1969. Still, falling unemployment rates did little to improve workers' wages. The average hourly earnings of production and non-supervisory workers corrected for inflation rose just 0.7% per year, slower than the 1.1% per year rate during the 120-month long expansion in the 1990s, and less than half of the 1.7% per year rate during the 106-month long economic expansion of the 1960s. Only the dismal wage growth during the expansion of the previous decade did worse.

All told, working people were tightening their economic belts even when the economy was expanding. Now that the Covid-19 economy is contracting at an alarming rate, we are in real trouble. But you probably didn't need the NBER to tell you that. ❑

Sources: "NBER Determination of the February 2020 Peak in Economic Activity," National Bureau of Economic Research, June 8, 2020; "The record-breaking US economic recovery in charts," by Robin Wigglesworth and Keith Fray, The Financial Times, July 4, 2019; Bureau of Labor Statistics, Total private: Average Hourly Earnings of Production and Nonsupervisory Employees, 1982-84 Dollars, Seasonally Adjusted. Federal Reserve Bank of St. Louis, Federal Reserve Economic Data (FRED), Real Gross Domestic Product, Billions of Chained 2012 Dollars, Quarterly, Seasonally Adjusted Quarterly; and, All Employees: Total Nonfarm Payrolls, Thousands of Persons, Monthly Seasonally Adjusted Monthly; Federal Reserve Bank of St. Louis, Federal Reserve Economic Data (FRED).

Article 3.2

GROWTH, GROWTH, GROWTH: WHAT WILL HAPPEN?

BY ARTHUR MacEWAN
May/June 2020

> Dear Dr. Dollar:
> *Infinite economic growth on a finite planet is impossible and ruinous. And yet the drumbeat goes on for growth, growth, growth. Surely it is true that the world is grossly overpopulated; it is projected to grow to nine billion by 2050. How will the current economy serve these billions? It won't work, and it wouldn't work even if there were no global climate change at all.* —Daniel Warner, via e-mail

Well, yes, growth of population and of production cannot go on forever. And, while the problem is broader than climate change, climate change has generated new attention to the issue.

At the same time, concern about this issue is not new. With the early economic expansion of the industrial revolution, in 1798 the English cleric and economist Thomas Malthus published *An Essay on the Principle of Population as it Affects the Future Improvement of Society*, in which he argued that food production could not keep up with the unchecked growth of population. The result would be periodic famines or plagues that would limit population growth and, Malthus's principal concern, prevent the "perfectibility of the mass of mankind":

> … it appears, therefore, to be decisive against the possible existence of a society, all the members of which should live in ease, happiness, and comparative leisure; and feel no anxiety about providing the means of subsistence for themselves and families.
>
> Consequently, if the premises are just, the argument is conclusive against the perfectibility of the mass of mankind.

Regardless of the possibility—and the meaning—of the "perfectibility of the mass of mankind," Malthus was wrong about the possibilities for the huge expansion of both production and population. He never would have conceived of our current world with 7.8 billion people, let alone the global population of nine billion projected for mid-century.

I bring up Malthus, whose argument has been repeated many times over the last 220 years, not because I want to debunk the problem of population growth or the devastation that economic growth is inflicting on our planet. Rather, the reference to Malthus leads us to look beyond the obvious (growth cannot go on forever) and include a more complex examination of what is going on and what can be done to improve the situation. The problem, it turns out, is not simply growth, growth, growth, but also the nature of growth.

While economic growth of any sort cannot go on forever on a finite planet, the actual nature of growth over the past 200-plus years has been particularly problematic. Three aspects of that growth are especially significant: its dependence on fossil fuels, the high degree of inequality that growth has continually generated, and the ability of producers to "externalize" the environmental costs of their activities.

The Fossil-Fuel Basis of Economic Growth

While economic activity has long been based on energy from fossil fuels, and this reliance on fossil fuels grew along with the industrial revolution, the increased use of fossil fuels exploded in the last several decades. Between 1950 and 2017, the world's use of fossil fuels (coal, crude oil, and natural gas, measured in terawatt hours of energy) increased six-and-a-half fold. During this same period, world output (inflation-adjusted Gross Domestic Product) rose roughly twelvefold. (Later on in this article I will return to the falling intensity of fossil fuel use.)

The great increase in the emission of carbon dioxide from the burning of fossil fuels has been the principal (though not the only) cause of climate change. And in addition to climate change, the pollution from the burning of fossil fuels creates major health problems, generating costs of nearly $200 billion annually in the United States, to say nothing of human suffering and deaths throughout the world.

Increasingly, alternatives to fossil fuels are emerging and are cost-competitive—particularly solar and wind energy (see Article 10.5, "Is a Rapid Green-Energy Switch Prohibitively Costly?"). These innovations will not eliminate the problems associated with economic growth, but they do portend a different basis for economic growth that could be much less damaging to the planet and the people who inhabit it.

But this shift is not happening fast enough, as the recent spate of severe hurricanes, huge wildfires, and the rising sea level demonstrates. While there are technical problems in a full transition to green energy, the main problems are political: the continuation of large subsidies to fossil fuel companies, the failure of government authorities to require that fossil fuel prices include social costs, and the limits—including actual rollbacks in the United States—of regulations requiring greater fuel efficiency in automobiles.

Economic Inequality and the Environment

It is well established that economic inequality contributes to the damage of the natural environment. As the economist James Boyce has pointed out:

> Those who are relatively powerful and wealthy typically gain disproportionate benefits from the economic activities that degrade the environment [e.g., oil company executives and stockholders], while those who are relatively powerless and poor typically bear disproportionate costs. All else equal, wider political and economic inequalities tend to result in higher levels of environmental harm.

It could be added that the wealthy, to a large extent, are able to avoid the negative impacts of environmental degradation—for example, by living in cleaner communities, away from the toxin-generating factories and refineries that they own.

Also, the impact of inequality on what people see as their needs is pervasive. Modern economists have built their analyses on the premise that there is no limit to human wants. More is better, and economic growth will be driven indefinitely by people's striving for greater income to provide for greater consumption.

But things aren't so simple. It is more accurate to see human wants as being created by society, by what people see that others have. With great inequality, people at all levels are driven to strive to gain what others have—and to keep from sliding down the very steep income ladder.

Classical economists, unlike their modern-day descendants, recognized the social bases of people's wants. For example, in his 1776 classic, *The Wealth of Nations*, Adam Smith writes:

> ... in the present times, through the greater part of Europe, a creditable day-labourer would be ashamed to appear in public without a linen shirt, the want of which would be supposed to denote that disgraceful degree of poverty which, it is presumed, nobody can well fall into without extreme bad conduct.

It is not the linen shirt per se that is the need; the need is the capability to appear in public without shame.

Karl Marx expresses the same basic idea in his 1847 essay, *Wage Labor and Capital*. Discussing how people determine their economic well-being, he writes:

> A house may be large or small; as long as the surrounding houses are equally small it satisfies all social demands for a dwelling. But if a palace arises beside the little house, the little house shrinks into a hut. ... Our needs and enjoyments spring from society; we measure them, therefore, by society and not by the objects of their satisfaction. Because they are of a social nature, they are of a relative nature.

In the modern era, the economist Richard Easterlin has developed the argument that:

> Economic growth in itself does not raise happiness. Evidence for a wide range of developed, transition, and developing countries consistently shows that higher growth rates are not accompanied by greater increments in happiness.

Easterlin has supported his argument with data from a wide range of countries, highly developed (e.g., the United States and the wealthier countries of Europe) and less developed (e.g., Mexico, Turkey, and China).

"Happiness" is hard to both define and measure, of course, and Easterlin's analysis has been disputed. Nonetheless, it is well established that a high degree of inequality within a country is associated with a high degree of stress at all levels. Stress and happiness would seem to be inversely related. And, data suggest that happiness seems to be connected more with relative economic equality than with a country's higher level of average income. For example, the World Happiness Report for 2019 (from the Center for Sustainable Development at the Earth Institute of Columbia University) ranked Finland as number one on its happiness index, while the United States ranked 19th. Per capita income in the United States is 30% higher than in Finland, but economic inequality in Finland is much less than in the United States. (The World Bank reports Gini coefficients, a common measure of a country's inequality ranging theoretically from zero, perfect equality, to one, all income going to one person. For almost all countries, the Gini coefficient is between 0.25 and 0.65. For Finland and the United States, the World Bank reports coefficients, respectively, of 0.274 and 0.414.)

At least in relatively high-income countries, it seems likely that economic inequality and the insecurity that accompanies it are stronger drivers of consumerism and the sense of a need for growth, growth, growth. Higher taxes on the wealth and income of the affluent, along with several other social policies (see Article 5.7, "Are Taxes the Best Way of Dealing with Inequality?") could, then, dampen the drive for economic expansion. Indeed, greater economic equality is probably a necessary condition for creating a sustainable economy.

"Externalizing" Environmental Costs

When I was growing up in Portland, Ore., during the 1950s, our family often drove across the Columbia River to Washington and into the wilderness northeast of Portland. While the wilderness had many attractions, my clearest memory of those trips is the stench from the paper mill in Camas, Wash. The mill's air pollution, I am pretty sure, was only its most obvious impact on the environment, as I believe its waste was also dumped into the Columbia River.

The Camas paper mill is only a small example of a much larger phenomenon, and more well-known examples include the tragedy at Love Canal and the devastation at some 40,000 Superfund clean-up sites around the country. The largest expression of this phenomenon is the discharge of greenhouse gases from the burning of fossil fuels.

When economic activity generates pollutants—from toxic waste to noxious odors and noise—those engaged in that activity will profit by placing those pollutants on society outside their operations. They usually could do otherwise—cleaning up the waste, filtering out the odors, blocking the noise—but this would impose costs. They could internalize those costs, but this would reduce profits. So they externalize the costs, imposing them on society at large.

Of course, regulations can force, and have forced, polluters to internalize costs. Due to many factors, the paper mill at Camas has dwindled to a fraction of its 1950s size, but one of those factors has been the increased cost of reducing its pollution as a result of regulation. Over recent decades, in the United States we have attained cleaner air and cleaner water as a result of these regulations.

Businesses have, however, achieved many successes in limiting the extent of environmental regulations and getting the public to bear the cost of pollution controls. For example, the Washington legislature provided tax exemption incentives for the installation of pollution control equipment at the paper mill in Camas. In recent years, the Trump administration has striven to reduce environmental protections in a wide range of activities. The most recent example is the administration's effort to eviscerate fuel efficiency requirements for automobiles.

Yet, the Trump administration aside, the development of effective, enforced regulation of pollution has been a slow and limited process. Firms continue to externalize much of the costs of their activity. Meaningful regulation might slow economic growth, but it would make economic growth less damaging.

No Growth?

Although the cessation of economic growth might have desirable consequences, there is no way that "no growth" could be accomplished in the foreseeable future. Also, it would likely have some quite negative consequences unless it was accomplished by a massive economic redistribution (which is itself hardly likely in the foreseeable future). For example, because of the economic insecurity that generally accompanies great inequality, efforts to stop environmentally destructive activity have sometimes been opposed by workers and their unions because they need to maintain their employment. One reply by workers to regulations that would limit global warming has been statements to the effect of: "They're worried about what will happen in 2050 and beyond. We're worried about putting food on the table next week."

Deniers of the dangers of unlimited growth argue that the market will take care of the problem. There are, in fact, some market phenomena, consequences of economic growth, that contribute to reducing the rate of increase of its negative impacts. As noted above, the intensity of fossil fuel use—that is, the decline in fossil fuel use per unit of output—has declined over time. This is probably due, first, to increased efficiency in the use of fossil fuels, which in some instances is a result of regulation (as with automobiles). More generally, firms find ways to reduce their costs by finding more efficient ways of using energy. Second, as economies grow, they shift toward greater service activity and proportionally less reliance on manufacturing—with the former generally being less energy intensive. Yet, at best, all these changes do is reduce the rate of increase of environmental damage relative to what it otherwise would have been.

It seems clear that an economy run on the basis of the unfettered seeking of profits will be incapable of sufficiently limiting the negative environmental destruction that comes with growth. The "external" impacts of market activity cannot be altered without some forms of government intervention. At times, that intervention can take the form of taxes—for example, by raising the price of fossil fuels, which will reduce their use. But direct regulation is widely needed to prevent damaging processes from taking place. Certainly, very substantial regulation will be needed to dramatically reduce reliance on fossil fuels and forestall severe global climate change.

It also seems clear that little can be accomplished without the significant reduction of economic inequality. Economic inequality not only generates the push for economic growth. In addition, the concentration of political power, which is the necessary concomitant of economic inequality, will prevent the needed changes.❑

Sources: Hannah Ritchie and Max Roser, "Fossil Fuels," Our World in Data, 2020 (ourworldindata. org); Max Roser, "Economic Growth," Our World in Data, 2020 (ourworldindata.org); James K.

Boyce, "Is Inequality Bad for the Environment?" Political Economy Research Institute, University of Massachusetts-Amherst, April 2007 (scholarworks.umass.edu); World Bank Indicators Data, (data.worldbank.org/indicator); Don Brunell, "Brunell: Camas paper mill may be harbinger," *The Columbian*, November 21, 2017 (columbian.com); World Happiness Report for 2019 (worldhappiness.report); Richard A. Easterlin, *Happiness, Growth, and the Life Cycle* (Oxford University Press, August 2016); Richard A. Easterlin, "Happiness, Growth, and Public Policy," The Institute for the Study of Labor, February 2013, (iza.org).

UPDATE: COVID-19 AND ECONOMIC GROWTH

This article on "Growth, Growth, Growth" was conceived well before the Covid-19 crisis dominated our lives, and it was mostly written as the crisis began to unfold. Commentators are fond of saying such things as, "This virus changes everything." Yet, had the virus exploded on us earlier, the basic points of this article would not have been any different.

The issues that are addressed here—fossil fuel-based growth, economic inequality, and firms' externalization of pollutants—will remain important issues after the Covid-19 crisis starts to fade from our daily lives. The need for change has not been altered by the crisis.

Yet, the experience of the Covid-19 pandemic has created some possibilities for progressive change. As a commentator in the *New York Times* stated in early May, we have been experiencing "a pandemic that is exposing nearly every systematic flaw in society." Exposing systemic flaws—and they have been dramatically exposed in recent months—can be an important step forward. Consider:

- On April 22, the Centers for Disease Control and Prevention reported on a study of the racial and ethnic makeup of those with Covid-19 at several hospitals. In the communities surrounding the hospitals, African Americans were 18% of the population, but they were 33% of those hospitalized. And on May 3, a story in the *New York Times Magazine* cited data from sites across the country showing the disparate impact of Covid-19 on African Americans. For example: "In Mississippi, black people are 38% of the population but 61% of the deaths ... [and in] New York, which has the country's highest numbers of confirmed cases and deaths, black people are twice as likely to die as white people."

- During the Covid-19 shutdown, CNN reported that people living in the cities and towns of Northern India 100 miles from the Himalayas have been able to see the mountains for the first time in decades. In New York City, according to a study released by IQAir on April 22, PM-2.5 (particulate matter with a diameter of less than 2.5 micrometers) was down by 29% as compared to the average of the preceding four years (2.5 micrometers is about 3% of the diameter of a human hair). The study reports similar, though varying, change in nine other cities around the world.

- While the poor response to Covid-19 in the United States can be partially attributed to the failures of the Trump administration, the weakness of the U.S. public health system is not new, and U.S. medicine has long been subordinated to the focus on profits rather than health. Just one example, provided by a story in *The New Yorker* on May 4. One doctor complained: "Why are nearly all the notes in Epic [the electronic medical record system] … basically *useless* to understand what's happening to a patient?" A colleague replied: "Because notes are used to bill, determine level of service, and document it rather than their intended purpose, which was to convey our observations, assessment, and plan. Our important work has been co-opted by billing."

These examples could be buttressed by numerous others, from the racial and class makeup of those who have lost their jobs in the crisis to the dramatic resource differences between hospitals that serve a low-income clientele and those that serve a high-income clientele. All of these phenomena are exposing the "systemic flaws" in our society. These flaws were evident before we heard of Covid-19, but the Covid-19 crisis has brought them dramatically to the fore. Perhaps the experience of the crisis can help generate the action and organizing that will lead to change. *—AM* ❏

Sources: Eliza Blue, "A Shortage of Steak? Yes, and Ranchers Knew It Was Coming," *New York Times*, May 1, 2020 (nytimes.com); Centers for Disease Control and Protection, "Covid-19 in Racial and Ethnic Minority Groups," April 22, 2020 (cdc.org); Linda Villarosa, "'A Terrible Price': The Deadly Racial Disparities of Covid-19 in America," *New York Times Magazine*, April 29, 2020; Rob Picheta, "People in India can see the Himalayas for the first time in 'decades,' as the lockdown eases air pollution," CNN, April 9, 2020 (cnn.com); IQAir, "Covid-19 Air Quality Report," April 22, 2020 (iqair.com); Siddhartha Mukherjee "What the Coronavirus Crisis Reveals About American Medicine," *The New Yorker*, May 4, 2020 (newyorker.com).

Article 3.3

A FUTURE FOR GROWTH—IF WE CHOOSE IT?

BY GERALD FRIEDMAN
July/August 2017

Defenders of capitalism argue that the hierarchy and inequality of the system are worth it because, as Austrian economist Ludwig von Mises put it, capitalism "delivers the goods"—high and rising living standards. The long-term slowdown of wage growth in advanced capitalist economies, then, poses a challenge to the system's defenders. If capitalism is not only hierarchical and unequal, but increasingly does not "deliver the goods" to most, might we be better off replacing it with a different form of economic organization?

To the extent that wage stagnation is due to the changing balance of power between labor and capital, this reflects the unfairness of capitalism and its unequal distribution of wealth and power. From this perspective, the "Golden Age" of the post-World War II decades, with rising wages and steady improvements in working-class living standards, reflected that period's strong unions and progressive politics. Meanwhile, the stagnant wages and living standards since the 1970s are the result of union weakness and the growing dominance of conservative politics since the collapse of the New Deal coalition in the 1970s. On the other hand, to the extent that wages have stagnated for reasons unrelated to the capitalist system, wage stagnation may be regrettable—but does not reflect on the political question of whether we might be better off replacing capitalism with a different economic system.

Economist and Northwestern University professor Robert Gordon has been a leading advocate of the view that wage stagnation is largely an unfortunate result of circumstances beyond anyone's control or political remedy. In his recent masterpiece, *The Rise and Fall of American Growth*, Gordon pulls together his analysis of earlier economic growth, driven by important innovations such as water supply networks, electricity, and the internal combustion engine, which he argues have had a vastly greater impact on economic growth than anything developed over the past 50 years. Because of the exhaustion of technological progress, growth in productivity (output per hour of work) and in overall output have slowed, and brought down the growth rate for wages and living standards. It is all unfortunate, in Gordon's view, but beyond the power of either the state or organized labor to change.

However, Gordon is wrong on both counts: the slowdown in productivity is not "exogenous"—it is not due to causes outside of the capitalist economy, nor does it explain the slowdown in wage growth. Instead, both the productivity slowdown and wage stagnation are due to the go-slow economic policies followed by the United States and its major trading partners since the 1970s, policies intended to fight inflation even at the cost of higher unemployment rates and slower economic growth, policies chosen because economic elites gain by hoarding a larger share of an ever slower-growing pie.

How much has economic growth slowed? Gordon's argument rests on familiar grounds: The relatively rapid growth in the American economy (and other affluent capitalist economies) from the end of World War II through the early 1970s has not been matched in the nearly half-century since. Between 1947 and 1972, per capita income in the United States increased at a rate of 2.4% per year. This slowed to 2.0% per year for 1972–96, and then to only 1.3% per year since. The slowdown after 1972 means a reduction in per capita income of over 25% by 2017: Instead of the nearly $70,000 that it would have been in 2017 at the 1947–1972 growth rate, it is only about $52,000.

PER CAPITA INCOME, 1947–2017

What accounts for the slowdown in growth? Gordon attributes the slowdown to various "headwinds," with a focus on a fall in technological progress after the 1960s. In the 1972–96 period, rising employment, especially of women, compensated somewhat for falling productivity. More total hours of work counteracted low growth in output per hour worked, and buoyed up the growth in total output. In the tech boom of the 1990s, computerization boosted productivity growth enough to get per capita income rising at the old rate, though only briefly. Since 2004, demographic conditions, Gordon argues, have led Americans to drop out of the labor force, and productivity has fallen off due to declining technological innovation.

Gordon's main mistake is that he does not take account of changing macroeconomic conditions or total ("aggregate") demand. While focusing on the growth in the supply of inputs, workers, machines, and innovative ideas, Gordon ignores the other side of markets, the demand for output. Rather than a slowdown in supply, slow growth since the 1970s reflects a shortfall in aggregate demand because governments and monetary authorities have slowed economic growth in order to restrain inflation. Slow growth in aggregate demand has meant that workers face higher unemployment and shorter hours, and companies reduce investment in physical plant and in research and development—leading to slower growth in productivity. The long-term slowdown in growth coincides with a rise in unemployment, mostly due to deficiency of demand, except in the 1996–2004 period. During those years, booming demand drove job creation, technological progress, and overall growth back up to their earlier levels.

GROWTH RATES SINCE 1972

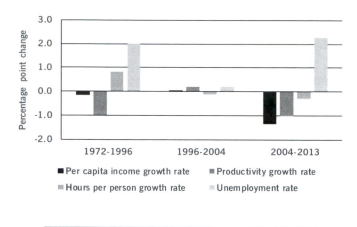

Why has productivity fallen? Loss of creativity or declining demand? Gordon's claim that technological progress has slowed for "exogenous" reasons—factors outside of the economic system, such as an exhaustion of ideas—is crucial to the argument that political decisions and the power of capital are not responsible for the slowdown in income and wage growth. The relationship between productivity growth and overall economic growth runs in both directions. Faster productivity growth may increase GDP growth, especially when falling costs may increase a country's exports. But faster overall economic growth, fueled by rising demand, also generates faster productivity growth by incentivizing productivity-enhancing investment and innovation. The relationship between productivity and GDP growth is strong enough to explain 60% of the decline in productivity between 1947–1972 and 1973–1996, and all of the decline in productivity since.

PRODUCTIVITY GROWTH AND GDP GROWTH, 1947–2017

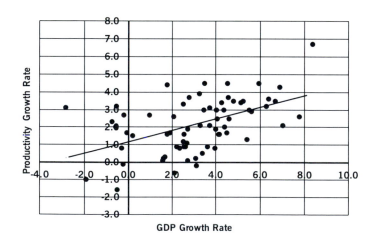

Since the 1970s, however, government macroeconomic policy has emphasized "inflation targeting"—achieving very low inflation rates—at the expense of growth in incomes and employment. Slower growth in demand, meanwhile, contributes to slower productivity growth by discouraging new investments—in physical plants, research and development, and worker training. In addition, when demand is weak, labor markets are "slack," and workers have little bargaining power. Lower wage pressure, in turn, means lower investment in labor-saving technologies. Capitalists have favored such policies for a simple reason—they have undermined workers' bargaining power and therefore tilted the distribution of income in the capitalists' favor.

Why don't Americans work as much as they used to? In addition to the decline in productivity, Gordon attributes the decline in output to falling employment, caused by the aging of the U.S. population. But an aging population is only part of the explanation. Into the 1990s, compared with other capitalist economies, the United States had high and rising employment rates with a rapidly increasing share of women in the paid labor force. This began to change after 1990, and changed more dramatically after 2000. Women's employment peaked in 2000 and has fallen since then, and men's employment and labor force participation have fallen sharply since around 1970. The United States' paid labor force has gotten dramatically smaller compared to its potential because of falling demand for goods and services, and therefore falling demand for workers. As a result, a significant share of the U.S. population has given up looking for work. The problem originates from a drop in demand, not a fall in supply. An aggressive fiscal policy, as was proposed by Senator Bernie Sanders (D-Vt.) in his 2016 presidential campaign, could help to bring more people into the workforce and into employment; and policies, like those in some Scandinavian countries, to help parents with childcare costs could, especially, help promote women's employment.

EMPLOYMENT RATES, FEMALE AND MALE, AGED 25–54

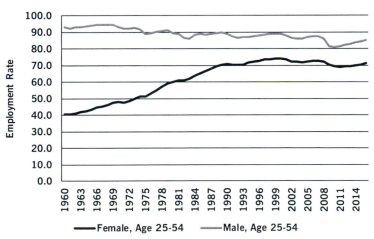

What about the distribution of income? Rising productivity is crucial for increasing national income but it does not necessarily determine the path of real wages. While for most of American history down to the mid-1960s, productivity and real wages grew together, since then they have diverged. From the mid-1960s through the mid-1970s, real wages grew by 1.5% a year but productivity grew nearly 1% a year faster.

For the next 20 years, however, real wages fell by around 0.5% a year even though productivity grew by over 1.7% a year; the slowdown in productivity growth of less than 1% a year was less than half the slowdown in wage growth of 2% a year. While wages have been rising since the mid-1990s, they have continued to grow at a much slower rate than productivity. Instead of leading to higher wages, rising productivity has fed growing corporate profits with a declining share of income going to labor. ❏

HOURLY EARNINGS VS. PRODUCTIVITY, 1964–2016

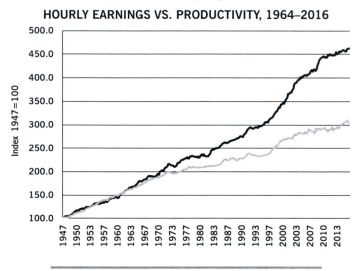

Sources: Llewellyn Rockwell, ed., *The Free Market Reader* (Ludwig von Mises Institute, n.d.); Jacob S. Hacker and Paul Pierson, *Winner-Take-All Politics* (Simon & Schuster, 2010); Robert B Reich, *Beyond Outrage* (Vintage Books, 2012); Richard D Wolff, *Capitalism Hits the Fan* (Olive Branch Press, 2010); David M. Kotz, *The Rise and Fall of Neoliberal Capitalism* (Harvard University Press, 2015); Robert Solow, "We'd Better Watch Out," *New York Times Book Review,* July 12, 1987; Robert J. Gordon, "Does the 'New Economy' Measure Up to the Great Inventions of the Past?," *Journal of Economic Perspectives* (December 2000); Robert J. Gordon, "Is U.S. Economic Growth Over?" Working Paper, National Bureau of Economic Research, August 2012 (nber.org); Robert J. Gordon, *The Rise and Fall of American Growth* (Princeton University Press, 2016); Nicholas Kaldor, *Causes of the Slow Rate of Economic Growth of the United Kingdom* (Cambridge University Press, 1966); R. Dixon and A. P. Thirlwall, "A Model of Regional Growth-Rate Differences on Kaldorian Lines," *Oxford Economic Papers* (1975); P. J. Verdoorn, "Verdoorn's Law in Retrospect: A Comment," *The Economic Journal* (1980); St. Louis Federal Reserve, Real gross domestic product per capita (fred.stlouisfed.org); Robert J. Gordon, "The Demise of U.S. Economic Growth: Restatement, Rebuttal, and Reflection," Working Paper, National Bureau of Economic Research, February 2014 (nber.org); Bureau of Labor Statistics, Nonfarm Business, Labor productivity (output per hour) (bls. gov); St. Louis Federal Reserve, Employment Rate: Aged 25-54: Males, Females for the United States (fred.stlouisfed.org).

Article 3.4

GROWING TOGETHER, FLYING APART
Regional Disparities in American Politics and Economics

BY GERALD FRIEDMAN
March/April 2018

For decades after the New Deal of the 1930s, the different states and regions of the United States grew together. As different regions—North and South, East and West—became more alike in their economies, they also came to resemble each other more in their politics and social attitudes. The Civil Rights revolution, of course, contributed to this by ending the South's peculiar system of *de jure* segregation. Also important in spreading economic development throughout the United States, however, were New Deal programs, including welfare spending, progressive taxation, and programs to promote development in rural and mountain areas. (These include the placing of military bases in southern and western states.)

During the post-World War II era, the New Deal continued to shape federal programs, raising income in poorer states, in rural regions, the South, and in the mountain West, and equalizing living standards throughout the United States. Beginning in the late 1970s, however, cutbacks in government social spending, changes in tax policy, and deregulation, including the opening of markets to foreign competition, reversed the narrowing of regional disparities. In recent decades, while goods-producing interior regions, including southern states, have suffered from foreign competition in manufacturing and other areas, richer coastal regions have benefited from deregulation, stronger protection of intellectual property, and the expansion of foreign trade in entertainment and financial and business services. These economic changes have contributed to a political upheaval where industrial regions in the South and Midwest have abandoned their traditional loyalty to the Democratic Party even while Democrats have gained in prosperous, export-oriented coastal regions.

THE REGIONS

Coastal: CA, CO, DE, DC, FL, HI, MD, MA, ME, NH, NJ, NY, NC, OR, PA, RI, VT, VA, WA
Deep South: AL, GA, LA, MS, SC
Border South: AR, KY, MO, OK, TN, TX, WV
Midwest: IL, IN, MI, OH, WI
Farm: IA, KS, MN, NE, ND, SD

Regional growth disparities have increased (see Figure 1). Starting in the 1970s, a larger share of economic growth began to go to export-oriented economies on the coasts and in the farm belt, less to other rural areas in the South and West and to the industrial Midwest. Before 2000, income generally grew faster in the poorer regions of the South than in the coastal regions. But since 2000, coastal entertainment, high tech, and financial centers like Los Angeles, New York, and San Francisco have boomed while income growth in the South has slowed and the industrial Midwest and the mountain West have continued to lag. Between 1963 and 2000, per capita income differentials narrowed, and the per capita income of the coastal states soared above nearly every other region's. In 1963, for example, the per capita income in coastal states was 48% above that of the Deep South and the differential fell to 34% by 2000. Moreover, by 2016 the per capita income in the coastal states rose to 28% above the industrial Midwest, up from -3% in 1963; 46% above the Border South states, up from 33% in 2000; and 33% above the Mountain states, compared to 15% in 2000. Only the export-oriented farm belt increased its relative income compared with the coastal states.

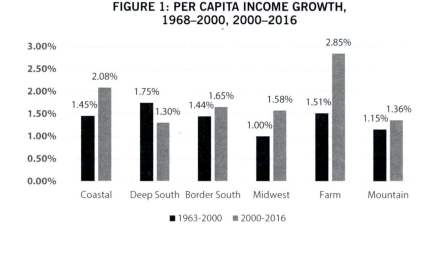

FIGURE 1: PER CAPITA INCOME GROWTH,
1968–2000, 2000–2016

Wall Street favors the urban coasts (see Figure 2). Economic policies favoring Wall Street (as well as entertainment and other professional types of employment) over Main Street benefit residents of coastal states more than those in the nation's interior. Different regions have been affected differently by economic policies benefiting the export of financial and professional services in exchange for imports of manufacturing goods. Regions with goods-producing industries, like manufacturing, have suffered from import competition. However, affluent coastal regions with fewer workers in manufacturing and mining have benefited from the export of financial and business services, which has allowed these regions to maintain employment-producing and hard-to-import services such as education, entertainment, and healthcare.

FIGURE 2: EMPLOYMENT MIX BY INDUSTRY AND REGION

Economic policies since the early 1970s have accelerated the decline of U.S. unions (see Figure 3). While the share of workers belonging to unions has declined in every state, the greatest absolute decline has been in the industrial Midwest, where the share of workers belonging to unions has fallen by nearly 14 percentage points, and the Deep South, where the union membership share has fallen by nearly 7 percentage points or 60%. By contrast, unions have fared better in the affluent coastal regions where total membership has been sustained by the growth of public-sector unions. Indeed, the coastal states are now the most unionized part of the United States. While national policies of free trade and industrial deregulation, combined with the hostility of economic and political elites to public-sector organization, have decimated unions throughout the rest of the United States, unions, especially public-sector unions, have fared better in affluent coastal states than elsewhere.

FIGURE 3: UNION SURVIVAL RATE
UNION MEMBERSHIP RATE 2016 COMPARED WITH 1983

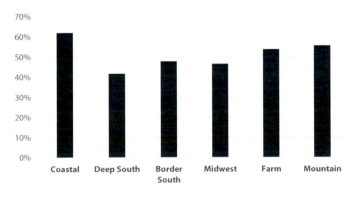

Regional economics affects politics (see Figure 4). Throughout the 1980s, the Democratic Party represented poorer parts of the country and campaigned for broad-based economic growth through pushing for industrial policies, business regulations, and income redistribution. Since the economic turmoil of the 1970s, however, and with the Democrats' embrace of the Civil Rights movement and the Republicans' embrace of Nixon's "Southern Strategy," the two parties have shifted. The Democrats now represent the more prosperous and cosmopolitan regions while Republicans represent the regions left behind by economic growth. The new (and influential) affluent component of the Democrats' base has pulled them away from policies that promote shared regional growth, such as support for managed trade or industrial policy, even while Republicans remain tied to neoliberal policies of fiscal austerity and industrial deregulation that hurt many of their own supporters. While the Democrats continue to support elements of the social safety net, such as Social Security, their support for income redistribution has been softened, as when democratic President Bill Clinton supported the repeal of the Aid to Families with Dependent Children program. ❑

FIGURE 4: DEMOCRATIC VOTE SHARE BY REGION, 1976–2016

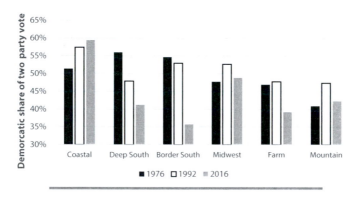

Sources: Figure 1: Spreadsheet "State exports" Tab "State GDP 1999–2016." Per capita income (PCY) from state GDP (from Bureau of Economic Analysis) divided by population (from the Census). The change in PCY is the 2016 level divided by the relative price increase 1978-2016, total divided by the 1978 level. The price level is from the BLS in tab CPI in the "State exports" spreadsheet. Annual change is the log of the change divided by the number of years.

Figure 2: Total Employment and employment by industry in 2016 is from the Bureau of Labor Statistics, Establishment Data, State Employment, Seasonally Adjusted, Table D1. Data are in spreadsheet "State Exports" tab "Employment Mix."

Figure 3: Union decline uses data from Union Stats. It is in spreadsheet "State exports" Tab "2017."

Figure 4: Spreadsheet "State Exports" Tab "Elections". Results for 1976 and 1992 are from U.S. Election Atlas. Results for 2016 are from the *New York Times*.

Chapter 4

UNEMPLOYMENT AND INFLATION

INTRODUCTION

In an introductory macroeconomics course, students are likely to hear that two key macroeconomic outcomes are the rates of unemployment and inflation, and that there is a trade-off between the two. In recent years, we have seen the seesaw of unemployment and inflation tilt very heavily in one direction. Unemployment in the United States and other countries has reached rates not seen since the Great Depression, while many countries have experienced not only very low inflation but even deflation for the first time in living memory. Moreover, the recent pandemic is upending some of the relative calm of the last decade, and it is bound to force macroeconomists and policymakers to rethink their assumptions.

Alejandro Reuss (Article 4.1) starts off this chapter by illustrating different ways in which the current pandemic has exposed the fault lines of our labor markets and the existing economic system in general. In the absence of a strong safety net, many low-income workers have been forced to continue to work in less-than-safe conditions. Others have become unemployed and have had to face the financial, physical, and psychological consequences of unemployment in a system that lacks universal health care and ties health insurance to employment (if at all).

Following a similar argument, Nicole Aschoff (Article 4.2) provides an overview of what employment has come to mean in the gig economy. She highlights how the precariousness of app workers has become evident during the pandemic, as well as the ways in which this new class of workers is fighting back.

When it comes to understanding the macroeconomy, it is important to understand the trade-off between inflation and unemployment described by the Phillips curve. Economist Ramaa Vasudevan (Article 4.3) takes a careful look at the relationship between inflation and unemployment and how that trade-off changed during two historical periods: the stagflation of the 1970s and the productivity boom of the 1990s. She attributes the sustained low inflation during the 1990s, despite low unemployment, to the relatively weak bargaining position of workers.

Next, economist Robert Pollin (Article 4.4) delves into why the textbook trade-off between inflation and unemployment affects the returns of stockholders and other investors. The answer, Pollin points out, is "all about class conflict."

Higher unemployment rates and fewer jobs eat away at the bargaining power of workers, keeping wage growth and inflation in check and corporate profit margins wide. As Pollin sees it, the unemployment rate consistent with price stability—the so-called "natural rate"—declined dramatically in the 1990s because workers' economic power eroded during that decade.

Then, in Article 4.5, John Miller examines how a $15 minimum wage would reduce poverty and increase the incomes of a large numbers of adult (not just teen) workers. Miller also highlights the fact that a growing body of research disputes the mainstream argument that minimum wage increases lead to an uptick in unemployment.

Next, in Article 4.6 Miller explains how enhanced unemployment benefits contribute to a more robust economic recovery. Contrary to the mainstream perspective of the *Wall Street Journal*, these benefits actually help workers make ends meet until jobs become available again.

Concluding the chapter, Alejandro Reuss (Article 4.7) turns to the writings of John Maynard Keynes and arguments about whether declining wages are the cure for unemployment. He outlines Keynes' classic arguments against conservative economists who believed that wage declines were part of the economy's "self-correction" during a depression, and that depression conditions worsen when wages drop.

Discussion Questions

1. (Article 4.1) According to Reuss, why should we not consider the human toll of the coronavirus pandemic a "natural disaster"?

2. (Article 4.2) Based on the arguments presented by Aschoff, how do you foresee the rise of the "app worker" shaping the overall nature of labor markets?

3. (Article 4.3) Why is there a "trade-off" between unemployment and inflation?

4. (Article 4.4) The economists who first posited the idea of a "natural rate of unemployment" certainly did not think they were devising a class-conflict theory. Yet Pollin says the "natural rate" is "all about class conflict." Why?

5. (Article 4.5) How do mainstream economists argue that minimum wage increases raise unemployment? What are the contemporary counter arguments? Why are minimum wage increases important for reducing inequality?

6. (Article 4.6) Why does the *Wall Street Journal* expect that enhanced unemployment benefits will prevent employees from working? How does the available evidence contradict that argument?

7. (Article 4.7) "Deflation" means a decrease in the overall price level. Lower prices sound good to most people. So, what's not to like about deflation?

Article 4.1

HOW THE CORONAVIRUS BECAME AN ECONOMIC CRISIS

BY ALEJANDRO REUSS
June 2020

S ome of the economic consequences of a massive communicable-disease crisis might arise in any society, regardless of the system of economic organization. Others, however, differ depending on the characteristics of the economic system. The particular ways that the coronavirus crisis has unfolded in
the United States should be understood as a series of shock waves, transmitted
through the structures of a capitalist economy and through the particular features of U.S. capitalism. In the United States and other countries, the coronavirus pandemic—in addition to being a public health disaster—has also triggered
a massive economic crisis. Overall economic output, income, and employment
have plummeted. The Congressional Budget Office (CBO) has predicted that
U.S. per capita GDP will decline at an annual rate of nearly 40% in the second
quarter of the year. That means that if the same rate of drop-off continued for
a full year, incomes would drop (on average) to only 60% of what they were a
year before.

Total employment, according to the Bureau of Labor Statistics (BLS) job
report for April, was down by more than 25 million compared to February. The
"headline" (or U-3) unemployment rate calculated by the BLS rose to nearly 15%.
That number, however, does not include jobless workers who have given up looking for work ("discouraged workers") or those who want to work full time but
can only find part-time work ("involuntary part-time workers"). The BLS's broad-
est unemployment measure (U-6), which adds those workers and some others
to the U-3 figure, surged to nearly 23% in April. The May report showed total
employment bouncing back somewhat, by about 4 million, still down by more
than 20 million compared to February. The headline unemployment rate, meanwhile, remained over 13% and the U-6 rate over 20%. However, we always need
to take official employment and unemployment figures with a grain of salt. This
is even more true now, as the coronavirus crisis has caused deviations from normal data collection methods and ambiguity about how some workers are counted
(the unemployment figures would be higher if "furloughed" employees who are
not getting paid were counted as unemployed). Moreover, we should not take the
bounce-back in the employment numbers in May as indicative that the economy
has turned the corner into recovery. That cannot be determined from one month
of data.

We can place the mechanisms that have turned the public health crisis in the
United States into a massive recession into two categories, those originating on
the demand side of the economy and those originating on the supply side. The
two sides are intertwined—changes in demand for goods and services affect the
amounts produced, and changes in supply conditions affect people's ability and
willingness to spend.

Demand-Side Effects

First, people have cut back on consumption activities that entail close contact with others and might lead to infection (such as dining out, attending events with large crowds, shopping at brick-and-mortar stores, etc.). In a capitalist economy, this is expressed as a decline in demand for those goods and services, a resulting decline in businesses' desired output, and, in turn, a decline in total work hours.

In an affected industry, owners and managers decide to reduce output, rather than have workers produce goods that cannot be sold. That means, in turn, that businesses reduce purchases of physical inputs (reducing or canceling orders for materials, energy, etc.) and labor power (cutting worker hours or laying workers off). Maintaining such purchases would only result in unnecessary expenses and larger business losses, which profit-seeking businesses aim to avoid.

The BLS employment data for April reflected the disproportional impact on the service sector, and especially on leisure and hospitality. Total private-sector employment was down by more than 20 million compared to February. In the leisure and hospitality sector alone, it was down by over eight million. In other words, while those industries accounted for only about 13% of total private employment before the massive job loss began, they were responsible for about 40% of the lost jobs. Businesses in the hard-hit sectors tried to adapt, like restaurants ramping up take-out and delivery services. Some other sectors (like supermarkets, online retail, package delivery, etc.) saw increases in demand and new hiring, but not nearly enough to offset the declines elsewhere. Leisure and hospitality employment recovered to a degree in May—by over one million jobs—but remained about seven million below the February level.

The effects of job loss in one sector can multiply across the economy: To the extent that affected workers cut back their spending, all industries that supply consumer goods and services face a decline in demand. Business owners and managers in those industries, therefore, also reduce output and work hours.

The magnitude of this second-order effect is not automatic or inevitable. It clearly depends on economic policies and institutions. The more replacement income laid-off workers get from "safety net" programs like unemployment insurance, the less they have to cut back their consumption spending. High levels of replacement income mean workers without jobs can still get the things they need to live, and workers in other industries are less likely to face layoffs or cuts in hours due to falling demand. For this reason, economists describe such policies as "automatic stabilizers." When there is a drop in demand, these policies automatically inject some spending back into the economy.

Income-replacement policies obviously do exist in capitalist economies. The current unemployment insurance system in the United States—a combination of federal and state policies—dates back to the 1930s. The federal government and some states have periodically expanded unemployment benefits, especially during crisis periods such as the Great Recession of 2007–2009 and its aftermath, and have done so again in the current crisis. The Coronavirus Aid, Relief, and Economic Security (CARES) Act increases benefit levels, the duration of benefits, and eligibility. Combined state and federal benefits, on average, will replace close to 100% of laid-off workers' lost pay through the end of July (not including the value of employer-provided benefits like health insurance). This does not necessarily mean, however, that demand for goods and services is unaffected by the surge in unemployment. Workers who have lost their jobs may still face a decline in their disposable incomes because of the loss of benefits like health insurance and the resulting increase in out-of-pocket costs. Workers experiencing cuts in work hours may not qualify for unemployment benefits. Some workers, such as undocumented immigrants, are denied federal benefits even when they are otherwise qualified. In addition, since the expanded benefits are only temporary, and future

---

What is Capitalism?

Mainstream economists don't tend to talk about "capitalism" very much, preferring terms like "market economy." They like to celebrate markets—unregulated "free markets" most of all—and to emphasize markets in describing modern economies like that of the United States. But there is more to capitalist economies than just markets. Economists of non-mainstream theoretical perspectives, known as "radical political economists," emphasize three major characteristics of capitalism—private property, wage labor, and production for profit. (For a more in-depth discussion, see Samuel Bowles, Richard Edwards, Frank Roosevelt, and Mehrene Larudee, "Capitalism as an Economic System," in *Understanding Capitalism: Competition, Command, and Change in the U.S. Economy*, 4th ed.)

1) Private property. When people think of private property, they may think first of personal belongings, such as their clothes, furniture, cars, or homes. Radical political economists, however, emphasize the economic and political importance of private ownership of the means of production (things that are used to produce other things, such as land, factories, machinery, raw materials, etc.). In the United States and other capitalist societies, these are owned mainly by private individuals or companies, and in fact by a relatively small percentage of the population. This is a familiar fact of life, yet there have been other societies, both ancient and modern, in which such resources cannot be privately owned, or at least some key resources cannot be privately owned. Critics of private ownership of the means of production, especially when highly concentrated, point to the enormous power that the control of resources gives to a relatively small number of capitalist owners, not least over the majority who have no other way to make a living but to work for them.

2) Wage labor. In capitalist economies, most employed people (as officially defined for purposes of employment statistics, those who work "for pay or profit") work for someone else for pay. They do not work for themselves, in their own businesses or on their own farms, but for some employer. Some wage or salary employees work for government agencies, but the vast majority work for private companies. In the United States and other similar economies, the predominance of wage labor has grown dramatically over time. Over the last couple of centuries, the U.S. economy has been transformed from one based on a combination of slavery, self-employment, wage labor, and unpaid household labor to one largely based on just the last two.

job prospects are so uncertain, many workers (employed and unemployed) may cut back their spending anyway.

In the United States, business owners and managers have historically been more successful than in other high-income capitalist countries in limiting unemployment insurance benefits. The eligibility duration and the replacement rates in the United States have generally been lower than for most other high-income countries. Since public "safety net" programs reduce workers' reliance on wage employment for income—and with it, employers' power over workers—capitalists have historically opposed such policies. Where unemployment insurance and other safety net programs do exist, business groups usually fight to keep benefits low and eligibility

---

With the rise of capitalism and its worldwide expansion, starting about 500 years ago, both wage labor and slavery expanded dramatically. (If we treat wage labor as a defining feature of capitalism, then an economy based on slavery is, by definition, not a capitalist economy. Some radical political economists, however, view the modern slavery-based economies in the Americas after colonization as examples of a different form of capitalism.) While slavery has by no means been eradicated, over the last couple of centuries wage labor has largely superseded slave labor. Small business ownership and self-employment was also much more prevalent in earlier times than it is today. As large capitalist enterprises came to dominate most industries, however, self-employment became quite marginal. The United States is not mainly a country of independent proprietors—however much nostalgia may exist for a bygone age of small farmers, craftspeople, and shopkeepers—but of wage and salary employees and capitalist employers. The capitalists own the means of production and the employees work for them.

3) Production for sale (with the aim of profit). The people who employ wage workers mostly do not directly consume the goods and services produced by those workers. In other economic systems, such as feudalism, those who appropriate goods produced by other people may aim primarily to keep those goods for their own enjoyment. The feudal lords, for example, might directly consume the crops produced by the serfs. Even today, in capitalist economies, some people are employed to directly produce goods and services for their employers' consumption (such as cooks, cleaners, drivers, and gardeners employed by the affluent).

For the most part, however, employers take possession of goods produced by wage and salary employees in order to sell them at a profit. The shareholders and executives of General Motors do not want the cars as such; the owners of McDonalds do not want the hamburgers. They want the profits from the sale of these goods. This means that overall investment, employment, and incomes in a capitalist economy are largely dependent on private business owners' and executives' expectations of future profits. This puts pressure on governments to create profitable conditions for private business, and gives owners and executives a great deal of power—extending way beyond the individual company or workplace to the politics of entire nations.

restrictive. Employers and the politicians beholden to them, moreover, typically push to keep the expansion of such programs during crisis periods strictly temporary. They do not want increased public economic security programs to become the "new normal."

Supply-Side Effects

Second, there are negative effects on overall economic output and employment due to disruptions on the supply side of the economy. Even in industries that involve little or no contact between workers and the public, for example, workers faced risk of infection if they went in to work and came into contact with other workers. Production in these industries has been interrupted by individual workers' decisions to stay away from work, groups of workers collectively demanding the suspension of work, and above all mandated public-health shutdowns of "nonessential" workplaces. Production and employment declined even if people were still able and willing to pay for the kinds of goods the affected industries produced—so this was not just a result of the fall in demand.

It may be possible for work to resume, for some occupations, with appropriate adaptations. The widespread, though highly unequal, transition to remote work is an example. Some forms of work might be compatible with new social distancing practices. Others might be safe with proper protective equipment. To the extent that production is interrupted, however, the total output of goods and services declines—as do the market incomes of employers and workers. Employees of shutdown businesses, whether formally laid off or "furloughed," do not get paid their wages. Expanded unemployment insurance benefits can reduce the impact on workers and the ripple effects across the economy. For reasons described above, however, job losses may still feed into a decline in demand, production, and employment across the economy.

In addition, people engage in specific kinds of consumption activities connected with their work lives. For example, most people normally have to get back and forth between home and the workplace. With millions working remotely, furloughed (with jobs but not actually working), or unemployed, people have been traveling much less. Along with a collapse in leisure travel, this has contributed to a dramatic fall in demand for gasoline, sending oil prices plummeting.

A decline in production in one industry, in addition, can have second-order effects on businesses in other industries. Businesses are connected to each other by input-output relations. A business in one industry, for example, buys needed inputs (machines, materials, etc.) from businesses in another industry. It may sell some of its output not to consumers but to other businesses, for which those outputs are needed inputs. Businesses where production has been interrupted (say, due to shutdown orders) will stop ordering inputs as normal, negatively affecting businesses in "upstream" industries. If they produce inputs used by other businesses, those "downstream" industries can be negatively impacted as well. When automakers shut down operations, for example, so do parts manufacturers. When meatpacking plants shut down, retail sales in supermarkets and take-out restaurants drop.

Limitations of the Demand-Boosting Playbook

There are well-known policy responses to recessions triggered by a collapse in overall demand in the economy, going back to the Great Depression of the 1930s. To inject additional demand into the economy, the government might:

- Purchase goods and services from private businesses
- Make cash payments to businesses, without requiring goods and services in return
- Make cash payments to individuals, without requiring work in return
- Directly employ individuals for pay
- Cut taxes to increase individuals' disposable incomes
- Increase the money supply, with the aim of reducing interest rates
- Directly make loans to businesses or individuals

We have already seen some of these demand-boosting policies put in place in the United States and elsewhere. The CARES Act included, for example, about $600 billion in direct cash payments to individuals. That mostly took the form of "stimulus checks" and increased unemployment benefits. (The stimulus checks are $1,200 one-time payments per single adult, $2,400 for married couples, and $500 paid to the parents of each child under 17. The amounts are lowered for individuals with incomes of $75,000 or more, or $150,000 or more for married couples.) It also included about $500 billion directly for large corporations, about $450 billion in loans and billions more in cash "grants" (much of that to passenger airlines and cargo carriers). Another $350 billion, mostly in the form of loans, was earmarked for small businesses. (Some corporations, by no means small, sparked an outcry by grabbing some of these "small business" funds. No surprise there.) In addition, the Federal Reserve launched an "unlimited" program to purchase financial securities—including bonds previously issued by the government and held by private financial institutions, bonds previously issued by private companies, etc.—with the aim of driving down interest rates. The idea is that lower rates will get private businesses and individuals to borrow and spend more. The Fed has also announced plans to purchase newly issued bonds on a large scale, directly channeling cash to the issuing businesses.

All of these policies could boost spending in the short run. When lower-income people receive additional income, they tend to spend most of it, so the demand boost is relatively large. Economist Mark Zandi estimated, during the Great Recession, that the spending impact of an extra $1 in unemployment benefits or nutrition assistance was between $1.60 and $1.75. That is because recipients spent most of the extra money, that spending became other people's incomes, they spent most of that, and so on. (This is known as a "multiplier effect.") The multiplier is smaller for extra income received by higher-income individuals, since they are likely to save more of it. Businesses that receive additional income may also refrain from spending it, especially if there is little reason to expand production, as during a recession. (Some of the bailout money, it should be noted, is tied to spending on wages and benefits. That may reduce businesses' cash hoarding.)

Further, an infusion of cash into the banking system does not always translate into substantial new lending. During the Great Recession, the Federal Reserve bought trillions in bonds, but the banks largely sat on the additional cash (holding it as "excess reserves").

The current crisis, in addition, poses some special complications, so standard demand-boosting policies might not quickly restore production and jobs. First, the sectors that are hardest hit—such as leisure and hospitality—might be slow to respond to the general sort of demand-boosting that's in the stimulus bill. This is true even aside from the impact of shutdown orders and the like. If people remain worried about coming into close contact with others, increased overall purchasing power may not translate quickly into more demand for restaurant meals, sporting events, concerts, or hotel accommodations. The recovery of employment in these sectors to their pre-crisis levels may be a long, drawn-out process. (It should be understood that, so long as the reopening of these sectors of the economy poses a serious health risk for workers and the public, the objective should not be the fastest possible recovery in production and employment. We are already seeing, as restrictions have been eased in many states, an alarming resurgence of infections.) Policies that boost demand across the board, of course, could stimulate increased production of other kinds of goods and services. Employers in those sectors might hire more workers, and some of the workers who have lost jobs in the hardest-hit sectors might get jobs as a result. Not all would, however, especially not in the short run.

Second, there are important constraints on supply, especially in the form of required shutdowns of nonessential businesses and widespread isolation requirements on workers. Some of the work that was done on-premises is now being done remotely, but certainly nowhere near all work affected by such requirements can be done remotely. Even if demand for some kinds of goods and services increased, it would not necessarily be possible for businesses to respond quickly with increased output and employment. (Again, nor would we want them to, as long as slowing the spread of the virus requires continued social isolation.)

For these reasons, responses to the crisis have to include adaptations to substantial declines in work hours and overall output, at least in the short to medium term. Demand-boosting policies can lessen the carnage. Not all policies out of the recession-response playbook, however, are equally effective in boosting demand. Nor are the various options equally good for other reasons. Some options, for example, reduce economic inequality; others increase inequality. Those that primarily benefit low- and middle-income people are better on both scores than those that benefit high-income individuals and giant corporations. Even if we cannot avoid declines in total output and income altogether, however, it is possible to manage significant declines in income without a disastrous toll in human terms. To accomplish this, the decline must not be borne disproportionately by a vulnerable group (like those who lose their jobs), and the most vulnerable must not bear any of the impact. ❏

Sources: Congressional Budget Office (CBO), Interim Projections for 2020 and 2021, May 2020 (cbo.gov); Bureau of Labor Statistics (BLS), The Employment Situation—April 2020, Released:

May 8, 2020 (bls.gov); Bureau of Labor Statistics, The Employment Situation—May 2020, Released: June 5, 2020 (bls.gov); Bureau of Labor Statistics (BLS), Employment and Earnings, Table B-1a. Employees on nonfarm payrolls by industry sector and selected industry detail, seasonally adjusted (bls.gov); Thomas Franck, "Here are the industries suffering the biggest job losses in an initial look at coronavirus impact," CNBC, April 3, 2020; Bureau of Labor Statistics, Current Employment Statistics, Charts: Employment change by industry with confidence intervals, March 2020, seasonally adjusted, in thousands, 1-month net change (bls.gov.ces); Alina Selyukh, "The Coronavirus Pandemic Hurts Some Industries, Benefits Others," Morning Edition, National Public Radio, March 24, 2020 (npr.org); Jessica Dickler, "Here 's who is hiring right now, amid a bleak jobs picture," CNBC, April 3, 2020 (updated April 6, 2020); Gary Burtless, "When the next recession hits, will unemployment benefits be generous enough? " Brookings Institution, November 28, 2018 (brookings.edu); Joshua Smith, Valerie Wilson, and Josh Bivens, "State Cuts to Jobless Benefits Did Not Help Workers or Taxpayers," Economic Policy Institute, July 28, 2014 (epi.org); Jennifer Valentino-DeVries, Denise Lu, and Gabriel J.X. Dance, "Location Data Says It All: Staying at Home During Coronavirus is a Luxury," *New York Times*, April 4, 2020; Christian Davenport, Aaron Gregg and Craig Timberg, "Working from home reveals another fault line in America 's racial and educational divide," *Washington Post*, March 22, 2020; Josh Mitchell, "State Shutdowns Have Taken at Least a Quarter of U.S. Economy Offline," *Wall Street Journal*, April 5, 2020; Jeffrey Bair, "Demand for Gasoline is Plummeting All Over the World," Bloomberg, April 6, 2020; Paul Krugman, *End This Depression Now!*, Chapter 2: "Depression Economics," (W.W. Norton & Co., 2012); Kristen Doerer, "What 's the Deal With Coronavirus Stimulus Checks, and How Do I Get One? " ProPublica, April 17, 2020 (propublica.org); Nick Routley, "The Anatomy of the $2 Trillion COVID-19 Stimulus Bill," Visual Capitalist, March 30, 2020; James Politi, Brendan Greeley, Colby Smith, and Joe Rennison, "Federal Reserve unleashes unlimited Treasury purchase plan," *Financial Times*, March 23, 2020; Jeff Cox, "The Fed says it is going to start buying individual corporate bonds," CNBC, June 15, 2020 (cnbc.com); Mark Zandi, "A Second Quick Boost From Government Could Spark Recovery," Edited excerpts of testimony before the U.S. House Committee on Small Business, July 24, 2008 (economy.com); Gerald Friedman, "Pushing on Strings," *Dollars & Sense*, May/June 2009; Samuel Bowles, Richard Edwards, Frank Roosevelt, and Mehrene Larudee, *Understanding Capitalism: Competition, Command, and Change*, 4th ed., Chapter 4: "Capitalism as an Economic System," (Oxford University Press, 2017).

Article 4.2

APP WORKERS IN THE COVID-19 ECONOMY
App-based companies "change the boundaries of the firm itself."

BY NICOLE ASCHOFF
May/June 2020

S martphones have become ubiquitous over the past decade, offering users unprec-edented access to each other, to information and entertainment, and to ser-vices, especially for well-off professionals. With a tap or a swipe people can restock milk and bread from Instacart; avoid the lunch-time rush with a tasty bite delivered through Seamless; or hail a Lyft when afterwork cocktails turn tipsy. Whatever you need—"there's an app for that!"

It's not entirely clear how many people are working in these app jobs—piece-work gigs mediated through a smartphone app. In the United States, estimates of "on-demand" app workers who earn money via online intermediaries such as Instacart and Uber vary widely. The Federal Reserve estimated that 16% of adults earned money from app jobs in 2017 while the Bureau of Labor Statistics estimates the number of contingent workers to be roughly six million people.

Even absent concrete numbers, it is clear that the emergence of app jobs in the past decade is a significant development in the evolution of work in the United States. In fact, app workers have become so important that many have been deemed "essential workers" in the battle to quell the coronavirus pandemic. As Americans grow increasingly wary of venturing outside, many are relying on their Instacart app to get groceries delivered to their homes. Some are even calling an Uber to take them to the hospital when they fall sick. A driver in San Francisco recalled how halfway through a ride his young passenger commented that he was worried that he had the coronavirus because he had been coughing up blood and was actually on his way to the hospital.

App jobs are part of what employment and labor market expert David Weil calls the "fissuring" of the workplace, whereby employers "change the boundar-ies of the firm itself" and "employment is no longer the clear relationship between a well-defined employer and a worker." The spread of multitier subcontracting has enabled companies to plan their budgets around paying for services rather than pay-ing wages. App jobs are the next step—a testing ground for companies to see how much they can force workers, consumers, and governments to take on the costs of production.

Pushing Costs onto Workers

Uber exemplifies the logic of app work. Drivers provide their own vehicle (paying for gas, repair costs, and insurance) and phone, while Uber provides only the soft-ware and its network. Uber takes a 25% cut from each ride, yet drivers are not con-sidered employees and the company is not responsible for their safety. Uber is also not responsible for the safety of its consumers (riders), nor the increased congestion and pollution it causes in urban centers. In San Francisco, for example, transportation experts concluded that transportation network companies such as Uber and Lyft were responsible for more than half of the increase in roadway congestion between 2010 and 2016.

App jobs are appealing at first glance. There are few barriers to entry. You can work when you're able, and the ads promise decent money. You just need a smartphone, often a car, and a willingness to work. Matthew Telles, a former Instacart "shopper" and member of the Gig Workers Collective, told *Democracy Now!* that, at first, he loved delivering for Instacart. It "paid great and gave me access to all the amazing buildings downtown, like the top of the Sears Tower." In a landscape of degraded work, app jobs can seem like a step up from the frustrating world of scheduling software and low-paid, irregular shifts that are common in the retail and fast-food sectors.

Some app jobs can even feel like being your own boss. Tech companies certainly push this interpretation, emphasizing how they provide the digital platform—the digital infrastructure that facilitates interactions (often commercial) between at least two people or groups—and you provide the hustle. Uber, for example, is adamant that it is not the employer of the roughly one million drivers worldwide who use its app to find people to ferry around.

Researchers at Carnegie Mellon's Human-Computer Interaction Institute aren't so sure. They call the Uber arrangement "algorithmic management." App workers who use these platforms to earn money don't have easy access to a flesh-and-blood manager. Instead they interact with an algorithm—a set of exact instructions to solve a problem or perform a computation. Algorithms can be written to perform simple tasks, like adding or subtracting numbers, or complex tasks, such as playing a video or, in the case of Uber, telling the driver where to drive, paying them what they are owed, and so forth. Algorithms effectively transform app workers' phones into their boss.

Turns out, it's not so great to have a smartphone as your boss. The modern work relationships enacted through our phones show not only how phones are a dream come true for the well-off, but also how the 21st-century working class is being made, and the divide between the haves and the have-nots is being reinforced.

In the United Kingdom, drivers for Deliveroo, a food delivery app—who are disproportionately immigrants and poor people of color—are closely monitored by Deliveroo's algorithm. They have 30 seconds to respond to the app when it pings them, and they don't know where they're going until they swipe "accept delivery." If the driver doesn't accept, or is too slow, meaning the "time to accept orders," "travel time to restaurant," "travel time to customer," or "time at customer" are longer than what the algorithm estimates they should be, her account can be deactivated.

Precarious Labor

Reliable data on how much pay app workers take home is hard to come by. Ridester's 2018 Independent Driver Earnings Survey found that drivers of Uber's most popular service, Uber-X, made a median wage of $14.73 an hour in 2018 after tips but before gas, insurance, and repairs—substantially less than a living wage. Pay can change from one day to the next following tweaks to the app by the company, and workers often have a hard time understanding how their pay is calculated. Last year Instacart and DoorDash drivers, for example, discovered that their companies had been routinely stealing the tips customers left them on the app.

In practice, app jobs are just the latest form of precarious labor. On-demand workers are not entitled to minimum wage, sick days, overtime pay, safety protections, unemployment or health insurance, a pension plan, or disability pay. App workers in service jobs are held hostage to the reviews of fickle customers, and if they have a problem, their app boss usually isn't much help. Stories abound of app workers who have found it difficult or impossible to get help from a real person at their companies when they needed it.

The coronavirus crisis is a real-time demonstration of just how vulnerable app workers are. After the pandemic brought the economy skidding to a halt, tens of millions of Americans have been thrown out of work, including app workers. The U.S. government passed a stimulus bill, providing federal unemployment payouts to ease the financial pain of the crisis. Significantly, in crafting the bill, app workers were recognized for the first time as real workers and made eligible for stimulus funds. Getting access to these funds has proven difficult, however. Outdated software, understaffed state agencies, and a delay by the Department of Labor in providing official guidance on how the program should be administered have meant relatively few app workers have received relief payments nearly two months into the shutdown.

Moreover, for the millions of app workers still working, a lack of safety equipment and workplace rights have made app jobs increasingly dangerous. In a Medium post, the Gig Workers Collective says Instacart has "turned this pandemic into a PR campaign, portraying itself [as] the hero of families that are sheltered-in-place, isolated, or quarantined." But Instacart, the collective argues, has "not provided essential protections to Shoppers on the front lines that could prevent them from becoming carriers, falling ill themselves, or worse."

Thousands of Instacart workers "walked out" on March 30, refusing to fill orders on the app in order to call attention to their concerns. They demanded sick pay, hazard pay ($5 extra per order and a minimum 10% tip per order), and personal protective equipment to be provided by the company. The company brushed off the action claiming the walkout represented only a small fraction of the company's 200,000 shoppers and did nothing to disrupt the app's functionality.

App workers aren't the only front-line workers who are anxious about safety and stress during the pandemic. Grocery store employees, health care providers, cleaners, warehouse workers, and truck drivers are just some of the workers dealing with a lack of protective equipment and demands to keep working while everyone else stays at home. This shared sense of struggle shaped the May Day walkouts and demonstrations by frontline workers at Amazon, Instacart, Whole Foods, Target, and FedEx. But app workers face additional challenges to organizing because they aren't officially recognized as employees and often the only thing connecting them to fellow workers is an app they don't control.

Organizing App Workers

Over the past few years app workers have been fighting back—demanding recognition and fair compensation for the work they do and developing strategies to overcome these organizing hurdles. In 2018 Uber and Lyft drivers, working with the New York City Taxi Workers Alliance and the Independent Drivers Guild, convinced the city to implement the country's first cap on drivers, limiting the number of ride-hail vehicles that could hit the streets in an effort to boost pay for all drivers. Last year California legislators approved Assembly Bill 5, a landmark bill that forces app-based service companies (such as Uber and Lyft) to reclassify their workers as employees rather than independent contractors.

Some more traditional labor unions have made tentative efforts to organize app workers. The United Food and Commercial Workers Local 1546 in Chicago, for example, is trying to sign up Instacart shoppers. App workers are also forming new organizations. The Gig Workers Collective is a nonprofit group that bills itself as a "first responder" designed to "take the lead in organizing immediate action to new grievances." A number of state-based groups have also emerged. In California, Gig Workers Rising and Mobile Workers Alliance organized a three-day caravan of Uber and Lyft drivers in support of Assembly Bill 5.

Platform companies who desperately want to maintain the digital piecework model are pushing back hard against these initiatives. In New York City, Uber and Lyft sued the city over the driver cap and implemented a punishing new tiered quota system for drivers. The rideshare companies also sued the state of California to prevent their drivers from being considered employees and are working on a ballot initiative to be exempted from the new regulations. In the meantime, they are simply ignoring the legislation, prompting California Attorney General Xavier Becerra to file a lawsuit against Uber and Lyft in San Francisco County Superior Court.

The federal government's belated recognition that app workers are real workers that deserve protection, even if only rhetorical at this point, is a positive shift, however. It is a signal that support for app workers is growing and that tech companies will find it more and more difficult to hide abusive employment relationships behind slick apps and feel-good stories. ❑

Note: This article is adapted from Aschoff's most recent book, *The Smartphone Society: Technology, Power, and Resistance in the New Gilded Age* (Beacon Press, 2020).

Sources: Board of Governors of the Federal Reserve System, "Report on the Economic Well-Being of U.S. Households in 2017-May 2018," May 2018; U.S. Bureau of Labor Statistics, "Contingent and Alternative Employment Arrangements News Release," June 7, 2018; Janet Burns, "'He was coughing up blood:' Uber and Lyft Drives Face Illness and Confusion Amid COVID-19 Outbreak," *Forbes*, March 17, 2020; David Weil, *The Fissured Workplace: Why Work Became So Bad for So Many and What Can Be Done To Improve It* (Harvard University Press, 2014); San Francisco County Transportation Authority, "TNCs & Congestion" draft report, October 2018; "Essential or Expendable? Gig Workers at Instacart & Grocery Stores Demand Safety Gear & Hazard Pay," *Democracy Now!*, April 20, 2020; Min Kyung Lee et al., "Working with Machines: The Impact of Algorithmic and Data-Driven Management on Human Workers," Carnegie Mellon University,

2015; Sarah O'Connor, "When Your Boss Is an Algorithm," *Financial Times*, September 8, 2016; Ridester, "Ridester's 2018 Independent Driver Earnings Survey," March 29, 2019; Rachel Siegel, "DoorDash to Change Its Controversial Tipping Policy After Outcry," *Washington Post*, July 24, 2019; Rebecca Rainey, "Millions of gig workers are still waiting for unemployment benefits," Politico, April 30, 2020; Gig Workers Collective, "Instacart Emergency Walk Off," Medium, March 27, 2020; Noam Scheiber and Kate Conger, "Strikes at Instacart and Amazon Over Coronavirus Health Concerns," *New York Times*, March 30, 2020; gigworkerscollective.org; Edward Ongweso Jr., "The Lockout: Why Uber Divers in NYC Are Sleeping in Their Cars," Vice, March 19, 2020; Cyrus Farivar and Olivia Solon, "Uber and Lyft Face Landmark lawsuit over gig worker classification," NBC News, May 5, 2020.

THE RELATIONSHIP OF UNEMPLOYMENT AND INFLATION

BY RAMAA VASUDEVAN
September/October 2006

> Dear Dr. Dollar:
> *Back in first-year economics we learned that there is a trade-off between un-*
> *employment and inflation, so you can't really have both low inflation and low*
> *unemployment at the same time. Do economists still consider that to be true?*
> —Edith Bross, Cambridge, Mass.

The trade-off between inflation and unemployment was first reported by A. W. Phillips in 1958—and so has been christened the Phillips curve. The simple intuition behind this trade-off is that as unemployment falls, workers are empowered to push for higher wages. Firms try to pass these higher wage costs on to consumers, resulting in higher prices and an inflationary buildup in the economy. The trade-off suggested by the Phillips curve implies that policymakers can target low inflation rates or low unemployment, but not both. During the 1960s, monetarists emphasized price stability (low inflation), while Keynesians more often emphasized job creation.

The experience of so-called stagflation in the 1970s, with simultaneously high rates of both inflation and unemployment, began to discredit the idea of a stable trade-off between the two. In place of the Phillips curve, many economists began to posit a "natural rate of unemployment." If unemployment were to fall below this "natural" rate, however slightly, inflation would begin to accelerate. Under the "natural rate of unemployment" theory (also called the Non-Accelerating Inflation Rate of Unemployment, or NAIRU), instead of choosing between higher unemployment and higher inflation, policymakers were told to focus on ensuring that the economy remained at its "natural" rate: the challenge was to accurately estimate its level and to steer the economy toward growth rates that maintain price stability, no matter what the corresponding level of unemployment.

The NAIRU has been extremely difficult to pin down in practice. Not only are estimates of it notoriously imprecise, the rate itself evidently changes over time. In the United States, estimates of the NAIRU rose from about 4.4% in the 1960s, to 6.2% in the 1970s, and further to 7.2% in the 1980s. This trend reversed itself in the 1990s, as officially reported unemployment fell. In the latter half of the 1990s, U.S. inflation remained nearly dormant at around 3%, while unemployment fell to around 4.6%. In the later Clinton years many economists warned that if unemployment was brought any lower, inflationary pressures might spin out of control. But growth in these years did not spill over into accelerating inflation. The United States, apparently, had achieved the Goldilocks state—everything just right!

What sustained this combination of low inflation and low unemployment? Explanations abound: a productivity boom, the high rates of incarceration of those who would otherwise fall within the ranks of the unemployed, the openness of the U.S. economy to world trade and competition, among others.

The full story, however, has to do with class conflict and the relatively weak position of workers in the 1990s. Both the breakdown of the Phillips curve in the 1970s and the recent "disappearance" of the natural rate of unemployment are in essence a reflection of institutional and political changes that affect the bargaining strength of working people—in other words, their ability to organize effective unions and establish a decent living wage.

Following the Reagan offensive against trade unions, workers' power fell dramatically. Consequently, unionization rates and the real value of the minimum wage each fell precipitously between the late 1970s and the 1990s. The period of stagflation, in contrast, had been one of labor militancy and rising wages. (Although "stagflation" has a negative ring, by many measures nonsupervisory workers—i.e., the vast majority of the U.S. labor force—fared better in the economy of the early- to mid-1970s than they do today, even after the long 1990s economic expansion.) Labor's weaker position in the 1990s meant that despite low unemployment, workers were not able to win higher wages that would have spurred inflation.

The long period of stable prices and low interest rates in the United States now seems to be coming to a close. The cost of the Iraq War and rising oil prices, among other factors, have fueled expectations of a resurgence of inflation. At the same time, the near jobless recovery from the last recession might suggest that the "natural rate" of unemployment is on the rise again—and that we are witnessing yet another twist in the strange history of the Phillips curve!

With inflation rising (albeit slowly, and still relatively mild at around 4.2%), some business sectors will no doubt begin clamoring for tighter monetary policies that sacrifice job creation and wage growth by slowing the economy growth. But these fears of inflation are probably misplaced. A moderate rate of inflation is conducive to the growth of real investment, and in the context of a decades-long squeeze on workers' wage share, there is room to expand employment without setting off a wage-price spiral. What workers need is not greater fiscal and monetary austerity, but rather a revival of a Keynesian program of "employment targeting" that would sustain full employment and empower workers to push for higher wages. It's not likely, however, that the owners of capital and their political allies would sit idly by were such a program to be enacted. ❑

Article 4.4

THE "NATURAL RATE" OF UNEMPLOYMENT
It's all about class conflict.

BY ROBERT POLLIN
September/October 1998

In 1997, the official U.S. unemployment rate fell to a 27-year low of 4.9%. Most orthodox economists had long predicted that a rate this low would lead to uncontrollable inflation. So they argued that maintaining a higher unemployment rate—perhaps as high as 6%—was crucial for keeping the economy stable. But there is a hitch: last year the inflation rate was 2.3%, the lowest figure in a decade and the second lowest in 32 years. What then are we to make of these economists' theories, much less their policy proposals?

Nobel prize-winning economist Milton Friedman gets credit for originating the argument that low rates of unemployment would lead to accelerating inflation. His 1968 theory of the so-called "natural rate of unemployment" was subsequently developed by many mainstream economists under the term "Non-Accelerating Inflation Rate of Unemployment," or NAIRU, a remarkably clumsy term for expressing the simple concept of a threshold unemployment rate below which inflation begins to rise.

According to both Friedman and expositors of NAIRU, inflation should accelerate at low rates of unemployment because low unemployment gives workers excessive bargaining power. This allows the workers to demand higher wages. Capitalists then try to pass along these increased wage costs by raising prices on the products they sell. An inflationary spiral thus ensues as long as unemployment remains below its "natural rate."

Based on this theory, Friedman and others have long argued that governments should never actively intervene in the economy to promote full employment or better jobs for workers, since it will be a futile exercise, and the end result will only be higher inflation and no improvement in job opportunities. Over the past generation, this conclusion has had far-reaching influence throughout the world. In the United States and Western Europe, it has provided a stamp of scientific respectability to a whole range of policies through which governments abandoned even modest commitments to full employment and workers' rights.

This emerged most sharply through the Reaganite and Thatcherite programs in the United States and United Kingdom in the 1980s. But even into the 1990s, as the Democrats took power in the United States, the Labour Party won office in Britain, and Social Democrats won elections throughout Europe, governments remained committed to stringent fiscal and monetary policies, whose primary goal is to prevent inflation. In Western Europe this produced an average unemployment rate of over 10% from 1990-1997. In the United States, unemployment rates have fallen sharply in the 1990s, but as an alternative symptom of stringent fiscal and monetary policies, real wages for U.S. workers also declined dramatically over the past generation. As of 1997, the average real wage for nonsupervisory workers in the United States was 14% below its peak in 1973, even though average worker productivity rose between 1973 and 1997 by 34%.

Why have governments in the United States and Europe remained committed to the idea of fiscal and monetary stringency, if the natural rate theory on which such policies are based is so obviously flawed? The explanation is that the natural rate theory is really not just about predicting a precise unemployment rate figure below which inflation must inexorably accelerate, even though many mainstream economists have presented the natural rate theory in this way. At a deeper level, the natural rate theory is bound up with the inherent conflicts between workers and capitalists over jobs, wages, and working conditions. As such, the natural rate theory actually contains a legitimate foundation in truth amid a welter of sloppy and even silly predictions.

The "Natural Rate" Theory Is About Class Conflict

In his 1967 American Economic Association presidential address in which he introduced the natural rate theory, Friedman made clear that there was really nothing "natural" about the theory. Friedman rather emphasized that: "by using the term 'natural' rate of unemployment, I do not mean to suggest that it is immutable and unchangeable. On the contrary, many of the market characteristics that determine its level are man-made and policy-made. In the United States, for example, legal minimum wage rates ... and the strength of labor unions all make the natural rate of unemployment higher than it would otherwise be."

In other words, according to Friedman, what he terms the "natural rate" is really a social phenomenon measuring the class strength of working people, as indicated by their ability to organize effective unions and establish a livable minimum wage.

Friedman's perspective is supported in a widely-read 1997 paper by Robert Gordon of Northwestern University on what he terms the "time-varying NAIRU." What makes the NAIRU vary over time? Gordon explains that, since the early 1960s, "The two especially large changes in the NAIRU ... are the increase between the early and late 1960s and the decrease in the 1990s. The late 1960s were a time of labor militancy, relatively strong unions, a relatively high minimum wage, and a marked increase in labor's share in national income. The 1990s have been a time of labor peace, relatively weak unions, a relatively low minimum wage and a slight decline in labor's income share."

In short, class conflict is the spectre haunting the analysis of the natural rate and NAIRU: this is the consistent message stretching from Milton Friedman in the 1960s to Robert Gordon in the 1990s.

Stated in this way, the "Natural Rate" idea does, ironically, bear a close family resemblance to the ideas of two of the greatest economic thinkers of the left, Karl Marx and Michal Kalecki, on a parallel concept—the so-called "Reserve Army of Unemployed." In his justly famous Chapter 25 of Volume I of *Capital*, "The General Law of Capitalist Accumulation," Marx argued forcefully that unemployment serves an important function in capitalist economies. That is, when a capitalist economy is growing rapidly enough so that the reserve army of unemployed is depleted, workers will then utilize their increased bargaining power to raise wages. Profits are correspondingly squeezed as workers get a larger share of the country's total income. As a result, capitalists anticipate further declines in profitability and they therefore reduce their investment spending. This then leads to a fall in job creation, higher unemployment, and a replenishment of the reserve army. In other words, the reserve army of the unemployed is the instrument capitalists use to prevent significant wage increases and thereby maintain profitability.

Kalecki, a Polish economist of the Great Depression era, makes parallel though distinct arguments in his also justly famous essay, "The Political Aspects of Full Employment." Kalecki wrote in 1943, shortly after the 1930s Depression had ended and governments had begun planning a postwar world in which they would deploy aggressive policies to avoid another calamity of mass unemployment. Kalecki held, contrary to Marx, that full employment can be beneficial to the profitability of businesses. True, capitalists may get a smaller share of the total economic pie as workers gain bargaining power to win higher wages. But capitalists can still benefit because the size of the pie is growing far more rapidly, since more goods and services can be produced when everyone is working, as opposed to some significant share of workers being left idle.

But capitalists still won't support full employment, in Kalecki's view, because it will threaten their control over the workplace, the pace and direction of economic activity, and even political institutions. Kalecki thus concluded that full employment could be sustainable under capitalism, but only if these challenges to capitalists' social and political power could be contained. This is why he held that fascist social and political institutions, such as those that existed in Nazi Germany when he was writing, could well provide one "solution" to capitalism's unemployment problem, precisely because they were so brutal. Workers would have jobs, but they would never be permitted to exercise the political and economic power that would otherwise accrue to them in a full-employment economy.

Broadly speaking, Marx and Kalecki do then share a common conclusion with natural rate proponents, in that they would all agree that positive unemployment rates are the outgrowth of class conflict over the distribution of income and political power. Of course, Friedman and other mainstream economists reach this conclusion via analytic and political perspectives that are diametrically opposed to those of Marx and Kalecki. To put it in a nutshell, in the Friedmanite view mass unemployment results when workers demand more than they deserve, while for Marx and Kalecki, capitalists use the weapon of unemployment to prevent workers from getting their just due.

From Natural Rate to Egalitarian Policy

Once the analysis of unemployment in capitalist economies is properly understood within the framework of class conflict, several important issues in our contemporary economic situation become much more clear. Let me raise just a few:

1) Mainstream economists have long studied how workers' wage demands cause inflation as unemployment falls. However, such wage demands never directly cause inflation, since inflation refers to a general rise in prices of goods and services sold in the market, not a rise in wages. Workers, by definition, do not have the power to raise prices. Capitalists raise prices on the products they sell. At low unemployment, inflation occurs when capitalists respond to workers' increasingly successful wage demands by raising prices so that they can maintain profitability. If workers were simply to receive a higher share of national income, then lower unemployment and higher wages need not cause inflation at all.

2) There is little mystery as to why, at present, the so-called "time-varying" NAIRU has diminished to a near vanishing point, with unemployment at a 25-year low while inflation remains dormant. The main explanation is the one stated by Robert Gordon—that workers' economic power has been eroding dramatically through the 1990s. Workers have been almost completely unable to win wage increases over the course of the economic expansion that by now is seven years old.

3) This experience over the past seven years, with unemployment falling but workers showing almost no income gains, demonstrates dramatically the crucial point that full employment can never stand alone as an adequate measure of workers' well-being. This was conveyed vividly to me when I was working in Bolivia in 1990 as part of an economic advising team led by Keith Griffin of the University of California-Riverside. Professor Griffin asked me to examine employment policies.

I began by paying a visit to the economists at the Ministry of Planning. When I requested that we discuss the country's employment problems, they explained, to my surprise, that the country *had no employment problems*. When I suggested we consider the situation of the people begging, shining shoes, or hawking batteries and Chiclets in the street just below the window where we stood, their response was that these people *were* employed. And of course they were, in that they were actively trying to scratch out a living. It was clear that I had to specify the problem at hand far more precisely. Similarly, in the United States today, we have to be much more specific as to what workers should be getting in a fair economy: jobs, of course, but also living wages, benefits, reasonable job security, and a healthy work environment.

4) In our current low-unemployment economy, should workers, at long last, succeed in winning higher wages and better benefits, some inflationary pressures are likely to emerge. But if inflation does not accelerate after wage increases are won, this would mean that businesses are not able to pass along their higher wage costs to their customers. Profits would therefore be squeezed. In any case, in response to *either* inflationary pressures or a squeeze in profitability, we should expect that many, if not most, segments of the business community will welcome a Federal Reserve policy that would slow the economy and raise the unemployment rate.

Does this mean that, as long as we live in a capitalist society, the control by capitalists over the reserve army of labor must remain the dominant force establishing the limits of workers' striving for jobs, security, and living wages? The challenge for the progressive movement in the United States today is to think through a set of policy ideas through which full employment at living wages can be achieved and sustained.

Especially given the dismal trajectory of real wage decline over the past generation, workers should of course continue to push for wage increases. But it will also be crucial to advance these demands within a broader framework of proposals. One important component of a broader package would be policies through which labor and capital bargain openly over growth of wages and profits after full employment is achieved. Without such an open bargaining environment, workers, with reason, will push for higher wages once full employment is achieved, but capitalists will then respond by either raising prices or favoring high unemployment. Such open bargaining policies were conducted with considerable success in Sweden and other Nordic countries from the 1950s to the 1980s, and as a result, wages there continued to rise at full employment, while both accelerating inflation and a return to high unemployment were prevented.

Such policies obviously represent a form of class compromise. This is intrinsically neither good nor bad. The question is the terms under which the compromise is achieved. Wages have fallen dramatically over the past generation, so workers deserve substantial raises as a matter of simple fairness. But workers should also be willing to link their wage increases to improvements in productivity growth, i.e., the rate at which workers produce new goods and services. After all, if the average wage had just risen at exactly the rate of productivity growth since 1973 and not a penny more, the average hourly wage today for nonsupervisory workers would be $19.07 rather than $12.24.

But linking wages to improvements in productivity then also raises the question of who controls the decisions that determine the rate of productivity growth. In fact, substantial productivity gains are attainable through operating a less hierarchical workplace and building strong democratic unions through which workers can defend their rights on the job. Less hierarchy and increased workplace democracy creates higher morale on the job, which in turn increases workers' effort and opportunities to be inventive, while decreasing turnover and absenteeism. The late David Gordon of the New School for Social Research was among the leading analysts demonstrating how economies could operate more productively through greater workplace democracy.

But improvements in productivity also result from both the public and private sector investing in new and better machines that workers put to use every day, with the additional benefit that it means more jobs for people who produce those machines. A pro-worker economic policy will therefore also have to be concerned with increasing investments to improve the stock of machines that workers have at their disposal on the job.

In proposing such a policy approach, have I forgotten the lesson that Marx and Kalecki taught us, that unemployment serves a purpose in capitalism? Given that this lesson has become part of the standard mode of thinking among mainstream economists ranging from Milton Friedman to Robert Gordon, I would hope that I haven't let it slip from view. My point nevertheless is that through changing power relationships at the workplace and the decision-making process through which investment decisions get made, labor and the left can then also achieve a more egalitarian economy, one in which capitalists' power to brandish the weapon of unemployment is greatly circumscribed. If the labor movement and the left neglect issues of control over investment and the workplace, we will continue to live amid a Bolivian solution to the unemployment problem, where full employment is the by-product of workers' vulnerability, not their strength. ❏

Sources: Robert Pollin, "The 'Reserve Army of Labor' and the 'Natural Rate of Unemployment': Can Marx, Kalecki, Friedman, and Wall Street All Be Wrong?," *Review of Radical Political Economics,* Fall 1998; Robert Pollin and Stephanie Luce, *The Living Wage: Building a Fair Economy* (New Press, 1998); David Gordon, *Fat and Mean: The Corporate Squeeze of Working Americans and the Myth of Managerial "Downsizing"* (Free Press, 1997; David Gordon, "Generating Affluence: Productivity Gains Require Worker Support," *Real World Macro,* 15th ed., 1998.

Article 4.5

GETTING UP TO SPEED ON THE MINIMUM WAGE

The Wall Street Journal *editors need to do their homework.*

BY JOHN MILLER
May/June 2021

> "The Young and the Jobless: The minimum wage hike has driven the
> wages of teen employees down to $0.00"
> The Editorial Board, *Wall Street Journal*, Oct. 3, 2009

> "Reality check for a $15 Minimum Wage: How many jobs for the young
> and un-skilled do Democrats want to lose?"
> The Editorial Board, *Wall Street Journal*, Feb. 8, 2021

> "Raising the Minimum Wage Definitely Costs Jobs"
> David Neumark, *Wall Street Journal*, March 18, 2021

In 2009, Congress raised the federal minimum wage to $7.25 per hour. In February of this year, the House of Representatives passed the Raise the Wage Act of 2021, which would double the $7.25 minimum wage to $15 by 2025. But the Senate declined to include raising the minimum wage in the American Rescue Plan it approved in March, although Senate Democrats are talking about adding the minimum wage increase to the Biden infrastructure proposal currently being considered by Congress.

Regardless of whether it is 2009 or 2021, the *Wall Street Journal* editors are still convinced that raising the minimum wage would mean unemployment for the very workers the legislation intends to help. The fact that it has been 12 years since Congress last increased the minimum wage, or that the current proposal would increase the minimum wage in gradual steps, isn't about to change their minds.

Why are the editors so cocksure that raising the minimum wage is a bad idea? That's easy. After all, anyone who has taken introductory economics was taught that imposing a wage floor in a low-wage labor market (above the equilibrium wage) would leave many workers without a job. And on top of that, for many years the consensus position of the economics profession was that minimum wage increases inevitably cause job losses, and the only question of interest was just how many jobs would be lost.

But just because the editors are wedded to their claim that the minimum wage is a jobs killer doesn't mean you should be, too. To begin with, the assumptions that underlie this simplistic introductory lesson about the minimum wage, which you saw illustrated on the chalkboard of old or on today's electronic whiteboard, are routinely violated. For one thing, labor markets are seldom competitive. Nor are all things held constant when the minimum wage increases, especially productivity and price levels. (More about that below.)

More importantly, the consensus among economists that the minimum wage inevitably destroys jobs has been steadily unraveling since the early 1990s. More and more evidence has piled up suggesting that the negative employment effect of increasing the minimum wage is negligible or even nonexistent.

But none of that has registered with the *Wall Street Journal* editors, who are content to recycle their editorials without a mention of this new minimum wage research. I doubt their recycling is good for the environment—and it is surely bad for honest discourse about the impact of increasing the minimum wage. Their ideological blindness contributes to, and, indeed, celebrates, the unwillingness of politicians to face up to the fact that the minimum wage is a poverty wage.

What Do We Know About the Minimum Wage?

Here's some of what the latest research tells us about the minimum wage:

- **A $7.25 minimum wage is indeed a poverty wage.** A minimum wage worker working 40 hours a week earns at most $15,000 a year. That income falls below the poverty line for a family with two or more members. An income of $15,000 a year is far less than the typical expenditures of a family of three as calculated by the Joint Economic Committee, and not even enough to cover the average cost of rental housing.
- **At $15 an hour the minimum wage would alleviate poverty.** It would exceed the poverty line for a family of four in 2021. A $15 minimum wage would lift 3.7 million people out of poverty, just over one-third of them children, according to the Economic Policy Institute. A recent Congressional Budget Office (CBO) study, even with its large estimates of job losses, still finds that a $15 minimum wage would lift 900,000 people out of poverty.
- **An increase in the federal minimum wage is long overdue.** The purchasing power of the minimum wage reached its peak in 1968—52 years ago—and has been on the decline ever since. If the minimum wage had kept up with inflation, it would be $11.90 today. If the minimum wage had also kept up with productivity gains since 1968, the minimum wage would have reached $31.67, according to calculations by economist Robert Pollin, who has written extensively about the minimum wage. Today, some 29 states and Washington, D.C., along with several cities, already have a minimum wage that is higher than $7.25.
- **Raising the minimum wage to $15 would boost the income of about one-fifth of the labor force.** Not only would minimum wage workers get a raise, but a higher minimum wage would also push up the wages of other low-income workers. The Economic Policy Institute estimates that by 2025, a $15 minimum wage would directly increase the wages of 22.1 million workers and push up the wages of another 10.1 million low-income workers—that's 32.2 million workers altogether. Even the recent CBO study, which the 2021 *Wall Street Journal* editorial relies upon,

allows that a $15 minimum wage would raise the wages of 27 million workers

- **The chief beneficiaries from increasing the minimum wage are adult workers, not teenagers.** What's more, women and minority workers will especially benefit from a wage increase. The vast majority of minimum wage workers are adults—just 20% are 16 to 19 years of age, according to the Bureau of Labor Statistics. The Economic Policy Institute reports that a $15 minimum wage would benefit 25.8% of all women workers and 31.6% of single parents. Also, 31.3% of Black workers would benefit, as would 26.0% of Hispanic workers.

- **Low wage workers would benefit from raising the minimum wage to $15 even if it caused large job losses.** No less than David Neumark, perhaps the preeminent defender of the traditional view of the minimum wage, allowed in his recent *Wall Street Journal* opinion piece that, "It's true that some workers would experience higher incomes and that, on net, incomes of low-wage workers would probably rise."

Outdated and in Need of Reconsideration

The "new literature" on the minimum wage is now nearly 30 years old. But it is still news to the *Wall Street Journal* editors.

At the beginning of this year, London School of Economics economist Alan Manning wrote honestly of the difficulty of discerning the "elusive employment effect" of the minimum wage, to use his words, in a leading economics journal. But instead of paying attention to the advances and limitations highlighted in Manning's article, the *Wall Street Journal* editors grabbed hold of the CBO's assessment of the budgetary effects of The Raise the Wage Act of 2021. The CBO report found that a $15 minimum wage would cost 1.4 million workers their jobs. For the editors, the report was a "Reality Check for a $15 Minimum Wage," which showed that "the gains would come at a high cost."

But nowhere do the editors mention the high degree of uncertainty around the CBO's employment loss estimates. For instance, the CBO's estimate of the median, or middle, estimate of the lost jobs from the increases in minimum wage in the studies they reviewed was 1.0 million. That was less than the average estimate of the number of lost jobs (which was pulled from a few studies that found extremely large job losses were likely). The report cautions that there is a one-third chance that the number of workers who lose their job from boosting the minimum wage would be between zero and 1.0 million workers.

Economist Michael Reich, a minimum wage expert at the University of California, Berkeley whose work is cited by the CBO, took issue with the report's pessimistic estimates. "A phased increase would likely be absorbed without detectable effects on employment," he said on a call to reporters.

Writing in the *Monitor Consult*, Reich explained that the CBO relied on state-level data on wages and employment. But in his research conducted with Anna

Godoey, Reich used more detailed data from over 150 counties and metropolitan areas in 45 states to assess the likely effect of increasing the minimum wage to $15 by 2025. They found that higher minimum wages do not have adverse effects on employment.

Their study found that consumers and the economy absorb higher wage standards. Higher minimum wages reduce employee turnover costs, reducing recruiting and training costs for firms, and increase worker productivity. In addition, low-wage employers, such as restaurants, absorb minimum wage costs through small price increases.

Godoey and Reich's findings are consistent with the increasing number of studies that have found little or no job loss as a result of minimum wage increases. Economists David Card and Alan Krueger conducted the first and still most important of these studies in 1994. Card and Krueger found that after New Jersey increased its minimum wage there were no job losses among fast-food workers; indeed, their level of employment actually increased relative to that of nearby fast-food workers in Pennsylvania.

Beyond a $15 Minimum Wage

As you can imagine, the new research on the minimum wage did not go down easy in the economics profession. But economists would do well to remember their own history of supporting the original minimum wage and other labor reforms of the Progressive Era a century ago. Leading labor economists of the day employed some of the same arguments used to support the current push for a living wage to make the case for a minimum wage, such as higher wages enhancing economic efficiency.

Many Progressive Era reformers considered any employer who paid less than a living wage to be a "parasitic" employer. Their low wages undercut the market share and profits of firms that were paying their workers a living wage. At the same time, it fell to the community and taxpayers to provide the support necessary to sustain employees who could not survive on low wages.

Combatting parasitic wages is no less of a compelling reason for raising the minimum wage today than it was for enacting a minimum wage a century ago. But that alone will not be enough. A $15 minimum wage would fall short of a living wage for a single adult in much of the country, and far short of a living wage for an adult with children. (For more detailed estimates by geographic location, see MIT's living wage calculator at livingwage.mit.edu.) Yet more needs to be done to counteract the decades old wage stagnation that has eroded the living standard of so many workers.

We should not let the chalk dust of introductory economics, or the outdated opinions of the Wall Street Journal editors, stand in the way of enacting these reforms.

We should not let the chalk dust of introductory economics, or the outdated opinions of the *Wall Street Journal* editors, stand in the way of enacting these reforms.□

Sources: David Neumark, "Raising the Minimum Wage Definitely Costs Jobs," *Wall Street Journal*, March 18, 2021 (wsj.com); "The Federal Minimum Wage," Joint Economic Committee, July 1, 2019 (jec.senate.gov); "Criticisms of Minimum Wage Increases Lag Behind Latest Research," Joint

Economic Committee, March 25, 2021 (jec.senate.gov); David Cooper, Zane Mokhiber, and Ben Zipperer, "Raising the federal minimum wage to $15 by 2025 would lift the pay of 32 million workers," Economic Policy Institute, March 9, 2021 (epi.org); C.J. Polychroniou, "Hiking the Minimum Wage to $15 is Key – But is hardly a living wage: Interview with Robert Pollin, Truthout, March 7, 2021 (truthout.org); David Card and Alan Krueger, "Minimum Wages and Employment: A Case Study of the Fast-Food Industry in New Jersey and Pennsylvania," *The American Economic Review*, Sept. 1994; Alan Manning, "The Elusive Employment Effect of the Minimum Wage," *Journal of Economic Perspectives*, Winter 2021; "The Budgetary Effects of the Raise the Wage Act of 2021," Congressional Budget Office, February 2021 (cbo.gov); Edward Lempinen, "A $15 minimum wage would costs jobs, right? Probably not, economists say," Berkeley News, March 18, 2021 (news.berkeley.edu); Michael Reich, "65 Billion Reasons why the Senate can pass a $15 minimum Wage by Reconciliation," Morning Consult, Feb. 4, 2021 (morningconsult.com); Anna Godoey and Michael Reich, "The US can raise the minimum wage to $15 without hurting jobs," CNN Business Perspectives, July 11, 2019 (cnn.com); Robert Prasch, "American Economist in the Progressive Era on the Minimum Wage," *Journal of Economic Perspectives*, Spring 1999; Marilyn Power, "Parasitic-Industries Analysis and Arguments for a Living Wage," *Feminist Economics*, Vol. 5, Issue 1, 1999.

Article 4.6

THE ACTUAL EFFECTS OF ENHANCED UNEMPLOYMENT BENEFITS

BY JOHN MILLER
November/December 2020

> The latest attempt to defy common sense is a study by Yale economists that purportedly finds the $600 federal enhancement to jobless benefits hasn't affected the incentive to work. But the study offers limited evidence for this conclusion, which is contradicted by other data and real-world evidence.
> —Editorial Board, "Economists vs. Common Sense: If you pay people not to work, fewer will work. Except at Yale, it seems," *Wall Street Journal*, August 2, 2020.

ARepublican cabal in the U.S. Senate has pledged to never renew the weekly $600 unemployment bonus that offered a lifeline to more than 25 million Americans as they weathered the economic devastation of the Covid-19 crisis. In the words of Republican Senator Lindsey Graham, the only way an extension of the $600 benefit would make it through the Senate is "over my dead body." The House of Representatives passed the extension of the $600 benefit in May (as part of the Health and Economic Recovery Omnibus Solutions, or HEROES, Act).

Republican opposition to $600 a week in enhanced unemployment benefits is fueled by their unwillingness to ease the draconian effects of the false choice between working and not working when there is no job to be had, and reinforced by the supposed "common sense" propagated by the *Wall Street Journal* editors, among others.

This is all pretty rich, especially coming from Graham, a senator who voted to raise his own salary three times (and who currently receives an annual salary of $174,000) and from the editors of the *Wall Street Journal*, who are far removed from the everyday world of Main Street common sense. The editors' "bedtime story"— to use a phrase from former Senior Advisor to the Treasury Department Ernie Tedeschi—makes little sense in an economy mired in the worst economic collapse since the Great Depression of the 1930s. And the loss of much-needed benefits only adds to the sleepless nights of those who are suffering the worst.

Overwhelming evidence supports quite a different bedtime story—one that calls for far more humane unemployment policies.

What Republican Nightmares Are Made Of

It is true. Many of the unemployed workers who received an extra $600 a week through the Coronavirus Aid, Relief, and Economic Security (CARES) Act, which was passed by Congress in March 2020, received more money than they had earned while working. Peter Ganong and two other University of Chicago economists found that was the case for about three-quarters (76%) of workers receiving weekly $600 payments and full state unemployment compensation from April through July. But Marokey Sawo and Michelle Evermore of the National Employment Law Project calculated that for just 40% of unemployed workers their benefits were greater than their previous total compensation (the sum of their wages and benefits).

The intent of the Federal Pandemic Unemployment Compensation (FPUC) program was to provide unemployment benefits that would fully replace the missing wages of unemployed workers. State unemployment compensation typically replaces about 40% to 45% of an unemployed worker's prior earnings, though benefits vary from state to state. With state employment agencies not up to the task of determining and distributing benefits that would match an unemployed worker's lost wages, Congress settled on adding a fixed benefit of $600 a week. The $600 weekly bonus payment (along with regular unemployment insurance benefits) would just replace the median weekly pay of U.S. workers, which is around $1,000. But the weekly $600 payment also pushed the total benefits of lower-income workers above their previous wages (or replaced more than 100% of their wages).

The FPUC benefits were critical to the survival of a range of workers. While the bulk of the $600 bonus went to unemployed workers receiving state unemployment benefits, workers who had exhausted their state unemployment benefits also received FPUC payments. So, too, did business owners and the self-employed, who received additional assistance from other CARES Act programs. But the $600 weekly FPUC payments ceased at the end of July and have yet to be renewed.

At Odds with the Evidence

The study conducted by the Yale economists that caught the attention of the *Wall Street Journal* editors is more credible than they suggest. The economists' conclusion that enhanced unemployment benefits have *not* led to fewer people looking for work has not been "contradicted by other data" as the editors claim. Multiple studies, using a variety of data sets, have confirmed that enhanced unemployment benefits, even those that exceeded the previous wages of the recipient, have not led to a decrease in the number of people looking for work, or increased the number of the unemployed. (Vice Chair of the Congressional Joint Economic Committee (JEC), Representative Don Beyer of Virginia, has summarized five of these studies, including the Yale Study, on the JEC website, jec.senate.gov.)

Let's look at a few of these studies, beginning with the Yale Study. Economists Dana Scott and Joseph Atlonji and several of their colleagues examined the weekly data from Homebase, a scheduling and timesheet system used by restaurants, bars, retail stores, and other service-sector businesses. They conclude that "the expansion in UI [Unemployment Insurance] replacement rates did not increase layoffs at the outset of the pandemic or discourage workers from returning to their jobs over time." The *Wall Street Journal* editors have clearly misread the Yale study, for the authors never claimed that their findings hold in all economic settings. The Yale authors emphasize that, "our results do not speak to the disemployment effects of UI generosity during more normal times, which is the subject of a vast literature."

In another study, Ernie Tedeschi, now Managing Director and Policy Economist at Evercore ISI, a financial consulting firm, examined Current Population Survey data (which is a key source for labor force statistics) for evidence that the effects of the ratio of unemployment benefits to previous wages had affected the likelihood that workers left a job or accepted a new one. He found no such evidence. Like the authors of the Yale Study, Tedeschi makes clear that his results are specific to the pandemic economy. He writes: "If the economy were at full employment, if there was no pandemic, and if the FPUC were permanent rather than a temporary component of the UI system, I'd expect an effect."

Finally, Ioana Marinescu, an economist at the University of Pennsylvania, and her co-authors, examined data on job listings and applications from the online platform Glassdoor from January to June 2020. They found that, after the unemployment bonus began in March, job applications stayed "relatively stable," job openings continued to decrease, and the ratio of applications per vacancy rose. They concluded that, "Employers who rely on online applications are not experiencing increased difficulties in finding applicants for their jobs after the CARES Act, which was a key concern with increasing benefits by $600 a week."

An Alternative Bedtime Story

Our alternative bedtime story begins this way: No matter how hard they search, unemployed workers can't find jobs that don't exist. The major cause of today's high unemployment is the lack of jobs, not workers who have stopped searching for work and have left jobs unfilled. By the end of July, there were still 11.1 million fewer jobs in the U.S. economy than there had been prior to the pandemic in January 2020.

Renewing the FPUC supplemental unemployment benefits would boost spending and create jobs. Economist Mark Zandi from Moody's Analytics estimates that $1 of renewed unemployment benefits would increase economic output by $1.64—a multiplier effect or bang for the buck that exceeds that of most forms of government spending. Harvard economists Marco Di Maggio and Amir Kerman calculate an even bigger effect, a $1.90 increase in output for each dollar of additional unemployment benefits. Extending the $600 a week enhanced benefit would have protected 1.7 to 2.8 million jobs and lowered the unemployment rate by between 1.1 and 1.8 percentage points, according to rough estimates from the JEC.

Workers will continue to return to work even if their unemployment benefits with the $600 a week FPUC supplement exceeds their previous wages. Tedeschi found that 70% of the unemployment insurance recipients who returned to work in June had been receiving unemployment benefits that were greater than their prior wages.

It makes sense, daresay, common sense: A job, even in today's economy, is more secure than enhanced unemployment benefits, and over time will pay more than unemployment insurance benefits. State unemployment benefits expire in less than a year, and in most states they expire within 39 weeks.

Our bedtime story, unlike the *Wall Street Journal* editors' "common sense," is consistent with the available evidence. And it supports generous unemployment insurance benefits that will contribute to a more robust economic recovery and actually help people get a good night's sleep. ❑

Sources: Dana Scott and Joseph Altonji et al., "Employment Effects of Unemployment Insurance Generosity During the Pandemic," Yale University, July 14, 2020; Arindrajit Dube, "The Impact of the Federal Pandemic Unemployment Compensation on Employment: Evidence from the Household Pulse Survey," University of Massachusetts Working Paper, July 31, 2020; Ioana Elena Marinescu, Daphné Skandalis, and Daniel Zhao, "Job search, job posting and unemployment insurance during the COVID-19 crisis," Social Science Research Network, July 20, 2020; Alexander W. Bartik et al., "Measuring the labor market at the onset of the COVID-19 crisis," NBER Working Paper No. 27613, July 2020; Ernie Tedeschi, "A short thread on the emergency $600 per week unemployment insurance payment, more formally known as Federal Pandemic Unemployment Compensation (FPUC)," July 26, 2020 (twitter.com/ernietedeschi); Peter Ganong, et al., "US Unemployment Insurance Replacement Rates During the Pandemic," Becker Friedman Institute, University of Chicago, August 24, 2020; Marokey Sawo and Michele Evermore, "Unemployed Workers and Benefit 'Replacement Rate,': An Expanded Analysis," National Employment Law Project and The Groundwork Collaborative, August 2020; Kate Davidson, "Is $600 a Week in Extra Unemployment Aid Deterring People From Seeking Work?," *Wall Street Journal*, July 29, 2020 (wsj.com); Patricia Cohen, "Do Jobless Benefits Deter Workers? Some Employers Say Yes. Studies Don't," *New York Times*, Sept. 10, 2020 (nytimes.com); Catherine Rampell, "The myth of unemployment benefits depressing work," *Washington Post*, August 3, 2020 (washingtonpost.com; Heather Long, "The controversial $600 unemployment aid debate, explained," *Washington Post*, August 6, 2020 (washingtonpost.com).

Article 4.7

KEYNES, WAGE AND PRICE "STICKINESS," AND DEFLATION

BY ALEJANDRO REUSS

August 2009

Most people are accustomed to worrying about inflation, which has been a durable fact of life in the United States for half a century. The overall price level in the U.S. economy (a sort of average of prices across the economy), as measured by the Consumer Price Index (CPI), has increased every calendar year since 1957. Or, rather, had increased every year since 1957, until 2008. Last year, as the U.S. economy went into its most severe recession since the Great Depression, the CPI declined by 0.2%. For the first time in decades, there is a reason for people in the United States to worry about the dangers of deflation.

Deflation: What's Not to Like?

Lower prices may sound appealing, but deflation can make a bad recession worse. Deflation can bring down overall demand. If individuals and firms expect prices to decline, they may postpone purchases. Why buy today, if the price will be lower tomorrow? Declining prices and wages can exacerbate firms' negative expectations about future sales and profits, discouraging current investment. If a firm does not think it will be able to sell future output at a sufficient profit, it will not make purchases of new plants and equipment now. Deflation can also make the cost of borrowing higher, and increase the burden of past debt. This can ruin debtors and bankrupt firms, as each dollar owed becomes harder to come by as prices drop. Over the three years with the sharpest drop in output and employment during the Great Depression, 1930–1933, the CPI dropped by over 25%. More broadly, a study by economists Michael Bruno and William Easterly of over 100 countries from the 1960s to 1990s showed that rates of deflation between 0% and 20% were associated with lower rates of economic growth than low to moderate rates of inflation (up to 30%) were.

Such concerns about deflation run sharply counter to the "mainstream" or neoclassical view of recessions. Neoclassical economists argue that the economy is "self-correcting," and that if it dips into recession it will quickly return itself to "full employment" without any need for deliberate government action. One of their main arguments for this view is that prices—including wages (the price of labor) and interest rates (the price of money)—are flexible. If there is excess supply of labor (unemployment), workers will reduce their wage demands, causing employers to want to hire more labor and workers to offer less labor for sale, until the surplus is eliminated. Likewise, if there is excess saving, the interest rate will decline, causing people to save less and borrow more, until that surplus is eliminated. In this view, a recovery (from a period of low employment and output) involves a decrease in the price level. Deflation, in other words, is the cure for what ails us.

What Is Price "Stickiness"?

One response to the neoclassical argument is that, in fact, prices are not perfectly flexible (they exhibit "stickiness"). For this reason, the economy is not self-correcting, at least not in the short run. Wages and prices may be "too high" (and, therefore, result in suppliers offering larger quantities for sale than demanders are able and willing to buy), but not come down quickly and eliminate the market surplus. This view has been widely attributed to John Maynard Keynes, and is, in fact, a key argument in what is known as "New Keynesian" economic theory. But this was not Keynes' argument.

Keynes expressed, in numerous passages in *The General Theory,* the view that wages were "sticky" in terms of money. He noted, for example, that workers and unions tended to fight tooth-and-nail against any attempts by employers to reduce money wages (the actual sum of money workers receive, as opposed to the real purchasing power of these wages, taking account of changes in the cost of living), even by a little bit, in a way they did not fight for increases in wages every time there was a small rise in the cost of living eroding their "real wages." Keynes argued emphatically, however, against the idea that the stickiness of money wages was the cause of unemployment, or that full flexibility of money wages (in particular, a decline in money wages) was likely to be a cure for depressions.

Is Wage Flexibility the Solution?

Keynes was careful to describe many different possible effects of declining money wages, some pointing towards increased consumption or investment (and therefore an increase in total output and incomes), and some pointing in the opposite direction. He pointed out two fundamental errors in the conventional view that lower money wages would necessarily result in increased employment. First, he noted that, while one worker could gain employment (at the expense of someone else) by accepting a lower wage, this did not automatically mean that lower money wages across the board would cause overall employment to increase. Second, he argued that, while decreased money wages would result in increased employment if total ("aggregate") demand were unchanged, there was no reason to believe that would be the case.

Keynes made at least four major arguments that declining money wages were not the cure for unemployment (and depressions) that classical economists thought:

1) Workers do not decide their level of real wages, and so cannot reduce these to a level that will ensure full employment. Keynes pointed out that particular workers (or groups of workers) and employers bargained not over real wages, but money wages. Real wages depended not only on these money-wage bargains but also on the overall price level. The price level, in turn, depended on money-wage bargains made between many different groups of workers and employers across the economy as a whole. Keynes argued that, if workers in general were to accept lower money wages, the overall price level could not possibly remain unchanged. The price level, instead, would decline by a similar proportion, so real wages might

not change very much at all. In that case, employers would not have an incentive to hire more workers, and overall employment would change very little.

2) Reductions in workers' money wages may result in decreased consumption, and therefore can result in lower incomes and output. Keynes argued that declines in money wages change the distribution of income—increasing the incomes of owners of other factors of production (capitalists and landowners) at the expense of workers, and those of rentiers (owners of money capital) at the expense of entrepreneurs (owners of businesses). These changes in distribution could result in a decrease in the "marginal propensity to consume" (the amount spent on consumption out of each additional dollar of income). Declining money wages (and the resulting decline in the price level) would tend to redistribute income from lower-income individuals (who tend to consume a very large proportion of their incomes) to higher-income individuals (who tend to consume lower proportions of their incomes, and to save higher proportions).

3) Declining wages can create incentives for employers to postpone purchases of durable equipment. Keynes argued that the effects of the reduction in money wages on the incentive for capitalists to invest (purchase durable equipment) depended on the expectations of future changes in money wages. If money wages declined, but capitalists expected them to go up in the immediate future (that is, money wages were thought to have "bottomed out"), Keynes argued, the effect on investment would be positive, since the cost of producing durable equipment now would be lower than in the future. However, if the decline in money wages made capitalists expect continued future declines, the effect on investment would be negative. Durable equipment purchased in the current period would, in Keynes' words, have to "compete ... with the output from equipment produced [in the future] ... at a lower labor cost." Owners of the more expensive equipment would have to cut their prices and accept lower profits to match the prices that owners of the less expensive equipment would be willing to accept (having the advantage of lower costs). This would produce an incentive to put off purchases of such equipment into the future.

4) A decline in the price level creates increased real burdens for debtors. When the price level goes down, the purchasing power of the currency increases. We would say, "a dollar becomes more valuable." Since most debts take the form of a specific sum of money owed, and the real purchasing power of this sum increases as the price level decreases, the real purchasing power that the debtor has to hand over also increases. Looked at another way, across-the-board deflation means that the debtor cannot charge as much for whatever she sells, but the amount of money she has to pay to the creditor does not change. Therefore, she now has to sell more units (of whatever it is she sells) to pay back the debt. Debt service will swallow up an increasing proportion of her gross income. "If the fall of wages and prices goes far ... those entrepreneurs who are heavily indebted," Keynes argues, "may soon reach the point of insolvency." That is, deflation can result in an epidemic of bankruptcies.

Keynes' arguments on the effects of declining wages and prices during a recession were part of his case, contrary to the mainstream economists of his time (and ours), that capitalist economies were not inherently "self-correcting." Depression conditions, Keynes argued, would not necessarily set off a chain of events pulling the economy back to its "full employment" level of output. Declining money wages and prices could, in fact, lead to a downward spiral that could plunge the economy into a deep recession. Capitalist economies could get stuck in a low-output, high-unemployment condition. Keynes believed that government action was necessary to guarantee a return to and maintenance of full employment. For this reason, he argued that the complacent attitude of conventional economists toward economic crises—that, eventually, the problem would solve itself—was not of much use. "Economists set them too easy, too useless a task," he wrote, "if in tempestuous seasons they can only tell us that when the storm is over the ocean is flat again." ❏

Sources: John Maynard Keynes, *The General Theory of Employment, Interest, and Money* (Harcourt, Inc., 1964); John Maynard Keynes, *A Tract on Monetary Reform* (MacMillan, 1923); Consumer Price Index, All Urban Consumers (CPI-U), Economagic; Michael Bruno and William Easterly, "Inflation Crises and Long-Run Growth," Policy Research Working Paper, World Bank, September 1995.

Chapter 5

WEALTH, INEQUALITY, AND POVERTY

INTRODUCTION

Wealth and inequality are both end products of today's patterns of economic growth. But while all macroeconomics textbooks investigate wealth accumulation, most give less attention to wealth disparities. The authors in this chapter fill in the gap by looking at who makes out, and who doesn't, in the accumulation of wealth.

During the start of the Covid-19 pandemic we were told that we were all "in the same boat." But as the weeks turned into months and with the economy in shutdown, it became obvious that some boats were significantly more pleasant than others. The wealthy have ample resources and can, over time, limit their exposure to the virus in luxury. Whereas, on the other end of the food chain, the "precariat" has found itself exposed, immiserated, and in imminent peril.

In Article 5.1, John Miller writes that in spite of a new-found appreciation for the "low-wage heroes" that are on the front lines of the Covid-19 pandemic, low-wage servitude is still being proposed by the *Wall Street Journal* and others as a necessary part of American economic growth. There are three major difficulties with attempting to resuscitate this tired and tortured ideological line. The first problem is factual. The second problem is social and institutional. And the third problem is one of having to acknowledge that "essential" workers are, in fact, "essential." If this is the case, the "Fight for $15" movement should be embraced by the *Wall Street Journal*—not dismissed.

Economist Chris Tilly (Article 5.2) then argues that rampant inequality is not necessary for economic growth, showing that among both developing and industrial economies and across individual countries' distinct regions, there is no correlation between higher inequality and faster economic growth. He contends that greater equality actually supports economic growth by bolstering spending, raising productivity, and reducing social conflict.

Next, Arthur MacEwan (Article 5.3) offers a compelling assessment of organized labor in the country. Is it possible to have both a decline and a resurgence of organized labor happen at the same time?

Then, economists Janelle Jones, John Schmitt, and Valerie Wilson track how the position of African Americans has changed since the Kerner Commission report of 1968 documented pervasive racial discrimination in U.S. society (Article 5.4). They find that, compared to 1968, African Americans today are much better educated, are healthier, and have higher incomes and are less often poor in absolute terms. At the same time, they find that large gaps between the economic, health, and educational outcomes of African Americans and whites still persist.

Article 5.5 is an interview with Michelle Holder that explores the persistent wage gap experienced by Black women in the labor force. What is this "double gap" that Black women experience? Holder walks us through her methodology and subsequent results on the subject.

An analysis of inequality would not be complete without considering the environmental dimensions of this problem. Frank Ackerman, in Article 5.6, presents different aspects through which inequality manifests itself in the environment. He identifies the long life of investments as the biggest economic obstacle to climate policy, and highlights a set of public policy strategies to overcome the challenges of outdated and unsustainable social and industrial structures.

We round out this chapter with Article 5.7, in which Arthur MacEwan weighs in on the question of income and wealth inequality and whether or not it can simply be addressed through raising taxes on the wealthy. MacEwan suggests that to sufficiently deal with the question, one has to address the many dubiously performing markets upon which the system relies. These markets themselves will continue to generate inequality no matter what the top marginal tax rate for individuals and corporations might be.

Discussion Questions

1. (General) The authors of this chapter believe that income and wealth distribution is as important as income and wealth creation, and consider greater economic equality an important macroeconomic goal. What are some arguments for and against this position? Where do you come down in the debate?

2. (General) "A rising tide lifts all boats," proclaimed President John F. Kennedy as he lobbied for pro-business tax cuts in the early 1960s. Have recent periods of economic growth (or "booms") lifted all boats? How have stockholders fared versus wage earners? How has the distribution of income and wealth by income group and by race changed?

3. (5.1) How has the Covid-19 pandemic affected workers at the bottom of the food chain? Has the "Fight for $15" movement increased its power?

4. (Article 5.2) Why do conservatives argue that inequality is good for economic growth? What counterarguments does Tilly use to challenge this traditional view of the "trade-off" between inequality and growth? What evidence convinces Tilly that equality is good for economic growth? Does that evidence convince you?

5. (Article 5.3) MacEwan suggests a number of reasons for the decline in organized labor. Have the lockdowns throughout the country during the Covid-

19 pandemic helped or hurt the prospects of increasing union membership and organizing? If so, how? What are "Right to Work" laws? How do they affect the ability to sustain unions?

6. (Article 5.4) In Table 1, which data indicate that since 1968 the position of African Americans has improved? In which areas do they still lag behind the position of whites? Which data indicate that the position of African Americans has gotten worse?

7. (Article 5.5) Holder proffers the concept of a "double wage gap" which is experienced by Black women. What is this "double gap"? Walk through the methodology that she uses to make this assessment. Is it sound? Why is this "double gap" so pervasive?

8. (Article 5.6) Why does Ackerman see the long life of many investments as the main obstacle to improved climate change policies?

9. (Article 5.7) MacEwan argues that while raising taxes for the wealthiest individuals and corporations might be a good start in addressing income inequality, simply increasing taxes is not a sufficient solution. According to MacEwan, the entire institutional and social structure of "the market" which generates this inequality needs to be addressed. How do each of the markets mentioned by MacEwan generate inequality? What would need to be done to adequately address this problem going forward?

Article 5.1

PUNDITS CLAIM FIGHTING INEQUALITY IS BAD FOR LOW-WAGE WORKERS

BY JOHN MILLER
March/April 2020

> The Sanders class-war story is wrong. … Over the past few years wages for workers toward the bottom of the income stream have been rising faster than wages for those toward the top.
>
> If you improve worker bargaining power, that may help a bit, but over the long run people can't earn what they don't produce. … The real solution, therefore, is not class war. It's to boost and expand productivity for everybody else.
> —David Brooks, "The Bernie Sanders Fallacy: No, Virginia, there is no class war," *New York Times*, Jan. 16, 2020

> During the Trump Presidency, wages for the bottom 10% of earners over age 25 rose an average 5.9% annually compared to 2.4% during Barack Obama's second term. Stressing growth [has] done more to reduce inequality than stress[ing] inequality at the expense of growth.
> —Editorial Board, "The Economy's Inequality Dividend: Growth is lifting low-income workers and the middle class," *Wall Street Journal*, Jan. 10, 2020

> "Since my election, the net worth of the bottom half of wage earners has increased 47%—three times faster than the increase for the top 1%."
> —Donald Trump, "Full Transcript: Trump's 2020 State of the Union Address," *New York Times*, Feb. 5, 2020

Long before the coronavirus went viral, an ideological virus infected much of the U.S. pundit class. *New York Times* columnist David Brooks, blinded to the systematic oppression of workers in today's unfettered capitalist economy, haughtily dismissed Senator Bernie Sanders's class war story as wrong. And the *Wall Street Journal* editors argued that "stressing growth does more to reduce inequality than stressing inequality at the expense of growth." In the White House, the ideological virus left the President babbling incoherently about the best economy ever.

The pundits' ideological blinders blocked out the fact that the growth- and productivity-enhancing policies they stress had driven inequality to the highest levels in nearly a century, even before the current crisis.

It is certainly time to up Brooks's and the editors' dose of antivirals and have them face up to how their ideological ravings have distorted their vision of what is actually happening in today's economy. But there just might not be a cure for President Donald Trump.

Low-Wage Workers Getting Rich?

Let's look first at Brooks and the *Wall Street Journal* editors' insistence that the wages of those near the bottom of our economy have been going up more quickly than the wages of those near the top during the Trump years. That is what the data say. But what lies behind those increases suggests something quite different about who benefits from today's economy than what Brooks or the editors suggest.

To start with, adjusted for inflation, the wage gains of the bottom 10% of wage earners in the last three years are just half (2.4%) of what the editors claim. Also, despite growing more quickly than the wages of the top 10% of wage earners, their wages remained just one-fifth of the wages of high-wage earners. That's hardly different than during the Obama years, and below where the ratio stood in 2007 prior to the Great Recession.

The low unemployment rates of the last three years helped to improve the position of low-wage workers, but it was increases in state minimum wages that pushed those wage gains above those of better-off workers.

While the federal minimum wage has been stuck at $7.25 per hour for over a decade, some 29 states (and several cities) now have hourly minimum wages higher than the federal minimum wage. As a result, for 89% of minimum-wage employees the minimum wage is higher that $7.25 an hour, and up to $13.50 an hour in Washington state.

Higher state minimum wages have made a real difference in the wages of those at the bottom. Economist Ernie Tedeschi, head of fiscal analysis at Evercore ISI, a macro advisory firm, found that wage growth near the bottom at the 10th percentile averaged 4.1% over the last two years. Tedeschi calculates that without the minimum-wage hikes their wages would have increased just 3.3%, which is less than the 3.6% wage growth of those near the top, at the 90th percentile

The wages of low-income workers went up more quickly in states that increased their minimum wage than in states that didn't. For workers near the bottom, in the 10th percentile, wages increased 3.2 percentage points in 2019. In years when the unemployment rates were higher and finding a job was more difficult, increases in the state minimum wage made an even greater difference. From 2013 to 2019, the wages of a worker at the 10th percentile, near the bottom, increased 17.6% in states that increased their minimum wage, but just 9.3% in states that didn't.

Nonetheless, as the Economic Policy Institute (EPI) reports, from 2007 to 2019, the wage gains of workers at the 10th percentile, near the bottom, averaged 0.6% a year, which fell well short of the average wage gains of workers at the 90th percentile, near the top, which were 0.9% a year. On top of that, the income of the richest 1%—much of which comes from investments, not wages—increased at a rate that dwarfed the income gains of all other groups during the Trump years. The income share of the top 1% rose from an outsized 20.7% in 2016 to 22.0% in 2018, as reported by economist Emmanuel Saez.

Is Wealth Trickling Down?

In his 2020 State of the Union address, President Trump insisted that his economy is enriching the bottom 50% of the population more quickly than that of the already wealthy. While more or less consistent with the wealth data collected by the New York Federal Reserve Board, Trump's claim is nothing more than a cynical fig leaf meant to cover up his gilded-age policies that have showered benefits on the super-rich and done precious little to improve the lot of most people.

Consider this. At the beginning of Trump's term, the aggregate wealth or net worth (the value of their assets less their debts) of the bottom half of the population was $1.1 trillion. By the third quarter of 2019 (the latest available data), that number was $1.7 trillion, or about 50% more. Nonetheless, most of those families had a negative net worth, having accumulated more debt than the value of their assets. And the aggregate wealth of the richest 1% of households, each with a net worth in excess of $10 million, was still 20 times that of the bottom 50% of the population.

Worse yet, the concentration of wealth at the top has intensified in the last three years. The share of the nation's wealth going to the top 1% has risen to 32.2%—more than any time prior to 1989. And while the wealth share of the bottom 50% reached 1.6% by the third quarter of 2019, that figure was still lower than any time since 1989–2008.

Getting Blood Out of a Stone?

My mother's response when we asked for what we didn't have was, "you can't get blood out of a stone." That's how Brooks responded to Sanders's push for more bargaining power for workers and higher wages: "People can't earn what they don't produce." The "real solution," Brooks claims, is to boost productivity.

Brooks is correct that wage levels often track closely with productivity levels. In most economic studies, productivity typically accounts for about 80% to 90% of the differences in wage levels across countries. But as economist Dani Rodrik has argued, the unaccounted portion of that variation (the remaining 10%–20%) "can move wage levels up or down in any country by 40% or more," depending on factors such as workers' bargaining power, labor regulations, and unionization levels.

But over the last five decades a yawning gap between wage gains and productivity growth has opened up in the United States. Hourly compensation (wages and benefits) of nonsupervisory workers in the private sector increased just 11.6% from 1979 to 2018, while productivity increased 69.8%, about six times more quickly.

That gap makes clear that it is not a lack of productivity gains that stands in the way of the gains that are necessary to reduce inequality.

Nonetheless, Brooks assures us that the link between wages and productivity remains strong. His claim is based on research by economists such as Michael Strain of the American Enterprise Institute. Strain finds that the pay-productivity gap has been nearly filled by payments to supervisory workers. But that group includes highly paid managers and even CEOs whose lavish stock options and bonuses are one of the drivers of today's inequality. By 2018, the ratio of CEO to worker compensation had reached 278-to-one, more than 10 times the 20.2-to-one ratio in 1965, as reported by EPI.

So, there is blood in the stone of productivity growth, but it has gone to fuel inequality—not reduce it.

The Right Class War Story

If Brooks's goal is to stop misguided class warfare, he has been asleep at the wheel. Today's plutocracy has been at war with everyday workers for decades, denying them their fair share of productivity gains, forcing them to endure stagnant wages, and leaving ever more of the population plagued by mounting economic insecurity and even declining life spans.

The data Brooks and the *Wall Street Journal* editors present show that focusing on growth alone does not reduce inequality. Economic growth must be accompanied by public policies such as boosting the minimum wage if it is to produce the dividend of lessening inequality.

If Brooks and the *Wall Street Journal* editors were to face up to the implications of their own evidence, they could start by joining the fight for a $15 federal minimum wage. They could also call for measures that improved workers' bargaining power, increased union representation, and enforced labor regulations—the very factors that account for gaps between wage levels and productivity in international studies. ❏

Sources: Ernie Tedeschi, "Pay is Rising Fastest for Low Earners. One Reason? Minimum Wages," *New York Times*, Jan. 3. 2020; Elise Gould, "State of Working America Wages," Economic Policy Institute, Feb. 20, 2020; Federal Reserve Board, "Distribution of Household Wealth in the United States since 1989," Jan. 6, 2020; Emmanuel Saez, "Striking it Rich," February 2020; Dani Rodrik, *The Globalization Paradox* (W.W. Norton, New York: 2011); Michael Strain, "The Link Between Wages and Productivity Is Strong," American Policy Institute, Feb. 4, 2019; Josh Bivens and Lawrence Mishel, "Understanding the Historic Divergence Between Productivity and A Typical Worker's Pay," Economic Policy Institute Briefing Paper, Sept. 2, 2015.

Article 5.2

GEESE, GOLDEN EGGS, AND TRAPS

Why inequality is bad for the economy.

BY CHRIS TILLY
July/August 2004

Whenever progressives propose ways to redistribute wealth from the rich to those with low and moderate incomes, conservative politicians and economists accuse them of trying to kill the goose that lays the golden eggs. The advocates of unfettered capitalism proclaim that inequality is good for the economy because it promotes economic growth. Unequal incomes, they say, provide the incentives necessary to guide productive economic decisions by businesses and individuals. Try to reduce inequality, and you'll sap growth. Furthermore, the conservatives argue, growth actually promotes equality by boosting the have-nots more than the haves. So instead of fiddling with who gets how much, the best way to help those at the bottom is to pump up growth.

But these conservative prescriptions are absolutely, dangerously wrong. Instead of the goose-killer, equality turns out to be the goose. Inequality stifles growth; equality gooses it up. Moreover, economic expansion does not necessarily promote equality—instead, it is the types of jobs and the rules of the economic game that matter most.

Inequality: Goose or Goose-Killer?

The conservative argument may be wrong, but it's straightforward. Inequality is good for the economy, conservatives say, because it provides the right incentives for innovation and economic growth. First of all, people will only have the motivation to work hard, innovate, and invest wisely if the economic system rewards them for good economic choices and penalizes bad ones. Robin Hood-style policies that collect from the wealthy and help those who are worse off violate this principle. They reduce the payoff of smart decisions and lessen the sting of dumb ones. The result: people and companies are bound to make less efficient decisions. "We must allow [individuals] to fail, as well as succeed, and we must replace the nanny state with a regime of self-reliance and self-respect," writes conservative lawyer Stephen Kinsella in *The Freeman: Ideas on Liberty* (not clear how the free woman fits in). To prove their point, conservatives point to the former state socialist countries, whose economies had become stagnant and inefficient by the time they fell at the end of the 1980s.

If you don't buy this incentive story, there's always the well-worn trickle-down theory. To grow, the economy needs productive investments: new offices, factories, computers, and machines. To finance such investments takes a pool of savings. The rich save a larger fraction of their incomes than those less well-off. So to spur growth, give more to the well-heeled (or at least take less away from them in the form of taxes), and give less to the down-and-out. The rich will save their money and then invest it, promoting growth that's good for everyone.

Unfortunately for trickle-down, the brilliant economist John Maynard Keynes debunked the theory in his *General Theory of Employment, Interest, and Money* in

1936. Keynes, whose precepts guided liberal U.S. economic policy from the 1940s through the 1970s, agreed that investments must be financed out of savings. But he showed that most often it's changes in investment that drive savings, rather than the other way around. When businesses are optimistic about the future and invest in building and retooling, the economy booms, all of us make more money, and we put some of it in banks, 401(k)s, stocks, and so on. That is, saving grows to match investment. When companies are glum, the process runs in reverse, and savings shrink to equal investment. This leads to the "paradox of thrift": if people try to save too much, businesses will see less consumer spending, will invest less, and total savings will end up diminishing rather than growing as the economy spirals downward. A number of Keynes' followers added the next logical step: shifting money from the high-saving rich to the high-spending rest of us, and not the other way around, will spur investment and growth.

Of the two conservative arguments in favor of inequality, the incentive argument is a little weightier. Keynes himself agreed that people needed financial consequences to steer their actions, but questioned whether the differences in payoffs needed to be so huge. Certainly state socialist countries' attempts to replace material incentives with moral exhortation have often fallen short. In 1970, the Cuban government launched the Gran Zafra (Great Harvest), an attempt to reap 10 million tons of sugar cane with (strongly encouraged) volunteer labor. Originally inspired by Che Guevara's ideal of the New Socialist Man (not clear how the New Socialist Woman fit in), the effort ended with Fidel Castro tearfully apologizing to the Cuban people in a nationally broadcast speech for letting wishful thinking guide economic policy.

But before conceding this point to the conservatives, let's look at the evidence about the connection between equality and growth. Economists William Easterly of New York University and Gary Fields of Cornell University have recently summarized this evidence:

- Countries, and regions within countries, with more equal incomes grow faster. (These growth figures do not include environmental destruction or improvement. If they knocked off points for environmental destruction and added points for environmental improvement, the correlation between equality and growth would be even stronger, since desperation drives poor people to adopt environmentally destructive practices such as rapid deforestation.)
- Countries with more equally distributed land grow faster.
- Somewhat disturbingly, more ethnically homogeneous countries and regions grow faster—presumably because there are fewer ethnically based inequalities.
- In addition, more worker rights are associated with higher rates of economic growth, according to Josh Bivens and Christian Weller, economists at two Washington, D.C., think tanks, the Economic Policy Institute and the Center for American Progress.

These patterns recommend a second look at the incentive question. In fact, more equality can actually strengthen incentives and opportunities to produce.

Equality as the Goose

Equality can boost growth in several ways. Perhaps the simplest is that study after study has shown that farmland is more productive when cultivated in small plots. So organizations promoting more equal distribution of land, like Brazil's Landless Workers' Movement, are not just helping the landless poor—they're contributing to agricultural productivity!

Another reason for the link between equality and growth is what Easterly calls "match effects," which have been highlighted in research by Stanford's Paul Roemer and others in recent years. One example of a match effect is the fact that well-educated people are most productive when working with others who have lots of schooling. Likewise, people working with computers are more productive when many others have computers (so that, for example, e-mail communication is widespread, and know-how about computer repair and software is easy to come by). In very unequal societies, highly educated, computer-using elites are surrounded by majorities with little education and no computer access, dragging down their productivity. This decreases young people's incentive to get more education and businesses' incentive to invest in computers, since the payoff will be smaller.

Match effects can even matter at the level of a metropolitan area. Urban economist Larry Ledebur looked at income and employment growth in 85 U.S. cities and their neighboring suburbs. He found that where the income gap between those in the suburbs and those in the city was largest, income and job growth was slower for everyone.

"Pressure effects" also help explain why equality sparks growth. Policies that close off the low-road strategy of exploiting poor and working people create pressure effects, driving economic elites to search for investment opportunities that pay off by boosting productivity rather than squeezing the have-nots harder. For example, where workers have more rights, they will place greater demands on businesses. Business owners will respond by trying to increase productivity, both to remain profitable even after paying higher wages, and to find ways to produce with fewer workers. The Congress of Industrial Organizations (CIO) union drives in U.S. mass production industries in the 1930s and 1940s provide much of the explanation for the superb productivity growth of the 1950s and 1960s. (The absence of pressure effects may help explain why many past and present state socialist countries have seen slow growth, since they tend to offer numerous protections for workers but no right to organize independent unions.) Similarly, if a government buys out large landholdings in order to break them up, wealthy families who simply kept their fortunes tied up in land for generations will look for new, productive investments. Industrialization in Asian "tigers" South Korea and Taiwan took off in the 1950s on the wings of funds freed up in exactly this way.

Inequality, Conflict, and Growth

Inequality hinders growth in another important way: it fuels social conflict. Stark inequality in countries such as Bolivia and Haiti has led to chronic conflict that hobbles economic growth. Moreover, inequality ties up resources in unproductive uses such as paying for large numbers of police and security guards—attempts to prevent individuals from redistributing resources through theft.

Ethnic variety is connected to slower growth because, on average, more ethnically diverse countries are also more likely to be ethnically divided. In other words, the problem isn't ethnic variety itself, but the racism and ethnic conflict that can exist among diverse populations. In nations like Guatemala, Congo, and Nigeria, ethnic strife has crippled growth—a problem alien to ethnically uniform Japan and South Korea. The reasons are similar to some of the reasons that large class divides hurt growth. Where ethnic divisions (which can take tribal, language, religious, racial, or regional forms) loom large, dominant ethnic groups seek to use government power to better themselves at the expense of other groups, rather than making broad-based investments in education and infrastructure. This can involve keeping down the underdogs—slower growth in the U.S. South for much of the country's history was linked to the Southern system of white supremacy. Or it can involve seizing the surplus of ethnic groups perceived as better off—in the extreme, Nazi Germany's expropriation and genocide of the Jews, who often held professional and commercial jobs.

Of course, the solution to such divisions is not "ethnic cleansing" so that each country has only one ethnic group—in addition to being morally abhorrent, this is simply impossible in a world with 191 countries and 5,000 ethnic groups. Rather, the solution is to diminish ethnic inequalities. Once the 1964 Civil Rights Act forced the South to drop racist laws, the New South's economic growth spurt began. Easterly reports that in countries with strong rule of law, professional bureaucracies, protection of contracts, and freedom from expropriation—all rules that make it harder for one ethnic group to economically oppress another—ethnic diversity has no negative impact on growth.

If more equality leads to faster growth so everybody benefits, why do the rich typically resist redistribution? Looking at the ways that equity seeds growth helps us understand why. The importance of pressure effects tells us that the wealthy often don't think about more productive ways to invest or reorganize their businesses until they are forced to do so. But also, if a country becomes very unequal, it can get stuck in an "inequality trap." Any redistribution involves a trade-off for the rich. They lose by giving up part of their wealth, but they gain a share in increased economic growth. The bigger the disparity between the rich and the rest, the more the rich have to lose, and the less likely that the equal share of boosted growth they'll get will make up for their loss. Once the gap goes beyond a certain point, the wealthy have a strong incentive to restrict democracy, and to block spending on education which might lead the poor to challenge economic injustice—making reform that much harder.

Does Economic Growth Reduce Inequality?

If inequality isn't actually good for the economy, what about the second part of the conservatives' argument—that growth itself promotes equality? According to the conservatives, those who care about equality should simply pursue growth and wait for equality to follow.

"A rising tide lifts all boats," President John F. Kennedy famously declared. But he said nothing about which boats will rise fastest when the economic tide comes in. Growth does typically reduce poverty, according to studies reviewed by economist Gary Fields, though some "boats"—especially families with strong barriers to participating in the labor force—stay "stuck in the mud." But inequality can increase at the same time that poverty falls, if the rich gain even faster than the poor do. True, sustained periods of low unemployment, like that in the United States during the late 1990s, do tend to raise wages at the bottom even faster than salaries at the top. But growth after the recessions of 1991 and 2001 began with years of "jobless recoveries"—growth with inequality.

For decades the prevailing view about growth and inequality within countries was that expressed by Simon Kuznets in his 1955 presidential address to the American Economic Association. Kuznets argued that as countries grew, inequality would first increase, then decrease. The reason is that people will gradually move from the low-income agricultural sector to higher-income industrial jobs—with inequality peaking when the workforce is equally divided between low- and high-income sectors. For mature industrial economies, Kuznets' proposition counsels focusing on growth, assuming that it will bring equity. In developing countries, it calls for enduring current inequality for the sake of future equity and prosperity.

But economic growth doesn't automatically fuel equality. In 1998, economists Klaus Deininger and Lyn Squire traced inequality and growth over time in 48 countries. Five followed the Kuznets pattern, four followed the reverse pattern (decreasing inequality followed by an increase), and the rest showed no systematic pattern. In the United States, for example:

- Incomes became more equal during the New Deal period of the 1930s and 1940s (a time that included economic decline followed by growth).
- From the 1950s through the 1970s, income gaps lessened during booms and expanded during slumps.
- From the late 1970s forward, income inequality worsened fairly consistently, whether the economy was stagnating or growing.

The reasons are not hard to guess. The New Deal introduced widespread unionization, a minimum wage, social security, unemployment insurance, and welfare. Since the late 1970s, unions have declined, the inflation-adjusted value of the minimum wage has fallen, and the social safety net has been shredded. In the United States, as elsewhere, growth only promotes equality if policies and institutions to support equity are in place.

Trapped?

Let's revisit the idea of an inequality trap. The notion is that as the gap between the rich and everybody else grows wider, the wealthy become more willing to give up overall growth in return for the larger share they're getting for themselves. The "haves" back policies to control the "have-nots," instead of devoting social resources to educating the poor so they'll be more productive.

Sound familiar? It should. After two decades of widening inequality, the last few years have brought us massive tax cuts that primarily benefit the wealthiest, at the expense of investment in infrastructure and the education, childcare, and income supports that would help raise less well-off kids to be productive adults. Federal and state governments have cranked up expenditures on prisons, police, and "homeland security," and Republican campaign organizations have devoted major resources to keeping blacks and the poor away from the polls. If the economic patterns of the past are any indication, we're going to pay for these policies in slower growth and stagnation unless we can find our way out of this inequality trap. ❑

Sources: William Easterly, *The Elusive Quest for Growth* (MIT Press, 2001); Gary S. Fields, *Distribution and Development* (MIT Press, 2001); Josh Bivens and Christian Weller, "Rights make might: Ensuring workers' rights as a strategy for economic growth," Economic Policy Institute 2003.

Article 5.3

CAN THE DECLINE OF UNIONS BE REVERSED?

BY ARTHUR MacEWAN
May/June 2021

> Dear Dr. Dollar:
> *It seems pretty clear that strong labor unions have been important in reducing economic inequality. But as labor unions have represented a declining share of workers, inequality has gotten worse and worse. Insofar as the decline of unions has been a result of globalization and technological change, the picture is pretty bleak. So am I right to be pessimistic about significant reductions of inequality, at least through the impact of unions?*
>
> —Taya Abbott, Brookville, Ind.

Yes, strong labor unions have been a force for reducing economic inequality. While various factors are involved in the relationship between unions and equality, both unions' ability to raise workers' wages and their impact on government are involved. And, yes, things have gotten worse over the last several decades, both in terms of union membership numbers and inequality.

But, no, pessimism is not necessarily justified, both because much more is involved than globalization and technology and because of some recent potentially positive developments.

Some Potential Progress?

The recent defeat of the union drive by Amazon at its huge Bessemer, Ala., warehouse was, of course, a significant blow against union organizing. The size and importance of Amazon and its history of strongly resisting the unionization of its facilities drew a great deal of attention. Moreover, Alabama has long been an environment quite hostile to unions. Nonetheless, the union drive at Bessemer had raised the hopes of unions and union supporter across the county. So it would be easy to draw pessimistic lessons from this experience.

Yet the defeat should not have come as a surprise, and understanding that defeat could lead to positive responses. The experience in Alabama highlights the challenges facing unions and could force unions to find ways to respond more effectively to those challenges.

One of those challenges is the ability of a powerful firm, Amazon in this case, to frame the debate around a union drive. For example, according to a spokesperson, not surprisingly, Amazon claimed, "Our employees choose to work at Amazon because we offer some of the best jobs available everywhere we hire, and we encourage anyone to compare our overall pay, benefits, and workplace environment to any other company with similar jobs." Actually, various analysts have made the comparison, and have found that when Amazon builds a distribution center in an area, wages in the area tend to fall. An example is provided by a 2018 report in the Economist magazine: "In the years since

Amazon opened its doors in Lexington County [South Carolina], annual earnings for warehouse workers in the area have fallen from $47,000 to $32,000, a decline of over 30%." It seems that because of its size, Amazon's role in local labor markets is to push wages down generally.

More particularly, at Bessemer, while Amazon's presence may not have pushed area wages down, according to a March New York Times article: "The most recent figure for the median wage in Greater Birmingham, a metropolitan area of roughly one million people that includes Bessemer, was near $3 [an hour] above Amazon's pay there according to the Bureau of Labor Statistics."

Be that as it may, at Amazon's Bessemer operation, according to a February 7 report by National Public Radio, workers expressed concerns over "grueling productivity quotas and had wanted more input in shaping the workplace including how people get disciplined or fired." In the era of Covid-19, workers in many plants have turned their attention to job safety and layoffs, and have found union protection an important benefit. Nonetheless, Amazon appears to have been able to convince a majority of workers at the Bessemer warehouse that they were well-paid and that pay and benefits outweighed these sorts of problems.

Beyond Amazon, in the decade leading up to 2020, union victories in elections resulting from union petitions rose from an average of 65.7% in the 2010–2012 period to an average of 71.4% in the 2017–2019 period—not huge, but nonetheless notable. Moreover, in January and February of 2020, before the pandemic came to dominance, unions won 78% and 94%, respectively, of elections brought about by their petitions. Covid-19 appears to have thrown a monkey wrench in union organizing efforts, as the number of union recognition elections resulting from union petitions fell sharply in the rest of the year.

Not Only at the Federal Level

At the state level, direct actions to weaken unions and prevent wage increases have been widespread. Several southern states have had "right to work" laws in place for decades, and recently, other states have enacted such laws. In 2011, the attacks on unions in Wisconsin highlighted this trend. A "right to work" law prohibits a union from establishing a contract with an employer that requires all workers in the establishment to join the union. The result is that, even when a majority of workers have voted the union into existence and voted for the contract, a worker can decline to join, not pay union dues, and still get the benefits bargained for by the union. The PRO Act, if enacted (see main article), would override state "right to work" laws.

In many cases, as authorities in cities and towns have enacted pro-labor regulations, state governments have overridden ("pre-empted") those local regulations. On issues ranging from raising minimum wages to mandating paid leave to establishing fair scheduling, from 1997 to 2017, 26 state governments overrode local actions a total of 67 times, with 55 of these pre-emptions coming since 2011.

Based on the Economic Policy Institute's "Worker Rights Preemption in the U.S.: A Map of the Campaign to Suppress Worker Rights in the States," November 2017, (epi.org).

The experience of the last decade does not signal a dramatic turnaround for the unionization of the U.S. workforce and does not negate what happened at Amazon, but it does temper pessimism.

Political Factors

There remain, of course, the forces of globalization and technological change. While there is dispute over the relative impact of these two factors on unionization, it is clear that both jeopardize jobs and provide employers with a means to undercut unions. There are, however, two other factors that have been important in weakening unions over recent decades: political decisions and the increasingly aggressive anti-union activity of employers. Understanding these factors is a first step in figuring out how to conduct more effective organizing.

One way that political decisions, at various levels of government, undermine unions is the way in which globalization has been structured. If we take globalization to mean an increasing engagement with the international economy, there are different ways that this engagement can be accomplished. The U.S. government has implemented this engagement in ways that favor large firms, making it easy for them to move operations abroad without requiring them to bear the social costs of the dislocation they leave behind, or the environmental costs of the long-distance transportation of goods. Also, the U.S. government has been miserly in providing training and other means of support for workers displaced through globalization—or through technological change, environmental regulation, or anything else.

And then there are the direct antiunion actions of government. For example, the actions of the National Labor Relations Board (NLRB) have been especially unfriendly to unionization, as exhibited in its failure to stop workers engaged in union organizing from being fired. During Republican administrations, the NRLB has been much worse on this issue than during Democratic administrations. Yet, since the early 1950s, there has been an upward trend in the risk of being fired for people engaged in union drives.

As to Congressional action, after the National Labor Relations Act of 1935 gave a major boost to unionization, in 1947, in a very different political climate, the Taft-Hartley Act created a legislative context unfavorable to labor that has lasted for decades. The Employee Free Choice Act (EFCA), introduced in 2007, 2009, and 2016, was an example of an effort to shift the ground in favor of labor, but it was repeatedly rejected by Congress. The EFCA would have allowed a union to be certified as the official union to bargain with an employer if the union collected the signatures of a majority of workers; and the existing right of an employer to demand an additional, separate ballot would have been eliminated.

Currently, the Protecting the Right to Organize Act (the PRO Act), passed by the House of Representatives in 2020 and again in 2021, would give workers more power during disputes at work and add penalties for companies that retaliate against workers who organize. The passage of the PRO Act in the House was a sign of progress for unions. However, it has little chance of getting through a Republican filibuster in the Senate.

The political context of union-management relations has both set the stage for and been encouraged by the efforts of management to combat unionization. And a political change has also taken place in operations at the firm level. Labor historian John Logan (writing in 2006) describes the burgeoning of the "union-avoidance industry" over the last several decades of the 20th century as involving consultants, law firms, industry psychologists, and strike management firms. He points out not only their success, but also that they have prospered in an atmosphere where he notes, quoting Fortune magazine, most U.S. employers "greet the prospect of unionization with the enthusiasm that medieval Europeans reserved for an outbreak of the Black Death." Logan concludes:

> Union avoidance experts have not been the major cause of union decline in the United States in the past half-century; nor have they been the sole source of the intensification of employer opposition to unionization since the 1970s...But they have contributed to the transformation of organizing campaigns into all-out struggles to the death.

What's the Point?

The point here is that the decline of unions and the difficulties that unions face in 2021 are not simply a result of some sort of inexorable forces, which is often how globalization and technological change are presented. The decline and difficulties have also been brought about by forces of political change, both through government and by the actions of employers and their allies in the union-avoidance industry.

What has been brought about by the force of political change can be reversed by political action, by more effective union organizing, including new approaches to organizing, and by greater pressure on the government by unions and their allies. This reality does not, perhaps, create a basis for optimism, but, along with some recent developments, leads to a rejection of pessimism.

In its efforts to prevent unionization at its Bessemer warehouse, Amazon hired the head of the consulting firm RWP Labor, one Russell Brown, who touts himself as "one of the nation's leading labor experts where he has worked with companies in maintaining a union-free workplace." As it turned out, the "expert" and the company were successful in this case, but that result was not automatic and can be reversed elsewhere. ❏

Sources: Celine McNicholas, Heidi Shierholz, and Margaret Poydock, "Union workers had more job security during the pandemic, but unionization remains historically low," Economic Policy Institute, Jan. 22, 2021 (epi.org); Jason Slotkin, "In Alabama, Workers At Amazon Warehouse Are Poised For Union Vote," NPR, Feb. 7, 2021 (npr.org); National Labor Relations Board, Election Reports, various years (nlrb.gov); "What Amazon does to Wages," *The Economist*, Jan. 20, 2018 (economist.com); Marshall Steinbaum, Eric Harris Bernstein, and John Strum, "Powerless: How Lax Antitrust and Concentrated Market Power Rig the Economy Against American Workers, Consumers, and Communities," Roosevelt Institute, Feb. 2018 (rooseveltinstitute.org); John Schmitt and Ben Zipperer, "Dropping the Ax: Illegal Firings During Union Election Campaigns, 1951–2007," Center for Economic and Policy Research, March 2009 (cepr.net); John Logan, "The Union Avoidance Industry in the United States, *British Journal of Industrial Relations*, December 2006 (jwj. org); Lee Fang, "Amazon hired Koch-backed antiunion consultant to fight Alabama warehouse organizing," The Intercept, Feb. 10, 2021 (theintercept.com); RWP Labor, rwplabor.com; Noam Scheiber, "Amazon Pay Isn't Highest," *New York Times*, March 19, 2021 (nytimes.com).

Article 5.4

FIFTY YEARS AFTER THE KERNER COMMISSION

African Americans are better off in many ways but are still disadvantaged by racial inequality.

BY JANELLE JONES, JOHN SCHMITT, AND VALERIE WILSON
February 2018, Economic Policy Institute

The year of 1968 was a watershed in American history and black America's ongoing fight for equality. In April of that year, Martin Luther King Jr. was assassinated in Memphis and riots broke out in cities around the country. Rising against this tragedy, the Civil Rights Act of 1968 outlawing housing discrimination was signed into law. Tommie Smith and John Carlos raised their fists in a black power salute as they received their medals at the 1968 Summer Olympics in Mexico City. Arthur Ashe became the first African American to win the U.S. Open singles title, and Shirley Chisholm became the first African-American woman elected to the House of Representatives.

The same year, the National Advisory Commission on Civil Disorders, better known as the Kerner Commission, delivered a report to President Lyndon Johnson examining the causes of civil unrest in African-American communities. The report named "white racism"—leading to "pervasive discrimination in employment, education, and housing"—as the culprit, and the report's authors called for a commitment to "the realization of common opportunities for all within a single [racially undivided] society." The Kerner Commission report pulled together a comprehensive array of data to assess the specific economic and social inequities confronting African Americans in 1968.

Where do we stand as a society today? In this brief report, we compare the state of black workers and their families in 1968 with the circumstances of their descendants today, 50 years after the Kerner report was released. We find both good news and bad news. While African Americans are in many ways better off in absolute terms than they were in 1968, they are still disadvantaged in important ways relative to whites. In several important respects, African Americans have actually lost ground relative to whites, and, in a few cases, even relative to African Americans in 1968.

The following are some of the key findings:

- African Americans today are much better educated than they were in 1968 but still lag behind whites in overall educational attainment. More than 90% of younger African Americans (ages 25 to 29) have graduated from high school, compared with just over half in 1968—which means they've nearly closed the gap with white high school graduation rates. They are also more than twice as likely to have a college degree as in 1968 but are still half as likely as young whites to have a college degree.

- The substantial progress in educational attainment of African Americans has been accompanied by significant absolute improvements in wages, incomes, wealth, and health since 1968. But black workers still make only 82.5 cents on every dollar earned by white workers, African Americans are 2.5 times as likely to be in poverty as whites, and the median white family has almost 10 times as much wealth as the median black family.

• With respect to homeownership, unemployment, and incarceration, America has failed to deliver any progress for African Americans over the last five decades. In these areas, their situation has either failed to improve relative to whites or has worsened. In 2017 the black unemployment rate was 7.5%, up from 6.7% in 1968, and is still roughly twice the white unemployment rate. In 2015, the black homeownership rate was just over 40%, virtually unchanged since 1968, and trailing a full 30 points behind the white homeownership rate, which saw modest gains over the same period. And the share of African Americans in prison or jail almost tripled between 1968 and 2016 and is currently more than six times the white incarceration rate.

TABLE 1: SOCIAL AND ECONOMIC CIRCUMSTANCES OF AFRICAN AMERICAN AND WHITE FAMILIES, 1968 AND 2018

	1968	2018 (most recent available data)	Change
High school graduate rate, adults ages 25–29 (%)			
Black	54.4%	92.3%	37.9 ppt.
White	75.0%	95.6%	20.6 ppt.
Gap (black as % of white)	72.6%	96.5%	
College graduate rate, adults ages 25–29 (%)			
Black	9.1%	22.8%	13.7 ppt.
White	16.2%	42.1%	25.9 ppt.
Gap (black as % of white)	56.0%	54.2%	
Unemployment rate (%)			
Black	6.7%	7.5%	0.8 ppt.
White	3.2%	3.8%	0.6 ppt.
Gap (ratio black to white)	2.1	2.0	
Median hourly wage (2016$)			
Black	$12.16	$15.87	30.5%
White	$17.06	$19.23	12.7%
Gap (black as % of white)	71.3%	82.5%	
Median household income (2016$)			
Black	$28,066	$40,065	42.8%
White	$47,596	$65,041	36.7%
Gap (black as % of white)	59.0%	61.6%	
Poverty rate (%)			
Black	34.7%	21.8%	-12.9 ppt.
White	10.0%	8.8%	-1.2 ppt.
Gap (ratio black to white)	3.5	2.5	

Educational Attainment

The most important development since 1968 is that African Americans today are much better educated than they were in 1968. These absolute improvements in educational attainment—including substantial increases in both high school and college completion rates—have opened important doors for black workers compared with their counterparts 50 years ago. In relative terms, African Americans today are almost as likely as whites to have completed high school. But even though the share of younger African Americans with a college degree has more than doubled, African Americans today are still only about half as likely to have a college degree as whites of the same age.

High School Graduation Rates
Over the last five decades, African Americans have seen substantial gains in high school completion rates. In 1968, just over half (54.4%) of 25- to 29-year-old African Americans had a high school diploma. Today, more than nine out of 10

	1968	2018 (most recent available data)	Change
Median household wealth (2016$)			
Black	$2,467	$17,409	605.7%
White	$47,655	$171,000	258.8%
Gap (black as % of white)	5.2%	10.2%	
Homeownership rate (%)			
Black	41.1%	41.2%	0.1 ppt.
White	65.9%	71.1%	5.2 ppt.
Gap (black as % of white)	62.4%	57.9%	
Infant mortality (per 1,000 births)			
Black	34.9	11.4	-67.4%
White	18.8	4.9	-74.0%
Gap (ratio black to white)	1.9	2.3	
Life expectancy at birth (years)			
Black	64.0 yrs.	75.5 yrs.	11.5 yrs.
White	71.5 yrs.	79.0 yrs.	7.5 yrs.
Gap (black as % of white)	89.5%	95.6%	
Incarcerated population (per 100,000)			
Black	604	1,730	286.3%
White	111	270	242.7%
Gap (ratio black to white)	5.4	6.4	

Notes: In the "Change" column, "ppt." indicates percentage point change—that is, the point difference (absolute difference) between two percentages; percentage (%) change indicates the relative difference between two numbers.

African Americans (92.3%) in the same age range had a high school diploma. (See Table 1 for all data presented in this report.)

The large increase in high school completion rates helped to close the gap relative to whites. In 1968, African Americans trailed whites by more than 20 percentage points (75.0% of whites had completed high school, compared with 54.4% of blacks). In the most recent data, the gap is just 3.3 percentage points (95.6% for whites versus 92.3% for African Americans).

College Graduation Rates

College graduation rates have also improved for African Americans. Among 25- to 29-year-olds, less than one in 10 (9.1%) had a college degree in 1968, a figure that has climbed to almost one in four (22.8%) today.

Over the same period, however, college completion expanded for whites at a similar pace, rising from 16.2% in 1968 to 42.1% today, leaving the relative situation of African Americans basically unchanged: In 1968 blacks were just over half (56.0%) as likely as whites to have a college degree, a situation that is essentially the same today (54.2%).

We would expect that these kinds of increases in the absolute levels of formal education would translate into large improvements in economic and related outcomes for African Americans. The rest of our indicators test the validity of this assumption.

Unemployment

The unemployment rate for African Americans in 2017 (the last full year of data) was 7.5%, 0.8% points higher than it was in 1968 (6.7%). The unemployment rate for whites was 3.8% in 2017 and 3.2% in 1968.

The unemployment data for these two years, almost 50 years apart, demonstrate a longstanding and unfortunate economic regularity: The unemployment rate for black workers is consistently about twice as high as it is for white workers.

Wages and Income

Hourly Wages

The inflation-adjusted hourly wage of the typical black worker rose 30.5% between 1968 and 2016, or about 0.6% per year. This slow rate of growth is particularly disappointing given the large increase in educational attainment among African Americans over these decades.

Even slower real wage growth (about 0.2% per year) for the typical white worker—albeit starting from a higher initial wage—meant that African Americans did modestly close the racial wage gap over the last five decades. But, in 2016, by the hourly wage measure used here, the typical black worker still only made 82.5 cents on every dollar earned by the typical white worker.

Household Income

The inflation-adjusted annual income of the typical African-American household increased 42.8% between 1968 and 2016, slightly outpacing income growth for the typical white household (36.7%). But the typical black household today still receives only 61.6% of the annual income received by the typical white household.

Poverty Rates

The share of African Americans living in poverty has declined substantially in the last five decades. Using the official federal poverty measure as a benchmark, over one-third (34.7%) of African Americans were in poverty in 1968. Today, the share of African Americans living in poverty is just over one in five (21.4%). For whites, the decline in the poverty rate was much smaller, from 10.0% in 1968 to 8.8% in 2016. In the most recent data, African Americans are about 2.5 times as likely to be in poverty as whites. (In 1968, they were 3.5 times as likely to be in poverty.)

Family Wealth

The typical black family had almost no wealth in 1968 ($2,467; according to 1963 data). Today, that figure is about six times larger ($17,409), but it is still not that far from zero when you consider that families typically draw on their wealth for larger expenses, such as meeting basic needs over the course of retirement, paying for their children's college education, putting a down payment on a house, or coping with a job loss or medical crisis.

Over the same period, the wealth of the typical white family almost tripled, from a much higher initial level. In 2016, the median African-American family had only 10.2% of the wealth of the median white family ($17,409 versus $171,000).

Homeownership

One of the most important forms of wealth for working- and middle-class families is home equity. Yet, the share of black households that owned their own home remained virtually unchanged between 1968 (41.1%) and today (41.2%). Over the same period, homeownership for white households increased 5.2 percentage points to 71.1%, about 30 percentage points higher than the ownership rate for black households.

Health

Infant Mortality

Over the last five decades, African Americans have experienced enormous improvements in infant mortality rates. The number of deaths per 1,000 live births has fallen from 34.9 in 1968 to 11.4 in the most recent data. Over the same period, whites have also seen dramatic reductions in infant mortality, with rates falling from 18.8 to 4.9 by the same measure.

In relative terms, however, African Americans have fallen behind. In 1968, black infants were about 1.9 times as likely to die as white infants. Today, the rate is 2.3 times higher for African Americans.

Life Expectancy

African Americans' life expectancy at birth has also increased substantially (up 11.5 years) between 1968 and today, outpacing the increase for whites (up 7.5 years). But an African American born today can, on average, still expect to live about 3.5 fewer years than a white person born on the same day.

Incarceration

The share of African Americans in prison or jail almost tripled between 1968 (604 of every 100,000 in the total population) and 2016 (1,730 per 100,000).

The share of whites in prison or jail has also increased dramatically, but from a much lower base. In 1968, about 111 of every 100,000 whites were incarcerated. In the most recent data, the share has increased to 270 per 100,000.

In 1968, African Americans were about 5.4 times as likely as whites to be in prison or jail. Today, African Americans are 6.4 times as likely as whites to be incarcerated, which is especially troubling given that whites are also much more likely to be incarcerated now than they were in 1968.

Appendix: Data Notes

Making comparisons over five decades is challenging. Data sources collected across so many years are not always directly comparable. One issue is that most government data in the 1960s grouped the population into only two groups: "white" and "nonwhite." Following the Kerner Commission and other researchers, our figures here use the "nonwhite" data as a proxy for the circumstances of African Americans at the time. We are confident that the "nonwhite" data do a reasonably good job capturing the experience of African Americans. The 1970 census, which included more detailed information on race than most government data in the 1960s, estimates that people from races other than white and African American (primarily Native Americans and Asians) constituted only about 1.4% of the U.S. population at the time. The 1980 census allowed respondents of any race to identify themselves as Hispanic, and in that year only about 7% did so.

A second issue is that data specifically for 1968 are not always available. In these cases, we either use data for the closest available year, or we use data for years before and after 1968 (usually 1960 and 1970) and interpolate. Our data for 2018 are the most recent data available for each of the indicators we examine, typically either 2015, 2016, or 2017 data. ❏

Sources: Report of the National Advisory Commission on Civil Disorders: Summary of Report, National Advisory Commission on Civil Disorders, 1968 (hsdl.org); "Table 104.20. Percentage of Persons 25 to 29 Years Old with Selected Levels of Educational Attainment, by Race/Ethnicity and Sex: Selected Years, 1920 through 2017," *2017 Tables and Figures*, National Center for Education Statistics, 2017 (nces.ed.gov); "Table B-43. Civilian Unemployment Rate by Demographic Characteristic, 1968–2009," *Economic Report of the President 2010* (gpo.gov); Bureau of Labor Statistics, , series ID LNU04000003 and LNU04000006 (bls.gov/data/#unemployment); "Current Population Survey," U.S. Census Bureau and the U.S. Bureau of Labor Statistics (census.gov); "Table H-5. Race and Hispanic Origin of Householder—Households by Median and Mean Income: 1967 to 2016," *Historical Income Tables*, U.S. Census Bureau (census.gov); "Table 2. Poverty Status of People by Family Relationship, Race, and Hispanic Origin: 1959 to 2016," *Historical Poverty Tables*, U.S. Census Bureau (census.gov); "Chart

3: Average Family Wealth by Race/Ethnicity, 1963–2016," *Nine Charts about Wealth Inequality in America, Urban Institute* (urban.org); Laurie Goodman, Jun Zhu, and Rolf Pendall, "Are Gains in Black Homeownership History?" Urban Institute (urban.org); "Table 11. Infant Mortality Rates, by Race: United States, Selected Years 1950–2015," *Health, United States, 2016—Individual Charts and Tables*, Centers for Disease Control and Prevention (cdc.gov); "Table 15. Life Expectancy at Birth, at Age 65, and at Age 75, by Sex, Race, and Hispanic Origin: United States, Selected Years 1900–2015," *Health, United States, 2016—Individual Charts and Tables*, Centers for Disease Control and Prevention (cdc.gov); Kris Warner, unpublished tabulations of incarcerated population data, using Bureau of Justice Statistics and U.S. Census Bureau data.

Article 5.5

UNDERVALUATION IS A CERTAINTY
Measuring Black Women's Wage Gap.

AN INTERVIEW WITH MICHELLE HOLDER
May/June 2021

We're all probably aware of gender wage gaps and racial wage gaps in the U.S. labor market, but amongst economists there are disagreements about how to measure and how to explain the reasons for those gaps. Zoe Sherman talked with Dr. Michelle Holder, associate professor of economics at John Jay College, part of the City University of New York, about her recent research, shared in her Roosevelt Institute paper, "The 'Double Gap' and the Bottom Line: African American Women's Wage Gap and Corporate Profits." She looks at the wage gap between African American women and their white male colleagues from several different angles to show the scale of the annually reoccurring loss to the Black community.

Dollars & Sense: To start us off, can you explain your use of the term "double gap"? What gap are we looking at and what about it is double? Please give us your headline finding here about just how big the gap is, too!

Michelle Holder: The term "double gap" is speaking to the wage penalty or the earnings penalty borne by Black women given both their race and their gender. As I'm sure most of your readers know, existing economic research shows that there is indeed a gender wage gap and there's a racial wage gap. The double gap, however, does not simply mean that you either double the gender wage gap, or you double the racial wage gap, and you know voilá you have estimated the wage penalty that the average Black female worker encounters in the U.S. labor force. The term double gap is simply codifying what the average Black woman worker in the U.S. labor market faces in terms of earnings penalties, given their gender and race.

For an individual Black woman who's a worker, the gap can be as low as $5,000 in certain low-wage occupations, or it can be as high as $50,000 to $75,000 in some high-wage occupations. More or less, on average, the gap is about $15,000 to $20,000 for your typical Black woman worker in in the U.S. workforce.

D&S: You also calculated the collective loss for Black women workers as a group, right? When you aggregated, what did you find for that total?

MH: I did aggregate it. I don't want to take complete credit for the work because I did enlist another researcher to compare my findings against his and to see how close they were, and they were pretty close. Using three different methodologies, when we aggregated [the estimates of] what I characterized as involuntarily forfeited wages, the aggregate loss to the Black community came to about $50 billion per year. This is an annually reoccurring loss. The analysis I did was for the year 2017.

This estimate has actually been criticized as being a lowball estimate, which I don't disagree with. It's a conservative estimate, in part because when I undertook this research I decided that I would only look at Black women who were more highly educated. Typically, economists look at occupations when they're looking at wages and wage differentials. I decided that for every occupation that I was examining I would only look at Black women between the 50th and 99th percentile in educational attainment in that occupation, so just the more educated Black women in that occupation. By using that approach, my overall estimate is quite conservative.

D&S: If we go back to that individual lens on the gap, you compared Black women workers to white non-Latinx male workers, and when we express it as a ratio you write that the simplest look gives us a $0.61 to $1 ratio. Many of us have seen that ratio reported somewhere. It's commonly reported, and it is important. Still, and you started to get into this in what you were just saying, you warned us that trying to boil down the whole issue to a single ratio is losing a lot of information. What are some of the issues that make that ratio hard to interpret? Why did you have to break it down by occupation?

MH: Thank you for raising that. I don't want to take away from that working figure. The $0.61 to $1 ratio is a useful metric. But it does obscure a couple of important things. One of the most important things a metric like that doesn't really get to is that normally, in the economics discipline, one will explain that wages, while driven by productivity, are informed by human capital attributes. One of the most important human capital attributes that a worker can possess is their level of education. Currently in the American labor market when comparing—I'm even going to take away the gender lens for a second and just compare Black and white workers in the American workforce—there's still a considerable educational attainment gap between Black and white workers in this country. Meaning that, if we look at all white non-Hispanic individuals in the United States 25 years of age and older, about 35% of them possess a bachelor's degree. But if you look at the African-American community, that number drops considerably to just over 20%, so there's a 14 to 15 percentage point differential there. That in and of itself explains some of the gap that we see between non-Latinx white male workers and Black female workers, given similar characteristics and similar jobs. It doesn't explain all of the gap, but it does explain some of the gap.

The other issue that just looking at that 61 cents to $1 metric doesn't really expose is that there is a difference, a not inconsiderable difference, between where men are situated in terms of their industrial and occupational distribution as workers and where women are situated … and, by extension, where white male workers are situated and where Black female workers are situated. It is the case that women are over-represented in low-wage occupations and industries, and there are systemic and historical reasons for that. When you start to talk about a simple metric like how Black women earn 61 cents for every dollar white men earn—and you know we've also heard the metric that women overall earn about 79 to 80 cents on the dollar that men earn overall—those metrics don't make clear that women and African Americans tend to be over-represented in low-wage industries and occupations. Part of that wage gap is explicable by these differences in occupational concentration and industrial concentration between white male workers and Black female workers.

But even once you take those factors into account, what remains at the end of the day is still a gap between Black women workers and white male workers that cannot be explained by the educational attainment gap, that cannot be explained by each respective group's industrial and occupational concentration, or by their age, or whether they are married, or how many children they have, or how long they've been working. Even after you take all of the potential factors that you can think of that would contribute to this wage differential between non-Latinx white men and Black women, there's still this residual factor that cannot be explained by any other characteristic that we can capture in the data.

This is why I think it's important to do this research: because there's pushback. When I suggest as an economist that discrimination is occurring against Black women in the U.S. workforce, the pushback is well, no, it isn't discrimination; it is weaker networks that Black women tend to have, it is that Black women may not have the same work ethic, all of these other "it's the fault of Black women" [explanations], [they claim that] the labor market is perfectly normal and competitive… and my research suggests that just isn't the case.

D&S: You are using the phrasing that this factor or that factor "explains," and my experience in trying to read this language is that often it feels like what that actually means is "explain away."

MH: Exactly, in a very nice way… and then let's just get back to business as usual. I think most Americans don't want to believe that there's a deliberate ef-

---

Methodologies

Methodologies: (1) Within each occupation, Holder took the most educated half of the Black women working in that occupation, then took an equivalently-educated sample of white men in that occupation and compared average wages of the two groups. (2) Within each occupation, she used a statistical technique called linear regression to explain wages as the sum of the effect of education plus the effect of job experience plus the effect of age, and so on. These are called the "control variables." Remaining differences in the data that aren't explained by the control variables can be interpreted as the effects of race and gender. (3) Colleague Tom Masterson at the Levy Institute at Bard College used a technique called statistical matching. He matched each Black female worker to a white male worker who closely resembled her in every dimension listed in method two and calculated the pairwise wage differences.

For more details see rooseveltinstitute.org/wp-content/ uploads/2020/07/RI_DoubleGap_ Report_202003.pdf.

fort to undervalue Black women workers. Whether or not the effort is deliberate, it is occurring and so we need to acknowledge that and not shy away from a very sensitive and difficult fact, as I see it, in the U.S. workforce.

D&S: Is it fair to say that your methods are isolating wage discrimination on the part of employers from all of these other things that you described?

MH: Yeah, it's pretty fair to say that. Three different methodologies were employed because I knew that there would be potential criticism about what this research was suggesting. Certainly, if you're using not one, not two, but three different methodologies, each one of them being completely independent, it's hard to knock down the findings out of hand.

All three methodologies yielded a gap of around $50 billion, with the estimates ranging from $49 billion to $58 billion, so those three methodologies came very close to each other, and as a result it was hard to dismiss these findings.

D&S: You mentioned also that your calculations are relevant to the debates over reparations, because you have identified a specific loss for which there could and should be restitution. Can you help us understand the magnitude of this loss? Most of us find that our brains start getting a little fuzzy when we think about $50 billion. On the one hand it's huge and on the other hand, as a share of GDP it's tiny, so what would it mean for a typical worker's household if this gap were closed? And what would it mean for these households if there were also retroactive reparations?

MH: One caveat is that I'm nowhere near as qualified as someone like William 'Sandy' Darrity to discuss the economics of reparations for the Black community, but the reason that I deliberately inserted the issue of reparations into my report is to bring up something that is occurring in the African-American community right now, which results in considerable monetary losses to our community, on the order of, minimally, $50 billion. That's in the aggregate, but by looking at it for individual Black women laborers and workers, that means roughly $15,000 to $20,000 per year that they should have been additionally compensated because their equal white male counterpart, that is ostensibly what he's receiving. But that's again for one year; over a lifetime that easily translates into a loss of over $1 million for Black women workers when compared to equally qualified, equally skilled, white male workers. You can imagine what could be done with resources like that on an individual basis, on a familial basis, and in terms of a community. I raised the issue of reparations partly because, as a community, we recognize that having been free labor for a few hundred years in this country resulted in riches for the country that we did not participate in. Similarly, today, the fact that Black female workers are undervalued results in a benefit to someone, but not to the Black community, and so from my perspective this seems quite similar to the situation that the current debate around reparations speaks to, which is not just the undervaluation but the outright confiscation of what should have been due to these workers: enslaved individuals were workers and today, Black women, we're still workers.

D&S: Picking up from there, because you're talking about how wealth is created and how it's not going to the workers who created it, I appreciated the way you framed your research. You're measuring the pay gap between demographic categories of workers, but you then directly connect that to the worker-owner divide. You talk about the bottom line in your title and in your subtitle about corporate profits. When you shared these findings with Ms. magazine, you argued that closing this gap should matter to all women. You noted in your paper that there has been long-term stagnation of wages for U.S. workers overall, while profits surge. This double gap that you calculated seems like it's just the tip of the maldistribution iceberg. I'm curious about how addressing this double gap then widens into other distributional issues and what kinds of opportunities for solidarity you see.

MH: First of all, thank you for raising the issue of the declining labor share. Other researchers have done a very good analysis of this declining labor share, which I cite in the paper. I'm going to probably pull a couple of things into my response to you on this one. The first one I'm going to reference is an economist by the name of Janelle Jones—she's now chief economist at the Department of Labor which is great, but she was the director of research at this organization called the Groundwork Collaborative in D.C.—and she put together a phrase called "Black women best." By that what she meant is if policymakers target and look at the condition and situation of Black women, particularly in the American workforce, and attempt to develop policies that would assist Black women workers in terms of fair wages and work conditions, these policies would help everyone. If we look at the American workforce simply through the lens of wages and we looked at it by gender, race, and ethnicity, what we would find is at the top of the hierarchy are non-Latinx white male workers, they are the best paid, and at the bottom of the hierarchy are women of color, African-American women, Latinas, and Native-American women. So according to Jones, if policymakers want to improve the conditions of all women workers, an easy way to do it is to target the least of these, which would be Black women workers. So, I draw from that. Any policy approach that would get at chipping away the double gap will help all women, there's no doubt about that.

But also, any policy approaches that would chip away at the double gap can only serve to strengthen the ties that bind all workers, because we are now in this post neoliberal, or still neoliberal, period where unionization has been on a steady decline in this country, both in the private and public sector, and workers are increasingly bargaining not as part of a union but as an individual with a corporation, with an agency, with an institution, and without the strength of other individuals to give that worker leverage. This double gap feeds into that because we have Black women workers who are singularly negotiating the terms and conditions of their employment both before they are hired and after they're hired. But we need to move away from this corporation versus individual worker approach and move back to the corporation versus the collective negotiating as the collective. Policies that would help alleviate this double gap that Black women workers face, I think, would go a long way in getting back to collective behaviors on the part of workers, rather than these individual [negotiations]. Not to say that workers prefer that, I don't think so, but this is where we're at today, is this one-on-one bargaining with owners, rather than collective bargaining with owners. I'm not sure if that quite answered your question?

D&S: Yes, I think it does, because if we're bargaining one on one, maybe relatively privileged workers are going to think, "Well, maybe I can gain something at the expense of my coworker?" But if their fortunes are bound together, then they're going to have to do it together. Is there anything else that I forgot to ask about that you want to make sure we include?

MH: I've talked to other Black women about my research, some of whom are academics, some of whom aren't, and this surprised me: While I think most Black women who work in this country get at some level that they probably aren't making the same as an equally qualified, equally skilled, equally educated white male worker, they didn't quite understand how big this gap can be. And that's because in this country, there's a real climate where we don't talk about income because it gets to the issues of status and respectability and importance. So even amongst friends and family members, we tend not to talk about what we earn, because then it's, "Oh well, you're making more than me, then that must mean your work is more important than mine, or you're doing better work than I'm doing, or you're just a better worker and I'm a slacker," and all those things. That's the climate in this country and it contributes to this lack of awareness on the part of Black women workers of how much they are undervalued. They were surprised by how big this gap is and how it's not just about the gap on a weekly basis or an hourly basis, even a yearly basis, but it's about the gap over a lifetime, the impact of it, and also the aggregation of the gap for the community and what it means in terms of losses to the community. When I go on my tour of speaking about my research, I really get bombarded by Black women who are like, "Wow, thank you for identifying the degree to which Black women are undervalued in the American workplace."

Finally, I think the last thing I would say is, when you are, as a female worker, in the position where you are negotiating your compensation…after you do all of your due diligence, you do your research, you talk to your friends and family, you tap into your networks, and you hit upon a figure that you think is a fair ask, add 5% to 10% on top of that. If the wage in whatever job you have to take is really sticky you may not get it, but what I tell people when I speak about this research is whether they are women of any race or specifically Black women, at some point during your work life, you will be underpaid, you will be undervalued. That is pretty much a certainty. ❑

Article 5.6

INEQUALITY, SUNK COSTS, AND CLIMATE JUSTICE

BY FRANK ACKERMAN
March/April 2019

Climate change is at once a common problem that threatens us all, and a source of differential harms based on location and resources. We are all on the same boat, in perilous waters—but some of us have much nicer cabins than others. What is the relationship of inequality to climate policy?

The ultimate economic obstacle to climate policy is the long life of so many investments. Housing can last for a century or more, locking residents into locations that made sense long ago. Business investments often survive for decades. These investments, in the not-so-distant past, assumed continuation of cheap oil and minimally regulated coal—thereby building in a commitment to high carbon emissions. Now, in a climate-aware world, we need to treat all fossil fuels as expensive and maintain stringent regulation of coal. And it is impossible to repurpose many past investments for the new era: they are sunk costs, valuable only in their original location or industry.

If we could wave a magic wand and have a complete do-over on urban planning, we could create a new, more comfortable, and more sustainable way of life. Transit-centered housing complexes, surrounded by green spaces and by local amenities and services, could offer convenient car-free links to major employment sites. Absent a magic wand, the challenge is how to get there from here, in a short enough time frame to matter for climate policy.

Space is the final frontier in energy use. Instead of shared public spaces for all, an ever-more-unequal society allows the rich to enjoy immense private spaces, such as McMansions situated on huge exurban lots. This leads to higher heating and cooling costs for oversized housing, and to higher infrastructure costs in general: longer pipes, wires, and travel distances between houses. And it locks in a commitment to low population density and long individual commutes. Outside of the biggest cities, much of the United States is too sparsely settled for mass transit.

Pushing Toward Clean Energy

Carbon prices and other incentives are designed to push people and businesses out of the most emissions-intensive locations and activities. Along with the wealthy exurbs, cold rural states, with high heating and transportation requirements per person, will become more expensive. So, too, will investment in emissions-intensive production processes, whether in electricity generation, heavy industry, or agriculture.

The art of policymaking requires a delicate balance. Too much pressure to make fuel expensive can produce a backlash, as in the yellow vest protests in France, which successfully blocked an increase in the price of gasoline. Too little pressure leads to complacency, and to the false belief that enough is already being done. Subsidies to support the transition may be useful but must be time-limited to avoid becoming a permanent entitlement.

The Green New Deal, the hopeful, if still vague, political vision that is now drawing widespread attention, calls for a transition to clean energy, investment in low-carbon infrastructure, and a focus on equality and workers' rights. A massive jobs program is inseparable from this proposal: Clean energy requires huge amounts of work in construction, steelmaking (all those wind turbines), many branches of electronics, new technologies for motor vehicles, and more. It would create substantial net benefits for the country and the economy.

A more fine-grained analysis is needed, however, to identify those who might lose from a Green New Deal. Their losses will loom large in the policy debate, regardless of the benefits to the rest of society. For example, as Robert Pollin and his colleagues have pointed out, after years of seniority-based cutbacks, many of the remaining workers in legacy energy industries (coal mines, oil wells, fossil-fueled power plants) are nearing retirement age. Pension guarantees, combined with additional funding to allow early retirement, may be more important to these workers. New green jobs will be more important to their children, to the small number of younger workers in at-risk jobs, and to those who have historically been excluded from or under represented in industrial employment.

Older residents who have spent their lives and invested their savings in a rural community, or have no assets except a farm, should be welcome to remain in those communities. But the lingering mystique of an almost-vanished rural America should not lead to new initiatives to attract younger residents back to an energy-intensive, emissions-intensive lifestyle.

Responding to Inequality

Energy use and carbon emissions are quite unequally distributed within, as well as between, countries. In all but the poorest countries, the rich spend more on energy in absolute dollar terms, but less than others as a percentage of income. As a result, any carbon price introduced in the United States or other high-income countries will be regressive, taking a greater percentage of income from lower-income households.

To address this problem, economist James Boyce proposes refunding carbon revenues to households on an equal per capita basis, in a cap-and-dividend system. Boyce's calculations show that most people could come out ahead on a cap-and-dividend plan: only the richest 20% of U.S. households would lose from paying a relatively high carbon price, if the revenues were refunded via equal per capita dividends.

Other authors have proposed that some of the revenues could go to basic research or to infrastructure development, accelerating the arrival of sustainable energy use. Any use of the revenues, except distribution in proportion to individual fuel use or emissions, preserves the incentive effect of a carbon price. The question of cap-and-dividend versus investment in sustainable energy is largely a debate about what will make a regressive carbon price politically acceptable.

Stranded Assets

It is not only households that have invested too heavily in now-obsolete patterns of energy use. The same pattern arises in a different context, in the energy sector itself. Electric utilities have often invested in fossil-fuel-burning plants, expecting to recover their investment over 20 to 30 years of use. Now, as changing prices and priorities shut down some of those plants before the end of their planned lifetimes, the unrecovered investment is a stranded asset, no longer useful for producers or customers.

The problem is further complicated by the regulatory bargains made in many states. Depending on utility regulations (which differ from state to state), a utility may have formally agreed to allow state regulators to set its rates, in exchange for an opportunity to recover its entire investment over a long period of years. What happens to that regulatory bargain when a regulated plant becomes uneconomic to operate?

Businesses whose investments have gone badly do not elicit the same degree of sympathy as individuals stuck in energy-intensive homes and careers. Indeed, Milton Friedman, the godfather of modern conservative economics, used to emphasize that private enterprise is a profit and loss system, where losses are even more important than profits in forcing companies to use their resources effectively.

Despite Friedman's praise of losses, demanding that a utility absorb the entire loss on its stranded assets could provoke political obstacles to clean energy and climate policy. Neither zero recovery nor full recovery of a utility's stranded assets may be appropriate in theory. Once again, it is the political art of the deal, not any fixed economic formula, that determines what should be done. Offering utilities too little provokes opposition and delay; offering them too much is unfair to everyone else and could encourage similar mistaken investments in the future.

What Does Global Sustainability Look Like?

Climate change is a global problem that can only be solved by cooperation among all major countries. The challenge for American policy is not only to reduce our own emissions, but to also play a constructive role in global climate cooperation. U.S. leadership, in cooperation with China and Europe, is crucial to the global effort to control the climate. Reviving that leadership, which had barely surfaced under President Barack Obama before being abandoned by President Donald Trump, is among the most important things we can do for the world today.

In the longer run, questions of climate justice and international obligations are among the most difficult aspects of climate policy. High-income countries such as the United States and northern Europe bear substantial responsibility for the climate crisis worldwide. Among other approaches, the Greenhouse Development Rights framework combines historical responsibility for emissions and current ability to pay for mitigation in assigning shares of the global cost of climate stabilization.

In the current political climate there is no hope of achieving complete consensus about international burden-sharing before beginning to address the climate crisis. The urgency of climate protection requires major initiatives as soon as possible, in parallel with (not waiting for the conclusion of) discussions of international equity. U.S. actions on both fronts are essential for global progress toward climate stabilization. Significant steps toward equity and burden-sharing may be required to win the support of emerging economies such as India, Indonesia, and Brazil.

Assuming it succeeds, what would global sustainable development look like? In view of the rapid urbanization of emerging economies, the key question is, what kind of low-carbon urban life can the world afford? The sprawling, car-intensive and carbon-intensive expanses of Los Angeles, Phoenix, or Houston seem like an amazingly expensive mistake. The compact, energy-efficient, transit-based urbanism of Tokyo or Hong Kong is at least a contender, a high-income life with much lower resource use per person.

The American example matters around the world: If our vision of the good life remains one of extravagant sprawl, others will try to imitate it. If we develop a more sustainable vision of our own future, the whole world will be watching. ❏

Sources: James Boyce, "Carbon Pricing: Effectiveness and Equity," *Ecological Economics*, 2018; Milton Friedman, "Chrysler: Are Jobs the Issue?," *Newsweek*, Sept. 10, 1979; P. Simshauser, "Monopoly regulation, discontinuity and stranded assets," *Energy Economics*, 2017; Paul Baer et al., "The greenhouse development rights framework: Drawing attention to inequality within nations in the global climate policy debate," Development and Change, 2009; Robert Pollin et al., "Green New Deal for U.S. States," Political Economy Research Institute, University of Massachusetts–Amherst, 2017 (perri.umass.edu).

Article 5.7

ARE TAXES THE BEST WAY OF DEALING WITH INEQUALITY?

BY ARTHUR MacEWAN
November/December 2019

> Dear Dr. Dollar:
> *What steps can we take to reduce extreme economic inequality? Are taxes on the rich, on their income and their wealth, the best option?*
> —Anonymous, via e-mail

Higher taxes on the rich would be a good start. During the mid-20th century, we had much less inequality (though still too much), and this was partly due to higher taxes on the rich. Today, the very rich pay lower tax rates than any other group. (There is, by the way, no evidence that those higher tax rates of earlier years harmed economic growth.)

Yet, there is a problem with relying on taxes to reduce economic inequality. Taxes can redistribute income, but relying on taxes means we are accepting the way the system works—the way markets operate—to create inequality in the first place. So instead of only focusing on taxes to *redistribute* income, we should also focus on reconstructing markets to *predistribute* income. As the saying goes, "An ounce of prevention is worth a pound of cure."

Not Natural, Not God-Given

There is a pernicious myth that affects the way we think about markets. According to this myth, markets are natural phenomena, there for us to work within and carry out our economic lives. The rules of markets are viewed as though fixed in stone, as though God-given. This leads to the view that, as long as we play by the rules, there is a certain justice in the outcomes, however unequal. In fact, markets are created by people, sometimes through the long development of decisions and practices by many people, but often directly by legislative action.

A few examples make the point:

The labor market and the role of unions. Before the 1930s, laws greatly constrained the unified action of workers. The National Labor Relations Act of 1935 established a new set of rules, facilitating a burgeoning of unions. Even after things moved in the other direction with the Taft-Hartley Act of 1947, which restricted the activities and power of unions, the labor movement remained relatively powerful in the post-World War II years—and the period from World War II to the 1970s was an era of less economic inequality as compared to later and earlier periods.

From the 1980s to the present, government actions (particularly via the National Labor Relations Board) have restricted union formation by, for example, ignoring illegal actions by employers during workers' efforts to unionize. Other factors have also weakened unions, including the nature of international trade agreements, which give employers relatively unfettered opportunities to close shop at home and employ low-wage workers abroad. This reconstruction of the labor market has directly and indirectly weakened unions and contributed to rising inequality.

The market for intellectual property and the role of patent and copyright laws. The U.S. system of intellectual property rights contributes to inflated profit rates and outsized executive salaries, especially in pharmaceutical and software firms. Patent and copyright laws protect the monopoly positions of these firms. Supporters of these laws argue that they encourage innovation, but the laws can also be used to prevent innovation, as large firms can stifle the operations of small competitors by claiming patent or copyright infringement. Also, even if the protections provided by these laws were useful for innovation, there is no reason that the protections need to last as long as they do in the United States. (See sidebar.)

There are, moreover, other ways to induce innovation. Indeed, much innovation is already based on research supported by the government through the National Institutes of Health, the National Science Foundation, the Defense Department, and other government agencies. In any case, regardless of whether one sees existing protections of intellectual property rights as good or bad, there is no disputing the point that the market in intellectual property is a constructed market, not "natural."

Free the Mouse!

In 1998, Congress passed the Sonny Bono Copyright Term Extension Act, extending existing copyright protections by an additional 20 years. Supporters claimed that passing the act was necessary to make sure that U.S. copyright holders had the same protection as those in the European Union, which were granted a 20-year extension in 1993. One of the prime beneficiaries of (and one of the strongest lobbyists for) this act was the Walt Disney Company; the act ensured that Disney's control over Mickey Mouse would not end in 2003, but would last until 2023—and Pluto, Goofy, and Donald Duck until 2025, 2027, and 2029, respectively.

Not surprisingly, the Copyright Extension Act aroused opposition, and critics campaigned under the banner of "Free the Mouse!" Along with popular efforts, the act was also challenged in the courts. While the challenge had particular legal nuances, it was based on the seemingly reasonable argument that the Copyright Extension Act, which protects creative activity retroactively, would do little to benefit the authors and composers who created their works in the first half of the 20th century, and would primarily enrich corporations and families that owned lucrative copyrights. The Supreme Court, apparently deciding that its view of the law trumped this reasonable argument, upheld the act.

Congress and the Court reconstructed the market for intellectual property in a way that provided a valuable handout to Disney and other firms, but it is hard to see how a 20-year extension of copyright protection will have any significant impact on creative efforts now or in the future.

Source: Arthur MacEwan, "Property: Who Has a Right to What and Why?" in *The Wealth Inequality Reader*, edited and published by *Dollars & Sense* and United for a Fair Economy (2004).

Financial markets. The operation of banks and other financial institutions doesn't simply "exist," but is organized with many regulations. Banks have to be chartered and follow various rules regarding reserves, reporting requirements, the purchase and sale of assets, etc. Also, they operate under certain practices widely recognized and accepted by financial institutions, as well as the government. A particularly important example is the "too big to fail" principle, which gives investors confidence that the federal government will step in to support large firms if they run into serious trouble. This practice provides an implicit subsidy to big banks, because investors are willing to provide funds to them on favorable terms, knowing that if things go wrong the government will step in and save the banks.

Fossil-fuel markets. Current regulations and subsidies in the oil and gas industry (including policies to encourage fracking) inflate the profits of energy companies, keep fuel prices low, encourage the overuse of fossil fuels, and harm the environment. A May 2019 working paper from the International Monetary Fund estimates fossil fuel subsidies for 2015:

> This paper updates estimates of fossil fuel subsidies, defined as fuel consumption times the gap between existing and efficient prices (i.e., prices warranted by supply costs, environmental costs, and revenue considerations), for 191 countries. Globally, subsidies remained large at $4.7 trillion (6.3% of global GDP) in 2015 and are projected at $5.2 trillion (6.5% of GDP) in 2017. The largest subsidizers in 2015 were China ($1.4 trillion), United States ($649 billion), Russia ($551 billion), European Union ($289 billion), and India ($209 billion).

These subsidies are a fundamental part of the construction of the fossil-fuel market, having negative impacts on both economic equality and the climate.

Schooling and the labor market. Schooling, from pre-K through college, shapes the labor market. The U.S. school system is a multi-tiered system, preparing people for different levels in the workforce. Certain areas of education receive attention—which means funds—according to the needs of employers, as demonstrated by the emphasis in recent years on STEM (science, technology, engineering, and math) education. The structure of the school system, good or bad, is not a "natural" phenomenon, but it greatly affects the operation of the labor market and the distribution of income.

Playing by the Rules They Set

These examples involve conscious action by groups with direct interests in the structure of these markets. Financial institutions, fossil fuel firms, pharmaceutical companies, software giants, and many others use their wealth and power to see that markets are constructed in ways that work for them. (An extreme example: Seats on the regional boards of the Federal Reserve Bank, which plays a major role in regulating banks, are reserved for bank representatives.) They get the rules made the way they want, play by the rules, and then claim they deserve what they get because they played by the rules. Nonsense, yes, but effective nonetheless.

Of course, it is difficult to fight these powerful firms and the individuals who reap their fortunes through these firms. They are quite powerful. But there is no reason to think it is more difficult than raising their taxes.

A first step is to establish a wide understanding of the fact that markets are social constructs and that they can be constructed differently. They have been structured differently in the past, and they can be structured differently in the future. For example, the health care system could be removed from market relations by the creation of "Medicare for All." This would not only alter the provision of medical care, but would reconstruct various related markets (e.g., the market for pharmaceuticals). Even if little change comes in the short run, it is important to send the message that just because firms and rich people play by the rules of the markets, this does not lead to the conclusion that the results are just. (And, of course, they often don't play by the rules!) ❑

Sources: Arthur MacEwan, *Neoliberalism or Democracy?*, Chapter 4, "The Construction of Markets," (Zed Books, 1999); David Coady et al., "Global Fossil Fuel Subsidies Remain Large: An Update Based on Country-Level Estimates," IMF Working Paper, Fiscal Affairs Department, May 2019 (imf.org); Emmanuel Saez and Gabriel Zucman, *The Triumph of Injustice: How the Rich Dodge Taxes and How to Make Them Pay* (W.W. Norton & Company, 2019).

Chapter 6

FISCAL POLICY, DEFICITS, AND AUSTERITY

INTRODUCTION

Most textbooks, at least to the extent that they are influenced by Keynesian economics, depict a macroeconomy stabilized by government intervention. They look at ways the government can use fiscal policy—government spending and taxation—to bolster a flagging economy. The recent shock associated with the Covid-19 pandemic is bound to put the effectiveness of these measures to the test.

What is the role of fiscal policy in this context? As the Great Recession worsened in the fall of 2008, the federal government increased spending and cut taxes. The fiscal stimulus, however, was both tilted too far toward tax cuts (which give the economy a smaller boost per dollar than spending increases) and just not large enough. It was enough to prevent a repeat of the Great Depression, but not enough to ignite the rapid economic growth necessary to put those who lost their jobs quickly back to work.

In the wake of the 2008 downturn, the federal budget went far into the red. While the increased spending played a role, it was mainly the collapse of the economy and the Bush administration's tax cuts and war spending that pushed up the deficit. The surge in government deficits and debt, however, somehow became the focus of macroeconomic policy debates in the United States, despite the persistence of historically high unemployment. The articles in this chapter contest the orthodox view that short-term deficit reduction should be a high priority, arguing that fiscal stimulus is necessary to tackle stagnant growth and promote a prompt recovery of employment.

We begin this chapter with an article by Gerald Epstein (Article 6.1), which addresses this question head on, in the context of the coronavirus pandemic. Epstein argues that we are in one of those moments in history when we can safely say that "we're all Keynesians now." The rapidly deteriorating economic conditions associated with the recent pandemic have led to an unusual consensus on the need for the government to spend to stimulate the economy. However, where disagreement arises is in terms of what to specifically spend these funds on. Expansionary fiscal policy that emphasizes the old trickle-down approach is bound to be ineffective, and to simply repeat the mistakes of the fiscal response to the Great Recession.

In Article 6.2, Amanda Page Hoongrajok explains how the Covid-19 pandemic and accompanying economic crisis have led to dramatic decreases in state and local revenues and expenditures. However, pandemic-related state and local revenue declines can be offset by federal government relief, since the federal government is able to borrow at very low interest rates. Additionally, states can also make up for revenue shortfalls by raising taxes on the wealthy. This kind of approach allows states to avoid austerity measures, which result in reduced education, health, infrastructure, and other important forms of spending.

Next, economist Marty Wolfson (Article 6.3) debunks the widespread myth, parroted by mainstream politicians and media commentators, that government spending cannot create jobs. He sees this as part of a conservative ideological campaign to prevent the government from doing just that. Government spending, he argues, need not be wasteful, and in fact is not necessarily less valuable than private spending. The government, he concludes, can and should be creating jobs.

Then, Alejandro Reuss (Article 6.4) takes a close look at what John Maynard Keynes actually had to say about the efficacy of fiscal policy in his most famous book, *The General Theory of Employment, Interest, and Money*. Keynes was a strong advocate of fiscal policy, especially government spending, as a response to business-cycle downturns. Reuss explains how Keynes challenged the "Treasury view" that government spending could not get the economy going because it would "crowd out" private investment, the same argument conservatives have invoked against fiscal stimulus policies today.

Next, Robert Pollin (Article 6.5) makes the case for the Green New Deal as an alternative to the prevailing neoclassical system. He argues that while the costs to adopt a more environmentally sustainable system will be high, the gains will be far superior. More importantly, we have no choice.

Then, Dean Baker (Article 6.6) explores the possible use of financial transaction taxes (FTT) to pay for President Joe Biden's infrastructure expenditures. Baker points out that deficit spending is only a problem if the economy is operating near full employment and therefore creating inflationary pressure. He also highlights the fact that increasing FTTs would reduce financial trading, which would free up additional resources in the economy.

Wrapping up the chapter, Jayati Ghosh (Article 6.7) then looks at tax policies on the global level. The pandemic and accompanying economic crisis, along with the Biden administration's proposed spending plans, create a great need to reduce tax avoidance by multinational companies and rich individuals. However, current international tax laws make avoidance far too easy, enabling multinational companies to shift profits to lower tax countries and making it possible for individuals to stash money in tax havens abroad. Ghosh suggests a number of steps countries and the international community could take to rectify these inequities and generate needed revenues.

Discussion Questions

1. (Article 6.1) According to Epstein, what type of medium- to long-term issues should be emphasized when implementing expansionary fiscal policy this time around?
2. (Article 6.2). How has the pandemic-related economic crisis impacted state and local finances? How might the federal government help? What can state and local governments do to compensate for revenue shortfalls?

3. (Article 6.3) What are the main arguments made by opponents of government "stimulus" spending? How does Wolfson refute each of these points?
4. (Article 6.4) Why did Keynes think that the dollar-for-dollar crowding-out argument (the "Treasury view") was mistaken? And how might Keynes respond to the arguments conservatives leveled against fiscal stimulus policies during the Great Recession?
5. (Article 6.5) What measures does Pollin propose for compensating the workers and communities that currently depend on fossil fuels?
6. (Article 6.6) What are financial transaction taxes (FFT)? How would FFTs reduce inflationary pressure when the economy is near full employment?
7. (Article 6.7) How have the pandemic and economic crisis intensified the need for the reform of international tax laws? What are base erosion and profit shifting (BEPS)? What policy suggestions does the author make for dealing with BEPS?

Article 6.1

THE CORONAVIRUS CONSENSUS: "SPEND, SPEND, SPEND"

BY GERALD EPSTEIN
March 2020

It's a Richard Nixon "We're all Keynesians now" moment. The forecasts for the U.S. and global economies are dire: There has been a record number of jobless claims—over 3 million workers. In a recent review entitled "The Lamps are going out across the economy," JP Morgan estimates that the unemployment rate will double in the next three months. Some are forecasting an unemployment rate in the United States as high as 20% within the next year, and the forecasts are getting more pessimistic by the day. For now, the raging battles among macroeconomic schools of thought have been submerged by the onslaught of the pandemic, producing a remarkable consensus on one general principle: Governments and central banks (in rich countries) should "spend, spend, spend."

And spend they will. The Federal Reserve announced a series of expansionary policies, many of them dusted off from its Great Financial Crisis of 2007–2008 playbook: lower key Fed interest rates to close to zero and pledge to keep it there; buy "at least" $700 billion worth of U.S. Treasury and mortgage-backed securities; continue its support of the short-term bank funding markets (REPO) to at least $30 billion per day; provide billions of dollars in credit lines (swaps) to a select group of foreign central banks; underwrite massive markets for short-term credit between corporations (commercial paper); and underwrite money market mutual funds. One can be sure this is just the beginning, as Treasury Secretary Steven Mnuchin calls for a $4 trillion Federal Reserve fund. And most recently, the Fed announced a Mario Draghi-style "we will do whatever it takes" to keep the financial system afloat. After some hiccups, the European Central Bank, under former International Monetary Fund managing director Christine Lagarde, pledged to "do whatever it takes" to limit the economic fall-out in eurozone countries from the pandemic, including up to 750 billion Euros of to expand quantitative easing and extend it to a major purchase of corporate bonds. The Bank of England has also pledged to make large liquidity interventions into financial markets.

Much of these central bank responses seem almost old-hat by now, reminiscent of their actions during the Great Financial Crisis. But where the new consensus really takes hold is in the area of fiscal policy: government taxing and spending. In the United States, the Democrats and Republicans in the House and Senate, though differing on many important details, are headed toward implementing, with President Trump's approval, a $2 trillion-dollar spending package including direct cash payments to individuals and households, with Republicans holding out for a heavy dose of corporate bailouts. In Europe, even deficit-maniacal Germany is increasing government spending substantially and has agreed to let the eurozone countries temporarily suspend their straitjacket fiscal rules that limit government budget deficits. Other European countries are following suit with large (and sure to be growing) fiscal packages. (The Political Economy Research Institute (PERI), among many others, have long insisted on the value of government spending to help generate full employment, reduce income inequality, and generate valuable long-term public investments that the capitalists will not make on their own.) As with John Maynard Keynes (see James Crotty's brilliant *Keynes Against Capitalism*, Routledge, 2019), skepticism abounds here with respect to the desirability or even feasibility of running limitlessly large government budget deficits in the absence of accompanying productive, and socially desirable, public investments, even for rich countries. And then there's Modern Monetary Theory (MMT), led by L. Randall Wray, Stephanie Kelton, and others who elevate the lack of concern over budget deficits and debts to a general principle for countries with "sovereign money," independent of circumstance and exigencies, save the condition of full employment. (See L. Randall Wray, *Modern Money Theory: A Primer on Macroeconomics for Sovereign Monetary Systems*, Palgrave Macmillan, 2012, for a classic statement). The validity of the MMT view as a general theory is highly suspect for a number of reasons, including its lack of attention to the globalization and size of highly speculative financial markets, and its lack of recognition of the special privileges the United States currently garners from the dominant global role of the dollar (for more, see my *What's Wrong with Modern Money Theory: A Policy Critique*, Routledge, 2019). But, as Keynes put it in his discussion of "classical economics" in the early chapters of *The General Theory of Employment, Interest, and Money*, MMT appears to be valid enough in the special case of the coronavirus economy, especially with respect to rich countries.

While important theoretical and practical differences remain among these "Keynesian groups" the conditions created by the coronavirus are so extreme and daunting, that the areas of common ground, even if they only apply in specific historical cases such as this one, have seemed to have all but disappeared as the current situation calls for apparently similar prescriptions.

These conditions include:

- Demand for goods and services (what economists call aggregate demand) are plummeting, which is creating a downward spiral of lost incomes and mass layoffs, leading to further declines in consumer spending and a massive drop in business spending as their profits tank and excess production capacity explodes. (To students of Econ 101 this is the interaction of the Keynesian "multiplier" and "accelerator.") The only counter for this is massive spending by the government to sustain the incomes and the ability of people to pay their bills.
- Orthodox economists have long argued that such massive government spending increases government budget deficits and raises interest rates, thereby "crowding-out" other spending. But interest rates have been extremely low, below 2%, for a decade; and now, the Federal Reserve and other central banks are pledging to keep interest rates near zero, and in some cases, they have already fallen below zero.
- Orthodox economists have argued that such low interest rates and expansionary central bank policies used to keep them low would lead to inflation, or even hyper-inflation. But Keynesian economists have long understood

that there is no automatic link between expansionary monetary and credit policy and inflation; much depends on the level of unemployment and excess production capacity. Unfortunately, we now have these in spades. Deflation is much more likely than inflation. In fact, deflation has been stalking major economies since the Great Financial Crisis, and some countries like Japan for much longer than that.

- Orthodox economists have argued that high levels of expansionary monetary policy could lead to a run on the currency and a collapse of the exchange rate. But this is not a serious concern for the United States, because the U.S. dollar is the key currency in the global economy and, in times like these, there is a huge dollar shortage: The dollar is in such massive demand that the Fed is taking extraordinary measures to provide dollars to major central banks around the world.

In short, there is broad agreement among these economists, and now extending beyond the "supply-side Republicans" to even the deficit hawk self-styled "adults in the room," that now is the time for governments and central banks to spend, spend, spend.

Where the Consensus Breaks Down

But, the kind of fiscal stimulus and the uses to which it is put matter enormously. It matters for who gets helped and who pays the price, and how catastrophic this health crisis becomes. And it matters for the long-term trajectory of the economy and our democracy. The apparent macroeconomic "consensus" goes only so far, and just beneath the surface are deep, deep differences of policy and perspective that stem from the deep political and economic divisions in our society. The struggle over macroeconomic policy may not be so much about the amount of spending but about the types and allocation of spending. It is obvious that the impact of the crisis will interact with the devastating inequalities and years of destructive economic and social policies that neoliberal economic policies by Republicans and Democrats have wrought in the United States, and in its allied countries around the world. The enormous political and policy battle will involve whether fiscal and monetary policy will reinforce these inequalities or ameliorate them, in the short and in the long run.

In fact, in the United States, these stark battle lines between the Trump administration, its Republican supporters, and some Democrats are manifest every hour in the fight over the government's fiscal package.

It is clear to most serious observers that millions of Americans' paychecks are evaporating into thin air, and that what is immediately needed is direct cash payments to workers and families to put food on their tables and keep a roof over their heads. Analysts at Cornell University estimate that over 37 million low-income workers are in industries that are directly affected by the shutdowns and demand collapses from the wake of the coronavirus. For millions of Americans, current plans to send a one-time check of $1,000–$2,500 are clearly inadequate in this context.

In addition, small businesses such as restaurants and other small businesses are threatened with bankruptcy as a result of the crisis. Small businesses have a huge employment footprint in the economy—by some measures they constitute as much as two-thirds of employment. If such businesses collapse, it will take much longer to revive the economy when the virus dissipates.

Senators Elizabeth Warren and Bernie Sanders, and many other Democrats on Capitol Hill, are calling for direct payments and the extension of unemployment benefits to all workers. They are also calling for regulations to prohibit evictions, suspend interest payments on student loans, and make medical care associated with the coronavirus free.

In addition, they and other Democrats are pushing for large federal payments to states and local municipalities, most of which have balanced budget restrictions, to help them pay the unemployment insurance and medical costs resulting from the crisis and to provide direct help for small businesses.

But the Republicans are pushing an almost entirely different agenda. Rather than delivering income to families and state and local governments, they are proposing massive payments to large corporations and, through the Federal Reserve, to banks and the financial markets. As Rana Foroohar of the *Financial Times*, among others, including economists at the Roosevelt Institute, the Center for Economic Policy Research, and PERI point out, this bailout, reminiscent of the bank bailouts of 2007–2008, without conditions attached, and at best with hopes of "trickle-down," would be an economic and political disaster.

Pointing out that many airlines, and corporate America in general, have gone on a massive spree of stock buybacks rather than preserving their income for productive investments and emergencies such as this, Warren, Sanders, Nancy Pelosi, Chuck Schumer, and other Democrats on Capitol Hill are all arguing for putting strong conditions on corporations in exchange for loans to help them get through the crisis. The key demand is for these corporations to maintain pay, health insurance, and pension coverage for their employees in exchange for financial support. The Republicans apparently will not have any of this.

These issues are also crucial in the evolving policies of the Federal Reserve and Treasury. Start with the financial system itself: Central banks are spending enormous resources plugging holes in the financial system that were largely caused by their failure to adequately regulate these banks and financial institutions after the Great Financial Crisis. Speculative investments by hedge funds, asset management firms, and foreign exchange traders, most of which were not regulated after the crisis, are forcing the hands of central banks to put up trillions of dollars in support. Excessive borrowing by non-financial corporations over the last decade has made things dramatically worse. As I indicated earlier, many of these corporations borrowed huge amounts while at the same time using cash to buy back their stocks.

Treasury Secretary Mnuchin, himself a hedge fund king who profited off of the financial crisis by foreclosing and reselling houses, is now evidently proposing as much as a $4 trillion Federal Reserve/Treasury fund to underwrite the financial system. Note that these massive sums will not help the macroeconomy or the health care system deal with the pandemic; the financial system itself does very little for the overall economy (see Gerald Epstein and Juan Antonio Montecino, "Overcharged:

The High Cost of High Finance," Roosevelt Institute, 2018). Rather, in committing these trillions of dollars, the central banks would be simply, at best, trying to prevent finance from messing everything up even more. The regulators should have taken care of this problem a decade ago. And, at most, it will keep the financial sector afloat so that these same bankers, like Mnuchin, who profited from the financial crisis, will have plenty of liquidity to stay afloat and profit again from this one.

Such expansionary Federal Reserve policy is also designed to prop up the stock market, which is of both political and, more importantly, financial interest to the corporate elite, including the Trumps. (In "Overcharged," Juan Antonio and I showed that quantitative easing by the Fed in 2009 and 2010 mostly helped the wealthy by raising asset prices such as stocks and bonds. This time around, the Republicans are hoping for a repeat.)

As in 2009–2010, the appropriate solution is to underwrite productive and necessary functions of the financial system while not bailing out the misbehavior — and adding to excessive profits and egregious incomes—of the bankers. In the short run, the Fed undoubtedly needs to provide sufficient liquidity so that the financial markets do not seize up. But the government should also create direct, public utility style banking, through the postal system, noprofit financial sector, or directly through the Fed.

And in exchange for any short-term financial assistance, the Dodd-Frank financial regulations, which have been dismantled since President Trump's election, should all be reinstated. And if massive support is provided, then equity stakes or even nationalizations and re-allocation of credit to socially productive investments would be promoted. (See Doug Henwood, "A Few Ambitious Points on Fighting the Crisis, Left Business Observer, March 2020.)

Global inequalities are another colossal inherited problem. The consensus of massive government spending cannot apply to poor countries because they do not have the financial or economic power to effectuate such spending. These countries would need enormous assistance from rich countries and international institutions to manage this crisis. The Federal Reserve, for example, as the issuer of the dominant global currency, the U.S. dollar, could use its billions to underwrite a fund for coronavirus aid to poor countries, rather than bailing out the speculative financial institutions of the major capitalist economies. (For problems facing developing countries see Jayati Ghosh's "The Covid-19 debt deluge," Social Europe, March 19, 2020.)

In the Medium to Longer Term

But there are longer term issues that must be addressed as we implement the solutions we need in the short term. As James Crotty has shown in his masterful new book on Keynes (*Keynes Against Capitalism*), even while Keynes was desperately fighting to save the United Kingdom from the ravages of the Great Depression, he also had his sights set on the longer-term transformations that were necessary to make the economy productive, fair, and sustainable. He focused on necessary public investments, fair wage initiatives, and central bank and financial policies that prevented speculation and fostered the allocation of credit for public purposes.

Progressives are arguing that policies must not only deal with the direct macroeconomic impacts on workers and poor people but must also begin to repair the deep structural flaws in our economy that underlie the devastation that the pandemic is producing. Senator Bernie Sanders has laid out a more structural vision that can be seen as building up institutions that are necessary in the longer term to restructure our economy: these include providing free coronavirus treatment through Medicare and Medicaid; creating a Reconstruction Finance style institution to finance needed spending for housing, hospitals, and health centers; using the Fed to support spending by state and local governments rather than just bailing out the big banks and hedge funds; prohibiting foreclosures; and eliminating interest on student loans, among many other needed structural changes.

Many have also proposed readying plans for a Green New Deal, and to make employment generation and green transition the centerpiece of the recovery plan as the crisis dissipates.

In short, the apparent consensus on the immediate need to "spend, spend, spend," is a good step in the right direction. But it leaves completely open what the money should be spent on, through what institutions it should be delivered, and in the service of whom. It leaves open what institutions will be built and enhanced as we deal with this problem. Perhaps most important, what precedents and power dynamics will be set up in the process? Will the response further entrench the Trumpists in the weeks ahead? Or will we lay the groundwork for the mobilization of more progressive political forces? We will all have to remain vigilant and active to push these responses in a progressive direction. ❑

Article 6.2

STATE AND LOCAL AUSTERITY
Are we doomed to repeat the mistakes of the past?

BY AMANDA PAGE HOONGRAJOK
January/February 2021

Since the onset of the Coronavirus recession, state and local governments across the United States have announced deep cuts in spending. The state-local government sector lost 1.5 million jobs in April and May. After a slight rebound, 320,000 additional jobs were cut between September and November. These cuts are occurring at the same time that public workers, such as school teachers and bus drivers, are risking their lives to provide essential services. A recent New York University study reported that nearly 25% of New York City transit workers have contracted Covid-19. Instead of receiving thanks and appreciation, these workers are getting laid off and furloughed en masse.

Not only have these cuts led to devastating job losses for government employees that are on the frontlines of the crisis, but they have also reduced the size and scope of public services just when all of us need them most. Are these layoffs and cuts on the state and local level inevitable, or are there ways to resist this austerity?

Balanced-budget rules are the key to making sense of why these cuts are happening. In the 1840s, the federal government ceased its tradition of bailing out states that were on the verge of bankruptcy. To try to avoid bankruptcy, many states then passed balanced-budget rules that constrained their legislatures' decisions about budgets. To this day, states adhere to this mindset, matching expenditures with revenues. Although the stringency of these rules varies across governments, balanced budgets are the norm. This means that without additional borrowing, any blow to revenues will severely impact a government's ability to spend.

Since the Covid-19 pandemic began, state and local government revenues have declined in lockstep with the decline in sales transactions and employment. The mandated lockdowns and ongoing quarantine measures have reduced consumption and overall economic activity. This, in turn, has led to layoffs that began in the leisure and hospitality sector and have spread to other industries as well. Sales and income tax revenue are two major sources of funds for state governments. As sales and incomes have declined, tax revenues have declined as well, creating a budget gap between expenditures and revenues.

Why is State and Local Austerity a Problem?

The federal government is usually thought of as "the" government, but in reality, people engage with state and local governments far more often. Local governments administer and manage essential services like public parks, libraries, K-12 education, and utilities while state governments handle larger programs like Medicaid, unemployment insurance, and public universities. To provide these vital services, state and local governments—which are together called "subnational" government—depend on federal government funds and the taxes they collect themselves such as sales, income, and property taxes. The aggregate state-local government sector represents all of the 50 state governments and 90,000 local governments, combined. This sector's spending has averaged about 11% of U.S. GDP from 1970 to 2020, meaning subnational government spending contributes substantially to economic output each year.

In the wake of the Great Recession, state and local governments made deep cuts to spending. From 2009 to 2019, state and local spending fell by about 2% of GDP, weakening overall demand and contributing to high unemployment rates. These spending contractions offset stimulus efforts on the federal level and slowed the recovery from the 2008–2009 downturn. One study by the Economic Policy Institute found that if state and local spending after the Great Recession had grown at a pace similar to previous recovery periods, unemployment rates would have reached their pre-recession levels by early 2013 instead of 2017. If the precedent set by the 2009 recovery continues, we can expect state and local government budget cuts to create even larger reductions in aggregate demand (the total quantity of goods and services demanded by households, businesses, government, and the international sector) and higher job losses. The job losses resulting from local cuts aren't just the lost government jobs, but ripple-effect losses as those newly unemployed teachers, bus drivers, sanitation workers, and City Hall clerks cut back on their spending, and then a line cook at their favorite diner gets laid off, or their barber's income drops. This is called the "multiplier effect" (see sidebar).

State and local austerity causes immediate and quickly multiplied pain and suffering, and it can also cause long-lasting damage to future growth and prosperity. Mass layoffs and decreased compensation reduce household incomes and the means to a decent standard of living. The typical "adjustment mechanisms," or ways that state and local governments close the gap between revenues and expenditures, is to cut education spending (both K-12 and higher education) and capital spending. For example, California's most recent budget included a $1 billion cut to higher education, while the University of Missouri system lost $40 million in state aid. The National League of Cities estimates that 65% of U.S. cities have cut spending on infrastructure and equipment. Education spending is a long-term investment in the care and well-being of children, while capital spending is a long-term investment in the physical infrastructure of the nation. Access to a quality education and freely accessible public goods like libraries, parks, and sturdy roads are not only desirable in a moral sense but increase the nation's productivity in the long run.

What Can We Do?

Coronavirus-induced revenue losses have created substantial budget gaps for state and local governments. Historically, governments have relied primarily on spending cuts to close these gaps. However, there are a number of alternative paths state and local governments can pursue to prevent the suffering from massive layoffs and losses of income associated with austerity.

The federal government should provide additional relief funds to help struggling governments stabilize their spending. The federal government can borrow at an ultra-low cost due to the Federal Reserve's control over short-term rates and the fact that investors across the world deem U.S. Treasury bonds as one of the safest assets available. State and local governments historically have not issued bonds to pay for operating expenses because of balanced-budget rules. However, even if they did, they would not be able to borrow at federal government debt rates. Therefore, it makes sense to have the borrowing occur at the federal level and have the federal government make transfers to state and local governments.

Opponents of federal relief sometimes claim that state and local governments will just save transfer funds instead of spending them. The data say otherwise. Research shows that state and local governments do rely on and use federal relief funds during downturns. A 2014 study by the Political Economy Research Institute at the University of Massachusetts-Amherst found that state governments spent two-thirds of the American Recovery and Reinvestment Act funds transferred to them during the Great Recession.

If Congress is unable (or unwilling) to provide these much-needed relief funds, it is worth asking what state and local governments can do independently to stimulate their local economies and hold back austerity. First, state and local governments could draw down their rainy-day funds. A "rainy-day fund" allows a government to save unexpected or above-average revenue for use at some point in the future when it is needed. During the Great Recession, state and local governments drew down their rainy-day funds before engaging in budget cuts. However, the savings they had accumulated before the downturn were woefully inadequate to cover the amounts needed to plug budget gaps. Although there is evidence that state and local governments built

The Multiplier Effect

To get a sense of the magnitude of output and job losses expected from state and local budget cuts, economists turn to the concept of the *multiplier*. An *output multiplier* estimates how much $1 of government spending increases output while a job multiplier estimates how much government spending it takes to create one new job. A 2019 study reviewed the existing empirical research on state government multipliers and estimates the output multiplier to be 1.5 and the cost per job to be $50,000. This means an additional $1 of state government spending is associated with an increase in state income of $1.50 and that $50,000 of state spending creates one additional job. The most conservative job multiplier from the studies reviewed was $125,000 of spending for one additional job. Using the cost-per-job figure of $125,000 and the multiplier estimate of 1.5, along with an expectation of how much state and local spending will decrease, allows economists to predict the output and employment losses from budget cuts. So, for example, if state and local government budgets were to decline by $500 billion over the next two years, state income could be expected to decline by $750 billion and produce job losses of about four million. These predictions closely match estimates made by Moody's Analytics.

up strong levels of reserves prior to the Covid-19 recession, the levels are still unlikely to adequately cover the massive losses in tax revenue.

Instead of cutting spending, another way to close a budget gap is to raise revenue. Traditionally, this is done through a tax increase. However, raising tax burdens across the board is not an ideal fix for a budget deficit for two reasons. First, increased tax burdens create additional hardships for individuals and families that are already struggling to make ends meet. Second, taxing people's income drains much-needed demand out of the economy. Higher taxes decrease disposable income, which means people have less money to buy goods and services.

However, tax increases that specifically target wealthier households are more desirable because they produce less of a drag on aggregate demand. Wealthier individuals and families spend smaller proportions of their disposable income than low-wealth households. Or, in economics jargon, the marginal propensity to consume is smaller for wealthier households. For example, a low-wealth household might spend 90 cents out of each additional dollar of disposable income they get, but a wealthier household might only spend 50 cents out of each additional dollar. One reason for this is that wealthier households are more likely to save or invest in financial assets. These actions do not directly contribute to aggregate demand or stimulate job growth. Taxing a wealthy household and using that money to keep a modestly paid municipal employee on the payroll will do more to keep the diner and the barbershop in business than leaving it in the wealthy household's savings account.

Tax increases on the wealthy are also more desirable in terms of equity. Wealthy households have more financial resources to weather downturns and therefore are more equipped to pay for tax increases. The Pew Research Centerrecently reported that about 44% of low-income adults have used money from savings or retirement accounts to pay their bills since the virus took hold in February. Additionally, about one-third of low-income individuals report having to get meals from a food bank or pantry. At the same time, the wealthy have seen their fortunes grow. Jeff Bezos's wealth alone has increased by $74 billion so far this year. Against the backdrop of this increasing inequality, popular support for a "millionaire's tax" has strengthened. A recent survey conducted by Ipsos found that 78% of New York City residents think there should be an additional tax on millionaires in order to help with the city budget deficit caused by Covid-19. As of September 2020, nine states were considering tax hikes on wealthy households, with potentially more on the way. As budget gaps continue to grow, state and local governments are increasingly looking for equitable ways to shore up more revenue.

The coronavirus-induced damage to state and local government budgets has pushed policymakers to think more creatively than ever about ways to avoid austerity. Although almost every state has a rule instructing governments to balance their budget with varying degrees of stringency, most of the compliance is derived from tradition and expectation. In other words, state and local governments feel compelled to balance their budgets not because they fear punishment, but because it is the political norm. At present, state and local governments that borrow to weather downturns are labeled "fiscally irresponsible" whereas governments that lay off public workers who have been risking their lives to provide vital services are viewed as "fiscally prudent." However, it may be time to rethink these labels. Governments that borrow during downturns can stabilize incomes and spending, reducing economic damage while governments that engage in austerity face a downward spiral of declining incomes, spending, and growth. During the current downturn, more cities and states have considered breaking the balanced-budget stranglehold. For example, New Jersey's most recent budget included $4.5 billion in borrowing for operating expenses, while New York City Mayor Bill de Blasio has also suggested borrowing to pay for the city's current bills.

Avoiding Past Mistakes

The Covid-19-driven lockdowns and quarantine measures have reduced transactions and employment, devastating sales and income tax revenue. If state and local governments choose to balance their budgets primarily with spending cuts, as was done in the last downturn, we can expect weak demand, high unemployment, and an overall sluggish recovery. However, the mistakes of the past do not have to be repeated. First, the federal government needs to provide additional relief funds to struggling governments. Not only are borrowing rates for the United States extremely low, research shows that state and local governments can and do spend relief funds. If the federal government will not provide additional funds, states and cities still have options to prevent austerity and stimulate their local economies. Progressive income taxes are an equitable way to raise revenue. As New Jersey's budget actions have shown us, engaging in austerity at the state-local level because "there are no other options" is no longer acceptable. ❑

Sources: Paul Berger, "Nearly 25% of New York City Transit Workers Cited Covid-19 Infections," *Wall Street Journal*, October 20, 2020 (wsj.com); Randall C. Henning and Martin Kessler, "Fiscal Federalism: US History for Architects of Europe's Fiscal Union," Peterson Institute for International Economics, January 2012 (piie.com); Katy Murphy, "Federal stimulus impasse endangers California budget relief," Politico, September 30, 2020 (politico.com); Austin Huguelet, "Missouri Gov. Parson halves cuts to state university, community college aid," *Springfield News-Leader*, October 8, 2020 (news-leader.com); National League of Cities, "Canceled Infrastructure Projects, Furloughs and Economic Ripple Effects: NLC Survey Shares Latest Financial Impacts of COVID-19," June 23, 2020 (nlc.org); Josh Bivens, "A prolonged depression is guaranteed without significant federal aid to state and local government," Economic Policy Institute, May 19, 2020 (epi.org); Gabriel Chodorow-Reich, "Geographic cross-sectional fiscal spending multipliers: What have we learned?," *American Economic Journal: Economic Policy*, May 2019 (aeaweb.org); Kate Davidson and David Harrison, "Coronavirus-Hit State Budgets Create a Drag on U.S. Recovery," *Wall Street Journal*, August 12, 2020 (wsj.com); Elizabeth McNichols, "Cuts in Services Have Been States' Primary Response to Budget Gaps, Harming the Nation's Economy," Center for Budget and Policy Priorities, April 18, 2012 (cbpp.org); Robert Pollin and Jeff Thompson, "State and municipal alternatives to austerity," *New Labor Forum*, October 2011, (journals.sagepub.com); Stephen Marglin and Peter Spiegler, "Did the states pocket the Obama stimulus money? Lessons from cross-section regression and interviews with state officials" PERI Working Paper, December 1, 2014 (peri.umass.edu); Elizabeth McNichol, Michael Leachman, and Joshuah Marshall, "States need significantly more Fiscal relief to slow the emerging deep recession," Center on Budget and Policy Priorities, April 14, 2020 (cosfp.org);

Christopher Carroll, Jiri Slacalek, Kiichi Tokuoka, and Matthew N. White, "The distribution of wealth and the marginal propensity to consume," *Quantitative Economics*, November 20, 2017 (onlinelibrary. wiley.com); Kim Parker, Rachel Minkin, and Jesse Bennett, "Economic Fallout From COVID-19 Continues To Hit Lower-Income Americans the Hardest," Pew Research Center, September 24, 2020 (pewsocialtrends.org); Rupert Neate, "Billionaires' wealth rises to $10.2 trillion amid Covid crisis," *The Guardian*, October 6, 2020 (theguardian.com); Mallory Newall and Sara Machi, "Cuomo earns high marks for COVID-19 handling in New York," Ipsos, October 21, 2020 (Ipsos.com); Robert Frank, "Taxes are likely to go up for the wealthy in these nine states," CNBC News, September 25, 2020 (cnbc. com); National Conference of State Legislatures, "NCSL fiscal brief: State balanced budget provisions," October 2010 (ncsl.org); Jake Blumgart, "This time could be different: Governments have alternatives to austerity," *City Monitor*, October 8, 2020 (citymonitor.ai).

Article 6.3

THE IDEOLOGICAL ATTACK ON JOB CREATION
Responding to Anti-Government Arguments

BY MARTY WOLFSON
May/June 2012

> "Government doesn't create jobs. It's the private sector that creates jobs."
> —Presidential candidate Mitt Romney, speaking at Wofford College,
> Spartanburg, S.C., January 18, 2012

It is jarring to hear pundits say that the government can't create jobs. It is even more jarring to hear the same refrain from someone whose job was created by the government! Perhaps Mitt Romney has forgotten, or would like to forget, that he used to have a government job as governor of Massachusetts.

But surely those currently on the government payroll have not forgotten, like the chairman of the House Republican Policy Committee, Rep. Tom Price (R-Ga.). He used the same talking points, "the government doesn't create jobs. It's the private sector that creates jobs," speaking on MSNBC's "Andrea Mitchell Reports" last June.

Price apparently thinks he doesn't have a real job, but what about teachers, firefighters, police officers, and school cafeteria workers? And what about the 2 to 4.8 million jobs—in both the public and private sectors—the U.S. Congressional Budget Office estimated were created by the 2009 U.S. economic stimulus package?

The "government doesn't create jobs" mantra is part of a coordinated right-wing campaign to *prevent* the government from creating jobs and promoting the interests of working families, and to instead encourage a shift in the distribution of income towards the wealthy. It is supported by ideologically motivated arguments and theories from conservative economists and anti-government think tanks. In what follows, these arguments are addressed and criticized, with the hope of clearing away some of the confusion undermining a vigorous government program to put people back to work.

The Argument That Government Spending Can't Increase Jobs

A senior fellow at the Cato Institute says the idea that government spending can create jobs "has a rather glaring logical fallacy. It overlooks the fact that, in the real world, government can't inject money into the economy without first taking money out of the economy." This argument is wrong for several reasons.

First, the government *can* inject money into the economy. It does so whenever it finances its spending by selling bonds to the Federal Reserve. In this case, money is created by the Federal Reserve when it buys the bonds. It creates a reserve account on its books; money is thus created without any reduction in money elsewhere in the economy.

Alternatively, the government can finance its spending through taxes or by selling bonds to the public. This is the case envisioned by the Cato analysis. The argument is that the money spent by the government is exactly balanced by a reduction in money in the pockets of taxpayers and bond buyers. However, if the taxpayers' or the bond buyers' money would otherwise have been saved and not spent, then there is a net injection into the economy of funds that can put people to work.

The argument made by the Cato Institute is actually a variation of another theory, known as "crowding out." In this theory, government spending creates competition for real resources that "crowds out," or displaces, private investment; private companies are unable to obtain the workers and capital they need for investment, so that any jobs due to government spending are offset by a decrease of jobs in the private sector.

This theory is valid only when there is full employment because there would be no idle resources, labor, or capital, to put to use. In that case, though, neither the government nor the private sector would be able to create net new jobs. In contrast, in a situation of unemployment, it is precisely because the government can access otherwise idle resources that it can create jobs.

And, of course, that is exactly the situation we are in. As of March, the official unemployment rate stood at 8.2 %. Adjusted for underemployment, e.g., by counting those discouraged workers who have dropped out of the labor force and those workers who are working part time but would like to work full time, the more accurate unemployment rate was 14.5%.

The Argument That Cutting Government Spending Creates Jobs

Consistent with anti-government ideology, conservative economics asserts not only that government spending can't create jobs, but also that cutting government spending creates jobs. Here's how the argument goes: less government spending will reduce the government deficit; smaller deficits will increase the confidence of businesses that will invest more and in that way create more jobs. According to John B. Taylor, an economist affiliated with Stanford's conservative Hoover Institution, "basic economic models in which incentives and expectations of future policy matter show that a credible plan to reduce gradually the deficit will increase economic growth and reduce unemployment by removing uncertainty and lowering the chances of large tax increases in the future." (Interestingly, an analysis by economist Robert Pollin of the Political Economy Research Institute at the University of Massachusetts-Amherst finds that Taylor's empirical model concludes that the stimulus bill was ineffective—but only because it included too much in tax cuts as opposed to direct government spending.)

This assertion is based more on wishful thinking than empirical validity, and has been criticized by Paul Krugman as depending on belief in a "confidence fairy." But it is not just liberal economists like Krugman who are critical of this theory. A confidential report prepared for clients by the investment bank Goldman Sachs concluded that a $61 billion cut in government spending from a bill passed by the House of Representatives in February 2011 (but not enacted into law) would lead to a decline in economic growth of 2%. And economist Mark Zandi, formerly an advisor to Republican presidential candidate John McCain, concluded that this $61 billion reduction in government spending could result in the loss of 700,000 jobs by 2012.

Ben Bernanke, chairman of the Board of Governors of the Federal Reserve System, stated that "the cost to the recovery [of steep reductions in government outlays now] would outweigh the benefits in terms of fiscal discipline." Even the International Monetary Fund, in its semiannual report on the world economic outlook, concluded that "the idea that fiscal austerity triggers faster growth in the short term finds little support in the data."

Also, in a review of studies and historical experience about the relationship between budget cutting and economic growth, economists Arjun Jayadev and Mike Konczal concluded that countries historically did not cut government spending and deficits in a slump and that there is no basis to conclude that doing so now, "under the conditions the United States currently faces, would improve the country's prospects."

The Argument That Private Spending Is Always Better than Public Spending

Another way that right-wing economics tries to discredit the idea that the government can create jobs is to assert that private spending is always preferable to public spending. There are several rationalizations for this view.

One is that private spending is more efficient than public spending. This ideological refrain has been repeated consistently, and gained a following, over the past 30 years. But repetition does not make it correct. Of course, the proponents of this argument can point to examples of government mismanagement, such as that following Hurricane Katrina. However, government bungling and inefficiency by an administration that did not believe in government does not prove the point. A much more grievous example of inefficiency and misallocation of resources is the housing speculation and financial manipulation—and eventual collapse that brought us to the current recession—due to a deregulated private financial system. Yet for free-market ideologues, this somehow does not discredit the private sector.

Some people think that economists have "proven" that "free" markets are efficient. The only thing that has been proven, however, is that you can arrive at any conclusion if your assumptions are extreme enough. And the assumptions that form the basis for the free-market theory are indeed extreme, if not totally unrealistic and impossible. For example: Orthodox free-market economics assumes perfectly competitive markets; perfect information; no situations, like pollution, in which private decision-makers do not take account of the societal effects of their actions; even full employment. But none of these assumptions hold true in the real world. Also, the distribution of income is irrelevant to the conclusions of this theory. The distribution of income is simply taken as given, so that the results of the theory are consistent with a relatively equal distribution of income as well as a very unequal distribution. As economist Joseph Stiglitz has said, "today, there is no respectable intellectual support for the proposition that markets, by themselves, lead to efficient, let alone equitable outcomes."

A second reason for supposing that private spending is to be preferred to public spending is the notion that public spending is less worthwhile than private spending. This means, for many people, reducing government spending as much as possible. For example, Grover Norquist, founder and president of Americans for Tax Reform and author of the anti-tax pledge signed by many members of Congress, said that he wanted to "shrink [the government] down to the size where we can drown it in the bathtub." The anti-tax, anti-spending crusade has in many cases been successful in reducing government budgets, on the national as well as the local level. This has resulted in a significant decrease in government services. Although some people are attracted to the view that government spending should always be reduced, they probably at the same time don't want to drive on roads and bridges that aren't repaired and they probably want fire trucks to arrive if their house is on fire. Perhaps, too, they wouldn't automatically prefer 12 kinds of toothpaste to schools, parks, and libraries.

The Argument That Government Spending Is Wasteful

Another argument contends that public spending is wasteful. Discussions of government accounts generally do not take account of public investment, so all public spending is essentially treated as consumption. As such, it is considered unproductive and wasteful by those who wish to disparage government spending. In other words, the government budget does not make a distinction between long-term investments and other spending as corporate budgets do.

One implication of treating all government spending as consumption is the notion that the federal government should maintain a balanced budget. To put this in accounting terms, on this view government accounts are considered to only have an income statement (which shows current revenues and current expenditures), not a balance sheet (which shows assets and liabilities).

Corporations, in contrast, maintain balance sheets. They don't balance their budgets in the way that the budget hawks want the government to do. Private investment in plants and equipment, for example, is accounted for on the asset side of the balance sheet; borrowing to finance this investment is accounted for on the liability side. Interest on the debt is accounted for on the income statement, and it is only the interest, not the outstanding debt balance, that has to be covered by current revenues. The assumption behind this accounting is that borrowing to finance productive investment will generate the revenue to pay off the borrowing.

In other words, corporations borrow on a regular basis to finance investment. So they only attempt to balance their current expenditures and revenues and not their capital budget.

Much confusion about private and public spending, and also about budget deficits, could be avoided if discussion focused on a federal government balance sheet. In that way, current spending that needs to be balanced with current revenue could be separated from long-term investments that will increase the productivity of the American economy. Such investments, in areas like infrastructure and education, can increase future economic growth and income, and thus generate more tax revenue to pay off the debt. Just like a private company's investments, they are legitimately financed by borrowing.

Government Can Indeed Create Jobs

The main point, though, is this: Whether financed by borrowing, taxes, consumption, or investment, government spending that increases the demand for goods and services in the economy is not wasteful. It has the ability to employ underutilized resources and create jobs.

Ultimately, a job is a job, whether created by the private or public sector. A job has the potential to enable workers to support themselves and their families with dignity. We should not let ideological arguments keep us from using every available means to promote the basic human right of employment. ❑

Sources: Congressional Budget Office, "Estimated Impact of the American Recovery and Reinvestment Act on Employment and Economic Output From April 2010 Through June 2010," August 2010; Daniel J. Mitchell, "The Fallacy That Government Creates Jobs," The Cato Institute, 2008; John B. Taylor, "Goldman Sachs Wrong About Impact of House Budget Proposal," Economics One blog, February 28, 2011; Paul Krugman, "Myths of austerity," *New York Times.* July 1, 2010; Jonathan Karl, "Goldman Sachs: House Spending Cuts Will Hurt Economic Growth," The Note, 2011; Mark Zandi, "A federal shutdown could derail the recovery," Moody's Analytics, February 28, 2011; Pedro da Costa and Mark Felsenthal, "Bernanke warns against steep budget cuts," Reuters, February 9, 2011; International Monetary Fund, *World Economic Outlook: Recovery, Risk, and Rebalancing,* 2010; Arjun Jayadev and Mike Konczal, "When Is Austerity Right? In Boom, Not Bust," *Challenge,* November-December 2010; Joseph Stiglitz, Foreword, in Karl Polanyi, *The Great Transformation: The Political and Economic Origins of Our Times* (Beacon Press, 2001); David Aschauer, "Is Public Expenditure Productive?" *Journal of Monetary Economics,* 1989; Robert Pollin, "US government deficits and debt amid the great recession: what the evidence shows," *Cambridge Journal of Economics,* Issue 36, 2012; Kelsey Merrick and Jim Horney, "Chairman Ryan Gets 62 Percent of His Huge Budget Cuts from Programs for Lower-income Americans," Center on Budget and Policy Priorities, March 23, 2012; Paul Ryan, The Path to Prosperity, March 20, 2012; Ethan Pollack, "Ryan's Budget Would Cost Jobs," The Economic Policy Institute, March 21, 2012.

Article 6.4

FISCAL POLICY AND "CROWDING OUT"

BY ALEJANDRO REUSS
May/June 2009

In response to the deepest recession in the United States since the Great Depression, the Obama administration proposed a large fiscal "stimulus" plan. (Fiscal policies involve government spending and taxation. A fiscal stimulus involves increases in government spending or tax cuts, or both.) The current stimulus plan, after some compromises between the Obama administration and Republicans in Congress, included both substantial tax cuts and increases in government spending. Together, they would increase the federal government deficit by over $700 billion.

A fiscal stimulus is a standard "Keynesian" response to a recession. The logic behind these policies is that recessions can be caused by insufficient total demand for goods and services. If saving (a "leakage" from demand) exceeds investment (an "injection" of demand), there will not be enough demand to buy all the goods and services that the economy is capable of producing at the "full employment" level. Some goods will go unsold, and firms will reduce output. They will cut jobs, cancel supply orders, and even close production facilities. The economy will spiral into a recession.

In standard Keynesian models, either tax cuts or increased government spending can increase total demand, and therefore total output and employment. An initial increase in spending (by either the government or the recipients of the tax cuts) results in new income for other individuals, who then go on to spend part (not all) of this income, which results in new income for still other individuals, and so on. Ultimately, this series of additions to income results in a total increase in gross domestic product greater than the original increase in government spending or reduction in taxes. The increase in real GDP divided by the initial spending increase is called the "multiplier." The standard Keynesian view implies a multiplier greater than one.

The Conservative Critique

Conservative economists, whose intellectual heritage includes decades-old attempts to refute Keynesian theory, disagree with this view. They argue that government spending cannot possibly increase overall economic activity, and that the stimulus plan is therefore doomed to fail. This position is sometimes known as the "Treasury view" (because it mirrors the arguments of the British Treasury Department during the Great Depression) or the theory of "crowding out." The new government spending, these economists argue, "has to come from somewhere," either from higher taxes or increased government borrowing. Either way, the increase in government spending will come at the expense of private spending.

If the spending is financed by tax increases, conservative economists argue, this will reduce individuals' after-tax incomes and therefore reduce their spending. If it is financed through borrowing, the increased government demand for loans will drive up interest rates, and this will "crowd out" private investment. (Some private investment projects that would have been profitable at lower interest rates would not be profitable at the higher rates, and therefore would not be undertaken.) Extreme versions of this theory, known as "dollar-for-dollar" crowding out, argue that the decrease in private investment will exactly offset the increase in government spending, and there will be no change in the overall output of goods and services.

Government intervention is not only incapable of pulling the economy out of a recession, conservative economists argue, it is also unnecessary. If there is more saving than investment, the quantity of funds people are willing to loan out will exceed the quantity that people are willing to borrow at the current interest rate. The surplus of loanable funds will drive down the interest rate. People will save less (since the reward for saving is lower) and borrow and invest more (since the cost of borrowing is lower), until the injection of investment and the leakage of saving are equal. In short, if insufficient demand ever caused a recession, the economy would quickly pull itself back to full employment without any need for government intervention.

Keynes' Rejoinder

Keynes agreed with the idea that saving equals investment. In his view, however, this is true not only when the economy is producing at its full-employment capacity, but also when it is producing at far less than its capacity. Keynes argued that the "classical" economists (as he called the conservative orthodoxy of his time) had an incorrect view of the relationship between interest rates and savings, and that this was at the heart of their errors about the possibility of prolonged recessions.

The classical economists believed that as interest rates increased, savings would increase, and that as interest rates declined, savings would decline. Keynes agreed that this was true at "a given income," but that a change in the interest rate would also affect the amount investment and therefore the level of income. A higher interest rate, he argued, was associated with lower investment, lower incomes, and therefore lower saving; a lower interest rate, with higher investment, higher incomes, and therefore higher saving. (As people's incomes increase, they spend more *and* save more; as their incomes decline, they spend less *and* save less.) In Keynes' view, saving will equal investment whether investment and saving are both high (at or near the full-employment level of output) or if investment and saving are both low (in a low-output, high-unemployment economy). In the latter case, Keynes believed, there was no guarantee that the economy would pull itself back to full employment.

Keynes was also well aware, long before his critics, that government borrowing could crowd out some private investment. In *The General Theory* itself, he noted that the effects of the government directly increasing employment on public works may include "increasing the rate of interest and so retarding investment in other directions." This does not imply, however, dollar-for-dollar crowding out. Keynes still believed, and the empirical evidence confirms, that under depression conditions an increase in government spending can result in an increase in total output larger than the initial spending increase (a multiplier greater than one).

Of Spending and Multipliers

In a January 2009 article in the *Wall Street Journal*, conservative economist Robert Barro declares, as a "plausible starting point," that the multiplier actually equals zero. That's what the dollar-for-dollar crowding-out theory means—an increase in government spending will be matched by equal decreases in private spending, and so will have zero effect on real GDP. When it comes to estimating the multiplier, based on historical data from 1943–1944, however, Barro finds that it is not zero, but 0.8.

First, contrary to Barro's intent, this is actually a disproof of dollar-for-dollar crowding out. It means that increased government spending brought about increased real GDP, though not by as much as the spending increase. It increased the production of public-sector goods by (much) more than it reduced the production of private-sector goods. Unless one views private-sector goods as intrinsically more valuable than public-sector goods, this is not an argument against government spending.

Second, Barro chose to base his study on two years at the height of the U.S. mobilization for World War II. When the economy is at or near full employment, the multiplier is bound to be small. If all resources are already being used, the only way to produce more of some kinds of goods (say, tanks and war planes) is to produce less of some others (say, civilian cars). Keynesian economists certainly understand this. Their point, however, is that government spending creates a large multiplier effect when the economy is languishing in a recession, not when it is already at full employment.

Economist Mark Zandi of Moody's economy.com reports much higher multipliers for government spending. Zandi estimates multipliers between 1.3 and 1.6 for federal aid to states and for government infrastructure expenditures. The multipliers are even larger for government transfers (such as food stamps or unemployment compensation) to the hardest hit, who are likely to spend all or almost all of their increase in income. Zandi estimates these multipliers at between 1.6 and 1.8. Tax cuts for high income individuals and corporations, who are less likely to spend their additional disposable income, have the lowest multipliers—between 0.3 and 0.4.

Why the *General* Theory?

The conservative case against standard Keynesian fiscal stimulus policy rests on the assumption that all of the economy's resources are already being used to the fullest. Keynes titled his most important work *The General Theory of Employment, Interest, and Money* because he thought that the orthodox economics of his time confined itself to this special case, the case of an economy at full employment. He did not believe that this was generally the case in capitalist economies, and he sought to develop a theory that explained this.

The argument conservatives make against government spending—"it has to come from somewhere"—is actually no less true for private investment. If dollar-for-dollar crowding out were true, therefore, it would be just as impossible for private investment to pull the economy out of a recession. This, of course, would be nonsense unless the economy was already at full employment (and an increase in one kind of production would have to come at the expense of some other kind of production).

If the economy were already operating at full capacity—imagine a situation in which all workers are employed, factories are humming with activity 24/7, and no unused resources would be available to expand production if demand increased—the argument that increased government spending could not increase overall economic output might be plausible. But that is manifestly not the current economic situation.

Real GDP declined at an annual rate of 6.3% in the fourth quarter of 2008. The official unemployment rate surged to 8.5%, the highest rate in 30 years, in March 2009. Over 15% of workers are unemployed, have given up looking for work, or can only find part-time work. Employment is plummeting by more than half a million workers each month. A theory that assumes the economy is already at full employment can neither help us understand how we got into this hole—or how we can get out. ❑

Sources: John Maynard Keynes, *The General Theory of Employment, Interest, and Money* (Harcourt, 1964); Associated Press, "Obama: Stimulus lets Americans claim destiny," Feb. 17, 2009; Paul Krugman, "A Dark Age of macroeconomics (wonkish)," Jan. 27, 2009 (krugman.blogs.nytimes.com); J. Bradford DeLong, "More 'Treasury View' Blogging," Feb. 5,2009 (delong.typepad.com); J. Bradford DeLong, "The Modern Revival of the 'Treasury View,'" Jan. 18, 2009 (delong.typepad.com); Robert J. Barro,"Government Spending is No Free Lunch," *Wall Street Journal*, Jan. 22, 2009 (wsj.com); Paul Krugman, "War and non-remembrance," *New York Times*, Jan. 22, 2009 (krugman.blogs.nytimes.com); Paul Krugman, "Spending in wartime," Jan. 23, 2009 (krugman.blogs.nytimes.com); Mark Zandi, "The Economic Impact of a $750 Billion Fiscal Stimulus Package," Moody's Economy.com, March 26, 2009; Bureau of Labor Statistics, Alternative measures of labor underutilization; Bureau of Labor Statistics Payroll Employment.

Article 6.5

THE GREEN NEW DEAL AS AN ANTI-NEOLIBERALISM PROGRAM

BY ROBERT POLLIN
November/December 2019

In 2007, Nicholas Stern, the prominent mainstream British economist and former chief economist at the World Bank, wrote that "Climate change is a result of the greatest market failure the world has seen." Stern's assessment was extreme, but not hyperbolic. This is for the simple reason that, if we take climate science at all seriously, we cannot avoid the conclusion that we are courting ecological disaster by not stabilizing the climate.

Neoliberalism is a driving force behind the climate crisis. This is because neoliberalism is a variant of classical liberalism, and classical liberalism builds from the idea that everyone should be granted maximum freedom to pursue their self interest within capitalist market settings. But neoliberalism also diverges substantially from classical liberalism: What really occurs in practice under neoliberalism is that governments allow giant corporations to freely pursue profit opportunities to the maximum extent, and governments even intervene on corporations' behalf when their profits might be threatened.

How the oil companies reacted to clear evidence of climate change represents a dramatic case study of neoliberalism in practice. In 1982, researchers working at the then Exxon Corporation (now Exxon Mobil) estimated that by about 2060, burning oil, coal, and natural gas to produce energy would elevate the planet's average temperatures by about 2° Celsius. This, in turn, would generate exactly the types of massive climate disruptions that we have increasingly experienced since the 1980s—i.e., heat extremes, heavy precipitation, droughts, rising sea levels, and biodiversity losses, with corresponding impacts on health, livelihoods, food security, water supplies, and human security. In 1988, researchers at the Shell Corporation reached similar conclusions. We now know what Exxon and Shell did with this information: They buried it. They did so for the obvious reason that, if the information were then known, it might have threatened their prospects for receiving massive profits from producing and selling oil.

There is no minimizing the fact that what Exxon and Shell did was immoral. But it is equally clear that both companies behaved exactly according to the precepts of neoliberalism—i.e., they acted to protect their profits. They also continued from the 1980s onward to behave according to the precepts of neoliberalism in extracting the largest possible subsidies that they could get from any and all governments throughout the world. Amid all of this, neither company has faced any government sanctions for their behavior. Quite the contrary, they have continued to earn huge profits and receive hefty government subsidies.

Defeating neoliberalism is clearly a political project of overwhelming significance. But we can't expect to defeat neoliberalism unless we have a viable alternative in place. This is where the idea of the Green New Deal becomes central.

The Green New Deal has gained tremendous traction as an organizing framework over the past couple of years. This alone is a major achievement. But it is still imperative that we transform this big idea into a viable program. In my view, putting meat on the bones of the Green New Deal starts with a single simple idea: We have to absolutely stop burning oil, coal, and natural gas to produce energy within the next 30 years at most; and we have to do this in a way that also supports increasing living standards and expanding opportunities for working people and the poor throughout the world.

This version of a Green New Deal program is, in fact, entirely realistic in terms of its purely economic and technical features. Clean renewable energy sources—including solar, wind, geothermal, and to a lesser extent small-scale hydro and low-emissions bioenergy—are already either at cost parity with fossil fuels and nuclear or they are cheaper. In addition, the single easiest and cheapest way to lower emissions is to raise energy efficiency standards through, among other measures, retrofitting existing buildings, making new buildings operate as net zero energy consumers, and replacing gas-guzzling automobiles with expanding public transportation and electric cars. Energy efficiency measures, by definition, will save people money—for example, your home electricity bills could realistically be cut in half without having to reduce the amount that you light, heat, or cool your house. So the Green New Deal will not cost consumers anything over time, as long as we solve the problem of funding Green New Deal investments through the cost savings we gain by raising efficiency standards and producing cheap renewable energy.

Through our work at the Political Economy Research Institute at UMass Amherst, my coworkers and I have estimated that building a 100% clean energy system will require about 2.5% of global GDP per year for roughly the next 30 years. Yes, that's a lot of money in dollar terms (roughly $2 trillion in 2021 and rising thereafter), but it does mean that 97.5% of global economic activity can still be devoted to things other than investments in clean energy.

In addition, these clean-energy investments will be a major source of job creation, in all regions of the globe. The critical factor is that clean-energy investments will create a lot more jobs than maintaining the existing dirty-energy infrastructure—in the range of two to four times more jobs per dollar of spending in all of the countries that we have studied, including Brazil, China, India, Indonesia, South Africa, Spain, and the United States.

Of course, jobs that are tied to the fossil fuel industry will be eliminated. The affected workers and their communities must be supported through generous "just transition" measures, including guaranteeing workers' pensions, moving people into new jobs without losing incomes, and investing in impacted communities. Land reclamation is just one such investment opportunity, including cleaning up abandoned coal mines and converting the residual coal ash into useful products, like paper.

In short, the Green New Deal offers a viable egalitarian and ecologically sane alternative to the reign of neoliberalism. However, to defeat neoliberalism will require unprecedented political organizing and breakthroughs along many fronts. This is obviously a daunting challenge. But as probably the most forceful proponent of neoliberalism, Margaret Thatcher, once famously declared, "There is no alternative." ❑

Sources: Naomi Oreskes and Erik Conway, *Merchants of Doubt: How a Handful of Scientists Obscured the Truth on Issues from Tobacco Smoke to Climate Change* (Bloomsbury Publishing, 2011); Robert Pollin, *Greening the Global Economy* (MIT Press, 2015); Robert Pollin, Jeannette Wicks-Lim, Shouvik Chakraborty, and Tyler Hansen, *A Green Growth Program for Colorado*, PERI, April 2019.

Article 6.6

FINANCIAL TRANSACTIONS TAXES
The Perfect Way to Pay for Biden's Infrastructure Package

BY DEAN BAKER
May 2021, Center for Economic and Policy Research

There has been a lot of silliness around President Joe Biden's proposed infrastructure packages and the extent to which they are affordable for the country. First and foremost, there has been tremendous confusion about the size of the package. This is because the media has engaged in a feast of really big numbers, where they give us the size of the package with no context whatsoever, leaving their audience almost completely ignorant about the actual cost.

We have been told endlessly about Biden's "massive" or "huge" proposal to spend $4 trillion. At this point, many people probably think that Biden actually proposed a "huge infrastructure" package, with "huge" or "massive" being part of the proposal's title.

While it would be helpful if media outlets could leave these adjectives to the opinion section, the bigger sin is using a very big number, which means almost nothing to its audience, without providing any context. In fact, much of the reporting doesn't even bother to tell people that this spending is projected to take place over eight years, not one to two years, as was the case with Biden's recovery package.

Over an eight-year period, Biden's proposed spending averages $500 billion annually. This is a period in which GDP is projected to be more than $210 trillion, meaning that his package is projected to be around 1.9% of GDP. While that is hardly trivial, military spending is projected to be around 3.3% of GDP over this period. This means that Biden is proposing to increase infrastructure spending by an amount that is roughly 60% of projected military spending.

It is infuriating that most of the reporting on these proposals make no effort to put the spending in any context that would make it meaningful for people. Reporters all know that almost no one has any idea what $4 trillion over eight years means (especially if no one tells them it is over eight years), yet they refuse to take the two minutes that would be needed to add some context to make such really big numbers meaningful. Therefore, we have a large segment of the population that just thinks the program is massive or huge.

What Paying for Spending Really Means

As our Modern Monetary Theory (MMT) friends constantly remind us, a government that prints its own money, like the United States, does not need tax revenue to pay for its spending. This distinguishes the U.S. government from a household or state and local governments. Households and state and local governments actually need money in the bank to pay their bills. For them, more spending requires more income or taxes and/or more borrowing. The federal government does not have this constraint.

Nonetheless, the federal government does face a limit on its spending: the ability of the economy to produce goods and services. If the federal government spends so much that it pushes the economy beyond its ability to produce goods and services, we will see inflation. If this excessive spending is sustained over a substantial period of time then we could see the sort of inflationary spiral that we had in the 1970s.

If the economy is already near its capacity when President Biden's infrastructure package starts to come on line in 2022 and 2023, an increase in spending of a bit less than 2.0% of GDP could be large enough to create problems with inflation. This is the reason that we have to talk about "paying for" the infrastructure package. We need not be concerned about getting the money in the bank, we have to reduce demand in the economy by enough to make room for the additional spending in Biden's infrastructure agenda. This is where a financial transactions tax comes in.

The Virtue of Financial Transactions Tax as a "Pay For"

The Biden tax proposals have focused on increasing the amount of money that corporations and wealthy individuals pay in taxes. This makes sense since they have been the big gainers in the economy over the last four decades.

Biden's tax increases will just take back a fraction of the income that has been redistributed upward through a variety of government policies over this period. And, in the case of the corporate income tax, his proposal will just be partially reversing a tax cut that was put in place at the end of 2017 by Donald Trump and a Republican Congress. While taxing the economy's big gainers is certainly fair, there is a problem with going this route to cover the cost of Biden's program: The rich don't spend a large share of their income.

This point is straightforward; if we give Jeff Bezos, Elon Musk, or any of the other super-wealthy another $100 million this year, it would likely not affect their consumption at all. They already have more than enough money to buy anything they could conceivably want, so even giving them a huge wad of money will not likely lead them to increase their consumption to any noticeable extent. Many of us are used to making this point when we argue that any stimulus payments in a recession should be focused on the middle class and the poor.

But this story also works in reverse, if we take $100 million away from the super-rich, it is not likely to reduce their spending to any noticeable extent. This means that Biden's tax increases are not likely to have as much impact on reducing demand as tax increases that hit the poor and middle class. This is not an argument for hitting the people who have not fared well over the last four decades, it is just noting the impact of taxing the super-rich.

Financial transactions taxes (FTT) are qualitatively different in this respect. While the immediate impact of a financial transactions tax is hugely progressive, in the sense that the overwhelming majority of stock trading is done by the rich and very rich, the impact on the economy makes FTTs look even better.

Most research shows that the volume of stock trading falls roughly in proportion to the increase in the cost of trading. This means that if a FTT raises the cost of trading by 40%, the volume of trading will fall by roughly 40%. For a typical investor, that implies that they (or their fund manager) will be paying 40% more on each trade, but they will be doing 40% fewer trades. In other words, the total amount that they spend on trades with the tax in place will be roughly the same as the amount that they spent on trades before the tax is in place.

And investors will not be hurt by less trading. Every trade has a winner and a loser. If I'm lucky and dump my hundred shares of Amazon stock just before the price drops, it means that some unlucky sucker bought the stock a day too soon. Every trade is like this. The reality is that for the vast majority of investors, trades are a wash. Half the time they end up as winners, and half the time they end up as losers.

However, they do end up as losers by doing lots of trading, which is because they are paying fees and commissions to the people in the financial industry carrying through the trades. This is why most financial advisers recommend that people buy and hold index funds so that they don't waste money on trading.

A FTT reduces the money going to the financial industry to carry through trades by reducing the volume of trading. This very directly frees up resources in the economy. The number of people employed to shuffle stocks, bonds, and various derivatives back and forth will be sharply reduced.

This is comparable to a situation where we found hundreds of thousands of people digging holes and filling them up again. A financial transactions tax, coupled with Biden's infrastructure proposals, will be a way to redeploy these people to productive work elsewhere in the economy.

There is also a substantial amount of money here. According to the Congressional Budget Office, a tax of 0.1$ (ten cents on $100) would raise almost $800 billion over the course of a decade. I've calculated that a graduated tax, with different rates on different assets (0.2% on stock transactions, lower on everything else) could raise an amount of revenue equal to almost 0.6% of GDP over the course of a decade, or $1.6 trillion. My friend and economist Bob Pollin has calculated that a somewhat steeper tax, along the lines proposed by Senator Bernie Sanders, could raise close to twice as much. In short, this is real money.

That doesn't mean that we should reject President Biden's proposals to increase corporate income taxes and taxes on the top 1% or 2%. (My route for taxing corporations is better than his.) Even if Musk might not change his consumption much as a result of paying another $100 million taxes, there are many moderately rich people, earning single-digit millions, who may have to forgo a third home or a live-in cook, if we raise their taxes as President Biden proposed.

The bottom line is that Biden's investment plan addresses longstanding needs in this country. We will likely have to reduce other spending in the economy to make room for it. A financial transactions tax is a great place to look for some of the offset. ❑

Article 6.7

REFORM OF GLOBAL TAXATION CANNOT WAIT

BY JAYATI GHOSH
December 2020, Social Europe

As the pandemic has raged around the world, releasing yet another wave of infections and associated deaths, economies have slumped, resulting in a massive loss of livelihoods. Material insecurities are increasing sharply, with more uncertainty, discord, and strife.

Yet, in the midst of all this, some corporations and individuals are doing better than ever—profiting immensely from the very forces that have laid everyone else low. And these same companies and wealthy individuals continue to pay much less in taxes relative to others, sometimes close to nothing.

The massive inequalities inherent in the global economic system have been evident for a while but they have been laid bare and intensified over the past year. The international tax architecture continues to aid and abet increasing inequality, because of anomalies which enable multinational companies to avoid paying the same rate of taxes local companies pay. It also allows very rich individuals to avoid paying even minimal wealth taxes in their own countries of residence, by stashing away money in tax havens and via other illicit financial flows.

We can no longer afford to allow this. This is not only because of concerns about the massive inequality it encourages, the injustice, and the absence of level playing fields for all taxpayers. Most important, right now, is that governments across the world—even those which have used central-bank liquidity to increase spending immediately—must make even larger expenditures in coming days.

They will have to deal with the pandemic and its effects on economies, support and provide social protection to those devastated by economic collapse, address and cope with the climate crisis, and try to meet the United Nations sustainable development goals, which have been hugely set back. No country can afford the luxury of coddling its richest residents and large corporations by allowing this tax avoidance and evasion—and the international community cannot continue to look the other way as vast sums are denied to governments and their citizens.

Stopping this bleeding in practical terms is not impossible—or even that difficult. Some solutions have been apparent and in the public domain for a while. The Independent Commission for the Reform of International Corporate Taxation (ICRICT) (of which I am a member) has suggested a set of comprehensive and fundamental reforms which incorporate basic principles of efficiency and fairness. These include enabling every country to tax the global profits of multinational companies (MNCs) by apportioning the profits according to a formula based on sales, employment, users (for digital companies), and capital, and with a global minimum tax rate of 25%.

This idea mimics a system already applied in the United States, which is very federalist and allows states to have different tax policies. The beauty of this is that it completely removes any incentive that MNCs have to engage in base erosion and profit shifting (BEPS)—artificially classifying profits to low-tax jurisdictions to avoid paying higher taxes in the countries where they actually operate.

Obviously, this is something most effectively done with international coordination, so ideally it should be organized under the aegis of the United Nations. Instead, the task was handed over to the Organization for Economic Cooperation and Development (OECD), which since 2013 has been working on a strategy for stopping global corporations from shifting profits to tax havens and ending the "race to the bottom" in corporate tax rates.

But the experience has been disappointing, to say the least. The OECD is a relatively closed club of mostly rich countries. The BEPS Inclusive Framework sought to include 135 countries and tax jurisdictions, but these were included only after the more important decisions on strategy were made, and most countries are still excluded from effective and equal participation.

A successful strategy to tackle tax avoidance, improve the coherence of international tax rules, and ensure a more transparent tax system necessarily requires both ambition and simplicity. Both have been lacking in the OECD process, possibly because of successful lobbying by large MNCs.

As a result, the OECD's proposals have been very delayed, very complicated (and therefore easier for corporations to game), and promoted only very marginal reform, which would barely skim the surface. Finally, even these modest and not so meaningful measures have not yet been finalized, despite years of deliberations.

Unilateral Moves

So how can governments and their citizens act, in the face of such inaction? Waiting for an international agreement is no longer desirable, as the need for public expenditure to support health, incomes, and employment becomes ever more pressing, and eventually these will have to be financed through taxes and other revenues. So governments should move unilaterally to introduce interim measures to ensure that profitable companies which have benefited from the pandemic—in particular those in the digital and tech sectors—contribute to a just recovery.

ICRICT has suggested five measures governments can undertake:

- Apply a higher corporate tax rate to large corporations in oligopolistic sectors with excess rates of return;
- Set a minimum effective corporate tax rate of 25% worldwide to stop base erosion and profit shifting;
- Introduce progressive digital services taxes on the economic rents captured by multinational firms in this sector;
- Require publication of country-by-country reports by all corporations benefiting from state support; and
- Publish data on offshore wealth to enable all jurisdictions to adopt effective, progressive wealth taxes on their residents and prevent or reduce illicit financial flows.

As long as wider reforms are blocked by leading OECD members, these measures will support governments in mobilizing much-needed additional revenue. In addition, unilateral measures such as these serve to bring effective pressure to bear on the international community for genuinely fair, international tax reforms.

With a change of guard at the White House, it is possible to be more hopeful than previously that some of this pressure will have positive effects. There is clearly broader public support for measures that would ensure that the rich (whether large MNCs or high-net-worth individuals) are taxed fairly and at similar rates to other companies and people.

This is clearly a *carpe diem* moment—not only because the stakes are so high and the costs of inaction so great, but because such measures are more feasible than ever. ❑

Chapter 7

MONEY AND MONETARY POLICY

INTRODUCTION

The Covid-19 pandemic has "shocked" the U.S. and global economy in a profound fashion. The Federal Reserve Bank has responded to the crisis with expanded access to liquidity (money) to attempt to stave off economic collapse.

The first two essays of this chapter specifically look at monetary policy and deficits in response to the pandemic.

In Article 7.1, Gerald Epstein chronicles the Federal Reserve Bank's response to the Covid-19 crisis. He provides a timeline for the introduction of the Paycheck Protection Program (PPP) as well as the creation of the "Paycheck Protection Program Liquidity Facility (PPPLF)." He also discusses the Coronavirus Aid, Relief, and Economic Security (CARES) Act, and the extent to which it helps out regular folks. It's hardly surprising that the level of relief that is available through PPP is directly related to a firm's size and political connections. Larger firms took advantage of this SBA Program at the expense of small businesses who were shut out of crucial loans as the larger, well-connected companies quickly gobbled up the available funds.

Next, Yeva Nersisyan and L. Randall Wray (Article 7.2) assess the critical underfunding of the American public health care system, which left the country vulnerable to the pandemic. Fiscal policy, which has been far too attuned to the interests of Wall Street over Main Street, has given deficit hawks excessive influence over policymaking. In times of crisis, according to Keynes, the state should run deficits to support necessary activities. In this article, Nersisyan and Wray introduce us to Modern Monetary Theory (MMT), and highlight this approach to addressing the profound public health crisis we find ourselves in.

Doug Orr (Article 7.3) takes us through the basics of money and the monetary system. We use money every day, but usually do not stop to think about what money is, how money is defined, how it has evolved historically, or how it is created today. Orr explains in everyday language what money is and how the Fed attempts to control the money supply.

Then in Article 7.4, Arthur MacEwan explains how a "fractional reserve" banking system works, and whether or not it is at the root of our current economic troubles.

The final three articles in this chapter step back to take a broader view of monetary policy historically. Gerald Friedman confirms that, in a "liquidity trap," monetary policy is bound to fail (Article 7.5). This was evident during the Great Recession, when the Federal Reserve attempted to increase the money supply through open-market operations only to generate an explosion in excess reserves held by U.S. commercial banks. The Fed can do little to get the economy going using conventional monetary policy if banks won't make loans.

Then, Alejandro Reuss (Article 7.6) looks at the key arguments made by John Maynard Keynes in *The General Theory of Employment, Interest, and Money*, and examines the limitations of monetary policy as a tool for reviving economies mired in depression conditions. Reuss applies lessons from Keynes's work to current problems in the U.S. economy.

To conclude the chapter, Arthur MacEwan provides an overview of the changing place of the dollar in the global economy—especially its "dominance" as the key currency in which international trade is conducted and reserves are held—over the span of more than 75 years (Article 7.7). He describes three critical moments: The first, near the end of World War II, when the Bretton Woods conference clearly established the dollar as the most important world currency; the next, in the early 1970s, when the "dollar crisis" led the United States to abandon the convertibility of dollars for gold at a fixed rate (the "gold standard"), yet the dollar remained the dominant currency. The third is happening right now, with the United States' dominant position in the global economy slipping, and the future role of the dollar unclear.

Discussion Questions

1. (Article 7.1) Was the Federal Reserve Bank's response to the Covid-19 pandemic adequate? Why or why not? And why, according to Epstein, is the challenge facing the Fed greater now than during the Great Financial Crisis?

2. (Article 7.2) From Nersisyan and Wray: "… the issue is one not of *finding funds* but of *finding and mobilizing real resources through spending*." What does this mean? How is this MMT approach also Keynesian?

3. (Article 7.3) What are the mechanisms the Fed uses to "control" the creation of money through the banking system? Why, according to Orr, is the Fed's control over the creation of money "limited"?

4. (Article 7.4) What is "fractional reserve" banking? Do banks "create money out of thin air"? In what ways, according to MacEwan, do U.S. economic problems go deeper than the monetary system?

5. (Article 7.5) Why does Friedman, like others before him, liken monetary policy to "pushing on a string"? What evidence does Friedman offer to show that this analogy is an apt description of monetary policy today?

6. (Article 7.6) What, according to Keynes, were the key limitations of monetary policy, as a response to an economic downturn? If these were well described many decades ago, why did governments rely on monetary policy in responding to the Great Recession?

7. (Article 7.7) What does it mean to say that the dollar is the "dominant" currency in the world? Why has this been the case for more than three-quarters of a century? Consider economic and political factors.

Article 7.1

THE FED AND THE CORONAVIRUS CRISIS

BY GERALD EPSTEIN
March/April 2020

For the second time in roughly 10 years, the Federal Reserve and other central banks around the globe are being asked by bankers and politicians to save them and also save the economy—in that order.

When the financial system was taken down in 2007–2008 by the outrageously reckless and corrupt behavior of regulator-enabled banks, the Fed, in partnership with the Treasury Department, committed, by some estimates, as much as $29 trillion to bail out the U.S. financial system. Other central banks took similar measures.

Now, the challenge facing the Fed and other central banks is likely to be even greater. This view might seem incorrect based on the claims of many commentators that the banks are stronger now than they were in the lead-up to the Great Financial Crisis of 2007–2008: they have less debt, have more capital buffers to stand between them and a taxpayer bailout, and have more ready cash (liquidity) to stem panic-driven runs. All of this is true.

But the problems facing the Fed come not just from banks, but also from the massive financial system outside of the banks: hedge funds, asset managers, corporate bond markets, and a shadow banking system that are barely regulated by the Fed or other financial regulators, even though they are integrally—and now dangerously—interdependent with the banks. According to the Financial Stability Board, this global shadow finance system has been growing twice as fast as global bank assets from 2012 to 2017. And even though this time around the source of the crisis is not the financial system, finance has become a massive crisis accelerator because it has gotten so large and has been allowed to become so speculative and vulnerable, while remaining at the center of our highly financialized capitalist system.

Meanwhile, the global economy is collapsing around us, even more so than during the last financial crisis. The Fed and other central banks are thus faced with a double dilemma. They hold the keys to monetary policy which, as one of the two tools of macroeconomic policy (along with fiscal policy), is tasked with maintaining high employment and stable prices—a tall order in the midst of this collapse of production, incomes, and employment. And at the same time, the Fed has to contend with preventing a meltdown of the financial system, which would make the underlying problem much, much worse. This is like being a parent and having one child who is terribly sick and needs care, while having a second child who is threatening to burn down the house unless he gets a huge treat. Can you deal with both? In what order?

During the Great Financial Crisis, the Fed made its choice. It bailed out the ornery kid and did very little for the rest of us.

This time around, we are still waiting to see how the Fed will respond. In recent weeks, the Federal Reserve has undertaken a series of extraordinary measures (see Deutsche Bank Research, "COVID-19: List of Monetary and Fiscal Policy

Responses by G20 Economies," March 30, 2020, for a very useful list). First, the Fed lowered their interest rates to practically zero and then restarted quantitative easing to buy government securities and mortgage bonds. Then they restarted the multiple facilities providing liquidity and implicitly guaranteeing the operation of multiple financial operations: these markets include the commercial paper market, money market mutual funds, mortgage-backed securities and others, all of which have come under stress. Among the biggest operations is in the so-called "repo" (repurchase agreement) market, which is the major way the shadow banking system (and banks) borrow and lend to each other over the short term. In fact, this market has been having trouble since September, long before the coronavirus crisis, but now it is under even more stress. According to Deutsche Bank Research, the Fed could end up lending as much as $5 trillion in this market.

In addition, there are new problems in the markets. Major corporations have been going on a borrowing spree in recent years, as global interest rates have remained low and corporations have been wanting to finance large payouts to their executives and stockholders. This corporate bond market is huge, $7 trillion or more, and is now in serious trouble as the profits of major corporations tank. The Fed has created two facilities to help provide liquidity to this market. In addition, in recent years investment banks have been engaging in securitizing and trading assets other than the famous sub-prime mortgages they got in trouble with 10 years ago: these include student loans and car loans. The Fed has now had to create a new facility for each of these.

But what about the states, localities, cities, and small businesses that are under enormous stress and need help to keep going and provide needed services? Last time around the Fed did little to help them. Now, the government has tasked the Fed with acting more like a public bank and an arm of the Treasury in order to funnel funds to these entities and markets. The Fed is developing facilities to give loan guarantees and credits to many of these. In addition, the Federal Reserve is expected to create a facility to give loans and loan guarantees to small businesses. In the $2.2 trillion Coronavirus Aid, Relief, and Economic Security (CARES) Act, the government, through the Treasury Department, is injecting an additional $454 billion dollars of capital into the Federal Reserve that can be leveraged up to as much as $4.5 trillion in lending to try to help Main Street, not just Wall Street.

Turning the Fed into a proper public financial system in the middle of a national crisis is, in fact, a good idea. That is what President Franklin D. Roosevelt did during World War II. Still, major questions of accountability and transparency abound. During the Great Financial Crisis, the Fed and the Treasury lent billions and even trillions of dollars with very little oversight. Senator Elizabeth Warren has called for much stricter oversight this time around. But how will this really occur? The Fed is a creature of Congress, and so the Congress must exercise this oversight in the name of the public.

The big and unasked questions, though, are: Why does the Fed have to bail out these massive financial markets yet again? How were these financial institutions and markets allowed to grow so massively over the last 10 years, with so little oversight? This time, wouldn't it be better to create substitute, public institutions and bring these wild financial markets under control? A few possible steps the U.S.

government could take include: nationalizing a bank or two and turning them into public utilities to support workers, families, and small business (as Doug Henwood has suggested recently); creating a postal banking system and supporting credit unions to provide small loans to households and small businesses; and directing a tightly accountable Federal Reserve to provide the liquidity and credit that we need to the "real economy" and to also provide dollar credit to underwrite international support for poor countries to help them survive the pandemic, while strictly limiting support to the massive global speculative financial system.

If we don't take these critical steps, we will just keep underwriting the bloated and unproductive global financial system—helping it to lurch, prosper, and crash, from crisis to crisis.

Sources: L. Randall Wray, "$29 trillion: A Detailed Look at the Fed's Bailout of the Financial System," Levy Economics Institute, December 2011 (levyinstitute.org); Financial Stability Board, Global Monitoring Report on Non-Bank Financial Intermediation, January, 2020; Deutsche Bank Research, "Covid-19: List of Monetary and Fiscal Policy Responses by G20 Economies," March 30, 2020; Doug Henwood, "A Few Ambitious Points on Fighting the Crisis," LBO News, March 20, 2020 (lbo-news.com).

Article 7.2

IT'S TIME TO DITCH "PAY-FOR" POLITICS
The Most Important Economic Lesson from the Covid-19 Crisis

BY YEVA NERSISYAN AND L. RANDALL WRAY
May/June 2020

In the early spring of 2020, the richest and most powerful country in the history of planet Earth was brought down by a virus. What the crisis made crystal clear is that the nation was monumentally unprepared to deal with an epidemic that scientists knew was a near statistical certainty—the question was never "if," but only "when." And when hit by a global pandemic, the U.S. health care system, which accounted for 17% of the nation's spending in 2018 (compared to an average of 8.8% among the Organization for Economic Cooperation and Development's 37 member countries), was unable to either slow its spread or to deal with its consequences. There were 30 cases of the disease in the United States on March 1. By the end of April, that had exploded to nearly a million confirmed cases and over 50,000 deaths.

By the beginning of April, New York City's hospitals had already reached full capacity—and the expectation was that the peak demand for beds was still three weeks away. New York State had 47,439 confirmed cases on April 1, a quarter of the U.S. total at that time—and at the then-current rate of expansion, New York City's prospects looked worse than those of the Chinese city of Wuhan. By the end of April, it had nearly 300,000 cases and over 17,000 deaths, and all but six states had more than 1,000 cases, ensuring that New York's plight was a harbinger of the fate of cities across the country.

The pandemic has brought to the surface the issues masked by our previously "roaring" economy, from the lack of federally mandated sick leave, to lack of access to health care, to the folly of tying retirement security to the stock market. It exposed our "just-in-time" economy, manifested in businesses (such as hospitals) operating with the minimum amount of personnel and barebones inventories and with tens of millions of workers living one paycheck away from homelessness. A failure of global supply chains threw the system into disarray as hospitals are struggling to procure protective equipment, just as the shutdown of the economy threatens to leave workers without food and shelter.

The crisis also exposed the hypocrisy of deficit hawks and supply-siders. Suddenly the U.S. government could spare $2 trillion for companies big and small, as well as for helicopter drops of cash for the rest of us. Suddenly the government is not the problem, but the solution. Leave it to the notorious supply-sider, Larry Kudlow, director of the United States National Economic Council, and a Republican administration to preside over the largest peacetime spending bill in history—in reaction to a monumental failure by our government to prepare for the calamity that had long been predicted.

From the beginning of the epidemic, the Trump administration declined to ramp up federal government involvement, preferring to rely on the market system.

President Donald Trump suggested that American entrepreneurs ought to profit from the disaster. Even as the nation's governors begged the administration to take a leading role, he deferred to a highly decentralized response to a national disaster (arguing, implausibly, that large parts of the nation would somehow escape). With medical supplies in short supply, the states started bidding against each other, driving the prices ever-higher. In early February Congressional offers of emergency funding were declined by administration officials. Weeks of broken promises to provide simple testing kits in sufficient quantities to assess the virus's spread ensued. Part of the reason the United States was slow to provide tests was because the administration refused to use tests developed abroad before domestic tests could be developed (which eventually turned out to be defective anyway).

Decades of Austere Budgets Created This Crisis

A *Washington Post* headline from March 29 said it all: "Desperate for Medical Equipment, States Find a Beleaguered National Stockpile," reflecting the catastrophic failure to prepare for a rapidly spreading crisis. As the article reported:

> States desperate for materials from the stockpile are encountering a beleaguered
> system beset by years of underfunding, changing lines of authority,
> confusion over the allocation of supplies, and a lack of transparency from the
> administration, according to interviews with state and federal officials and public
> health experts.

The problem with our health care system extends well beyond the dearth of medical supplies, hospitals beds, and caregivers to a payments system that relies far too heavily on for-profit private insurance. Even those with coverage fear seeking help because of the uncertainty of coverage, high deductibles, and out-of-pocket costs. And despite Obamacare, over 27.5 million people had no health insurance in 2018. The number of uninsured people is sure to skyrocket as workers lose their jobs and health insurers drop coverage during the crisis. (Those insurers are making out like bandits as almost all medical procedures unrelated to the coronavirus are being postponed, and they are pushing costs associated with the virus onto patients. They've already discussed steep insurance rate hikes next year.)

This pandemic was not the first time the government botched the response to a crisis. On a more localized scale, the nation's lack of preparation for disaster had already been exposed numerous times—by hurricanes Katrina (2005) and Maria (2017), by tornadoes in Tuscaloosa, Ala. (April 2011) and Joplin, Mo. (May 2011), and the Yarnell Hill Fire (2013), Cedar Fire (2003), and Camp Fire (2018). In every case, these disasters were foreseen and not only caused death and destruction, but also wrecked economic havoc that took years to overcome. In the case of these "natural" disasters, the economic destruction was localized—and largely borne by those least able to do so. In the case of the coronavirus, the economic effects have already been felt across the entire nation—and it is going to get much worse.

But how could the country that became the "Arsenal of Democracy" during World War II in a matter of a few short years be so unprepared to deal with foreseen disasters big or small? The answer lies in the rise of the twin ideologies of free markets and balanced budget conservatism. It started with Reaganomics in the 1980s, but has since become the dominant approach to the economy espoused by both political parties. Over the past few decades we have witnessed the gradual dismantling of government institutions put in place during the New Deal and soon after World War II to control unfettered capitalism. While some of the destruction of public institutions has been explicit, such as the deregulation of finance and cuts to government programs (e.g., the welfare reform of 1996), a lot of it has taken the form of underfunding programs to support the claim that government programs don't work (e.g., the Veteran's Administration).

The Neoliberal Balanced-Budget Conservatism That Created This Disaster

For generations Americans have been told that our government doesn't have the money to pay for public services, provide health care, invest in our infrastructure, or provide income for seniors and low-income families. Just like a household, we are told, the government must balance its budget or else risk running up inflation and high levels of debt—and ultimately bankrupting our nation. We are at the mercy of bond markets and our biggest creditor, China, for our continued ability to borrow and keep the government open.

Republicans never really believed it—as evidenced by a long stream of targeted tax cuts, courtesy of Presidents Ronald Reagan through George W. Bush to Donald Trump. Each gave lip service to the Laffer curve—which is supposed to show that tax cuts for the rich will goose growth and increase tax revenues, just as jobs trickle down to the poor—but there's no evidence that any of their tax cuts did that; indeed inequality continued to grow on trend and the tax cuts never "paid for" themselves. The Republican anti-deficit stance is based purely on a desire to constrain government—what they call a "starve the beast" strategy: cut taxes to increase deficits that can then be used as justification for cutting social spending.

Paradoxically, Democrats—supposedly the Keynesian party—are the true believers of fiscal austerity. When they are in power, they really do aim for smaller deficits—and insist on "pay-fors" to offset any desirable proposals to help average folks. The original PayGo (Pay As You Go) legislation, enacted as part of the Omnibus Budget Reconciliation Act of 1990, required that legislation be "paid for" either through tax increases or cuts to other spending; otherwise it would trigger a sequestration, a process of across-the-board cuts in most government programs. It expired in 2002 but was renewed in 2010 by President Barack Obama with the support of the majority of Democrats. While some Democrats see PayGo as a way to prevent Republicans from cutting taxes without paying for them, in reality it never prevented "unfunded" tax cuts—with Trump's recent tax cuts for the rich the latest example.

Even some progressive economists maintain that spending has to be "paid for." They resist the call for a payroll tax holiday out of the fear it will bankrupt Social Security. They insist on tying popular progressive policies to new taxes on the rich or on financial transactions. They believe that while deficits may be necessary in times of crises or emergencies and low interest rates, it is irresponsible to run up Federal government debt. Even in the case of the Green New Deal (GND)—something that is literally critical to human survival—some progressive economists have formulated "pay-fors" as, for example, Robert Pollin does in his 2019 *American Prospect* article, "How Do We Pay for a Zero-Emissions Economy?." There he worries about "where to get $100 billion a year in new federal government funds" to pay for a U.S. GND, arguing that "these funds will need to come from someplace." He proposes to finance the GND—capable of delivering a zero emissions U.S. economy by 2050—through three public funding mechanisms: 50% of the funds through Federal Reserve green bond purchases; 25% through shifting funds out of the military budget; and 25% through a carbon tax. By contrast, our Modern Monetary Theory (MMT) approach argues that the challenge ahead is not to find the *funding* for the GND, but rather to move *resources* to the GND. We could support taxes, transfers of funds out of defense, or bond sales if they released resources to be used for the GND effort. But in our view, the issue is one not of *finding funds* but of *finding and mobilizing real resources through spending*.

The MMT Approach to Living Within Our Means

These economists are wrong. Government spending doesn't have to be "paid for" in the same way that households must finance their spending, as MMT has long explained. MMT, a macroeconomic theory which has risen to prominence since the Global Financial Crisis, holds that this difference between households and the sovereign issuer of the currency holds true in times of crises and also in normal times, regardless of the level of interest rates and existing levels of outstanding government bonds (i.e., national debt). The sovereign can never run out of finance. Period.

MMT has been thrust into the limelight with the response to the pandemic. Not only have Democrats and Republicans alike suddenly discovered a love for trillions of dollars of "unfunded" spending, but they are invoking MMT arguments, to boot. Even President Trump argued in defense of an unprecedented fiscal stimulus, saying that "[i]t's our money … it's our currency."

As they say, in the foxhole, there are no atheists. Everyone now suddenly seems to be a believer. But what many of the people now believe is not really MMT. Those who've jumped on the bandwagon take one of two positions (or both) on what MMT supposedly says:

- That deficits are okay in a recession;
- That deficits should be financed by "helicopter money" printing by the central bank.

As MMT has long demonstrated, a government with its own sovereign currency is not financially constrained, since it has a monopoly over the issuance of its currency. It's nonsensical to say that the government has run out of money, since a sovereign government spends its IOUs into existence. Further, there is no such thing as a "helicopter money" alternative to financing a fiscal stimulus package. "Helicopter money," a term coined by Milton Friedman, originally implied direct central bank payments to households. Today people use the term mostly to mean fiscal spending financed by "printing money." MMT does not propose to finance government spending by "printing money." Government spending always happens in the same way: Congress appropriates, then the Treasury and its fiscal agent—the Fed—ensure that the necessary payments are made. This involves the Fed crediting bank reserve accounts at the Fed, and banks crediting the demand deposits of recipients of Treasury spending. (Tax payments, on the other hand, lead to debits to both checking accounts and bank reserve accounts at the Fed.) A deficit implies a net credit to both checking and reserve accounts, while bond sales simply convert these into government bonds (i.e., savings accounts at the Fed). Government never spends by dropping bags of cash from helicopters. And it never spends by running the printing press. All government spending—including the stimulus spending that is already showing up in people's bank accounts—takes the form of credits by the Fed to bank reserves, and credits by private banks to the accounts of recipients.

Further, for MMT, a budget deficit is an outcome, not a goal or even a policy tool to be pulled out of the closet during a recession. Government should formulate its budget to pursue the public purpose: rising living standards, greening for sustainability, accessible health care for all, a social safety net for those who need it, and a job guarantee program to ensure that anyone who wants to work can find a good one at a living wage.

Most progressives also advocate for a strongly countercyclical role for spending (rising in bad times, falling in good)—and MMT agrees, and, indeed, sees the job guarantee as an essential component of that. Tax policy should also be set to achieve the public purpose: to promote equity and fairness (this means imposing progressive taxes), to incentivize behavior (promote the good, punish the bad), and to prevent inflation. That last one also plays a cyclical role: taxes should rise in robust expansions to dampen demand and fall in recessions to reduce "fiscal drag."

If spending is countercyclical (moving in the opposite direction of the business cycle) and taxing is procyclical (moving in the direction of the business cycle) to stabilize the economy, this does mean that the government's budget will be strongly countercyclical (moving toward surplus in expansions and toward deficit in recessions). This is desired by Keynesians and MMTers alike. But MMT argues that there's no such thing as some special kind of "deficit spending" to be used in a downturn or even a crisis. Indeed, when tax law and the budget are formulated, there is no way to know what the budgetary outcome will be—whether balanced, in surplus, or in deficit. We won't know until the end of the fiscal year (and even then, it will just be a first estimate) as the outcome will depend on the performance of the economy. And the spending will already have occurred before we even know the end-of-the-year budget balance.

The only sense in which government "pays for" spending is in terms of mobilizing real resources; a nation always pays for things in terms of the real output it can produce or can net import from others. When the economy is below full employment, as it certainly was even before the current crisis, government spending creates "free lunches" as it utilizes resources which would otherwise be left idle. Only at full employment does a country face trade-offs for real resource uses. Unemployment, therefore, indicates that a country lives below its means, leaving real output that could be produced "on the table." Full employment—the only measure that matters—means that the nation is living up to its means.

The Coronavirus and MMT Lessons

So what are some of the lessons we should learn so far from the coronavirus crisis?

Everyone now accepts that in a time of crisis, we throw fiscal austerity to the wind. It would be literally insane to let the economy crash and to doom millions of people to untimely death on the argument that we need "pay-fors" before we can attempt to counter the destruction wrought by the virus.

Yet, note that, if anything, the real constraints on government are actually more severe in a crisis like this than they are in normal times. Tens of millions of workers are sidelined and millions of business are completely shuttered. Our nation's ability to supply output has taken a huge hit. Our problem right now is that we may not be able to produce enough (or import enough—given that the pandemic is global) to satisfy our needs. Our problem really is not lack of finance, but lack of the real output we desperately need: hospital beds, masks, testing kits, safe places to quarantine those who are infected, and maybe even food, shelter, and clothing to support our population. In spite of all these real constraints, government has discovered that its ability to provide financial help is unlimited. Thank goodness!

In some sense we should be relearning the forgotten lessons of World War II. The war taught us that the constraint to government spending is the availability of real output—not a lack of finance. Keynes understood it and so did U.S. Treasury officials planning for the war. As Keynes aptly explained in *How to Pay for the War*, if available resources fall short of what is needed for the war effort and for civilian uses, the solution could not be found in finance. In this competition for limited resources, the government can always outbid the private sector. Prosecuting the war without an appropriate reduction or delay in private spending would simply cause inflation. Thus taxation and bond sales have to be implemented with a view of reducing and delaying demand, not to raise revenue for Treasury spending.

But the most important lesson we must learn is that the ability of the government to run deficits is not limited to times of crisis. We must finally accept that deficits are fine in normal times, just as we accept them to be necessary in times of crises and wars. Indeed, it was always crazy to think that in the normal times before this crisis hit, our government's ability to mobilize underutilized resources was limited by financial constraints. The real limits faced by government before the pandemic were far less constraining than the limits faced after the virus had brought a huge part of our productive capacity to a halt.

If we can learn this lesson, it will allow us to replace our reactive, "band-aid" approach to policymaking with a proactive use of the fiscal tools of spending and taxation with a view to their functions and the goal of ensuring full employment and other public purpose. In normal times we must build up our supplies, our infrastructure, and institutions to be able to deal with crises, whatever form they may take. We must not let mistaken analogies of household budgets to government budgets prevent us from preparing for the next inevitable disaster.

Our analysis above has important implications for policy proposals, such as the GND. Once the current crisis passes, detractors will predictably claim we can't afford the GND as government deficits and debt will surely have increased. We must not fall into that trap again; the size of the deficits or debt does not determine the nation's fiscal space. The latter is always about real resources. Further, we can push out those real resource constraints with appropriate policies, since there is nothing natural about them. Indeed, our refusal to fully utilize our capacity, whether labor or plant and equipment, leads to a loss of capacity and productivity, thus shrinking what really matters. If we have the real capacity and know-how to implement a GND, which we do have according to the experts, then we can afford it. The affordability of the GND is about real resources, not finance. It is irrational to fear deficits more than we fear the annihilation of human civilization.

Progressives have tried for decades to play the "pay-for" game. At best this has yielded subpar policy outcomes, such as Obamacare. At worst, these half-measures have prevented real solutions, such as Medicare for All, to even have a chance. Going forward, it is essential to decouple government spending and taxation and evaluate them based on their impact on the economy. Government must spend and tax with a view of achieving the public purpose, rather than abiding by some imaginary financial constraint. Disposing of the myths and acknowledging the real constraints will allow us to put our resources to work—and to keep them at work—to prepare for challenges, big or small. ❑

Sources: "Coronavirus in the U.S.: Latest Map and Case Count," *New York Times* website (ongoing updates); Suzanne Smalley, "Senator says White House turned down emergency coronavirus funding in early February," Yahoo News, March 29, 2020; Amy Goldstein, Lena H. Sun, and Beth Reinhard, "Desperate for Medical Equipment, States Find a Beleaguered National Stockpile," *Washington Post*, March 28, 2020; President Donald J. Trump, White House briefing, March 27, 2020; Robert Pollin, "How Do We Pay for a Zero-Emissions Economy?" *The American Prospect*, December 5, 2019; Peter Borfinger, "Coronavirus crisis: now is the hour of Modern Monetary Theory, International Politics and Society, March 27, 2020; John Maynard Keynes, *How to Pay for the War*, (MacMillan & Co., 1940); Yeva Nersisyan and L. Randall Wray, "How to Pay for the Green New Deal," Levy Institute Working Paper, May 2019; Willem H. Buiter, "The Helicopters Are Coming," Project Syndicate, March 26, 2020; Sam Levey, Modern Money and the War Treasury, Global Institute for Sustainable Prosperity Working Paper No. 123, August 2019.

Article 7.3

WHAT IS MONEY?

BY DOUG ORR
November/December 1993; revised October 2010

We all use money every day. Yet many people do not know what money actually is. There are many myths about money, including the idea that the government "prints" all of it and that it has some intrinsic value. But actually, money is less a matter of value, and more a matter of faith.

Money is sometimes called the universal commodity, because it can be traded for all other commodities. But for this to happen, everyone in society must believe that money will be accepted. If people stop believing that it will be accepted, the existing money ceases to be money. Recently in Poland, people stopped accepting the zloty, and used vodka as money instead.

In addition to facilitating exchanges, money allows us to "store" value from one point in time to another. If you sell your car today for $4,000, you probably won't buy that amount of other products today. Rather, you store the value as money, probably in a bank, until you want to use it.

The "things" that get used as money have changed over time, and "modern" people often chuckle when they hear about some of them. The Romans used salt (from which we get the word "salary"), South Sea Islanders used shark's teeth, and several societies actually used cows. The Three Wise Men brought gold, frankincense, and myrrh, each of which was money in different regions at the time.

If money does not exist, or is in short supply, it will be created. In prisoner of war camps, where guards specifically outlaw its existence, prisoners use cigarettes instead. In the American colonies, the British attempted to limit the supply of British pounds, because they knew that by limiting the supply of money, they could hamper the development of independent markets in the colonies. Today, the United States uses a similar policy, through the International Monetary Fund, in dealing with Latin America.

To overcome this problem, the colonists began to use tobacco leaves as money. This helped the colonies to develop, but it also allowed the holders of large plots of land to grow their own money! When the colonies gained independence, the new government decreed gold to be money, rather than tobacco, much to the dismay of Southern plantation owners. Now, rather than growing money, farmers had to find or buy it.

To aid the use of gold as money, banks would test its purity, put it in storage, and give the depositor paper certificates of ownership. These certificates, "paper money," could then be used in place of the gold itself. Since any bank could store gold and issue certificates, by the beginning of the Civil War, over 7,000 different types of "paper money" were in circulation in the United States, none of it printed by the government.

While paper money is easier to use than gold, it is still risky to carry around large amounts of cash. It is safer to store the paper in a bank and simply sign over its ownership to make a purchase. We sign over the ownership of our money by writing a check. Checking account money became popular when, in an unsuccessful attempt to control the amount of money created by banks, the government outlawed the printing of paper money by private banks in 1864.

How Banks Create Money

Banks are central to understanding money, because in addition to storing it, they help to create it. Bankers realize that not everyone will withdraw their money at the same time, so they loan out much of the money that has been deposited. It is from the interest on these loans that banks get their profits, and through these loans the banking system creates new money.

If you deposit $100 cash in your checking account at Chase Manhattan Bank, you still have $100 in money to use, because checks are also accepted as money. Chase must set aside some of this cash as "reserves," in case you or other depositors decide to withdraw money as cash. Current regulations issued by the Federal Reserve Bank (the Fed) require banks to set aside an average of three cents out of each dollar. So Chase can make a loan of $97, based on your deposit. Chase does not make loans by handing out cash but instead by putting $97 in the checking account of the person, say Emily, who is taking out the loan. So from your initial deposit of $100 in cash, the economy now has $197 in checking account money.

The borrower, Emily, pays $97 for some product or service by check, and the seller, say Ace Computers, deposits the money in its checking account. The total amount of checking account money is still $197, but its location and ownership have changed. If Ace Computer's account is at Citibank, $97 in cash is transferred from Chase to Citibank. This leaves just $3 in cash reserves at Chase to cover your original deposit. However, Citibank now has $97 in "new" cash on hand, so it sets aside three cents on the dollar ($2.91) and loans out the rest, $94.09, as new checking account money. Through this process, every dollar of "reserves" yields many dollars in total money.

If you think this is just a shell game and there is only $100 in "real" money, you still don't understand money. Anything that is accepted as payment for a transaction is "real" money. Cash is no more real than checking account money. In fact, most car rental companies will not accept cash as payment for a car, so for them, cash is not money!

As of June 2010, there was $883 billion of U.S. currency, i.e., "paper money," in existence. However, somewhere between 50% to 70% of it is held outside of the United States by foreign banks and individuals. U.S. $100 bills are the preferred currency of choice used to facilitate illegal international transactions, such as the drug trade. The vast majority of all money actually in use in the United States is not cash, but rather checking account money. This type of money, $1,590 billion, was created by private banks, and was not "printed" by anyone. In fact, this money exists only as electronic "bits" in banks' computers. (The less "modern" South Sea Islanders could have quite a chuckle about that!)

The amount of money that banks can create is limited by the total amount of reserves, and by the fraction of each deposit that must be held as reserves. Prior to

1914, bankers themselves decided what fraction of deposits to hold as reserves. Since then, this fraction has been set by the main banking regulator, the Fed.

Until 1934, gold was held as reserves, but the supply of gold was unstable, growing rapidly during the California and Alaska "gold rushes," and very slowly at other times. As a result, at times more money was created than the economy needed, and at other times not enough money could be created. Starting in 1934, the U.S. government decided that gold would no longer be used as reserves. Cash, now printed by the Fed, could no longer be redeemed for gold, and cash itself became the reserve asset.

Banks, fearing robberies, do not hold all of their cash reserves in their own vaults. Rather, they store it in an account at a regional Fed bank. These accounts count as reserves. What banks do hold in their vaults is their other assets, such as Treasury bonds and corporate bonds.

The Fed and Bank Reserves

The only role of the government in creating money is indirectly through the Fed, which is controlled by neither the Congress nor the executive branch. If the Fed wants to expand the money supply, it must increase bank reserves. To do this, the Fed buys Treasury bonds from a bank, and pays with a check drawn on the Fed itself. By depositing the check in its reserve account at the Fed, the bank now has more reserves, so the bank can now make more loans and create new checking account money.

By controlling the amount of reserves, the Fed attempts to control the size of the money supply. But as recent history has shown, this control is limited. During the late 1970s, the Fed tried to limit the amount of money banks could create by reducing reserves, but banks simply created new forms of money, just like the POW camp prisoners and colonial farmers. In 1979, there was only one form of checking account money. Today, there are many, with odd names such as NOWs, ATSs, repos, and money market deposit accounts. If there is a profit to be made creating money, banks will find a way.

In 2010, we have the opposite problem. The Fed is trying to expand the money supply, but banks are refusing to create new money. In good times, banks hold as few reserves as possible, so they can profit from making loans. In times of crisis, banks fear that we will lose faith in the commercial banking system and all try to take out our "money" as cash. Since there is far more electronic money than cash, this is impossible. But if the bank cannot give us our money in the form we want it, the bank fails and ceases to exist. Since the start of 2007, over 300 banks, with assets totalling more than $637 billion, have failed.

Since all banks fear they will be next, they want as many reserves as possible. Excess reserves are any reserves above those required by the Fed. During the 1990s, these averaged about $1 billion for the entire banking system. During the crisis of 2001, they spiked to the then unheard of level of $19 billion. As of June 2010, excess reserves in the banking system were $1,035 billion! This is the classic case of trying to push on a string. The Fed can create reserves, but only banks can create money and they are not yet willing to make any new loans.

These amorphous forms of money function only because we believe they will function, which is why the continued stability of the banking system is so critical. While it is true that the bailout of the banking system was not handled very well, and that many people who created the crisis are still profiting from it, the bailout was a necessary evil. In a modern market economy, banks create the money, and no market economy can function without its money. Money only exists if we believe in it, so we have to maintain the faith. To maintain the faith we need more democratic control over money creation, which can only come if regulation of the financial system is greatly expanded. ❏

Sources: Money supply: Federal Reserve Board, www.federalreserve.gov/releases/h6/current/; excess reserves: St. Louis Federal Reserve Bank, research.stlouisfed.org/fred2/series/EXCRESNS; bank failures: Federal Deposit Insurance Corporation (FDIC), www.fdic.gov/bank/individual/failed/banklist.html.

Article 7.4

SHOULD WE BLAME "FRACTIONAL RESERVE" BANKING?

BY ARTHUR MacEWAN
May/June 2013

> Dear Dr. Dollar:
>
> *I have seen various arguments (on the internet, for example) that a prime cause of our economic problems (inequality, crises, mass unemployment, the immense power of the banks, etc.) is our monetary system. In particular, that it is a "fractional reserve system," in which "money is created out of thin air." Could you comment?*
>
> —Mike Smith, New York, N.Y.

The last several years, when banks and the whole financial system have been at the core of economic disruption, could easily lead one to see the monetary system as central to our economic problems.

Keep in mind, however, that we have had essentially the same monetary system for decades, the Federal Reserve has existed for 100 years, and the "fractional reserve" system existed before the Fed. During these earlier eras, including periods when we relied on the gold standard as the basis of our monetary system, we have had depressions, inflation, severe inequality, and excessive power in the hands of finance and large corporations generally. We have also had some relatively good times—periods of stable economic growth, less economic inequality, lower unemployment, and less power and profits for the banks. So, whatever is wrong with our monetary system (and there are certainly things that are wrong), the explanation of our economic problems must be more complex.

But what is the fractional reserve system? Basically, it is the system by which banks keep as reserves only a fraction of the amount of deposits that their customers have with the banks. Banks can do this because at any time their customers will demand only a fraction of those total obligations. When, for example, you deposit $100 in the bank, the bank will loan out to someone else perhaps $90 of that $100. This $90 is new money that the bank has created. The person or business taking this loan then deposits the $90 in another account with the bank or another bank altogether, allowing a new loan of $81 to be generated by the banking system; the remaining $9 (10% of the deposit) will be kept as reserves. And so on.

By this process, if people are willing to take out the loans, the banks can create an additional $900 of money based on an original deposit of $100. This is sometimes called "creating money out of thin air." In fact, it is creating money on the basis of 10% reserves.

If banks were left to their own devices, competition would create pressure to push down the reserve ratio—they could, for example, make twice the amount of loans were they to reduce their reserves from 10% to 5% of obligations. However, the Federal Reserve has a great deal of authority over what the banks can do. It sets the reserve ratio. Banks cannot simply lower the amount of reserves to make more loans. (The actual reserve ratio varies depending on type of obligation; 10% is just an example that makes calculations easy.) Most frequently, the Fed affects the supply of money by buying bonds from the banks, thus increasing the banks' reserves (and enabling them to lend more), or selling bonds to the banks, thus reducing the banks' reserves.

That's the formal way it works. Although critics of a fractional reserve system claim it "debases the currency" (i.e., leads to inflation), it does not automatically allow the banks to create more and more money without limits, which could indeed generate severe inflation. The U.S. economy has experienced mild inflation for most of the last century (averaging 3.2% annually), but fractional reserve banking is not generally associated with high "runaway" inflation. Ironically, in light of the claims of the critics, the Fed has often followed policies that work in exactly the opposite direction—restricting the banks' ability to create money, thus restricting the loans they can make, and restraining economic growth and employment. (After all, neither banks nor other large corporations like severe inflation.)

But of course the formal way the system works is not the whole story. The banks themselves and other big firms have a great deal of influence over what the Fed does. So the Fed usually regulates the banks with a very light hand. In the Great Recession, in particular, the Fed (along with the U.S. Treasury) provided the banks with funds to meet their obligations when many of those banks would have otherwise failed. In this respect, the way the Fed works is not so different from the way the government works in general—money has a great deal of influence over policy.

It would be nice if our economic problems were so simple that they could be solved by some reorganization of our monetary system. But the problems are bigger and deeper. ❑

Article 7.5

PUSHING ON STRINGS

The explosion of U.S. banks' excess reserves since 2008 illustrates the dramatic failure of monetary policy.

BY GERALD FRIEDMAN
May/June 2009; updated June 2018

Monetary policy is not working. Since the economic crisis began in July 2007, the Federal Reserve has dramatically cut interest rates and pumped out over $1 trillion, increasing the money supply by over 15% in less than two years. These vast sums have failed to revive the economy because the banks have been hoarding liquidity rather than lending.

The Fed requires that banks hold money on reserve to back up deposits and other bank liabilities. In the past, beyond these required reserves, banks would hold very small amounts of excess reserves, holdings that they minimized because reserves earn very little or no interest. Between the 1950s and September 2008, U.S. banks held over $5 billion in total excess reserves only once, after the September 11 attacks. This changed with the collapse of Lehman Brothers. Beginning with less than $2 billion in August 2008, excess reserves soared to $60 billion in September and then to $559 billion in November before peaking at $798 billion in January 2009. (They had dropped to $644 billion by the time this article was written.)

This explosion of excess reserves represents a signal change in bank policy that threatens the effectiveness of monetary policy in the current economic crisis. Aware of their own financial vulnerability, even insolvency, frightened bank managers

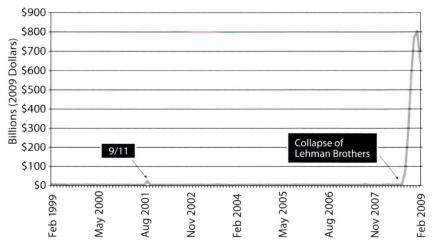

BANK EXCESS RESERVES SINCE 1999

Source: "Excess Reserves of Depository Institutions," Federal Reserve Bank of St. Louis, research.stlouisfed.org.

responded to the collapse of major investment houses like Lehman Brothers by grabbing and hoarding all the cash that they could get. At the same time, a general loss of confidence and spreading economic collapse persuaded banks that there are few to whom they could lend with confidence that the loans would be repaid. Clearly, our banks have decided that they need, or at least want, the money more than consumers and productive businesses do.

Banks could have been investing this money by lending to businesses that needed liquidity to buy material inputs or pay workers. Had they done so, monetarist economists would be shouting from the rooftops, or at least in the university halls, about how monetary policy prevented another Great Depression. Instead, even the *Wall Street Journal* is proclaiming that "We're All Keynesians Again" because monetary policy has failed. Monetary authorities, the *Wall Street Journal* explains, can create money but they cannot force banks to lend or to invest it in productive activities. The Federal Reserve confronts a reality shown in the graph above: it can't "push on a string," as Fed Chair Marriner Eccles famously put it during his testimony before Congress in 1935, in the depths of the Great Depression.

If the banks won't lend, then we need more than monetary policy to get out of the current crisis. No bailout, no Troubled Asset Relief Program (TARP), can revive the economy if banks hoard all of the cash they receive. The Obama-era stimulus was an appropriate response to the failure of string-pushing. But much more government stimulus will be needed to solve a crisis this large, and we will need programs to move liquidity from bank vaults to businesses and consumers. It may be time to stop waiting on the banks, and to start telling them what to do with our money.

Update, June 2018

Ten years after the onset of the Great Recession, sometimes called the Lesser Depression, we can better appreciate the limits of monetary policy in stimulating a depressed economy. Four years after the 2008 crash, the Federal Reserve pushed money into the economy in hopes of stimulating investment. While not a complete failure, the Fed's monetary policy did little to stimulate the economy, with investment demand in particular continuing to lag in what has been the slowest economic recovery since World War II. The failure of monetary policy, not only in the United States but in Japan and Europe as well, has led even many orthodox economists, notably Paul Krugman and Larry Summers, to warn that the United States has entered a period of "secular stagnation" where the rate of return has fallen so low that the interest rate cannot drop to a level where capitalists can profit from new investment. With the return on investment this slow, the economy has fallen into what John Maynard Keynes, and Krugman, call a "liquidity trap," a situation where there is so little demand for investment that further increases in the money supply will simply go into idle cash reserves rather than new economic activity. In such a situation, monetary authorities can do little but "push on strings" because only active fiscal policy can provide economic stimulus by substituting government spending for failing private investment. Inadequate fiscal stimulus in the United States and, even more, in Europe, accounts for the slow economic recovery from the Lesser Depression despite active monetary stimulus. ❑

Article 7.6

KEYNES AND THE LIMITS OF MONETARY POLICY

BY ALEJANDRO REUSS
April 2009

As the United States has plunged into financial crisis and the deepest recession since the Great Depression, the U.S. Federal Reserve (the "Fed") has pursued an aggressively "expansionary" monetary policy. Monetary policy refers to government policies affecting the money supply or interest rates. Expansionary monetary policy is aimed at increasing the money supply or lowering interest rates. The idea is that, by lowering interest rates, the government can stimulate investment (such as firms' purchases of new equipment and construction of new plants). Projects that would not be profitable for a company if it had to borrow at a higher interest rate could be profitable if borrowing were less costly. Policymakers at the Fed hope, then, that lower interest rates will encourage investment and bring about renewed economic growth.

The main interest rate that the Fed targets is the "federal funds rate," the interest rate that banks charge each other for overnight loans. For all of 2006 and 2007, the federal funds rate stood at over 4%. Throughout 2008, as the financial crisis and recession grew deeper, the Fed moved aggressively to cut interest rates. By the end of the year, the federal funds rate was 0.0%–0.25%, where it remains today. Even with the federal funds rate basically at zero, however, the economy has spiraled deeper into recession. Gross domestic product (GDP) shrank at an annual rate of 6.2% in the fourth quarter of 2008 and the official unemployment rate climbed to 8.5% by March 2009.

Are Interest Rates Coming Down?

Firms and consumers cannot borrow at the federal funds rate. Then why does the Fed try to bring down the federal funds rate when it wants to stimulate economic activity? Fed policymakers hope that by pulling down very short-term interest rates that do not directly affect firms and consumers, they can indirectly pull down longer-term interest rates that are important to firms and consumers.

Interest rates on 30-year fixed-rate mortgages have declined, reaching historic lows under 5% in March 2009. The low mortgage rates, however, may be deceptive. Mortgage lenders have generally tightened lending standards, and the low rates are only available to borrowers that banks consider very safe. Other borrowers may pay rates several percentage points higher, or be unable to borrow at all. Meanwhile, banks have raised credit card interest rates and dramatically tightened borrowing limits.

Key corporate interest rates have not come down as the Fed hoped. Moody's AAA bond rate, an index of the interest rates on long-term bonds for low-risk corporate borrowers, was about the same in March 2009 as in January 2008 (about 5.3%). Moody's Baa bond rate, the equivalent index for higher-risk corporate borrowers, has gone from about 6.5% in January 2008 to over 8% in March 2009. The spreads between these rates and the federal funds rate have increased dramatically as the federal funds rate has fallen.

That would come as no surprise to John Maynard Keynes. Keynes argued, in *The General Theory of Employment, Interest, and Money*, that during boom periods the general estimation of risk by both lenders and borrowers is "apt to become unusually and imprudently low." Lenders loan out money freely, even recklessly, accepting a low rate of interest relative to the risk involved. During crisis periods, on the other hand, lenders often become much more risk averse, parting with their money less freely, and insisting on a higher rate of interest in exchange for the risk of not being paid back. This is sometimes known as the "flight to liquidity" or "flight to safety." Keynes' analysis suggests that during economic crises the interest rates on assets that are considered very safe—like government bonds—are apt to go down, since people are looking to avoid losses and willing to accept a low rate of return to do so. But the interest rates on riskier assets may go up. A rise in the interest rates that firms or consumers pay would tend to deepen—rather than correct—an economic downturn.

Can't the Fed Do More?

If interest rates are not low enough to turn the economy around, then why doesn't the Fed increase the money supply some more—until interest rates *are* low enough? The answer is that nominal interest rates can reach a lower bound below which they cannot decline further. (The "nominal" interest rate, in contrast to the "real" interest rate, does not account for changes in the purchasing power of the dollar due to inflation.) This lower bound can be greater than 0%, but cannot be lower than 0%. The federal funds rate is now about 0%. When interest rates reach this lower limit, the economy is commonly described as being caught in a "liquidity trap."

People hold their wealth in the form of bonds rather than money because they can earn interest on bonds. For example, you may be able to buy a bond for $100 that promises a payment of $110 in one year. That gives you a 10% annual interest rate (you loaned the bond issuer $100 for a year, and at the end of the year you get your $100 back plus $10 in interest). That is the incentive to buy the bond instead of just holding money.

Suppose the Fed wants to lower interest rates to stimulate spending. It offers to buy government bonds (previously sold to the public) at a higher price, driving down the interest rate. For instance, the Fed might offer $110 for bonds that promise $110 in one year. If you were to buy such a bond at the new price of $110, you would receive the same amount of money back a year later. The interest rate on that bond is now 0%. The idea of the policy is that banks will sell their government bonds to the Fed at the new higher price, take the money and buy other bonds (such as those issued by corporations), driving up their price and lowering the interest rate on those bonds.

Imagine that the Fed, however, decided that an interest rate of 0% was not low enough, and decided instead to pay banks $120 for bonds that promise $110 in a year. The banks would gladly sell their bonds, so the money supply would increase. But they would not loan out the money they received at a negative interest rate (paying consumers or firms to borrow from them). They would be better off just keeping the money in their vaults. In other words, once the interest rate reaches 0%, there is nothing more that the government can do with conventional expansionary monetary policy. That is the liquidity trap—any extra liquidity (money) the Fed makes available gets trapped, instead of being loaned out.

Monetary Policy and Interest Rates Today

Economic journalists and commentators have inaccurately described "interest rates" as being at or near 0% these days. The federal funds rate has hit rock bottom, but other interest rates clearly have not. Keynes was acutely aware that, when monetary authorities limit themselves to buying short-term securities, the "effect may ... be mainly confined to the very short-term rate of interest and have but little reaction on the much more important long-term rates of interest."

In a famous passage in *The General Theory*, Keynes notes the possibility that "after the rate of interest has fallen to a certain level ... almost everyone prefers cash to holding a debt which yields so low a rate of interest." This passage is often taken to be Keynes' description of the liquidity trap. He goes on to say that he did not know of any case when this had actually happened and notes that it is not likely to happen "owing to the unwillingness of most monetary authorities to deal boldly in debts of long term." It is clear from this passage that Keynes was not describing merely a situation in which certain short-term interest rates targeted by the government (such as the federal funds rate) were pushed to their lower limits, but rather one in which all interest rates hit rock bottom—a different situation from what is commonly referred to as a "liquidity trap" today.

Keynes viewed monetary policymakers' focus on certain short-run interest rates not as an inherent limitation in monetary policy, but as a limitation in the ways monetary policy was conventionally practiced. He notes that governments did not usually buy long-term bonds and drive down long-term interest rates, but that there was no reason they could not. In March, the Fed actually began to do just that, buying billions in long-term government securities in an attempt to bring down long-term rates. The 10-year Treasury bond rate dropped dramatically (from about 3% to 2.5%) the day the purchases began. It has increased somewhat since then, but remains lower than it was before November 2008.

Any attempt to revive private investment by manipulating interest rates, however, faces at least two additional barriers:

First, the interest rates consumers and firms pay do not move in lockstep with interest rates on government securities, either short-term or long-term. The contrast between short-term and long-term bonds is not the same as the difference between relatively safe government bonds and riskier corporate bonds or consumer loans. As we have seen, interest rates on corporate bonds have failed to decline, even as rates on long-term government bonds have declined. Banks' consumer lending standards, likewise, have tightened even as the Fed has driven down interest rates on government bonds.

Second, economic activity simply may not change dramatically in response to changes in interest rates, especially during a recession. Expectations of future sales and profits are extremely negative, so firms are dramatically slashing payrolls and investment spending. Total employment has decreased by over half a million people for each of five consecutive months from November 2008 to March 2009. Nonresidential fixed investment decreased by over 20% in the last quarter of 2008; investment in nonresidential structures by nearly 10%. Firms have inventories they cannot sell, are laying off workers, and are producing below their existing productive capacity. Most of them are not going to make large investments in new plants and equipment under such conditions.

For these reasons, Keynesian economists have advocated a very large fiscal stimulus. Fiscal policy, in contrast to monetary policy, involves government spending and taxation. A fiscal stimulus program involves increases in government spending or reductions in taxes. Keynesian economists, believing that monetary policy is not adequate to pull the economy out of its current crisis, have argued especially for a dramatic increase in government spending as the surest way to revive overall spending, production, and employment. ❏

Sources: John Maynard Keynes, *The General Theory of Employment, Interest, and Money* (Harcourt, 1964); The Federal Reserve Bank, Intended federal funds rate, Change and level, 1990 to present; Bureau of Economic Analysis, News Release: Gross Domestic Product (GDP) and Corporate Profits, March 26, 2009; Bureau of Labor Statistics, Table A-12, Alternative measures of labor underutilization; Luke Mullins, "Banks Tighten Mortgage Lending Standards," *U.S. News & World Report*, Feb. 2, 2009; Jeannine Aversa and Alan Zibel, "Mortgage rates down, but standards remain high," Associated Press, Press-Telegram, March 19, 2009; Bob Tedeschi, "Mortgages: 'Cashing Out' is Now Harder," *New York Times*, March 19, 2009; Kathy Chu, "Changing credit card terms squeeze consumers," *USA Today*, Dec. 16, 2008; Jane J. Kim, "BofA to Boost Rates on Cards With Balances," *Wall Street Journal*, April 9, 2009; Federal Reserve Bank of St. Louis, Moody's Seasoned Aaa Corporate Bond Yield; Federal Reserve Bank of St. Louis, Moody's Seasoned Baa Corporate Bond Yield; Paul Krugman (blog), "Spreads," Jan. 19, 2009; Jon Hilsenrath, "Fed in Bond-Buying Binge to Spur Growth," *Wall Street Journal*, March 19, 2009; Paul Krugman, "Return of depression economics," *New York Times*, March 4, 2009; Federal Reserve Bank of St. Louis, Ten-Year Treasury Constant Maturity Rate; Bureau of Labor Statistics, Payroll Employment; Bureau of Economic Analysis, News Release: Gross Domestic Product (GDP) and Corporate Profits, March 26, 2009.

Article 7.7

DOLLAR DOMINANCE

BY ARTHUR MacEWAN
January/February 2015

> Dear Dr. Dollar:
> *What does it mean that the dollar is the "dominant" global currency? Why does this situation exist? And how does it matter?*
> —Anonymous

Suppose that, when you paid for things with checks, all the recipients of those checks believed that you were a very responsible person, and that you would keep plenty of money in the bank to honor those checks. Moreover, not only did the check recipients believe in you, but people in general had this same opinion.

Under these circumstances, the people holding your checks wouldn't have to cash them in. Those checks could simply be used as money. The checks themselves would be acceptable in transactions among all those people who believed you were so responsible.

This situation would be nice for you because you could write plenty of checks and not worry about those checks being cashed in against your account, which would also mean that you would have extra buying power. At the same time, the people who used your checks as money would have an easier time with transactions, having your checks as a widely acceptable form of currency—i.e., they would have more "liquidity." Also, holding onto your checks—keeping them "in reserve"—would be a safe way for people to store money for when they needed it.

Fiction and Reality

To a large extent, this fictional situation with your checks is analogous to the real situation of the U.S. dollar in global commerce. With people and banks around the world using dollars and holding dollars, not "cashing them in" for U.S. goods, the United States—primarily its government and businesses—is able to spend more abroad without giving up so much in goods and services produced in the United States. Governments, businesses, and people around the world have more liquidity than they would otherwise, and they have more confidence than they would otherwise in the value of the currency (dollars) they are using and holding in reserve.

Like you in the fictional scenario, the U.S. government in the real scenario is viewed as "responsible." An important part of the U.S. government being viewed as "responsible" is that it would keep the value of the dollar relatively stable—i.e., not much inflation (at least compared to other currencies). This organization of the global finance system, with the dollar in this special, or dominant, position has an interesting history—and some powerful implications.

Where Did This System Come From?

The crucial formal step in creating the dollar-dominated system came at the end of World War II, with the United States in an extremely strong economic position. Indeed, the high level of government spending on the war had brought the U.S. economy out of the Great Depression, while other high-income countries (and many low-income countries) had had their economies physically decimated by the war. Combined with this economic power, the United States had extreme military power. Thus, the era following World War II came to be called "The American Century" (of course it was not really a full century, but let's not quibble).

As the end of the war was coming into sight, in July 1944, representatives of the U.S. government and of 43 allied governments (over 700 delegates in all) met over three weeks at the Mt. Washington Hotel in Bretton Woods, N.H. The purpose of this conference was to set up the arrangements for the operation of the global economy in the postwar era. Although the Soviet Union and China were both represented at the Bretton Woods conference, in subsequent years they did not take part in the arrangements. (Today you can go to Bretton Woods and, at the entrance to the hotel's driveway, see the sign commemorating this conference, but you have to pay an entrance fee to actually get onto the hotel grounds.)

Unsurprisingly, given the relative economic and political power of the allied governments, the U.S. government basically dictated the conference outcomes, arrangements by which commerce among capitalist countries would be organized in the decades following World War II—the "Bretton Woods era." The central feature of these arrangements was that the dollar would be at the core of global commerce. Other countries' currencies would be "pegged" to the dollar, which meant that each government would set the value of its currency in terms of the dollar. For example, in 1949 the French franc was pegged at $0.37 and the British pound at $2.80. The dollar itself was set in relation to gold: $34 to the ounce. Other countries' banks could redeem their dollars for gold at this rate, but, as with your checks, they generally didn't do so. When the gold redemption promise was terminated in 1971, it turned out not to make much difference—more on that in a moment.

Of course, economies change in relation to one another. In the postwar era, different rates of inflation and different rates of productivity growth meant that the values of the currencies in terms of the dollar had to be changed from time to time. For example, if France was running a trade deficit with the rest of the world (importing more than it was exporting), this meant that the value of its franc was too high in relation to the dollar—i.e., in terms of dollars, the cost of French goods was too high and France's exports would be low, while the cost for France of goods from elsewhere would be too low and France's imports would be high. Moreover, with French exports not paying for its imports, France would necessarily build up a foreign debt to pay for the excess imports.

One could look at this franc-dollar relationship another way: instead of the franc being too high, one could say that the dollar was too low. But the rules that were established at Bretton Woods excluded the dollar from having to adjust. In this example, it was the French who would have to adjust the value of their currency—i.e., France would have to devalue its currency. And, importantly, it would have to borrow to cover the foreign debt it had built up. The U.S. economy, on the other hand, was protected from the disruption that would have been caused by changing the value of the dollar.

The International Monetary Fund (IMF) was established at Bretton Woods to provide countries in this kind of situation with the loans they needed. The IMF provided these loans, but with various conditions—in particular that the country taking the loans would have to take steps to reorganize their economies, generally in ways that opened them to more foreign commerce, trade, and investment.

While the IMF did play a role in European adjustments, its actions became especially important in lower-income countries, where it used its loan conditions to push countries towards a greater openness to international investment and trade—very much in the interests of multinational firms based in the richer countries. (The World Bank was also created at Bretton Woods, but its role is not a central part of the story here.)

Change Without Change

The Bretton Woods rules of the game worked fairly well for 25 years. In fact, from the perspective of the United States, one might say they worked too well. While the Bretton Woods system promoted U.S. commerce, opening up trade and investment opportunities around the (capitalist) world, it also provided a stability in global affairs in which firms based elsewhere—in Japan and Europe—were able to also expand and ultimately challenge the dominant position of U.S firms.

A critical juncture in global commercial arrangements then came in 1971: the Bretton Woods system fell apart. A combination of heavy spending abroad by the U.S. government (on the Vietnam War), the economic challenge from other rich countries, and inflation in the United States led the U.S. government to drop its promise of redeeming dollars for gold. Yet, while the system fell apart, there was surprisingly little change in international trade and investment. The relative economic and military power of the United States, though not as extreme as it had been in the immediate post-World War II era, continued. And the perceived threat of the Soviet Union served as a glue, binding the world's major capitalist powers in Europe and Asia to the United States, and leading them to accept continued U.S. economic, as well as military, dominance.

After 1971, various new arrangements were put in place—for example, a system of partially managed "pegs" was established. Yet the dollar remained the central currency of global commerce. Prices of internationally traded goods—most importantly oil—continued to be set in dollars, and countries continued to hold their reserves in dollars.

Although 1971 marked the beginning of a new era in international financial arrangements, the dollar retained its dominant position. Regardless of the various economic problems in the United States, the dollar has remained both relatively stable and in sufficient supply to grease the wheels of international commerce. Indeed, an ironic example of the continuing role of the dollar came in the Great Recession that began in 2008. Even while the U.S. economy was in the doldrums, businesses and governments elsewhere in the world were buying U.S. government bonds—a principal means of holding their reserves in dollars—since they still considered these the safest assets available.

Power and a Symbol of Power

In the years leading up to the Great Recession, China entered the global for-profit economy and was exporting at a high rate, exceeding its imports. The Chinese government used the extra money that China was obtaining from its trade surplus to heavily invest in U.S. government bonds. That is, China built up extensive reserves in dollars. In effect, China was loaning money to the United States—loans which filled both the federal budget deficit and the U.S trade deficit. What many observers decried as a dangerous situation (We are becoming indebted to the Chinese! Horror!) in fact served both the U.S. and Chinese governments quite well.

The international role of the dollar is a symbol of U.S. power and is based on that power. At the same time, the dollar's role works to enhance that power, giving the U.S. government and U.S. businesses the liquidity needed for carrying out global operations—everything from wars to benign commerce.

There are problems with the system. The continued role of the dollar depends to a large extent on the avoidance of significant inflation in the United States. Yet restraints on inflation—e.g., the Federal Reserve raising interest rates—generally work against expanding employment. So maintaining the role of the dollar can come at the expense of most people in the country.

Also, there is always the risk of change. Just as the position of the dollar supports U.S. power in world affairs, if that position is undermined, U.S. power would suffer. In recent years, there has been some threat that other governments would challenge the dollar with their own currencies. China, in particular, has attempted to establish its own positon in world affairs, which, if successful, could ultimately undercut the dominance of the dollar. Indeed, the fear associated with China holding reserves in dollars (i.e., as U.S. government bonds) is to some extent based on concern about the potential implications of China shifting out of dollars (or threatening to do so). Yet, especially with the recent weakening of the Chinese economy, this particular challenge does not appear likely in the near future.

Over the last several decades, the role of the dollar in world affairs has become like the role of the English language. Both developed as a consequence of the extreme power of the United States in the global economy, and both give advantages to the U.S. government, U.S. firms, and to any individuals engaged in international activities. Most important, the roles of both the dollar and the English language have become thoroughly entrenched. Even as the power of the United States weakens, those roles are likely to continue for some time to come. ❏

Chapter 8

FINANCE, SAVINGS, AND INVESTMENT

INTRODUCTION

In the orderly world of neoclassical macroeconomics, capital markets—governed by all-powerful interest rates—work seamlessly to assure that savings is matched by investment, fueling growth in the private economy, which in turn guarantees full employment. Should the flow of saving exceed the uptake of investment, falling interest rates automatically solve the problem.

In the real world, economies are far messier than neoclassical macroeconomics suggests. Keynes argued that there is no neat connection, or "nexus," between savings and investment in a modern financial economy. Savings often sit, hoarded and uninvested. And interest rates, no matter how low, seldom coax reluctant investors to lay out their money in a weak economy. In the Keynesian world, economies regularly suffer from investment shortfalls that lead to recessions and cost workers their jobs.

Ramaa Vasudevan (Article 8.1) provides a primer on the increased importance of financial markets, financial institutions, and financial elites in today's economy and its governing institutions. The fact that failed financial corporations have received massive bailouts, for Vasudevan, only underlines the power they wield in the era of "financialization."

Next, Gerald Epstein (Article 8.2) discusses not only the dramatic growth in the size of the financial sector, but also the transformation from regulated "boring" banking to deregulated "roaring" banking. Epstein argues that the current system has ill-served the economy and society, and calls for the regulation of private finance and the development of alternative financial institutions as two parts of the needed solution.

Then, in Article 8.3, John Miller examines the stock market in the wake of the Covid-19 pandemic, and why the stock market doesn't reflect the on-the-ground reality that many in the United States face. He points to the absence of other investment opportunities, as well as Fed policies that have kept interest rates down, as two of the causes of this discrepancy. Miller also explains how this has contributed to further increases in inequality.

Next, Arthur MacEwan (Article 8.4) tackles the issue of stock "buybacks" by corporations, which have grown dramatically in recent years. Stock buybacks serve several purposes for corporations, such as reducing the number of outstanding shares of stock (and so pushing up the company's earnings per share), boosting the stock price, and funneling income to top executives (whose compensation is tied to the stock price). There is little evidence, however, that stock buybacks fuel productive investment or "trickle down" to workers.

Another dubious practice of financial markets is the practice of "shorting" financial assets. MacEwan (Article 8.5) walks us through the steps of "betting to lose." "Shorting" is no longer just the practice of high-risk gamblers and gangsters; the largest financial services companies in the world (Goldman Sachs) also engaged in these underhanded if not outright fraudulent practices leading up to, during, and after the 2008 financial crisis.

Then, Alejandro Reuss (Article 8.6) looks back at economist John Maynard Keynes's understanding of financial instability, especially financial "bubbles"—a major problem in the U.S. economy. Reuss argues that bubbles have been a key driver of demand in the U.S. economy in recent decades, and so it will require deeper changes than just financial regulation to solve this problem.

Robert Pollin reviews the insights of post-Keynesian economist Hyman Minsky on the tendency toward excessive financial risk-taking during economic booms (Article 8.7). Minsky offers us a hypothesis of endogenous instability within financial markets. Minsky pointed to government regulation as a necessary substitute for the discipline of the market (which reins in risk-taking only through ruinous financial crashes).

Bringing the chapter to a close, MacEwan (Article 8.8) responds to the question: Why is student debt cancelation such a big deal? MacEwan begins the article by focusing on the need for higher education to enable students to compete for well-paying jobs. He then discusses the dramatic growth of student debt and some of the factors that have contributed to it. Finally, after reviewing some of the impacts of high student debt (which is especially burdensome for low-income students) he discusses various debt reduction proposals.

Discussion Questions

1. (Article 8.1) What is "financialization"? How does it manifest itself in today's economy? How did it contribute to the 2008 financial crisis?

2. (Article 8.2) "Roaring" sounds better than "boring." But why does Epstein believe that "boring" banking is better than "roaring" banking?

3. (Article 8.3) How have stock prices behaved during the pandemic? What factors have contributed to increases in stock prices? And why do low interest rates raise stock prices? Finally, how do rising stock prices contribute to increasing inequality?

4. (Article 8.4) What are stock "buybacks," and what, in MacEwan's view, are their economic consequences?

5. (Article 8.5) How could large financial services companies enrich themselves at their clients' expense through "shorting"? What does this practice say about the viability of the "efficient market hypothesis" of finance?

6. (Article 8.6) Some economists argue that financial market instability is the result of "irrational" investor behavior. Did Keynes agree?

7. (Article 8.7) Why do financial companies tend to engage in excessive risk-taking during economic booms? If financial crashes are too harmful to tolerate, and bailouts (to prevent or contain a crash) only encourage further risky behavior, what are the alternatives?

8. (Article 8.8) Compare the rationale for free K-12 education in the early 20th century with the argument for free college education today. What factors have contributed to the recent rapid rise of student debt? Identify some of the negative impacts of high student debt. Which debt reduction proposals make the most sense?

Article 8.1

FINANCIALIZATION: A PRIMER

BY RAMAA VASUDEVAN
November/December 2008

Y ou don't have to be an investor dabbling in the stock market to feel the power
of finance. Finance pervades the lives of ordinary people in many ways, from
student loans and credit card debt to mortgages and pension plans.

And its size and impact are only getting bigger. Consider a few measures:

- U.S. credit market debt—all debt of private households, businesses,
  and government combined—rose from about 1.6 times the nation's
  gross domestic product in 1973 to over 3.5 times GDP by 2007.
- The profits of the financial sector represented 14% of total corporate
  profits in 1981; by 2001–2002 this figure had risen to nearly 50%.

These are only a few of the indicators of what many commentators have labeled
the "financialization" of the economy—a process University of Massachusetts economist Gerald Epstein succinctly defines as "the increasing importance of financial
markets, financial motives, financial institutions, and financial elites in the operation of the economy and its governing institutions."

In recent years, this phenomenon has drawn increasing attention. In his latest
book, pundit Kevin Phillips writes about the growing divergence between the real (productive) and financial economies, describing how the explosion of trading in myriad
new financial instruments played a role in polarizing the U.S. economy. On the left, political economists Harry Magdoff and Paul M. Sweezy had over many years pointed to
the growing role of finance in the operations of capitalism; they viewed the trend as a reflection of the rising economic and political power of "rentiers"—those whose earnings
come from financial activities and from forms of income arising from ownership claims
(such as interest, rent, dividends, or capital gains) rather than from actual production.

From Finance to Financialization

The financial system is supposed to serve a range of functions in the broader economy. Banks and other financial institutions mop up savings, then allocate that capital, according to mainstream theory, to where it can most productively be used. For
households and corporations, the credit markets facilitate greatly increased borrowing, which should foster investment in capital goods like buildings and machinery,
in turn leading to expanded production. Finance, in other words, is supposed to facilitate the growth of the "real" economy—the part that produces useful goods (like
bicycles) and services (like medical care).

In recent decades, finance has undergone massive changes in both size and
shape. The basic mechanism of financialization is the transformation of future
streams of income (from profits, dividends, or interest payments) into a tradable asset

like a stock or a bond. For example, the future earnings of corporations are transmuted into equity stocks that are bought and sold in the capital market. Likewise, a loan, which involves certain fixed interest payments over its duration, gets a new life when it is converted into marketable bonds. And multiple loans, bundled together and then "sliced and diced" into novel kinds of bonds ("collateralized debt obligations"), take on a new existence as investment vehicles that bear an extremely complex and opaque relationship to the original loans.

The process of financialization has not made finance more effective at fulfilling what conventional economic theory views as its core function. Corporations are not turning to the stock market as a source of finance for their investments, and their borrowing in the bond markets is often not for the purpose of productive investment either. Since the 1980s, corporations have actually spent more money buying back their own stock than they have taken in by selling newly issued stock. The granting of stock options to top executives gives them a direct incentive to have the corporation buy back its own shares—often using borrowed money to do so—in order to hike up the share price and allow them to turn a profit on the sale of their personal shares. More broadly, instead of fostering investment, financialization reorients managerial incentives toward chasing short-term returns through financial trading and speculation so as to generate ballooning earnings, lest their companies face falling stock prices and the threat of hostile takeover.

What is more, the workings of these markets tend to act like an upper during booms, when euphoric investors chase the promise of quick bucks. During downturns these same mechanisms work like downers, turning euphoria into panic as investors flee. Financial innovations like collateralized debt obligations were supposed to "lubricate" the economy by spreading risk, but instead they tend to heighten volatility, leading to amplified cycles of boom and bust. In the current crisis, the innovation of mortgage-backed securities fueled the housing bubble and encouraged enormous risk-taking, creating the conditions for the chain reaction of bank (and other financial institution) failures that may be far from over.

Financialization and Power

The arena of finance can at times appear to be merely a casino—albeit a huge one—where everyone gets to place her bets and ride her luck. But the financial system carries a far deeper significance for people's lives. Financial assets and liabilities represent claims on ownership and property; they embody the social relations of an economy at a particular time in history. In this sense, the recent process of financialization implies the increasing political and economic power of a particular segment of the capitalist class: rentiers. Accelerating financial transactions and the profusion of financial techniques have fueled an extraordinary enrichment of this elite.

This enrichment arises in different ways. Financial transactions facilitate the reallocation of capital to high-return ventures. In the ensuing shake-up, some sectors of capital profit at the expense of other sectors. More important, the capitalist class as a whole is able to force a persistent redistribution in its favor, deploying its newly expanded wealth to bring about changes in the political economy that channel even more wealth its way.

The most symbolic instances of the structural changes that paved the way for financialization were the squashing of working-class aspirations during the Reagan-Thatcher years, and the defeats of the miners' strike in England and of the air traffic controllers' (PATCO) strike in the United States. At the same time, these and other governments increasingly embraced the twin policy mantras of fighting inflation and deregulating markets in place of creating full employment and raising wages. Corporations pushed through legislation to dismantle the financial regulations that inhibited their profit-making strategies.

Financialization has gathered momentum amid greater inequality. In the United States, the top 1% of the population received 14.0% of the national after-tax income in 2004, nearly double its 7.5% share in 1979. In the same period the share of the bottom fifth fell from 6.8% to 4.9%.

And yet U.S. consumption demand has been sustained despite rising inequality and a squeeze on real wages for the majority of households. Here is the other side of the financialization coin: A massive expansion of consumer credit has played an important role in easing the constraints on consumer spending by filling the gap created by stagnant or declining real wages. The credit card debt of the average U.S. family increased by 53% through the 1990s. About 67% of low-income families with incomes less than $10,000 faced credit card debt, and the debt of this group saw the largest increase—a 184% rise, compared to a 28% increase for families with incomes above $100,000. Offered more and more credit as a privatized means of addressing wage stagnation, then, eventually, burdened by debt and on the edge of insolvency, the working poor and the middle class are less likely to organize as a political force to challenge the dominance of finance. In this sense, financialization becomes a means of social coercion that erodes working-class solidarity.

As the structures created by financial engineering unravel, the current economic crisis is revealing the cracks in this edifice. But even as a growing number of U.S. families are losing their homes and jobs in the wake of the subprime meltdown, the financial companies at the heart of the crisis have been handed massive bailouts and their top executives have pocketed huge payouts despite their role in abetting the meltdown—a stark sign of the power structures and interests at stake in this era of financialization. ❑

Sources: Robin Blackburn, "Finance and the Fourth Dimension," *New Left Review*, Issue 39, May-June 2006; Robert Brenner, "New Boom or Bubble," *New Left Review*, Issue 25, Jan-Feb 2004; Tamara Draut and Javier Silva, "Borrowing to make ends meet," *Demos*, Sept 2003; Gerald Epstein, "Introduction" in G. Epstein, ed., *Financialization and the World Economy* (Edward Elgar Publishing, 2006); John Bellamy Foster, "The Financialization of Capitalism," *Monthly Review*, April 2007; Gretta Krippner, "The financialization of the US economy," *Socio-Economic Review*, Issue 3, Feb. 2005; Thomas Palley, "Financialization : What it is and why it matters," Political Economy Research Institute Working Paper #153, November 2007; A. Sherman and Arin Dine, "New CBO data shows inequality continues to widen," Center for Budget Priorities, Jan. 23, 2007; Kevin Phillips, *Bad Money: Reckless Finance, Failed Politics, and the Global Crisis of American Capitalism* (Viking, 2008).

Article 8.2

FROM "BORING" BANKING TO "ROARING" BANKING
How the financial sector grew out of control, and how we can change it.

AN INTERVIEW WITH GERALD EPSTEIN
May/June 2015

Gerald Epstein is a professor of economics and a founding co-director of the Political Economy Research Institute (PERI) at the University of Massachusetts-Amherst. He has written extensively about U.S. and global finance and recently delivered the Distinguished Faculty Lecture at UMass-Amherst titled "When Big is Too Big: Do the Financial System's Social Benefits Justify Its Size?" In April, he sat down with Dollars & Sense co-editor Alejandro Reuss to discuss major themes in his current research—the dramatic growth in the financial sector, the transformation from regulated "boring" banking to deregulated "roaring" banking, the ways the current system has ill-served the economy and society, and the need for regulation of private finance and development of alternative financial institutions.

Dollars & Sense: What should we be looking at as indicators that the financial sector has grown much larger in this most recent era, compared to what it used to be?

Gerald Epstein: There are a number of different indicators and dimensions to this. The size of the financial sector itself is one dimension. If you look at the profit share of banks and other financial institutions, you'll see that in the early postwar period, up until the early 1980s, they took down about 15% of all corporate profits in the United States. Just before the crisis, in 2006, they took down 40% of all profits, which is pretty astonishing.

Another measure of size is total financial assets as a percentage of gross domestic product (GDP). If you look at the postwar period, it's pretty constant from 1945 to 1981, with the ratio of financial assets to the size of the economy—of GDP—at about four to one. But starting in 1981, it started climbing. By 2007, total financial assets were ten times the size of GDP. If you look at almost any metric about the overall size of the financial sector—credit-to-GDP ratios, debt-to-GDP ratios, etc.—you see this massive increase starting around 1981, going up to a peak just before the financial crisis, in 2006.

Two more, related, dimensions are the sizes of the biggest financial firms and the concentration of the industry. For example, the share of total securities industry assets held by the top five investment banks was 65% in 2007. The share of the total deposits held by the top seven commercial banks went from roughly 20% in the early postwar period to over 50%. If you look at derivatives trading, you find that the top five investment banks control about 97% of that. So there's a massive concentration in the financial system, and that hasn't declined—in some ways, it's gotten worse—since the financial crisis.

D&S: Could you describe the qualitative changes in financial institution behavior in this same era, and the origins of these changes? When we hear that year 1981, we immediately think of deregulation. Is it just deregulation, or is there more to it than that?

GE: We can roughly think about two periods of banking and finance in the post-World War II era. Coming out of the Great Depression, when there was a lot of financial regulation, the Glass-Steagall Act separated investment from commercial banking, there were rules governing the issuing of complex and risky securities, rules for different kinds of financial institutions in terms of what kinds of assets they could hold. Savings and loans could mostly focus on housing, commercial banks primarily on business loans, investment banks couldn't take deposits and mostly engaged in underwriting and those kinds of activities. There were interest-rate ceilings, high capital requirements, leverage requirements. During this period, most of the activity of banks, commercial banks particularly, was in terms of taking in deposits and making individual loans—business loans, mortgages, real estate loans. Many people call this the age of "boring banking." It was also called the age of "3-6-3" banking—bankers paid 3% interest, lent out at 6%, and got to the golf course by 3 p.m.

Then starting in the late 1970s and early 1980s, their activities really changed, partly as a result of financial deregulation, partly as a result of increased competition from other kinds of financial institutions. Relatively unregulated banks could pay depositors higher interest rates, could charge higher interest rates on their loans, and could engage in new kinds of financial innovation—such as securitization, which is placing a bunch of loans into a bundle, such as an asset-backed security or mortgage-backed security, and selling these things off. "Boring banking" could no longer compete, so instead of engaging in one-to-one lending, they started engaging in more activities with the capital markets—bundling up or securitizing loans, selling them off, using derivatives to hedge risks but also to make bets. They kind of became like hedge funds in the sense of doing a lot of trading, buying and selling a lot of derivatives, and engaging with the securities and capital markets. But they still had the government guarantees like they were banks.

D&S: How does finance measure up, during this most recent era of deregulated finance, against the key claims that are made about its socially constructive role?

GE: If you look at the textbook description of the positive roles that finance plays, basically it comes down to six things: channel savings to productive investment, provide mechanisms for households to save for retirement, help businesses and households reduce risk, provide stable and flexible liquidity, provide an efficient payments mechanism, and come up with new financial innovations that will make it cheaper, simpler, and better to do all these other five things. If you go through the way finance operated in the period of "roaring" banking, one can raise questions about the productive role of banking in all of these dimensions.

Taking the first role, channeling finance to productive investment, in the early post-war period, nonfinancial corporations on average got about 15%–20% of their funding for productive investment from outside sources, from banks and from the capital markets. For the rest, they used retained earnings. In the latter period, after around 1980 or so, this was cut more or less in half—to 7%–10%. So finance didn't really provide a huge percentage of funds for nonfinancial corporate investment in the age of roaring banking. So you have this paradoxical situation where the income going to finance grew significantly while the real contribution to providing funding for investment went down. During the 1960s, finance got about 40 cents for every dollar they gave to nonfinancial corporations for investment. By the 2000s, it was up to 66 cents.

What was finance doing instead? As Juan Montecino, Iren Levina, and I point out in a paper we wrote, they started lending to each other, instead of to the real economy or nonfinancial corporations. So we looked at intra-financial sector lending as a share of total lending from 1950 to 2010 and we found that, from 1950 up to around 1980 or so, they were only doing about 10% of total lending to each other. Just before the crisis in 2008, they were doing almost 30% of all lending to each other. This lending to each other really was a way of providing finance for derivatives trading and other kinds of betting, rather than financing real investment.

The second role is providing mechanisms for households to save for retirement. There are a lot of studies that show that banks didn't do a very good job in the period of roaring banking. Part of the problem is that the savings vehicles that finance provides for households come at a very high cost. If you put your money in a mutual fund, say, with Fidelity or one of these other companies, oftentimes the fees that you have to pay are very high, and the returns that you get aren't any better—sometimes worse—than if you put your money in a broad portfolio of stocks, like the S&P 500 or something like that. There are a lot of studies that show that the returns that you get from putting your money in these active funds is more than 2% less than if you just put it into a broad stock portfolio. Well, this 2% is going directly to the company, to Fidelity and the people who work for them, so it's a way that finance is overcharging.

The way in which finance has failed in helping households save for retirement is even more stark if you realize that, for most households in the United States, most of the wealth that people have is in their homes. If you think about what the financial sector did to people's savings in their houses in that period, it's a pretty dismal record—especially for African American, Hispanic, and other minority households, much more so than for white households. Already, African Americans' wealth is

---

How the Banks Broke Out of Regulations

D&S: You talk about banks that had been comfortably and profitably engaging in highly regulated "boring" activities coming under competitive pressure. How much of this is coming from new players and how much is it the banks themselves finding those niches to evade the regulations that existed at the time?

GE: It's both, for sure. I can't really tell you about the relative weights of those two factors, but certainly both are going on. So for example, one of the key restrictions that commercial banks were working under was the "Regulation Q ceiling." There were limits on what they could pay for deposits. In the late 1960s and 1970s, when inflation began taking off, savers were finding that the real interest rates they were getting from their deposits with banks were turning negative, banks couldn't raise the interest rates they paid to keep depositors. And these aren't small savers. We're talking about big corporations and wealthy people. Financial institutions were able to find niches outside the regulations, particularly money market mutual funds and other innovations. Fidelity Investments, for example, was able to create a checking account

just a fraction of white wealth, and most of their wealth was in their houses. The financial crisis of 2006–2007 pretty much wiped out a large percentage of African-American wealth during this period. So clearly, roaring banking didn't do much to help households save for retirement.

The third role is to reduce risk. You just need to look at the kinds of financial products that banks were selling under the guise of reducing risk—like credit default swaps, mortgage-backed securities, asset-backed securities, etc. These products lost enormous amounts of value during the financial crisis, and would have lost almost all of their value if the government hadn't bailed them out. The financial sector was a source of enormous risk, rather than a source of reducing risk.

The same can be easily said of the fourth function, providing stable and flexible liquidity. If you look at the housing bubble and the tremendous run-up in asset prices provided by the tremendous increase in liquidity from the financial sector—through asset-backed securities, subprime lending, and so forth—you realize that it was not stable. It was actually what led to the asset bubble and crash. So private banking does not provide stable or flexible liquidity. In the end, in 2008, the Federal Reserve had to come in and provide enormous amounts of liquidity to the system to keep it from melting down entirely.

For the fifth role, to provide an efficient payments mechanism, we see a similar kind of thing. The only thing that kept the payments system operating after the financial crisis was the enormous amounts of liquidity that the Federal Reserve flooded into the financial system. Moreover, if anyone has ever tried to transfer money from one bank to another, or overseas, you realize that our payments mechanism—even in normal times—is very inefficient. Banks can hold onto your funds for two or three or four days before making them available to you, when you try to transfer from one bank to another, just as a way of extracting more money from households. Both in abnormal times and in normal times, the payments mechanism in the period of roaring banking is very poor.

---

based on a money market mutual fund. They could start offering much higher interest rates.

But the banks themselves also found ways of breaking out of this, primarily through the Eurodollar market that developed in the mid-1960s. Citibank, Bank of America, and all of these other banks were able to develop these same kinds of financial products overseas, where they weren't subject to the same kinds of restrictions. Of course, it wasn't really overseas, it was just accounting changes on their books. One set of accounts was the Eurodollar market and another set of accounts was domestic, but they were all really in the same place, in New York or wherever. They were able to develop these kinds of new products and able to keep their commercial customers and others by setting up in the Eurodollar market rather than in New York.

Citibank was one of the examples of a bank that started pushing the envelope in various ways, to set up these accounts in the United States. The Federal Reserve essentially looked the other way—gave them an administrative pass—in the late 1970s. This just started opening up a floodgate. So it was a combination of new players coming in and developing these kinds of things and the old players figuring out ways around restrictions, primarily by booking all of this in overseas accounts.

Finally, that brings us to banking innovations. Paul Volcker famously told a group of bankers in 2009 that the only financial innovation that he could see in the last 20 years that had been at all efficient was the ATM. There's no evidence that financial innovations have led to more economic growth. Jim Crotty and I did a literature survey that at least 30%–40% of the financial innovations over the last 20 years are used at least to some extent, if not largely, to evade regulations or to evade taxes—that is, to shift around pieces of the pie from the public to the banks, rather than to increase the size of the pie.

In short, roaring banking has done a pretty dismal job of providing any of these functions that the textbook case says finance should provide.

D&S: Of course, bubbles burst and exacerbate the severity of downturns. One of the amazing things about the aftermath of the recent crisis has been the apparent imperviousness of the financial sector to serious reform—especially in contrast to the Great Crash of 1929 and the Great Depression. How do you make sense of that?

GE: You have to use a political economy approach to understand the sources of political support for finance. I call these multilayered sources of support the "bankers' club."

The lead group in the bankers' club is the bankers themselves, and the politicians that they're able to buy off with financial contributions and so forth. Their ability to do that, of course, has become much greater with changes in the campaign finance reform laws and Citizens United and so forth, so it makes it much easier for the banks to throw enormous amounts of money at politicians and prevent significant reform. This is true for both parties, for the Republicans and for the Democrats. We know how important finance was to President Bill Clinton's political coalition in raising money. That's been true for Democrats for many years, not just Republicans.

The bankers have a lot of other support as well. Historically, the Federal Reserve has been one of the main orchestrators of the bankers' club. You can clearly see that in the role that Timothy Geithner played—when he was at the New York Fed, and then after when he became Treasury Secretary under President Barack Obama—in fighting tooth-and-nail against any significant reform. He was one of the main figures in opposition to tough reform through the Dodd-Frank Act. The Federal Reserve, through many mechanisms—the "revolving door" mechanism, the fact that they regulate banks, and so on—is a very strong member of the bankers' club.

A perhaps surprising group in the bankers' club has been many economists, especially academic economists who work on finance. Some of them take quite a bit of money from financial firms as consulting fees or are on the boards of directors of financial firms. Jessica Carrick-Hagenbarth and I studied this, looking at a group of 19 well-known academic economists who were working with two groups, the Pew Charitable Trusts Financial Reform Project and the Squam Lake Working Group on Financial Regulation, on financial reform issues. And they were coming up with financial reforms that, while some of them were OK, a lot really lacked teeth. We found that many of them, if not most of them, had some kind of association with financial firms, but were not disclosing this when they would write their academic papers speak on the radio or on TV or give testimony.

An important source of power of the bankers' club is that banks can threaten to fail if we don't bail them out. They can threaten to leave—to move to London, Frankfurt, Hong Kong, or Shanghai—if we don't give them what they want. So this threat is the ultimate "club" that the bankers hold over our heads, and they use that all the time in the fight over financial reform.

On top of that, there's an important member of the bankers' club that in the 1930s wasn't a member—nonfinancial corporations. This time around, if you look at the fight over Dodd-Frank, you find very little opposition to banks from other members of the capitalist class. They were either silent or supported the banks. This is a big contrast to the 1930s when a lot of industrial firms did not support the banks, and in fact joined with President Franklin D. Roosevelt on financial regulation. Why is this? Why didn't we see more opposition from other capitalists to what the banks had done? After all, what the banks did led to this massive recession and hurt profits, at least initially, created all sorts of problems for nonfinancial corporations—and yet they supported the banks. Part of the answer may be that nonfinancial corporations have now become financialized themselves. The CEOs of these corporations get a lot of their incomes and wealth through stock options and other kinds of financial activities. Some nonfinancial firms have large financial components themselves. General Electric Co., for example, is now spinning off its financial subsidiary, GE Capital. But for many years it was getting quite a lot of income from GE Capital. And it's not just GE but also many other large nonfinancial corporations.

So there was a united front among the capitalists to oppose strong financial reform. Finance had plenty of money to buy off politicians. And while there was a strong and valiant effort on the part of Americans for Financial Reform, Better Markets, some academic economists who were opposing what the banks did, and important roles played by Senator Elizabeth Warren (D-Mass.) and some other politicians—it just wasn't enough, given this united front of capitalists, the money machine, and the academic economists who were giving legitimacy to what the banks were doing.

D&S: That brings us to the question of a reform agenda for now. We've heard a lot about the need for reregulation of finance, with an eye toward the restoration of the boring banking of the 1950s–1970s. The other question is whether the functions of finance require capitalist banks at all, even within a capitalist economy. Could all the functions of finance be done better by public and cooperative financial institutions, rather than private capitalist banks?

GE: The way I've been thinking about it is that we need both—that they're complements to each other. Short of the complete overthrow of capitalism, and having a totally socialist economy, which is unlikely to happen in the immediate future, what I think we should argue for is both reregulation of private finance and a much stronger push for what I call "banks without bankers." We need to have reregulation of private finance as long as it continues to exist, for two reasons.

First, as we've seen—and as John Maynard Keynes and Hyman Minsky and others argued—private finance can create a lot of problems if it's not regulated. As

---

Did the U.S. Economy Rely on a Financial "Bubble Machine"?

D&S: What would you think of the characterization that—within the context of U.S. capitalism becoming reliant on asset bubbles for achieving anything close to full-employment output—finance played the role of being the "bubble machine"? So, finance functions as an essential cog of a bigger dysfunctional system.

GE: My colleague Robert Pollin wrote a great book about this called *Contours of Descent*, about the Clinton administration and its role in creating this bubble machine. One of the impacts of all this roaring banking and this "pro-cyclical" liquidity creation—massive liquidity on the way up and then withdrawal of liquidity on the way down—was that it did have a huge levitating effect on wealth and, through this wealth effect, led to significant consumption particularly among the wealthy. And that helped to propel the economy forward in the 1990s.

Sometimes, people talk about this as if capitalism needed this to survive and that's why it's happened that way. I don't like that type of thinking methodologically. The questions that we need to answer are: What is the counterfactual? What would have happened if the bubble machine weren't operating? Would the economy have slid into a long period of stagnation, or would there have been economic and political forces that would have generated a much healthier type of growth? These are things that we can't know, though which are certainly worth asking. But the characterization that bubbles had that kind of effect—of generating these booms, particularly during the Clinton years—is certainly correct.

Keynes put it, when "enterprise is a bubble on a whirlpool of speculation," we're in big trouble. You have to bring private finance under control so that it can't continue to generate these massive bubbles and then crashes, which create enormous problems for workers and for households all over the world.

Second, as long as there's private finance out there and the bankers are making enormous profits and incomes, not only does that generate a worsening of the income distribution—it's an engine for inequality—it also makes it hard to have a stable and productive public financial sector. If you have public or cooperative banks, and you have people running those institutions and they think of themselves as financiers or bankers, and they realize that they could jump ship and work for the private financial sector and make five, 10, 15, 20 times what they're making in the public interest, this can be extremely tempting. Or it can get them to reorient the activities that they engage in to make them more profitable and look more like private banks. This is what happened to a number of public financial institutions around the world in the run-in up to the financial crisis. The first financial institution that really got into trouble, or one of the first, was Bayerische Landesbank, a regional provincial public bank in Germany that was supposed to be making boring banking investments, but instead was making roaring banking investments, because they wanted to keep up with the private financial institutions.

You can't let there be too big a gap between the activities and the incomes and pay between the public sector and the private sector if the public sector is going to do the job it needs to do. Of course, you can have a gap, and it can be somewhat large, but it can't get as big as it got in the 2000s. So for both of those reasons I do think that we need to control private finance.

But in order to break up the bankers' club and to provide the real kind of finance that society needs, we do need to promote more cooperative finance and public finance. How do you do that? Well, there are a bunch of different ways. For example, there's the State Bank of North Dakota, and there are a number of organizations that are trying to promote state banks in other states. I know there's been an organization in Massachusetts, for example, that's been trying to do this. There are credit unions all over the country, so building the credit unions by having a national credit union bank to support them is another option. These are all things that should be done.

The government should stop subsidizing the "too big to fail" banks by bailing them out. This lowers the cost of funds for these banks, allows them to grow larger and squeeze out cooperative and other kinds of community banks. So the government should end too big to fail as a way to make more room for these other kinds of public and cooperative banks. The Federal Reserve could serve as a backstop for these types of banks, by agreeing to act as a lender of last resort, to let them use their securities as collateral for borrowing. So there are all different kinds of ways that the government could support the creation or expansion of these sorts of institutions.

I think that's necessary for us to get out of the trap that we're in. ❑

Article 8.3

THE STOCK MARKET AND THE CORONAVIRUS CRISIS
Wall Street demands your money and *your life.*

BY JOHN MILLER
January/February 2021

"**Y**our money or your life" is the threat petty criminals brandish when they shake down a victim on the street. If the street is Wall Street the threat is even more chilling: "Your money *and* your life."

That's what has transpired since the Covid-19 pandemic struck down so many in the United States, sickened others, and crippled the health care system. The economy collapsed and then struggled to recover. The stock market crashed and then soared to record highs. And the U.S. economy became yet more unequal.

When the novel coronavirus hit in February and March, the economy closed down, spending evaporated, and output plummeted, declining 10.1% in just two months. That was twice as far as output fell during the Great Recession of the last decade. Jobs disappeared. In two months, over 25 million jobs were gone, nearly three times the number of jobs lost in the Great Recession. The unemployment rate increased more in three months than it did during the first two years of the Great Depression of the 1930s. The official unemployment rate reached 14.7% in April, but that measure was undoubtedly a gross underestimate of the number of workers in need of a job.

This economic catastrophe brought the stock market stumbling down in tandem. Stock prices fell more quickly than even during the Great Depression. From February 19 to March 23, nearly $10 trillion of market value evaporated as stock prices dropped 34%, measured by the broad-based Standard and Poor's (S&P) 500 Index.

But the economy and the stock market soon parted ways. As businesses opened back up and the federal government's $2.2 trillion stimulus package (the Coronavirus Aid, Relief, and Economic Security Act, or CARES Act) took hold, the economy began to recover. It grew quickly in June and July and then more slowly. By the end of September, economic output was still 3.5% below its pre-crisis level, disturbingly close to the 4% drop in output during the Great Recession. In November, half a year into the recovery, there were still nine million fewer jobs in the economy than at the onset of the pandemic. That was more jobs than had been lost during the Great Recession.

Meanwhile, the stock market soared. Within five months, stock prices had returned to their pre-pandemic level, and by early December the S&P 500 Index was 9% above its pre-pandemic high. The rapidity of the recovery was unprecedented. It took five-and-a-half years before stock prices returned to their pre-crises level after the Great Recession, and 25 years before stock market prices fully recovered after the Great Depression.

How Could That Be?

But how could the stock market recover so quickly, while the economy struggled to make up the ground it had lost? For starters, the stock market is not the economy—but the stock market and the economy are connected. For instance, the S&P 500 Index was pushed up by the rapid rise in the stock prices of the tech giants Apple, Microsoft, Alphabet (Google), and Facebook along with the ecommerce behemoth Amazon, all corporations positioned to do well in the pandemic. At the same time, the sectors struck hardest by the pandemic, such as restaurants, movie theaters, and parts of retail, don't have much of an effect on the stock market.

But most importantly, the stock market did so well because the economy did so poorly, as Keynesian economist Paul Krugman put it. With much of the economy in trouble, there were few profitable investment outlets other than the stock market. And when the Federal Reserve Board pumped money into the tanking economy it made the bonds market, the chief alternative investment outlet to the stock market, less profitable. The Fed's easy-money policies lowered interest rates in the hope of coaxing along the spending needed to support the failing economy. But interest rates are the rate of return that investors make on buying bonds. With a lower rate of return, investment money moved out of the bond market and into the stock market, driving up stock prices.

But even with few alternatives, why would an investor buy corporate stock in a failing economy? One reason is that the Fed purchased the corporations' bonds, saving them billions in borrowing costs, protecting them from bankruptcy, and making their stock a better investment. By June, the Fed had added $2.8 trillion of bonds, loans, and other assets to its holdings during the pandemic. That included lots of Treasury bonds that went to finance the federal government deficit and loans to county and state governments to cover their losses.

Yet More Inequality

U.S. inequality worsened as the stock market and the economy went their separate ways. Rising stock prices have benefitted the wealthy. The richest 1% of households alone own two-fifths of stocks by value, while one-half of U.S. households own no stock. A recent report from Americans for Tax Fairness and the Institute for Policy Studies estimates that the net worth of the 651 U.S. billionaires increased from $2.95 trillion in March to $4.01 trillion in December.

At the same time, the pandemic inflicted its worst pain on the economically vulnerable. From February to August, 18.9% of workers with less than a high school diploma lost their jobs, but that number was just 0.1% for workers who had graduated from college. *The Monthly Labor Review*, a publication of the Bureau of Labor Statistics, reports that 67.5% of workers with a college degree could do their jobs from home, while that was true for only 24.5% of workers with a high school diploma.

In the same period, 11.2% of Black workers were turned out of their jobs, but only 6.4% of white workers faced unemployment. On top of that, more than half of the white workers who lost their jobs during the pandemic had returned to work by September, while Black workers recovered just a third of their lost jobs.

With women overrepresented in the industries hardest hit in the pandemic, such as hospitality and food service, 7.8% of women workers lost their jobs, while 6.7% of male workers lost their jobs. Some 80% of the workers who dropped out of the labor force in September were women. Those women stepped up to fill the gap created by the closing of childcare centers, schools, and camps. At the same time, women continued to hold the majority of the jobs designated as essential by the Department of Homeland Security.

It Didn't Have to Be This Way

Had our government kept its eye on the disappearing jobs and had provided the work-a-day economy with the unqualified and unstinting support it lavished on the financial markets, the economic pain of the pandemic crisis would have been far less and would have subsided sooner. But the cost of being held up on Wall Street is truly your money and your health, if not your life. ❏

Sources: Edward Wolf, "The Asset Prices Meltdown and the Wealth of the Middle Class," National Bureau of Economic Research Working Paper, No. 18559; "The Recession and Recovery in Perspective," Federal Reserve Bank of Minneapolis; Dorothy Neufeld, "How the S&P 500 Performed During Major Market Crashes," The Visual Capitalist, August 5, 2020; Steven Rattner, "Lofty Stock Prices Don't Stem From a Strong Recovery," stevenrattner.com, September 1, 2020; Paul Krugman, "Crashing Economy, Rising Stocks: What Going On?" *New York Times*, April 30, 2020; Bureau of Labor Statistics, "Ability to work from home: evidence from two surveys and implication for the labor market in the COVID-19 pandemic," June 2020; Heather Long et al, "The covid-19 recession the most unequal in modern U.S. history," *Washington Post*, September 30, 2020; Stephanie Ebbert, "Women are leaving the workforce in droves," *Boston Globe*, October 2, 2020; David Dayen, "How the Fed Bailed Out the Investor Class Without Spending a Cent," *The American Prospect*, May 27, 2020; "Net Worth of U.S. Billionaires Has Soared by $1 Trillion," Americans for Tax Fairness, December 9, 2020.

Article 8.4

STOCK BUYBACKS: ANY POSITIVE OUTCOME?

BY ARTHUR MacEWAN
November/December 2016; updated June 2018

> Dear Dr. Dollar:
> *When a corporation buys back some of its own stock, is there any positive*
> *outcome (for the economy) other than making upper management richer?*
> — Julia Willebrand, New York, N.Y.

In early 2018, shortly after Congress and President Donald Trump enacted sweeping new tax legislation, the Apple corporation said it would use $100 billion of its gains from the new tax laws to buy back shares of its own stock. Apple is not new to the buyback game, but this 2018 action takes it to a new high. Exxon, which before Apple held the top buyback position, was spending *only* $20 billion per year on buybacks before 2015.

According to research by the Morgan Stanley bank, corporations expect to spend 43% of their tax cut gains on buybacks. They expect that another 26% will go to paying down debt and to mergers and acquisitions, whereas capital spending would account for 17%. Only 13% would go to wage increases. (The extent to which wages will be increased by investment is an open question; but new investment is a relatively small share of firms' tax change gains.) Yet although buybacks are a major part of the tax change story in 2018, they are not a new phenomenon.

Usually we think of firms issuing—i.e., selling—shares of stock to raise money for their investments. However, firms can also buy back those shares, which are shares of ownership in the firms. In recent years, buybacks have become a big deal. From 2006 to 2015, U.S. nonfinancial corporations' total net equity issues—new share issues minus shares taken off the market through buybacks and merger-and-acquisition deals—averaged negative $416 billion per year.

These buybacks, this reversal of the conventional view of how firms operate, do not generate a positive outcome for the economy. That is, these buybacks do not lead to economic growth or other changes that would benefit those of us who neither manage a company nor hold large amounts of its stock—just about everybody. Certainly, a firm's executives can gain through buybacks. As can some shareholders, both the ones who sell their shares in the buyback and the ones who, continuing to hold the company's stock, may see its value rise.

A driving force in the buyback game is that it generally serves to raise the incomes of companies' top executives. They are gaming the system to raise their own incomes. Yet, top executives have always wanted more income, and buybacks were relatively insignificant until the mid-1980s. So why have stock buybacks become so substantial in more recent years?

In a 2014 article in the *Harvard Business Review*, William Lazonick, a professor at the University of Massachusetts-Lowell emphasizes two new developments. The first is Wall Street's increasing focus on earnings per share (EPS) as a princi-

TOP 5 INDIVIDUAL FIRMS AND TOTAL OF TOP 50 FIRMS WITH LARGEST AMOUNT SPENT ON BUYBACKS FROM 2006–2015

	Spending on buybacks (millions of dollars)	Spending on buybacks as percentage of net income
ExxonMobil	$206,253	59.2%
Microsoft	$123,640	71.1%
IBM	$119,497	88.8%
Apple	$103,468	45.5%
Proctor & Gamble	$72,487	69.2%
Top 50	$3,739,442	59.8%

pal means to evaluate the well-being of a firm. EPS is the amount of net earnings (i.e., profits after taxes) divided by the total number of shares of stock outstanding, usually calculated for a three-month period. A firm's spending on buybacks is not counted as an operating expense and therefore does not affect net earnings, but the buybacks do reduce the number of shares outstanding. So the buybacks increase EPS.

Focusing on EPS means focusing on the immediate or short run performance of a firm, and it tells little about the firm's long-run prospects. Furthermore, the firm's long-run prospects can be harmed by the buybacks, since, though not counted as an operating expense, the buyback expenditure reduces the firm's retained earnings that are the financial foundation for investing in productive capabilities.

Associated with this EPS emphasis is that the salaries of top executives are often tied to their firms' EPS. Moreover, executives are often paid in company stock. By buying back a firm's stock (i.e., raising demand for the stock), executives are able to lift the stock price, even if only temporarily. So buybacks and the consequent increase in a firm's EPS are a way that top executives can game the system all the way to the bank.

The second factor that Lazonick points to in explaining the change is that in 1982, the Securities and Exchange Commission (SEC) instituted Rule 10b-18 of the Securities Exchange Act, which greatly facilitated stock buybacks without meaningful regulation. Lazonick points out: "In essence, Rule 10b-18 legalized stock market manipulation [by a firm] through open market purchases." (An "open market" purchase is the purchase of a company's stock in the securities market or, if the purchase is directly between the buyer and seller, at the securities market price.)

There is also a third factor, which helps explain the surge of buybacks in the most recent years—namely the poor performance of the U.S. economy. In a slow-growth economy, the opportunities to profit from productive investment are limited, which raises the relative appeal of gaming the system through buybacks and other means. Yet, devoting funds to buybacks and abandoning productive investment contributes to the economy's poor performance.

During the decade ending in 2015, large firms with familiar names dominated in terms of the amount spent on buybacks (as shown in the table). ExxonMobil led, spending $206.3 billion on buybacks during this period, amounting to nearly 60% of its net income (profits after taxes). Then came Microsoft and IBM, with the latter's spending on buybacks amounting to 89% of its net income. For the top 50 firms in terms of amount spent on buybacks, the total spending was $3.7 trillion in the years 2006–2015, an amount equal to 60% of their total net income over that period. In more recent years, as noted above, Apple has become the leader of the pack.

In a 2016 paper, which supplies additional data and analysis of buybacks, Lazonick sums up the phenomenon: "Given the importance of these corporations to the operations and performance of the economy, it is fair to say that the 21st century U.S. industrial economy has become a 'buyback economy.'"

Of course, there are those who claim that buybacks are good for the economy. In a rather trite attack on Lazonick's *Harvard Business Review* article, Greg Satell in a *Forbes* article claims that buybacks can put more "excess cash" in the hands of investors who will be able "to create new value." One wonders: If so many major firms themselves cannot find, or choose not to find, productive investments "to create new value," why will those who sell stock back to the firms make productive investments? Most likely, they, too, will use the funds to game the system, entering into the grand casino we call "Wall Street." ❑

Sources: William Lazonick, "How Stock Buybacks Make Americans Vulnerable to Globalization," AIR Working Paper #16-0301, March 2016 (theairnet.org); William Lazonick, "Profits without Prosperity," *Harvard Business Review*, September 2014 (hbr.org); Greg Satell, "Why Stock Buybacks Are Good For The Economy And The Country," *Forbes*, May 9, 2015 (forbes.com); Steven Rattner, "Testimony Before the House Ways and Means Committee," May 16, 2018 (waysandmeans.house.gov); Jack Nicas, "Apple Says It Will Buy Back $100 Billion in Stock," *New York Times*, May 1, 2018 (nytimes.com).

Article 8.5

IS "SHORT SELLING" BAD FOR THE ECONOMY?

BY ARTHUR MacEWAN
November/December 2018

> Dear Dr. Dollar:
>
> *Many a Wall Street investor makes money by "short selling," which, as I understand it, involves buying stocks that the investor believes are likely to fall in value in the near future. How do they manage to make a profit by buying stocks whose value is likely to fall? Does this practice threaten the health of the larger economy or is it relatively harmless?*
>
> —Clifford Anderson, Sacramento, Calif.

Yes, short sellers take action when they believe a stock's price will fall in the near future. But they don't buy the shares of the stock; they borrow the shares. They sell the borrowed shares of stock at the existing price. Then, when the price falls, they purchase the shares of stock at the now lower price and return them to the lender (plus some interest or fee). The amount of money (profit) that the short seller makes is the difference between the price at which the shares were sold and the price at which they were later purchased times the number of shares involved (minus the interest or fees).

For example, a short seller borrows 100 shares of a stock at a current price of $75 a share. The shorter immediately sells the stock for $7,500. Then, as the short seller had hoped, the price drops to $50 a share. So the short seller buys 100 shares for $5,000 and returns the shares to the lender. The profit is $2,500 (minus the interest or fees).

If, contrary to the short seller's expectation, the price of the stock rises, she/he suffers a loss instead of a gain. While the profits in the above example are limited to $7,500, because the price cannot drop below zero, the loss is, in theory, unlimited—i.e., there is no limit on how high the price could go. In practice, however, if the price starts to rise significantly, the short seller can cut her/his losses by buying and suffering only a small loss. Nonetheless, short selling is risky.

Short selling is one way to bet (speculate) against a stock (or, for that matter, other assets such as bonds or various kinds of financial instruments), but it is not the only way. For example, if a speculator believes the price of a stock will fall, she/he can buy a "put"—the right, but not the obligation, to sell the stock at a fixed price at a certain date in the future. If the price falls below the price agreed upon in the "put," the buyer can buy at this lower price and sell at the "put" price, making a profit. If the price does not fall below the "put" price, the sale doesn't take place. The person who bought the "put" only loses what she/he paid for it. All the risk is born by the seller of the put.

A speculator can also buy a "credit default swap," which is essentially an insurance policy on a security. If the price of the security drops (or, in the case of a bond, if there is a complete default), the buyer of the "swap" gets the par value of the security (i.e., its value as originally issued). The speculator does not actually have to buy the security to buy the "swap," the de facto insurance policy. Betting against a security in this manner is a bit like buying fire insurance on the house of a neighbor who you know smokes in bed at night.

Broader Impacts?

Because short selling can be so risky, with possible losses far exceeding possible gains, many analysts warn against it. Clearly, it is a dangerous practice for the amateur investor. But aside from what's bad or good for the individual, what about the broader impact?

Critics of short selling argue that it creates undesirable and excessive ups and downs in securities markets, and that unstable securities markets are bad for the wider economy. Also, when there is significant short selling of the stock of a particular company, the short selling itself may cause the value of that stock to fall. Investors who learn about the short sells might believe the short seller knows something they don't. So these other investors sell their shares, the stock price falls, and the short seller wins. Again, the problem is excessive gyrations of securities markets.

Defenders of short selling see it as a useful practice, a method of forcing companies to operate effectively. If the companies don't operate well, short sellers will bet against them. In this view, short selling is seen as desirable because it forces companies to be accountable for their errors—which is supposedly good for the economy in general.

Whether one likes it or not, it is hard to see how securities markets could exist without winners and losers, without some investors having different appraisals of particular companies than other investors. So short selling seems to be part of the necessary operations of the casino-like financial markets.

Short selling—or, more generally, betting against a security—becomes a real problem when used in ways to game the system. One of these ways is "short and distort." A large investor—a hedge fund, for example—can short the stock of a company and then undertake a campaign to discredit the operation of the company. If the campaign generates a fall in the price of the company's stock, the investor wins—but not because of any real weakness of the company.

An Odious Example

Another, especially odious example of using negative speculation was an operation by the investment bank Goldman Sachs in the early 2000s. During the housing bubble that led to the financial crisis and Great Recession, Goldman Sachs created packages of mortgaged-backed securities—collateralized debt obligations (CDOs)—that it sold to its clients, which included pension funds, insurance companies, and various other investors. Believing these CDOs were good investments, presumably because Goldman Sachs was urging their purchase, the clients spent billions buying them. For a while the clients made money off these investments.

Then, according to the *New York Times*, "worried about a housing bubble, top Goldman executives decided in December 2006 to change the firm's overall stance on the mortgage market, from positive to negative, though it did not disclose that publicly"—that is, the firm did not tell its clients. So Goldman Sachs started making CDO investments (i.e., shorting the CDOs) that would pay off only if the housing bubble deflated.

When the housing market started to go bust and the CDOs did fall in value, Goldman Sachs made billions and its clients lost billions. Goldman Sachs was not the only financial institution to profit from this sort of duplicitous practice. Others, according to the *Times*, included Deutsche Bank and Morgan Stanley, as well as some smaller firms.

On January 13, 2010, at hearings of the Financial Crisis Inquiry Commission, whih was established by Congress to investigate the crisis, the commission's chair, Phil Angelides, confronted the head of Goldman Sachs, Lloyd Blankfein, on this issue: "I'm just going to be blunt with you. It sounds to me a little bit like selling a car with faulty brakes and then buying an insurance policy on the buyer of those cars … It doesn't seem to me that's a practice that inspires confidence in the market." ❏

Sources: Gretchen Morgenson and Louise Story, "Banks Bundled Bad Debt, Bet Against It and Won," *New York Times*, December 23, 2009 (nytimes.com); Caitlin Kenney, "Financial Crisis Inquiry Commission Day One," NPR, January 13, 2010 (npr.org).

Article 8.6

BUBBLE, BUBBLE, TOIL, AND TROUBLE
Keynes and Financial Instability

BY ALEJANDRO REUSS
October 2013

In recent years, the United States has experienced major "bubbles"—increases in asset prices fueled by nothing more than the expectation that in the future others will be willing to pay even more—in the stock market and in real estate markets. The S&P Composite Index, a broad index of stock prices, stood at less than 850 in early 2003, after the "dot.com" crash. By 2007, it had ballooned to over 1,500. The real estate bubble saw the Case-Shiller 20-City Home Price Index, the main index of U.S. housing prices, more than double from 100 at the beginning of 2000 to over 206 in the middle of 2006. Both have crashed since then. The Case-Shiller Index fell to less than 150 by January 2008. The S&P lost about half its value, down to a little more than 750, between its 2007 peak and March 2009.

Sources of Market Volatility

In the words of former Federal Reserve Chair Alan Greenspan, a wave of "irrational exuberance" fueled the stock market boom. It is easy to believe that daredevil risk-taking, an unreasoning faith that prices will keep rising and rising, and possibly testosterone intoxication, are responsible for asset "bubbles." That may not be entirely false, but we chalk up bubbles exclusively to irrational behavior at the peril of ignoring the element of individual rationality in joining into a bubble and fueling its growth. In *The General Theory*, John Maynard Keynes argued that financial market instability, in particular, was due not merely to some "wrongheaded propensity" on the part of the individuals involved, but to the organization of financial markets themselves.

Conventional economic theory of asset markets is dominated by the "efficient markets hypothesis." Proponents of this view argue that the price of a financial asset at any given moment reflects all the available information about its true value (e.g., stock prices at any given moment reflect all of the available information about the value of a company, or real estate prices about the value of those properties). When new information becomes available, either about a particular asset or about the national or world economy, this causes market participants to revalue the asset, and the price goes up or down accordingly. If it were possible to know now that a stock's price would, say, go up to a specific level the next day, people would buy it now in anticipation of the rise, bidding up the price today. We would not have to wait until tomorrow to get to the new, higher price. In this view, stock prices reflect the real values of the assets being traded, so far as the available information allows, and price fluctuations on the stock market and other asset markets originate from outside the markets themselves.

Critics of the efficient markets hypothesis have argued that it underestimates the instability generated within asset markets. Price fluctuations are caused not only by newly available information, but by market participants' reactions to previous price fluctuations and prediction of how other participants will react to those fluctuations. Market participants are concerned, in Keynes' view, not with correctly ascertaining the long-term value of an asset, but primarily with guessing what others will be willing to pay for it in the short run. They buy and sell, Keynes argued, not on the basis of "what an investment is really worth to [someone] who buys it 'for keeps'," but on the basis of "what the market will value it at … three months or a year hence."

Keynes' Beauty Contest

In *The General Theory*, Keynes famously compared financial markets to a strange sort of beauty pageant run by London newspapers in his time. The papers published an array of photos, and readers could enter a contest in which the winner was the reader who guessed which faces would be chosen the most by other readers. (Keynes was not commenting, one way or another, about the existence of these or other "beauty contests." In fact, he was not focused on this as a contest between the women pictured, but as a contest between the readers doing the guessing.) As Keynes pointed out, it would not do to simply choose the photo that one found most attractive, for one's own tastes might not match those of other entrants. Neither, however, should one choose the photo that one thought other entrants would find most attractive (for they would not themselves be choosing the one they found most attractive). Each entrant would, rather, be trying to guess what other entrants would guess about which photos most other entrants would choose.

In the same way, participants in the stock market, Keynes argued, did not generally attempt to estimate the likely returns from a company's investments (often referred to these days as its "fundamentals"), but to "guess better than the crowd how the crowd will behave." If other market participants are, for whatever reason, buying a particular kind of asset and driving up its price, rational participants would decide to buy as well (to benefit from the short run increase in prices) as long as they expected that the price would continue to rise.

This makes sense, from the standpoint of an individual buyer, even if the buyer, in some sense, knows better—that is, believes that the company in question has bad long-term prospects, that "the market" has overpriced the stock, that other buyers are acting unwisely, and so on. For example, you may not think that Springfield Nuclear Power is a very well-run company, but as long as you think other people are (unwisely) going to buy its stock, pushing up the stock price, it makes sense for you to buy the stock and profit from these future price increases. As more people buy in to take advantage of a crowd-induced rise in prices, of course, they further fuel the growth of the bubble. These price increases, in turn, may induce still others to buy the stock in anticipation of further increases, and so on.

This process can dramatically unhitch the price of an asset from its "fundamentals," at least for a time. To show that the price of a stock, of houses, or of some other asset has grown out of all due proportion, however, we must have some basis for estimating the "correct" value. For stocks, one comparison is the "price-earnings (P/E) ratio" (the ratio of the stock price to the corporation's profits, on which stocks ultimately are a claim). For housing, one can use a ratio between housing prices and "owner's equivalent rent" (how much it would cost to rent a similar house), or the "price-rent ratio." By these measures, U.S. stocks and housing have been grossly overvalued during the bubbles of recent years.

Economist Robert Shiller, a leading authority on asset bubbles, notes that price-earnings ratios in the mid 2000s are above historical norms. In 2007, the P/E ratio peaked over 27. (It had peaked at over 44 in late 1999, during the dot.com bubble.) The price-rent ratio, likewise, went way above historical norms in 2007. The national average for the 15 preceding years was less than 17. In mid 2007, it was nearly 23.

Bubbles and the Real Economy

Some people will profit in any bubble. But bubbles do not go on forever. Some end with a fizzle (prices stop rising, and inflation gradually erodes the value of the asset); others, with a dramatic crash, as the U.S. stock market and housing markets did in 2008. As a bubble bursts, however, the price may not simply return to the "right" level. Instead, market participants may believe that price declines now mean that prices are likely to continue to fall in the future (in effect, this is a bubble in reverse, known as a "panic sell-off"). As the price of an asset declines, more and more people sell to avoid getting stuck with it, fueling a further decline, and so on. Falling asset prices may, in short, overshoot the mark in the other direction.

Keynes was concerned that the "daily revaluations of the Stock Exchange … inevitably exert a decisive influence of the rate of current investment"—that fluctuations in stock prices affect real economic activity. Rising stock prices, which make it possible for a company to raise capital cheaply by issuing new shares, have the same effects as falling interest rates. Some investment projects, which would be unprofitable if the cost of capital were greater, will be undertaken. Plummeting stock prices, on the other hand, are like increasing interest rates. They make it more expensive for companies to raise capital, and may therefore result in decreased real investment.

The collapse of the stock and housing bubbles reverberated on real economic activity in at least two more ways.

First, people's consumption spending is affected not only by their current incomes, but also their wealth (the value of the assets they own, minus their debts, at any given time). As people's wealth increases, they spend more freely; if their wealth decreases, they curtail their spending. This is known as the "wealth effect." Keynes described this phenomenon in *The General Theory*, writing that the "consumption of the wealth-owning class may be extremely susceptible to unforeseen changes in the money-value of its wealth." The stock market and real estate bubbles certainly fueled increased consumption. Many people simply spent more freely because they felt financially secure. Some borrowed against the rising values of their homes, often for consumption spending. As the values of these assets have plummeted, people have cut back dramatically on spending.

Second, the collapse of the housing market detonated a major financial crisis. Banks had bet heavily on the continued rise in real estate prices. They extended mortgage loans indiscriminately. They bought enormous amounts of mortgage-backed securities (which pay returns to their owners based on payments made on an underlying set of mortgages). When real estate prices plummeted and mortgage defaults skyrocketed, banks were left holding assets that were plummeting in value and were basically unsellable. Many curtailed their lending dramatically, trying to build their cash reserves as a guard against bankruptcy. The resulting tightening of credit made it difficult for consumers and firms to borrow, further dragging down spending and contributing to the deepening recession.

Is Regulation the Answer?

In the parts of *The General Theory* focused on financial instability, Keynes argued that the speculative short-term speculative buying and selling of securities disconnected financial markets from any real evaluation of the long-term prospects of different investments. While this was, in Keynes' view, harmless enough if the speculation existed on the surface on a "steady stream of enterprise," it could be very harmful if enterprise became the surface on top of a "whirlpool of speculation."

It's easy to see the relevance of this analysis to the current economic crisis. From the 1940s to the 1970s, banks, insurance companies, and other financial institutions were highly regulated, and financial crises were relatively rare. Since the deregulation of finance in the 1980s, the nonregulation of ever-more-exotic financial securities and the creation of a vast world of "shadow banking" have made crises much more frequent. Enterprise (that is, the real economy) seems to have been dragged down, as Keynes foresaw, into the whirlpool.

The chain reaction of excessive financial risk-taking, the eruption of the financial crisis, and the deepest recession since the 1930s has resulted in calls for renewed financial regulation. As of yet, only partial and inadequate measures have been adopted, and the largest banks are flying higher than ever. Even if there were robust new financial regulation, however, that would not solve the problems that cause the Great Recession in the first place—since these problems went way beyond just excessive financial speculation or risk-taking.

Economic growth in capitalist economies depends on growing demand for goods and services to match the growing productive capacity of an economy. From the late 1940s to the early 1970s, the rate of productivity growth was matched by the rate of real wage growth. Ordinary workers, then, largely created the demand for the goods that they were producing in ever-greater abundance. Since then, however, real wage growth has stagnated, while productivity and total output have kept right on rising. The demand for these goods and services had to come from somewhere. In part, it came from the wealthy who, enjoying a growing share of the total income, spent more. In part, it came from working families that made up for stagnant wages with more hours of paid work (especially by women) and more and more debt. In large measure, though, it also came from bubbles! Remember, growing asset prices encourage people to spend more. Unsustainable asset bubbles are not just a way that the U.S. economy has *failed* over the last few decades—they are a way that it has *worked*.

This way of structuring a capitalist economy, however, is prone to periodic crises that inflict an enormous human toll. Creating an economy that does not depend on the next bubble, however, requires much more than just an overlay of financial regulation. ❏

Sources: John Maynard Keynes, *The General Theory of Employment, Interest, and Money* (Harcourt, 1964); S&P/Case-Shiller Home Price Indices; "Stock Market Winners Get Big Payoff—In Testosterone," *Scientific American,* April 21, 2008 (scientificamerican.com); Robert Shiller, Online Data; Robert Shiller, *Irrational Exuberance*, 2nd ed. (Princeton University Press, 2000).

Article 8.7

WE'RE ALL MINSKYITES NOW

BY ROBERT POLLIN
October 2008; The Nation

As the most severe financial crisis since the 1930s Depression has unfolded over the past 18 months, the ideas of the late economist Hyman Minsky have suddenly come into fashion. In the summer of 2007, the *Wall Street Journal* ran a front-page article describing the emerging crisis as the financial market's "Minsky moment." His ideas have since been featured in the *Financial Times*, *BusinessWeek* and *The New Yorker*, among many other outlets. Minsky, who spent most of his academic career at Washington University in St. Louis, Mo. and remained professionally active until his death, in 1996, deserves the recognition. He was his generation's most insightful analyst of financial markets and the causes of financial crises.

Even so, most mainstream economists have shunned his work because it emerged out of a dissident left Keynesian tradition known in economists' circles as post-Keynesianism. Minsky's writings, and the post-Keynesian tradition more generally, are highly critical of free-market capitalism and its defenders in the economics profession—among them Milton Friedman and other Nobel Prize-winning economists who for a generation have claimed to "prove," usually through elaborate mathematical models, that unregulated markets are inherently rational, stable and fair. For Friedmanites, regulations are harmful most of the time.

Minsky, by contrast, explained throughout his voluminous writings that unregulated markets will always produce instability and crises. He alternately termed his approach "the financial instability hypothesis" and "the Wall Street paradigm."

For Minsky, the key to understanding financial instability is to trace the shifts that occur in investors' psychology as the economy moves out of a period of crisis and recession (or depression) and into a phase of rising profits and growth. Coming out of a crisis, investors will tend to be cautious, since many of them will have been clobbered during the just-ended recession. For example, they will hold large cash reserves as a cushion to protect against future crises.

But as the economy emerges from its slump and profits rise, investors' expectations become increasingly positive. They become eager to pursue risky ideas such as securitized subprime mortgage loans. They also become more willing to let their cash reserves dwindle, since idle cash earns no profits, while purchasing speculative vehicles like subprime mortgage securities can produce returns of 10% or higher.

But these moves also mean that investors are weakening their defenses against the next downturn. This is why, in Minsky's view, economic upswings, proceeding without regulations, inevitably encourage speculative excesses in which financial bubbles emerge. Minsky explained that in an unregulated environment, the only way to stop bubbles is to let them burst. Financial markets then fall into a crisis, and a recession or depression ensues.

Here we reach one of Minsky's crucial insights—that financial crises and recessions actually serve a purpose in the operations of a free-market economy, even while they wreak havoc with people's lives, including those of tens of millions of innocents who never invest a dime on Wall Street. Minsky's point is that without crises, a free-market economy has no way of discouraging investors' natural proclivities toward ever greater risks in pursuit of ever higher profits.

However, in the wake of the calamitous Great Depression, Keynesian economists tried to design measures that could supplant financial crises as the system's "natural" regulator. This was the context in which the post-World War II system of big government capitalism was created. The package included two basic elements: regulations designed to limit speculation and channel financial resources into socially useful investments, such as single-family housing; and government bailout operations to prevent 1930s-style depressions when crises broke out anyway.

Minsky argues that the system of regulations and the bailout operations were largely successful. That is why from the end of World War II to the mid-1970s, markets here and abroad were much more stable than in any previous historical period. But even during the New Deal years, financial market titans were fighting vehemently to eliminate, or at least defang, the regulations. By the 1970s, almost all politicians—Democrats and Republicans alike—had become compliant. The regulations were initially weakened, then abolished altogether, under the strong guidance of, among others, Federal Reserve Chair Alan Greenspan, Senator Phil Gramm (R-Texas), and Clinton Treasury Secretary Robert Rubin.

For Minsky, the consequences were predictable. Consider the scorecard over the 20 years before the current disaster: a stock market crash in 1987; the savings-and-loan crisis and bailout in 1989–1990; the "emerging markets" crisis of 1997–1998—which brought down, among others, Long-Term Capital Management, the super-hedge fund led by two Nobel laureates specializing in finance—and the bursting of the dot-com market bubble in 2001. Each of these crises could easily have produced a 1930s-style collapse in the absence of full-scale government bailout operations.

Here we come to another of Minsky's major insights—that in the absence of a complementary regulatory system, the effectiveness of bailouts will diminish over time. This is because bailouts, just like financial crises, are double-edged. They prevent depressions, but they also limit the costs to speculators of their financial excesses. As soon as the next economic expansion begins gathering strength, speculators will therefore pursue profit opportunities more or less as they had during the previous cycle. This is the pattern that has brought us to our current situation—a massive global crisis, being countered by an equally massive bailout of thus far limited effectiveness.

Minsky's Wall Street paradigm did not address all the afflictions of free-market capitalism. In particular, his model neglects the problems that arise from the vast disparities of income, wealth, and power that are just as endemic to free-market capitalism as are its tendencies toward financial instability, even though he fully recognized that these problems exist. Yet Minsky's approach still provides the most powerful lens for understanding the roots of financial instability and developing an effective regulatory system.

Minsky understood that his advocacy of comprehensive financial regulations made no sense whatsoever within the prevailing professional orthodoxy of free-market cheerleading. In his 1986 magnum opus, *Stabilizing an Unstable Economy*, he concluded that "the policy failures since the mid-1960s are related to the banality of orthodox economic analysis. ... Only an economics that is critical of capitalism can be a guide to successful policy for capitalism." ❑

Article 8.8

WHY IS STUDENT DEBT CANCELATION SUCH A BIG DEAL?

BY ARTHUR MacEWAN
March/April 2021

> Dear Dr. Dollar:
> *Now that President Joe Biden is in office, I've noticed news reports about the possible cancellation of student debt. Why has this become such a big deal recently? And would cancelling these debts actually help?*
> —Betty Timmons, Lindenwold, N.J.

At its core, the argument for cancelling student debt has arisen from the belief that higher education should be free, just like pre-K through high school education. Also, the extremely rapid growth of student debt since the early 2000s has made the issue a "big deal." And, still further, the perilous state of the economy—which means the perilous state of many people's lives—has brought a special urgency to the issue.

If High School, Why Not College?

Throughout the 19th century, high schools were not a substantial part of the public education provided to the majority of the population. Early in the 20th century, however, it became increasingly the case that this secondary education was important in preparing young people for employment, and states rapidly expanded high schools. Still, by 1940, only 38% of 25–29-year-olds held high school diplomas. By 2018, 93% of these young adults had completed high school.

But it is clear today that having only a high school diploma does not get one very far in the job market, and a college degree (at least) is considered necessary by employers for almost everything that would be considered a well-paying job. Indeed, in 2019, the average earnings of a person with a bachelor's degree (and no higher degree) was 67% more than the average for a person with only a high school degree ($1,248 per week compared to $746 per week).

Implicit, then, in the argument for abolishing student debt is that those holding the debt shouldn't have had to pay for college in the first place. Their attendance in college, like attendance in high school 100 years ago, was necessary for the economy to function effectively. As the whole society paid for high schools then, the argument is that the whole society should pay for college now.

Removing student debts would move things toward a more legitimate situation—which is to say that, since the students' education is good for the whole society, the society as a whole should pay for it. Our current system does provide some aspect of less costly higher education, especially for low-income students, through partially funding public institutions, scholarships, and subsidized loans. But most students and their families still have to pay substantial amounts. Yet there is no more rationale for this approach than there would be if only the poor could go to elementary and high school for free.

This position was, in effect, endorsed over 200 years ago, in 1785, by John Adams (who later became the second president of the United States):

> The whole people must take upon themselves the education of the whole people and be willing to bear the expenses of it. There should not be a district of one mile square, without a school in it, not founded by a charitable individual, but maintained at the public expense of the people themselves.

Rapidly Rising Debt

Aside from this fundamental issue about how to pay for higher education, student loan debt is a "big deal" because it has been rising so rapidly. In 2003, total student debt outstanding in the United States was $246 billion, which seems like a lot of money, but it was less than 3% as large as the country's total personal disposable income (PDI—what people have after paying taxes). By 2019, student debt had increased more than sixfold, to $1.54 trillion, and amounted to over 9% of PDI. (Interest payments on the debt amounted to about $90 billion annually.) In this period, all other categories of household debt grew by only 70%, while PDI rose by 92%. (These increases may seem large, but that is because all these figures are in current dollar amounts, that is, not adjusted for inflation. Data for 2020 are not available at this writing, but data for the first three quarters of 2020 show that the changes from 2003 to 2020 were pretty much the same as the changes from 2003 to 2019.)

As the figures above demonstrate, at the beginning of the 21st century, student debt was certainly a problem for some people, but it was not a major burden overall. Now it has become a more serious problem for many, many people and an overall burden on the economy. The debt falls heavily on people as they enter the paid labor force. They are forced to take jobs they would otherwise avoid, simply to pay their debts; by inhibiting movement in the labor force, the debt harms productivity. Also, heavy debt leads young workers to delay buying homes, having children, and creating stable lives. This situation tends to undermine aggregate consumer demand, and, of course, people with unstable lives are less effective economic actors.

Several factors account for the rapid increase of student loan debt: the rising cost of a college education; the reduction in states' support for their public higher education institutions; the relative stagnation of incomes for a large segment of the population; the increasing need for a college degree to obtain good jobs; and the greater availability of government loans.

For the roughly 42 million people who owe on student loans, the average debt is about $36,500. (This average is for all demographic groups taken together—but see below.) The average, however, can be somewhat misleading. People with very large loan amounts pull up the average. Half of the people in debt for their student loans owe only about half of the average (around $17,000 to $18,000). That is, the median is far less than the average (mean). Any way we look at it, however, for tens of millions of people, paying off these student loans is a big burden.

The Impact

Whether we look at the average or the median, these figures are too simple to tell us what is happening to people. To appraise the hardships that lingering student debt is creating, more data on who owes the debt would be needed but is not readily available.

One thing we do know is that the debt burden falls disproportionately on African Americans. According to a 2016 Brookings Institution report: "Four years after graduation, Black graduates have nearly *$25,000* more student loan debt than white graduates: $52,726 on average, compared to $28,006 for the typical white graduate [emphasis in original]." While there are various explanations for this large racial debt gap, probably the major factor is the huge racial wealth gap. According to another Brookings Institution Report:

> A close examination of wealth in the U.S. finds evidence of staggering racial disparities. At $171,000, the net worth of a typical white family is nearly ten times greater than that of a Black family ($17,150) in 2016. Gaps in wealth between Black and white households reveal the effects of accumulated inequality and discrimination, as well as differences in power and opportunity that can be traced back to this nation's inception. The Black-white wealth gap reflects a society that has not and does not afford equality of opportunity to all its citizens.

To the extent that high levels of debt are strongly associated with low levels of family wealth, it is reasonable to infer that many other people who owe large amounts of student debt are from low-income families of all races. To be sure, there are people with heavy debt loads who have become doctors and others who are in a good position to pay off their debts. But, in the overall picture of things, these well-off people are more than offset by the roughly 40% of students who start college but never finish, many of whom take on debt but do not obtain the better-paying jobs that tend to come with a college degree. This is a group in which African Americans and, more generally, people from low-income families make up a substantial share.

It certainly appears that the system that has evolved for financing college, in which students take on large amounts of debt, regenerates the racial and class inequalities of our society.

The Proposals

Reduction or cancellation of most student debt could be accomplished by the president, without any act of Congress. Many progressive activists, as well as Senators Bernie Sanders and Elizabeth Warren, have argued for a general cancellation of student debt. President Joe Biden has called for cancelling $10,000 of debt for each student. A general cancellation of the debt can be justified because students never should have had to pay for college in the first place and because the debt places a severe burden on millions of people, especially people from low-income families. Nonetheless, it is important to recognize that even Biden's more modest proposal would reduce the debt burden quite significantly for many people. After all, with the median debt at $17,000 to $18,000, the cancellation of $10,000 would mean eliminating more than half the burden for more than half the people who owe student debt. (A proposal by Chuck Schumer, the new majority leader of the Senate, calls for forgiving $50,000 of student debt for each person. This would eliminate the debt for the substantial majority of student loan debtors.)

Whatever is done about the debt, a recent article in the *New York Times* offered a cautionary point: "…debt forgiveness alone would be like treating a contaminated river without stopping the source of the pollution." The most straightforward and readily supportable way to eliminate the student debt problem is to make higher education free for all students and publicly supported, like pre-K through high school education.□

Sources: New York Fed Consumer Credit Panel, "Household Debt and Credit," Federal Reserve Bank of New York (newyorkfed.org); Federal Reserve Bank of St. Louis, "Employed full time: Median usual weekly real earnings: Wage and salary workers: 16 years and over," (fred.stlouisfed.org); U.S. Bureau of Labor Statistics, "Median usual weekly earnings of full-time wage and salary workers by educational attainment," (bls.gov); Mel Hanson, "Student Loan Debt by Race and Ethnicity," Education Data, September 24, 2020 (educationdata.org); Kevin Carey, "Forgiveness of Loans Wouldn't Tackle Roots of Student Debt Crisis," *New York Times*, November 21, 2020 (nytimes.com); Zack Friedman, "Student Loan Debt Statistics In 2020: A Record $1.6 Trillion," *Forbes*, February 3, 2020 (forbes. com); Digest of Education Statistics, "Percentage of persons 25 to 29 years old with selected levels of educational attainment, by race/ethnicity and sex: Selected years, 1920 through 2018," National Center for Education Statistics, 2018 (nces.ed.gov); Judith Scott-Clayton and Jing Li, "Black-white disparity in student loan debt more that triples after graduation," Brookings Institution, October 20, 2016 (brookings.edu); Kriston McIntosh et al., "Examining the Black-white wealth gap," Brookings Institution, February 27, 2020 (brookings.edu).

Chapter 9

THE GLOBAL ECONOMY

INTRODUCTION

When it comes to the global economy, most textbooks line up behind the "Washington Consensus"—a package of free-trade and financial-liberalization policies that the U.S. Treasury Department, the International Monetary Fund (IMF), and the World Bank have prescribed for the world's developing economies. Mainstream textbook discussions of exchange rates, international trade, and economic development policies almost always promote a market-dictated integration into the world economy. Outside of the classroom, however, popular discontent with the Washington Consensus has spawned worldwide movements calling into question the myth of self-regulating markets on which these policies rest.

The chapter begins with two articles by economist Jayati Ghosh on the impact of the pandemic on the global economy and the relationship between neoliberalism and neocolonialism.

In the context of the Covid-19 pandemic, Ghosh (Article 9.1), examines the ways in which this crisis will continue to sharply increase global inequality. While the United States, as the holder of the world's reserve currency, is able to spend trillions of dollars to prop up its economy, developing countries are unable to access the liquidity they need to provide much-needed services to an increasingly beleaguered population. Ghosh calls for the IMF to issue Special Drawing Rights (SDRs) to ensure that global international economic transactions simply do not seize up even after the lockdowns are lifted, and that developing countries are able to engage in international trade.

Then, in Article 9.2, Ghosh argues that imperialism has not disappeared, but simply changed shape. The direct military conquest and control of economic territory by the great powers has given way (at least some of the time) to control through multilateral agreements and international institutions. It may still mean the seizure of land, mines, or oil fields—but it also may mean the privatization of public assets and services, or the extension of intellectual property rights to new realms. Where the "labor aristocracy" of the imperialist countries once shared in the bounty of empire, the new incarnation of empire as "globalization" has helped grind away the incomes and status they once enjoyed.

While the doctrines of free trade and international financial deregulation are seldom questioned in mainstream economics textbooks, both are scrutinized here. Economist Arthur MacEwan (Article 9.3) shows how industrialized economies developed by protecting their own manufacturing sectors—never preaching the "gospel of free trade" until they were highly developed. Today, he argues, mainstream economists and pundits prescribe free trade not because it's the best way for others to develop, but because it gives U.S. corporations free access to the world's markets and resources, which in turn strengthens the power of businesses against workers.

Next, economist Thomas Palley examines how globalization has led to further divisions among workers (Article 9.4). Palley uses the hands of a clock to illustrate how the uneven effects of globalization foster divisions among workers and leave them isolated. The fact that workers benefit as consumers when exploitative conditions allow them to buy cheap goods stands in the way of overcoming those divisions and isolation, making it difficult for them to undertake collective action that would improve the conditions of most workers.

Next are two articles that address underlying questions related to inequality and trade. Is trade truly fair and equal, with all parties mutually benefitting (Article 9.5)? And how has the pandemic affected Mexican labor on both sides of the U.S. border (Article 9.6)? Mateo Crossa and James M. Cypher examine the unprecedented role that the U.S. government and corporations played in pressuring the Mexican government to reopen hundreds of factories that process meat, build cars, and create myriad other products by classifying them as "essential" in the midst of the coronavirus pandemic.

Rounding out this chapter, in Article 9.7, economist Smriti Rao presents us with a case study of India's response, or lack thereof, to the Covid-19 pandemic. The "stress test" of the Covid-19 pandemic has exposed many authoritarian regimes as criminally negligent and institutionally incompetent in protecting the public's health and safety. Prime Minister Narendra Modi's regime in India has delivered a remarkably large body count.

Discussion Questions

1. (Article 9.1) According to Ghosh, how does the "exorbitant privilege" of the United States as the holder of the world's reserve currency impact the Covid-19 recovery in the United States, as compared to developing countries?

2. (Article 9.2) Ghosh states that imperialism has not disappeared, but simply changed shape. What have been the results of this change in shape on workers in the most powerful countries?

3. (Article 9.3) "Free trade" policies, MacEwan argues, give businesses greater power relative to labor. Why is this so? Is this a good reason to oppose such policies?

4. (Article 9.4) How does Palley use the hands of a clock to illustrate how the uneven effects of globalization increase divisions among workers?

5. (Article 9.5) According to MacEwan, how has U.S. firms' reliance on the exploitation of people and resources evolved over time? In your view, can future economic prosperity in the United States be promoted without a model of global exploitation?

6. (Article 9.6) How, specifically, did the U.S. government and corporations get the Mexican government to reopen hundreds of factories by classifying them as "essential" in the midst of the coronavirus pandemic?

7. (Article 9.7) Rao notes the remarkable turnaround in India's response to the Covid-19 pandemic. What does Rao mean by describing this response as "stringent, stingy and severe"? Analyze each one of these three terms and how they each relate to the Indian government's Covid-19 response.

Article 9.1

THE PANDEMIC AND THE GLOBAL ECONOMY

BY JAYATI GHOSH
April 2020, Dissent

There are still many uncertainties about the Covid-19 pandemic: about the extent of its spread, its severity in different countries, the length of the outbreak, and whether an initial decline could be followed by a recurrence. But some things are already certain: we know that the economic impact of this pandemic is already immense, dwarfing anything that we have experienced in living memory. The current shock to the global economy is certainly much bigger than that of the 2008 global financial crisis, and is likely to be more severe than the Great Depression. Even the two world wars of the 20th century, while they disrupted supply chains and devastated physical infrastructure and populations, did not involve the restrictions on mobility and economic activity that are in place in the majority of countries today. This is therefore an unprecedented global challenge and requires unprecedented responses.

This very severe economic impact largely stems not from the pandemic itself, but from measures that have been adopted across the world to contain it, which have ranged from relatively mild restrictions on mobility and public gatherings to complete lockdowns (and clampdowns) that have brought to a halt most economic activity. This has meant a simultaneous attack on demand and supply. During lockdowns, people (especially those without formal work contracts) are deprived of incomes and joblessness increases drastically, causing huge declines in consumption demand that will continue into the period after the lockdown is lifted. At the same time, production and distribution are halted for all but essential commodities and services—and even for these sectors, supply is badly affected because of implementation issues and inadequate attention to the input-output linkages that enable production and distribution. Previous regional and global crises have not entailed this near-cessation of all economic activity. The deadly combination of collapses in both demand and supply is why this time is truly different and has to be dealt with differently.

World trade in both goods and services is already collapsing. The World Trade Organization (WTO) expects trade to fall anywhere between 13% and 32% in 2020. But even these dismal projections could well be underestimates, because they implicitly rely on relatively rapid containment of the virus and the lifting of lockdown measures by late summer. Exports of goods—other than those deemed "essential"—have effectively ceased; travel has declined to a tiny fraction of what it was, and tourism has also stopped for the time being; various other cross-border services that cannot be delivered electronically are contracting sharply. Trade prices have collapsed and will continue to decline. In the month leading up to March 20, 2020, primary commodity prices fell by 37%, with energy and industrial metals prices falling by 55%.

Within countries, economic activity is contracting at hitherto unimaginable rates, bringing about not only a dramatic immediate collapse but the seeds of future contraction as negative multiplier effects start playing out. In the United States alone, around 22 million people lost their jobs in four weeks, with GDP estimated to contract by 10% to 14% from April to June. Elsewhere the pattern is no different, probably worse, as most countries are facing multiple forces of economic decline. The International Monetary Fund (IMF) predicted on April 14 that global output will fall by 3% in 2020, and as much as 4.5% in per capita terms—and this is based on the most optimistic projections.

These collapses in economic activity necessarily affect global finance, which is also in disarray. The classic point about financial markets being imperfect not only because of asymmetric but also incomplete information is being borne out in practice: these markets are all about time, and now we must painfully accept that no one can know the future, even a few months ahead. Financial bets and contracts made just a few months ago now appear completely implausible to sustain. Most debts are clearly unpayable; insurance claims will be so extreme as to wipe out most insurers; and stock markets are collapsing as investors realize that none of the assumptions on which earlier investments were made are valid anymore. These negative forces together amount to humongous losses that could threaten the very viability of the global capitalist order (an order that was already struggling to show any dynamism over the past decade).

Unequal Effects

In an already very unequal world, this crisis already has and will continue to sharply increase global inequality. A large part of this is because of the very different policy responses in most developing countries (other than China, the origin of the pandemic, which has managed to contain its spread and revive economic activity relatively quickly) as compared to advanced economies. The sheer enormity of the crisis has apparently registered with policymakers in the developed world, who have (probably temporarily) abandoned all talk of fiscal austerity and suddenly appear to have no problem simply monetizing their government deficits. It is likely that the global financial system would have collapsed in the panic that arose in the third week of March without massive intervention by the major central banks of the developed world—not just the U.S. Federal Reserve but the European Central Bank, the Bank of Japan, the Bank of England, and others.

The "exorbitant privilege" of the United States as the holder of the world's reserve currency obviously gives it greater freedom to prop up its own economy. But other developed countries are also putting forward fairly large fiscal packages, from 5% of GDP in Germany to 20% in Japan, in addition to various other expansionary and stabilizing measures through their central banks.

By contrast, most developing countries have much less leeway to engage in such policies, and even those larger developing economies that could do so appear to be constrained by the fear of financial markets punishing them further. This is terrible: their economic challenges are already much greater than those in the developed world. Developing countries—many of which have yet to experience the full force of the spread of the virus—have been hit by a perfect storm of collapsing global trade, falling remittances, sharp reversals of capital flows, and currency depreciation. In just the month of March, capital flight from emerging market assets was an estimated $83 billion, and since January nearly $100 billion has flown out—compared to $26 billion after the 2008 financial crisis. Portfolio investment is down by at least 70% from January to March 2020, and spreads on emerging market bonds have risen sharply. Currencies of developing countries have mostly depreciated sharply, other than in China. The foreign exchange crunch is generating serious problems in servicing external debt, which is harder to do because of shrinking foreign exchange inflows and rising domestic costs for servicing them. By early April, 85 countries had approached the IMF for emergency assistance because of severe problems in meeting foreign currency payment obligations, and that number is likely to rise.

These external pressures, which are already together much greater than anything experienced during the Great Depression, have come to bear on economies that are already struggling with the terrible domestic economic consequences of their virus-containment strategies. The burden of these processes has fallen massively upon informal workers and self-employed people, who are being deprived of their livelihoods and falling into poverty at very rapid rates. Informal workers make up 70% of the labor force in developing countries, and they are unlikely to be paid at all during lockdowns in which they are forced to be inactive. Workers with formal contracts have also started losing their jobs. The International Labour Organization estimated in early April that more than four out of every five workers in the world are facing the adverse impacts of the pandemic and associated policy responses, and most of them reside in the developing world. Women workers are more likely to be disproportionately adversely affected: more likely to lose jobs and experience major pay cuts, more likely to be rationed out of labor markets when jobs do become available, more likely to suffer during lockdowns because of enhanced possibilities of domestic abuse, and more likely to suffer from inadequate nutrition in a time of household food shortages.

In many countries, livelihood losses are associated with dramatic increases in the extent of absolute poverty and growing hunger, even among those previously not classified as poor. Indeed, the re-emergence of hunger on a global scale is likely to be an unfortunate legacy of the pandemic and the containment measures that resulted. To add to all of this depressing news, most states in developing countries will not be able to indulge in the necessary levels of deficit financing (by borrowing from central banks) to enable the required increases in public expenditure, because of foreign exchange constraints and greater surveillance of financial markets over their deficits.

The Aftermath

This, unfortunately, is just the beginning. What of the aftermath, when the pandemic is brought under control? It bears reiterating that after a seismic shock of this magnitude, economies across the world will not simply be able to carry on as before, picking up where they had left off before this crisis. Over the coming year, many things are likely to change, including global reorganization of trade and capital flows. International trade will remain subdued for a while. Most commodity prices will also remain low, because global demand will take some time to pick up. This will affect commodity exporters' revenues, but it need not provide much advantage for commodity importers because of the overall deflationary pressures stemming from depressed demand.

On the other hand, the breaking of supply chains could well lead to specific shortages, including of some essential items, generating cost-push inflation especially in developing countries. Cross-border capital flows will be volatile and unstable, and most developing countries will struggle to attract sufficient secure capital on terms that would make it beneficial to add to domestic savings and meet trade financing costs. The steep currency depreciations that have already occurred are unlikely to get completely reversed and could even accelerate further, depending upon what strategies are pursued in both developed and developing countries. These falling currency values, higher margins on interest paid, and rising yields on bonds will all continue to make debt servicing a massive problem. Indeed, most developing country debt will be simply unpayable.

In addition to problems in domestic banks and non-bank lenders because of likely large-scale defaults, there will be massive problems in insurance markets, with the failure of some insurance companies and rising premiums that could be a disincentive for most medium and small enterprises to be insured at all. Travel and tourism revenues will also be significantly curtailed over the medium term, as the earlier confidence underlying such travel will have eroded. Similarly, many migrants will have lost employment. Demand for foreign labor is likely to decline in many host countries, so remittances will also decline. All of this will continue to put pressure on government finances especially (but not only) in the developing world.

Averting Catastrophe

This litany of horrors is well within the realm of the possible. The saving grace is that these outcomes are not inevitable: they depend crucially on policy responses. The terrible consequences described above are predicated on international institutions and national governments not taking the measures that could ameliorate the situation. There are both national and global policies that could help, but they must be implemented quickly, before the crisis generates even more humanitarian catastrophe. It is essential to ensure that the policy responses do not (as they currently do) increase national and global inequalities. This means that recovery strategies must be reoriented away from handouts to large corporations without adequate regulation of their activities, and toward enabling the survival, employment, and continued consumption demand of poor and middle-income groups, and the survival and expansion of tiny, small, and medium enterprises.

There are some obvious steps that the international community needs to take immediately. These steps rely on the existing global financial architecture—not because this architecture is just, fair, or efficient (it is not), but because, given the need for a speedy and substantial response, there is simply no possibility of constructing meaningful alternative institutions and arrangements quickly enough. The existing institutions—especially the IMF—have to deliver, which requires that they shed their pro-capital bias and their promotion of fiscal austerity.

The IMF is the only multilateral institution that has the capacity to create global liquidity, and this is the moment when it must do so at scale. An immediate issue of Special Drawing Rights (SDRs), which are supplementary reserve assets (determined by a weighted basket of five major currencies), would create additional international liquidity at no extra cost. Since a fresh issue of SDRs must be distributed according to each country's quota in the IMF, it cannot be discretionary and cannot be subject to other kinds of conditionality or political pressure. At least 1 to 2 trillion SDRs must be created and distributed. This will have a huge impact in ensuring that global international economic transactions simply do not seize up even after the lockdowns are lifted, and that developing countries are able to engage in international trade. Advanced economies with international reserve currencies are much less likely to need to use them, but they can be a lifeline for emerging markets and developing economies, providing additional resources to fight both the pandemic and the economic disaster. They are much better than depending on the IMF to provide loans, which often require conditionalities. (Insofar as additional emergency loans from the IMF are required, they must also be provided without conditionality, as purely compensatory financing for this unprecedented shock.) The issuance of more SDRs is also preferable to allowing the U.S. Federal Reserve to play the role of sole stabilizer of the system. The Fed's swap lines are currently providing central banks of a few chosen countries with dollar liquidity as it becomes scarce in this crisis. But this is not a norm-based multilateral allocation; these swaps reflect the strategic national interests of the United States, and therefore reinforce global power imbalances.

One reason why there has been only limited issue of SDRs so far (the last increase was after the 2008 crisis, but to the tune of only around 276 billion SDRs) is the fear that such an increase in global liquidity would stoke inflation. But the world economy has just experienced more than a decade of the largest increases in liquidity ever due to "quantitative easing" by the U.S. Fed without inflation, because global demand remained low. The current situation is only different because it is more acute. If additional liquidity is used to invest in activities that would ease the supply shortages likely to come up because of lockdowns, then it could also ease any cost-push inflation that might emerge.

The second important international measure is dealing with external debt problems. There should immediately be a moratorium or standstill on all debt repayments (both principal and interest) for at least the next six months as countries cope with both the spread of the disease and the lockdown effects. This moratorium should also ensure that interest payments do not accrue over this period. It is obvious that very few developing countries will be in any position to service their loans when foreign exchange inflows have effectively stopped. But in any case, if everything else is on hold in the global economy today, why should debt payments be any different?

A moratorium is a temporary move to tide these countries over during the period when the pandemic and the closures are at their peaks. But eventually substantial debt restructuring is likely to be necessary, and very substantial debt relief must be provided especially to low-income and middle-income countries. International coordination would be much better for all concerned than the disorderly debt defaults that would otherwise be almost inevitable.

Within nation-states, the institution of capital controls would enable developing countries to deal at least partly with these global headwinds by stemming the volatility of cross-border financial flows. Such capital controls must be explicitly allowed and encouraged, in order to curtail the surge in outflows, to reduce illiquidity driven by sell-offs in emerging markets, and to arrest declines in currency and asset prices. Ideally, there should be some cooperation among countries to prevent any one country from being singled out by financial markets.

The aftermath of this crisis is also going to require a revival of planning—something that had almost been forgotten in too many countries in the neoliberal era. The collapse of production and distribution channels during lockdowns means that defining and maintaining the supply of essential commodities is of critical importance. Such supply chains will have to be thought through in terms of the input-output relationships involved, which in turn requires coordination between different levels and departments in governments as well as across provinces—and possibly at the regional level as well.

The pandemic is likely to bring about a change in attitudes to public health in almost all countries. Decades of neoliberal policy hegemony have led to drastic declines in per capita public health spending in rich and poor countries alike. It is now more than obvious that this was not just an unequal and unjust strategy but a stupid one: It has taken an infectious disease to drive home the point that the health of the elite ultimately depends on the health of the poorest members of society. Those who advocated reduced public health spending and privatization of health services did so at their own peril. This is true at a global scale as well. The current pathetically nationalist squabbles over access to protective equipment and drugs betray a complete lack of awareness of the nature of the beast. This disease will not be brought under control unless it is brought under control everywhere. International cooperation is not just desirable but essential.

While pushing for these major strategies for national governments and international organizations, we need to be conscious of some concerns. One is the fear that governments across the world will use the opportunity presented by the pandemic to push for the centralization of power, with significantly increased monitoring and surveillance of citizens, and increased censorship and control over information flows to reduce their own accountability. This has already started in many countries, and fear of infection is causing many people across the world to accept invasions of privacy and forms of state control over individual lives that months ago would have been seen as unacceptable. It will be harder to sustain or revive democracy in such conditions. Much greater public vigilance is required both at present and after the crisis has ended.

There is also a fear that the increased inequalities thrown up by this crisis will reinforce existing forms of social discrimination. In principle, a virus does not respect class or other socio-economic distinctions. But there are well-known negative feedback loops between the squalor associated with income poverty and infectious diseases. In our unequal societies, poor and socially disadvantaged groups are more likely to be exposed to Covid-19 and are more likely to die from it, because people's ability to take preventive measures, their susceptibility to disease, and their access to treatment all vary greatly according to income, assets, occupation, and location. Perhaps even worse, Covid-19 containment policies within countries show extreme class bias. "Social distancing" (better described as physical distancing) implicitly assumes that both residences and workplaces are not so crowded and congested that the prescribed norms can be easily maintained, and that other essentials like access to soap and water are not limited. The fear of infection during the pandemic has brought out some more unpleasant forms of social discrimination and prejudice in many countries, from antipathy to migrants to differentiation on the basis of race, caste, religion, and class. At a time when the universality of the human condition is highlighted by a virus, responses in too many countries have been focused on particularistic divisions, which bode ill for future progress.

Despite these depressing possibilities, it is also true that the pandemic, and even the massive economic crisis it has brought in its wake, could also bring about some changes in attitudes that point to a more hopeful future. Three aspects of this deserve comment.

The first is the recognition of the essential nature and social significance of care work and the greater respect and dignity accorded to paid and unpaid care workers. This could result in societies increasing the number of paid care workers, providing required training for them because of greater appreciation of the skills involved in such labor, and offering these workers better remuneration, more legal and social protection, and greater dignity.

Second, the wider realization among the public of the real possibility that unthinkable events can occur and unimaginably dreadful processes can be unleashed by our ways of life may also bring home the reality of climate change and the disasters it will bring in its wake. This could make more people conscious of the need to change how we live, produce, and consume, before it is too late. Some of the less rational aspects of global supply chains, especially in the multinational food industry (which has encouraged produce from one part of the world to be shipped to another part of the world for processing, before coming back to places near its origin to be consumed), will be questioned and could decline in significance. Other changes in lifestyle and consumption and distribution patterns could follow.

Finally, on a more philosophical level, existential threats like pandemics encourage more recognition of the things that really matter in human existence: good health, the ability to communicate and interact with other people, and participation in creative processes that bring joy and satisfaction. These realizations could encourage the first steps toward civilizational shifts that lead to the reorganization of our societies. There is an opportunity to move away from dominant assumptions about individualistic utility maximization and the profit motive to more caring and cooperative social frameworks. ❑

Article 9.2

NEOLIBERALISM AS NEOCOLONIALISM

BY JAYATI GHOSH
May/June 2020

The damaging effects of neoliberalism—and the terrible legacy it leaves behind even for governments trying to change their countries' economic directions— are by now well known: growing domestic wealth and income inequalities, the erosion of regulations on capital, the elimination of protections for workers, the increased instability of economic life (with periodic business-cycle crises), the obsession with fiscal austerity policies that dismantle the welfare state and deprive citizens of their economic rights, and ever-deepening and spreading financialization. All of these features of neoliberalism are now generally accepted, even by some of its defenders. Now the Covid-19 pandemic is bringing home the fact that neoliberalism is posing a massive danger to public health and, therefore, to the very survival of societies.

One feature that is less remarked upon—and often even less noticed—is the role that neoliberal policies have played globally, in reinforcing contemporary imperialism. This has occurred through the way neoliberalism operates in developing countries, including in so-called "emerging markets." This tendency of neoliberalism is often disguised by the recent "rise" of some Southern powers, most of all China, and the perception that these changes make earlier notions of imperialism outdated. Yet in many ways, current global economic structures impose constraints upon developing countries that are so severe that they are actually quite similar to the constraints that are characteristic of the period of direct colonial control. Neoliberalism has created a revamped form of neocolonialism.

Financialization and Neocolonialism

The first and most obvious route through which neoliberalism imposes a new colonial-like control is through financial liberalization and the associated financialization of much of economic life. Financialization has been marked not just in advanced economies but in many developing countries as well. Financial deregulation has undermined the diversity of financial structures, suited to the particular national context and to the advancement of economic development objectives, created in the newly independent developing countries in the mid-20th century. Developing countries—even those at relatively low levels of economic development and diversification—were told, instead, that financial liberalization was essential for them to attract external capital that, in turn, was supposedly essential to finance economic development. Indeed, the International Monetary Fund (IMF) and the World Bank have actively pushed financial liberalization on developing countries, regardless of their specific contexts and degree of development, and particularly in the wake of balance-of-payments crises that revealed their external vulnerability.

There are, of course, several other ways in which the new global architecture of trade, investment, and finance has reduced the policy autonomy of developing countries and undermined their prospects for productive diversification and sustainable economic expansion. For example, intellectual property rights and the monopoly privileges they confer on multinational companies—mostly based in the global North—have been significant, by sharply reducing the possibilities of emulation that formed the basis of almost all successful industrialization from the 19th century onwards, in currently rich countries like Germany, the United States, Japan, and so on. Trade liberalization and export obsession empowered extractive industries (like mining, petroleum, forestry, etc.) and forced a shift back to primary product exports in many developing countries, thereby stalling and in some cases even reversing their attempts at economic diversification and structural transformation. But in this piece, I will focus specifically on financial liberalization and its effects.

Policymakers across the developing world, and especially those in finance ministries, internalized the view that financial liberalization was necessary to improve the functioning of the financial sector. This was supposed to be the key to increased profitability and competitiveness. It was supposed to make financial intermediation—the linkage between savers and borrowers—more effective. It was also the supposed key to attracting international capital and thereby increasing the resources that were available for domestic investment. These ideas were usually supported by the media, which caters to the elite in most developing countries. Their constant reiteration ensured that such measures had wide support among both elites and the middle class, who often have the most political voice in these countries.

As a result, many key features of existing financial structures and policies in developing economies were eliminated. Developing-country governments had directed credit to specific key industries. Without such policies no country has successfully industrialized. They had created financial institutions to serve specific development purposes, such as development banks and other institutions to finance long-term investment. They had imposed domestic regulations that prevented financial fraud and the siphoning off of savings for private gain rather than social purpose. They had imposed controls on cross-border capital flows to reduce vulnerability to global economic conditions. They had established controls on foreign ownership of financial assets, preventing the external takeover of key resources. It is worth noting that the one major economic success story of recent decades—the People's Republic of China—did not embark on financial liberalization policies. Even now the Chinese state retains significant control over domestic financial institutions and cross-border movements of capital.

The effects of financial liberalization across the developing world are, sadly, now only too obvious. Globally, there are three major consequences: First, the international financial system has been transformed in ways that substantially increase systemic risk, and make the system more crisis-prone. Within the financial world, there is a complex web of entanglement, with all firms mutually exposed to different kinds of risks, but each individual firm exposed in differing degrees to particular financial entities. It is difficult to judge the actual risk exposure of individual financial institutions. This makes a mockery of prudential regulation, such as "capital adequacy" ratios, which have supposedly become stricter over time, since it is difficult to actually define or measure the extent of capital when risk weights can be changed and assets themselves are loosely defined. The process of financial consolidation has substantially increased the risks associated with the system.

Second, for developing countries, there were further dangers associated with exposure to new kinds of risk. Financial liberalization creates a propensity to financial crisis, both external and internal. Such crises can have a deflationary impact on real economic activity and reduce access to funds for small-scale producers, both urban and rural. This in turn has major social effects in terms of loss of employment and the decline of standards of living for most citizens. Financial liberalization also reduces developing countries' domestic policy autonomy. With increased exposure to global financial markets, and completely unbridled international capital flows, it is no longer possible for a country to control the amount of capital inflow or outflow. Both movements can create undesirable consequences. If, for example, international investors suddenly flood a country with foreign portfolio investments, it can cause the national currency to appreciate. Unless the capital inflows are simply (and wastefully) stored up in the form of accumulated foreign exchange reserves, they are necessarily associated with current account deficits. This occurs because, as the exchange rate appreciates, exports become more expensive, and imports become cheaper, making domestic production less competitive, and shifting production away from traded goods (imports and exports) to non-traded activities (including finance and real estate). Over time, this can also derail the project of industrialization, especially when dynamic economies of scale are involved so that lower production reduces opportunities of learning by doing and production synergies. Financial liberalization has therefore created a new problem which is analogous to what economists dubbed "Dutch disease," (so called because of the experience of the Netherlands with the sudden discovery of North Sea oil that increased oil exports and rendered other forms of domestic production less competitive) with capital inflows causing an appreciation of the real exchange rate that, in turn, causes changes in the real economy.

Third, an even more powerful impact of financial liberalization is that it forces governments to adopt deflationary fiscal policies to appease financial interests. To begin with, the need to attract internationally mobile capital means that there are limits to taxation, especially on capital. Typically, trade liberalization has already reduced the indirect tax revenues (as from tariffs) of states undertaking financial liberalization. With financial liberalization creating pressures to limit other taxes, the overall tax-to-GDP ratio often deteriorates. This imposes limits on government spending, since finance capital is generally opposed to large fiscal deficits. Financial liberalization, therefore, reduces both the possibilities for countercyclical macroeconomic policies—where the state increases spending to boost demand during an economic downturn—and the developmental or growth-oriented activities of the state.

Finance and Development

Financial liberalization can dismantle the very financial structures that are crucial for economic growth and development. While the relationship between financial structure, financial growth, and overall economic development is complex, the basic issue of financing for development is how to mobilize or create real resources. In the classical development literature of the mid-20ᵗʰ century, finance in the sense of money or financial securities came into play only when looking at the ability of the state to tax away a part of the surplus to finance its development expenditures, given the obstacles to deficit-financed spending. By and large, the financial sector was seen as adjusting to the requirements of the real economy.

In this brave new world of today, when the financial sector is increasingly left unregulated or minimally regulated, market signals determine the allocation of investible resources. It was earlier believed that this is both desirable and more efficient, but both actual historical experience and analyses since then have under-lined that the most successful development experiences have emerged from "getting prices wrong," that is, moving away from market signals. Financial deregulation means that available savings are allocated by financial intermediaries to the sectors that are most profitable. In other words, private benefits, rather than overall social benefits, determine the allocation of savings and investment. Credit is directed to non-priority and import-intensive but more profitable sectors. Investible funds are concentrated in the hands of a few large players. Savings are directed to already well-developed centers of economic activity. The socially desirable role of financial intermediation therefore becomes muted.

Financial liberalization also has a negative impact on any medium-term strategy of ensuring growth in particular sectors through directed credit, which had been the basis for the industrialization process through much of the 20ᵗʰ century. In a large number of developing countries in the past, the finan-cial structure was developed with economic development objectives in mind. Financial structures were created to deal with the difficulties associated with late industrial entry.

Small Producers Under Financial Liberalization

In the developing world, financial liberalization has especially negative effects on employ-ment-intensive sectors such as agriculture. For small-scale producers, the transaction costs of borrowing tend to be high, the risks are many, and collateral is not easy to come by. The agrarian crisis in most parts of the developing world is at least partly, often sub-stantially, related to the decline in peasant farmers' access to institutional finance, which is the direct result of financial liberalization. Reductions in state-directed credit toward peas-ant farmers and other small producers have contributed to rising costs of credit, greater difficulty accessing necessary working capital for cultivation and other activities, and the reduced economic viability of cultivation.

All of these effects have added directly to rural distress. In India, for example, the deep crisis of the cultivating community has been associated with farmer suicides, mass out-migrations from rural areas, and even deaths from starvation. There is strong evidence that, in different parts of rural India, these and other forms of distress have been related to the decline of institutional credit, which has forced farmers to turn to private moneylend-ers and involved them once more in interlinked transactions to their substantial detriment.

By the 20th century, minimum capital requirements for entry in most sectors were high because technology for factory production had evolved in a capital-intensive direction since the Industrial Revolution. Competition from more established producers meant that firms had to concentrate on production for a protected domestic market or be supported with finance to survive long periods of low capacity utilization (during which they could find themselves a foothold in world markets). Not surprisingly, therefore, most late industrializing countries created strongly regulated and even predominantly state-controlled financial institutions aimed at mobilizing savings and using the allocation of credit to influence the size and structure of investment. They did this through directed credit policies and differential interest rates, and the provision of investment support to the nascent industrial class in the form of equity, credit, and low interest rates.

By dismantling these structures, financial liberalization destroys important policy instruments that historically evolved in late industrializers. This reduces their ability to ensure economic growth through the diversification of production, given the difficulties generated by international inequality (and especially by the fact that other countries have already industrialized). Financial liberalization is therefore likely to have depressing effects on growth for other reasons than just deflationary bias. It keeps countries stuck in their positions in the global value-added ladder, or may even cause regression and downward movement, much as direct colonial control did in an earlier age.

All of this is even more significant because the process of financial liberalization across the globe has not generated greater net flows of capital into the developing world, as was expected by its proponents. Rather, for the past several years, the net flows have gone in the reverse direction. Even the "emerging markets," which have been substantial recipients of capital inflows, have not experienced increases in overall investment rates, and have built up their external reserves instead. This is only partly because of precautionary measures to guard against possible financial crises; it also indicates prior excess of savings over investment resulting from the deflationary macroeconomic stance.

The workings of international financial markets have actually contributed to international concentration. Developing countries, particularly those in Asia, hold their reserves in U.S. Treasury bills and other safe securities. This contributes to the U.S. economy's absorption of more than two-thirds of the world's savings over the past two decades. At the same time, developing countries are losing out from holding their reserves, these very-low-yielding "safe" assets, while capital inflows into these same countries generally reap much higher rates of interest. This undesirable form of financial intermediation is in fact a direct result of the financial liberalization measures which have simultaneously created deflationary impulses and increased financial fragility across the developing world.

Financialization and Political Control

Other aspects of global financial markets—for example the very unequal and unjust treatment of the sovereign debt of developing countries, which typically ensures the assets of North-based creditors while forcing citizens in poor countries to bear the costs of adjustment and repayment—also contribute to the several ways in which the period of neoliberal globalization has worsened the relative position of such countries and hampered the development project. Without the more obvious political control evident under colonialism, neoliberalism has enabled the flourishing of colonial-style economic relations between countries.

These tendencies have become more apparent—and indeed intensified—in the current Covid-19 pandemic that is sweeping across the globe. While some core advanced countries are currently adversely hit by the spread of the virus, the economic fallout in the developing world has already been far more disastrous, even in countries that have not yet been very badly hit by the contagion. Sharp reversals of capital flows, collapses in export and tourism revenues, currency depreciations, and resulting problems of debt servicing have created a perfect storm for developing countries, many of whom are also imposing severe containment measures like lockdowns that are destroying domestic economic activity. Already, capital movements have indicated a global "flight to safety" to U.S. Treasury Bills, which enable the U.S. government to institute a massive stimulus program of government spending and even larger interventions of bond purchases by the U.S. Federal Reserve. Such strategies are simply not available to other countries, particularly developing countries that will face massive external headwinds even as they struggle to cope with the potential havoc created by large-scale infection and the economic consequences of lockdowns.

If anything, current tendencies therefore reaffirm the basic point made in this article: While current structures of imperialist political control are not as explicit and obvious as those of direct colonial control, they nevertheless still function to enforce global inequality, the global division of labor, and imperialist exploitation of the resources and labor of the "periphery." ❑

Sources: Alice Amsden, *Asia's Next Giant* (Oxford University Press, 1989); Erik Reinert, *How Rich Countries Got Rich and Why Poor Countries Stay Poor* (Anthem Press, 2007); United Nations Conference on Trade and Development (UNCTAD), Trade and Development Report (2016).

Article 9.3

THE GOSPEL OF FREE TRADE: THE NEW EVANGELISTS

BY ARTHUR MacEWAN
November 1991; updated June 2018

Note: This article, originally written in 1991 and updated in 2009, is followed by an af-
terword that takes into account the sharp changes in U.S. international economic policy
that have developed under the Trump administration. — Eds.

F ree trade! With the zeal of Christian missionaries, for decades the U.S. government has been preaching, advocating, pushing, and coercing around the globe
for "free trade."

As the economic crisis emerged in 2007 and 2008 and rapidly became a global
crisis, it was apparent that something was very wrong with the way the world economy was organized. Not surprisingly, as unemployment rose sharply in the United
States, there were calls for protecting jobs by limiting imports and for the government to "buy American" in its economic stimulus program. Similarly, in many other
countries, as unemployment jumped upwards, pressure emerged for protection—
and some actual steps were taken. Yet, free-trade missionaries did not retreat; they
continued to preach the same gospel.

The free-traders were probably correct in claiming that protectionist policies would
do more harm than good as a means to stem the rising unemployment generated by the
economic crisis. Significant acts of protectionism in one country would lead to retalia-
tion—or at least copying—by other countries, reducing world trade. The resulting loss
of jobs from reduced trade would most likely outweigh any gains from protection.

Yet the argument over international economic policies should not be confined
simply to what should be done in a crisis. Nor should it simply deal with trade in
goods and services. The free-traders have advocated their program as one for long
run economic growth and development, yet the evidence suggests that free trade is
not a good economic development strategy. Furthermore, the free-traders preach
the virtue of unrestricted global movement of finance as well as of goods and services. As it turns out, the free flow of finance has been a major factor in bringing
about and spreading the economic crisis that began to appear in 2007—as well as
earlier crises.

The Push

While the U.S. push for free trade goes back several decades, it has become more
intense in recent years. In the 1990s, the U.S. government signed on to the North
American Free Trade Agreement (NAFTA) and in 2005 established the Central
American Free Trade Agreement (CAFTA). Both Republican and Democratic presidents, however, have pushed hard for a *global* free trade agenda. After the demise
of the Soviet Union, U.S. advisers prescribed unfettered capitalism for Eastern and
Central Europe, and ridiculed as unworkable any move toward a "third way." In low-

income countries from Mexico to Malaysia, the prescription has been the same: open markets, deregulate business, don't restrict international investment, and let the free market flourish.

In the push for worldwide free trade, the World Trade Organization (WTO) has been the principal vehicle of change, establishing rules for commerce that assure markets are open and resources are available to those who can pay. And the International Monetary Fund (IMF) and World Bank, which provide loans to many governments, use their financial power to pressure countries around the world to accept the gospel and open their markets. In each of these international organizations, the United States—generally through the U.S. Treasury—plays a dominant role.

Of course, as with any gospel, the preachers often ignore their own sermons. While telling other countries to open their markets, the U.S. government continued, for instance, to limit imports of steel, cotton, sugar, textiles, and many other goods. But publicly at least, free-trade boosters insist that the path to true salvation—or economic expansion, which, in this day and age, seems to be the same thing—lies in opening all markets to foreign goods. Get rid of trade barriers at home and abroad, allow business to go where it wants and do what it wants. We will all get rich.

Yet the history of the United States and other rich countries does not fit well with the free-trade gospel. Virtually all advanced capitalist countries found economic success through heavy government regulation of their international commerce, not in free trade. Likewise, a large role for government intervention has characterized those cases of rapid and sustained economic growth in recent decades—for example, Japan after World War II, South Korea in the 1970s through the 1990s, and China most recently.

Free trade does, however, have its uses. Highly developed nations can use free trade to extend their power and control of the world's wealth, and businesses can use it as a weapon against labor. Most important, free trade can limit efforts to redistribute income more equally, undermine social programs, and keep people from democratically controlling their economic lives.

A Day in the Park

At the beginning of the 19th century, Lowell, Mass., became the premier site of the U.S. textile industry. Today, thanks to the Lowell National Historical Park, you can tour the huge mills, ride through the canals that redirected the Merrimack River's power to those mills, and learn the story of the textile workers, from the Yankee "mill girls" of the 1820s through the various waves of immigrant laborers who poured into the city over the next century.

During a day in the park, visitors get a graphic picture of the importance of 19th-century industry to the economic growth and prosperity of the United States. Lowell and the other mill towns of the era were centers of growth. They not only created a demand for Southern cotton, they also created a demand for new machinery, maintenance of old machinery, parts, dyes, *skills*, construction materials, construction machinery, *more skills*, equipment to move the raw materials and products, parts maintenance for that equipment, *and still more skills*. The mill towns also created markets—concentrated groups of wage earners who needed to buy products to sustain themselves. As centers of economic activity, Lowell and similar mill towns contributed to U.S. economic growth far beyond the value of the textiles they produced.

The U.S. textile industry emerged decades after the industrial revolution had spawned Britain's powerful textile industry. Nonetheless, it survived and prospered. British linens inundated markets throughout the world in the early 19th century, as the British navy nurtured free trade and kept ports open for commerce. In the United States, however, hostilities leading up to the War of 1812 and then a substantial tariff made British textiles relatively expensive. These limitations on trade allowed the Lowell mills to prosper, acting as a catalyst for other industries and helping to create the skilled workforce at the center of U.S. economic expansion.

Beyond textiles, however, tariffs did not play a great role in the United States during the early 19th century. Southern planters had considerable power, and while they were willing to make some compromises, they opposed protecting manufacturing in general because that protection forced up the prices of the goods they purchased with their cotton revenues. The Civil War wiped out the planters' power to oppose protectionism, and from the 1860s through World War I, U.S. industry prospered behind considerable tariff barriers.

Different Countries, Similar Experiences

The story of the importance of protectionism in bringing economic growth has been repeated, with local variations, in other advanced capitalist countries. During the late 19th century, Germany entered the major league of international economic powers with substantial protection and government support for its industries. Likewise, in 19th-century France and Italy, national consolidation behind protectionist barriers was key to economic development.

Britain—which entered the industrial era first—is often touted as the prime example of successful development without tariff protection. Yet, Britain embraced free trade only after its industrial base was well established; as in the United States, the early and important textile industry was erected on a foundation of protectionism. In addition, Britain built its industry through the British navy and the expansion of empire, hardly prime ingredients in any recipe for free trade.

Japan provides an especially important case of successful government protection and support for industrial development. In the post-World War II era, when the Japanese established the foundations for their economic "miracle," the government rejected free trade and extensive foreign investment and instead promoted its national firms.

In the 1950s, for example, the government protected the country's fledgling auto firms from foreign competition. At first, quotas limited imports to $500,000 (in current dollars) each year; in the 1960s, prohibitively high tariffs replaced the quotas. Furthermore, the Japanese allowed foreign investment only insofar as it contributed to developing domestic industry. The government encouraged Japanese companies to import foreign technology, but required them to produce 90% of parts domestically within five years.

The Japanese also protected their computer industry. In the early 1970s, as the industry was developing, companies and individuals could only purchase a foreign machine if a suitable Japanese model was not available. IBM was allowed to produce within the country, but only when it licensed basic patents to Japanese firms. And IBM computers produced in Japan were treated as foreign-made machines.

In the 20th century, no other country matched Japan's economic success, as it moved in a few decades from a relatively low-income country, through the devastation of war, to emerge as one of the world's economic leaders. Yet one looks back in vain to find a role for free trade in this success. The Japanese government provided an effective framework, support, and protection for the country's capitalist development.

Likewise, in many countries that have been latecomers to economic development, capitalism has generated high rates of economic growth where government involvement, and not free trade, played the central role. South Korea is a striking case. "Korea is an example of a country that grew very fast and yet violated the canons of conventional economic wisdom," writes Alice Amsden in *Asia's Next Giant: South Korea and Late Industrialization,* widely acclaimed as perhaps the most important analysis of the South Korean economic success. "In Korea, instead of the market mechanism allocating resources and guiding private entrepreneurship, the government made most of the pivotal investment decisions. Instead of firms operating in a competitive market structure, they each operated with an extraordinary degree of market control, protected from foreign competition."

Free trade, however, has had its impact in South Korea. In the 1990s, South Korea and other East Asian governments came under pressure from the U.S. government and the IMF to open their markets, including their financial markets. When they did so, the results were a veritable disaster. The East Asian financial crisis that began in 1997 was a major setback for the whole region, a major disruption of economic growth. After extremely rapid economic growth for three decades, with output expanding at 7% to 10% a year, South Korea's economy plummeted by 6.3% between 1997 and 1998.

Mexico and Its NAFTA Experience

While free trade in goods and services has its problems, which can be very serious, it is the free movement of capital, the opening of financial markets, that has sharp, sudden impacts, sometimes wrecking havoc on national economies. Thus, virtually as soon as Mexico, the United States, and Canada formed NAFTA at the beginning of 1994, Mexico was hit with a severe financial crisis. As the economy turned downward at the beginning of that year, capital rapidly left the country, greatly reducing the value of the Mexican peso. With this diminished value of the peso, the cost of servicing international debts and the costs of imports skyrocketed—and the downturn worsened.

Still, during the 1990s, before and after the financial crisis, free-traders extolled short periods of moderate economic growth in Mexico —3% to 4% per year—as evidence of success. Yet, compared to earlier years, Mexico's growth under free trade has been poor. From 1940 to 1990 (including the no-growth decade of the 1980s), when Mexico's market was highly protected and the state actively regulated economic affairs, output grew at an average annual rate of 5%.

Most important, Mexico's experience discredits the notion that free-market policies will improve living conditions for the masses of people in low-income countries. The Mexican government paved the way for free trade policies by reducing or eliminating social welfare programs, and for many Mexican workers wages declined sharply during the free trade-era. The number of households living in poverty rose dramatically, with some 75% of Mexico's population below the poverty line at the beginning of the 21st century.

China and Its Impact

Part of Mexico's problem and its economy's relatively weak performance from the 1990s onward has been the full-scale entrance of China into the international economy. While the Mexican authorities thought they saw great possibilities in NAFTA with the full opening of the U.S. market to goods produced with low-wage Mexican labor, China (and other Asian countries) had even cheaper labor. As China also gained access to the U.S. market, Mexican expectations were dashed.

The Chinese economy has surely gained in terms of economic growth as it has engaged more and more with the world market, and the absolute levels of incomes of millions of people have risen a great deal. However, China's rapid economic growth has come with a high degree of income inequality. Before its era of rapid growth, China was viewed as a country with a relatively equal distribution of income. By the beginning of the new millennium, however, it was much more unequal than any of the other most populous Asian countries (India, Indonesia, Bangladesh, and Pakistan), and more in line with the high-inequality countries of Latin America. Furthermore, with the inequality has come a great deal of social conflict. Tens of thousands of "incidents" of conflict involving violence are reported each year, and most recently there have been the major conflicts involving Tibetans and Uighurs.

In any case, the Chinese trade and growth success should not be confused with "free trade." The foundation for China's surge of economic growth was established through state-sponsored infrastructure development and the vast expansion of the country's educational system. Even today, while private business, including foreign business, appears to have been given free rein in China, the government still plays a controlling role—including a central role in affecting foreign economic relations.

A central aspect of the government's role in the county's foreign commerce has been in the realm of finance. As Chinese-produced goods have virtually flooded international markets, the government has controlled the uses of the earnings from these exports. Instead of simply allowing those earnings to be used by Chinese firms and citizens to buy imports, the government has to a large extent held those earnings as reserves. Using those reserves, China's central bank has been the largest purchaser of U.S. government bonds, in effect becoming a major financer of the U.S. government's budget deficit of recent years.

China's reserves have been one large element in creating a giant pool of financial assets in the world economy. This "pool" has also been built up as the doubling of oil prices following the U.S. invasion of Iraq put huge amounts of funds in the pockets of oil-exporting countries and firms and individuals connected to the oil industry. Yet slow growth of the U.S. economy and extremely low interest rates, resulting from the Federal Reserve Bank's efforts to encourage more growth, limited the returns that could be obtained on these funds. One of the consequences—through a complex set of connections—was the development of the U.S. housing bubble, as financial firms, searching for higher returns, pushed funds into more and more risky mortgage loans.

It was not simply free trade and the unrestricted flow of international finance that generated the housing bubble and subsequent crisis in the U.S. economy. However, the generally unstable global economy—both in terms of trade and finance—that has emerged in the free-trade era was certainly a factor bringing about the crisis. Moreover, as is widely recognized, it was not only the U.S. economy and U.S. financial institutions that were affected. The free international flow of finance has meant that banking has become an increasingly global industry. So as the U.S. banks got in trouble in 2007 and 2008, their maladies spread to many other parts of the world.

The Uses of Free Trade

While free trade is not the best economic growth or development policy and, especially through the free flow of finance, can precipitate financial crises, the largest and most powerful firms in many countries find it highly profitable. As Britain preached the loudest sermons for free trade in the early 19th century, when its own industry was already firmly established, so the United States—or at least many firms based in the United States—find it a profitable policy at the beginning of the 21st century. The Mexican experience provides an instructive illustration.

For U.S. firms, access to foreign markets is a high priority. Mexico may be relatively poor, but with a population of 105 million it provides a substantial market. Furthermore, Mexican labor is cheap relative to U.S. labor; and using modern production techniques, Mexican workers can be as productive as workers in the United States. For U.S. firms to obtain full access to the Mexican market, the United States has to open its borders to Mexican goods. Also, if U.S. firms are to take full advantage of cheap foreign labor and sell the goods produced abroad to U.S. consumers, the United States has to be open to imports.

On the other side of the border, wealthy Mexicans face a choice between advancing their interests through national development or advancing their interests through ties to U.S. firms and access to U.S. markets. For many years, they chose the former route. This led to some development of the Mexican economy but also—due to corruption and the massive power of the ruling party, the Institutional Revolutionary Party (also known as the PRI)—to huge concentrations of wealth in the hands of a few small groups of firms and individuals. Eventually, these groups came into conflict with their own government over regulation and taxation. Having benefited from government largesse, they came to see their fortunes in greater freedom from government control and, particularly, in greater access to foreign markets and partnerships with large foreign companies. National development was a secondary concern when more involvement with international commerce would produce greater riches more quickly.

In addition, the old program of state-led development in Mexico ran into severe problems. These problems came to the surface in the 1980s with the international debt crisis. Owing huge amounts of money to foreign banks, the Mexican government was forced to respond to pressure from the IMF, the U.S. government, and large international banks which sought to deregulate Mexico's trade and investments. That pressure meshed with the pressure from Mexico's own richest elites, and the result was the move toward free trade and a greater opening of the Mexican economy to foreign investment.

Since the early 1990s, these changes for Mexico and the United States (as well as Canada) have been institutionalized in NAFTA. The U.S. government's agenda since then has been to spread free-trade policies to all of the Americas through more regional agreements like CAFTA and ultimately through a Free Trade Area of the Americas. On a broader scale, the U.S. government works through the WTO, the IMF, and the World Bank to open markets and gain access to resources beyond the Western Hemisphere. In fact, while markets remain important everywhere, low-wage manufacturing is increasingly concentrated in Asia—especially China—instead of Mexico or Latin America.

The Chinese experience involves many of the same advantages for U.S. business as does the Mexican—a vast market, low wages, and an increasingly productive labor force. However, the Chinese government, although it has liberalized the economy a great deal compared to the pre-1985 era, has not abdicated its major role in the economy. For better (growth) and for worse (inequality and repression), the Chinese government has not embraced free trade.

Who Gains, Who Loses?

Of course, in the United States, Mexico, China, and elsewhere, advocates of free trade claim that their policies are in everyone's interest. Free trade, they point out, will mean cheaper products for all. Consumers in the United States, who are mostly workers, will be richer because their wages will buy more. In Mexico and China, on the one hand, and in the United States, on the other hand, they argue that rising trade will create more jobs. If some workers lose their jobs because cheaper imported goods are available, export industries will produce new jobs.

In recent years this argument has taken on a new dimension with the larger entrance of India into the world economy and with the country's burgeoning information technology industry, which includes programming and call centers. This "outsourcing" of service jobs has received a great deal of attention and concern in the United States. Yet free-traders have defended this development as good for the U.S. economy as well as for the Indian economy.

Such arguments obscure many of the most important issues in the free-trade debate. Stated, as they usually are, as universal truths, these arguments are just plain silly. No one, for example, touring the Lowell National Historical Park could seriously argue that people in the United States would have been better off had there been no tariff on textiles. Yes, in 1820, they could have purchased textile goods more cheaply, but in the long run the result would have been less industrial advancement and a less wealthy nation. One could make the same point with the Japanese auto and computer industries, or indeed with numerous other examples from the last two centuries of capitalist development.

In the modern era, even though the United States already has a relatively developed economy with highly skilled workers, a freely open international economy does not serve the interests of most U.S. workers, though it will benefit large firms. Today, U.S. workers are in competition with workers around the globe. Many different workers in many different places can produce the same goods and services. Thus, an international economy governed by the free-trade agenda will tend to bring down wages for many U.S. workers. This phenomenon has certainly been one of the factors leading to the substantial rise of income inequality in the United States during recent decades.

The problem is not simply that of workers in a few industries—such as auto and steel, or call centers and computer programming—where import competition is an obvious and immediate issue. A country's openness to the international economy affects the entire structure of earnings in that country. Free trade forces down the general level of wages across the board, even of those workers not directly affected by imports. The simple fact is that when companies can produce the same products in several different places, it is owners who gain because they can move their factories and funds around much more easily than workers can move themselves around. Capital is mobile; labor is much less mobile. Businesses, more than workers, gain from having a larger territory in which to roam.

Control Over Our Economic Lives

But the difficulties with free trade do not end with wages. In both low-income and high-income parts of the world, free trade is a weapon in the hands of business when it opposes any progressive social programs. Efforts to place environmental restrictions on firms are met with the threat of moving production abroad. Higher taxes to improve the schools? Business threatens to go elsewhere. Better health and safety regulations? The same response.

Some might argue that the losses from free trade for people in the United States will be balanced by gains for most people in poor countries—lower wages in the United States, but higher wages in Mexico and China. Free trade, then, would bring about international equality. Not likely. In fact, as pointed out above, free-trade reforms in Mexico have helped force down wages and reduce social welfare programs, processes rationalized by efforts to make Mexican goods competitive in international markets. China, while not embracing free trade, has seen its full-scale entrance into global commerce accompanied by increasing inequality.

Gains for Mexican or Chinese workers, like those for U.S. workers, depend on their power in relation to business. Free trade or simply the imperative of international "competitiveness" are just as much weapons in the hands of firms operating in Mexico and China as they are for firms operating in the United States. The great mobility of capital is business' best trump card in dealing with labor and popular demands for social change—in the United States, Mexico, China, and elsewhere.

None of this means that people should demand that their economies operate as fortresses, protected from all foreign economic incursions. There are great gains that can be obtained from international economic relations—when a nation manages those relations in the interests of the great majority of the people. Protectionism often simply supports narrow vested interests, corrupt officials, and wealthy industrialists. In rejecting free trade, we should move beyond traditional protectionism.

Yet, at this time, rejecting free trade is an essential first step. Free trade places the cards in the hands of business. More than ever, free trade would subject us to the "bottom line," or at least the bottom line as calculated by those who own and run large companies.

Afterword

The gospel of free trade remained the dominant policy outlook of business and political elites in the United States well into the 21st century. Both Democrats and Republicans in the White House and Congress pushed ahead with "free-trade agreements." And they had wide support among economists. True, there was some opposition from the lower ranks of the Democratic Party, from unions, and from some businesses directly harmed by foreign competition. But this opposition had limited effect.

Then, in 2016, the chickens came home to roost. People who had been left behind by the economic changes of recent decades—wage stagnation and rising inequality, combined with the decline of manufacturing—had come to view their condition as being the result of free trade or, more generally, "globalization." While their economic difficulties had multiple causes, "unfair" competition from China, Mexico, and elsewhere was readily identified and became the focus of their grievances.

In his ride to the White House, Donald Trump was able to combine this hostility to globalization with underlying racism and xenophobia. In his demagoguery, the United States was the victim in the world economy. And many people, some who really were the victims of the policies of free trade, bought the story. Trump promised to rip up NAFTA and withdraw from the Trans-Pacific Partnership (TPP) pursued by the Obama administration.

Upon taking office, President Donald Trump did abandon the TPP, and in 2018 it appears that NAFTA is on the verge of demise. More generally, as this update is being written in June 2018, the Trump administration has initiated a set of classical protectionist policies, imposing tariffs on many goods—not only from China, Mexico, and other low-wage countries, but also from Canada and the European Union.

While these actions appeal to his "base" and to workers and businesses that will directly benefit from a reduction in competition, the Trumpian counter to free trade will harm most workers and the U.S. economy generally. For example, jobs in the steel industry (a focus of the new tariffs) will increase somewhat, but more jobs will be lost in industries—particularly the auto industry—where higher prices for steel will yield production cutbacks. Also, as other countries impose retaliatory tariffs on U.S. exports, still more jobs in the United States will be lost. Most generally, the changes and unpredictability of the Trump administration's actions generate economic uncertainty, which is bad for business.

Few members of the political and business elite and few economists have voiced support for the reemergence of classical protectionism. For them, the gospel of free trade remains a gospel.

For most people, however, neither free trade nor classical protectionism is a reasonable way for the United States to engage with the global economy. There are other options. To develop these options, to build a progressive trade policy, it is useful to recognize that jobs are changing all the time due to several causes—international trade, but also technological change, and new wants and needs. It would not be useful to stop this change, but it is essential that in the process of these changes workers be protected. This means supporting meaningful and extensive retraining programs, job transfer programs, and ample funds for workers in transition. The goal should be to protect workers, which is not the same as protecting jobs.

Further, a progressive trade policy would take into account the conditions under which imported goods are produced—especially the impact on workers and on the environment. Restrictions would be placed on the import of goods produced under conditions where workers are denied basic human rights. Likewise, restrictions would be placed on the import of goods produced in an environmentally destructive manner. In both cases, the restrictions could be absolute or could be accomplished by tariffs that eliminated the cost advantages attained by abrogating labor rights and ignoring environmental concerns.

Engagement with the economies of the rest of the world can be quite valuable, both for narrow economic reasons and more broadly for many cultural, educational, and intellectual reasons. There is an important exception: International financial activity should be severely restricted because it removes a country's ability to control its own economy. But overall, a progressive policy is a policy of global engagement, not isolation. ❏

Article 9.4

THE GLOBALIZATION CLOCK

BY THOMAS PALLEY
May/June 2006; revised November 2018

Over the past 40 years, real wages have stagnated in developed economies, and there has also been a massive increase in income and wealth inequality. Those developments are substantially attributable to the neoliberal economic policy paradigm which has dominated policymaking. Globalization is a critical element of that paradigm, and it has been a major contributing factor to wage stagnation and increased inequality.

The neoliberal policy era did not happen in a vacuum. Instead, it needs to be explained by political economy, which shows how particular economic interests triumphed in capturing political power and the world of economic ideas (i.e., economic theory), and how those ideas and policies were accepted by society. The Globalization Clock provides a metaphor for understanding that political process as it relates to globalization. It helps explain why globalization has been so politically difficult to turn back despite its injurious effects. A key reason is globalization's adverse impact on political solidarity, with globalization aggravating the preexisting decline in solidarity caused by the rise of the consumer society.

Political economy has historically been constructed around the divide between capital and labor, with firms and workers at odds over the division of the economic pie. Within this construct, labor is usually represented as a monolithic interest, yet the reality is that labor has always suffered from internal divisions—by race, by occupational status, and along many other fault lines. Neoliberal globalization has in many ways sharpened these divisions, which helps to explain why corporations have been winning and workers losing.

One of these fault lines divides workers from themselves: Since workers are also consumers, they face a divide between the desire for higher wages and the desire for lower prices. Historically, this identity split has been exploited to divide union from nonunion workers, with anti-labor advocates accusing union workers of causing higher prices. Today, globalization is amplifying the divide between people's interests as workers and their interests as consumers through its promise of ever-lower prices.

Consider the debate over Walmart's low-road labor policies. While Walmart's low wages and skimpy benefits have recently faced scrutiny, even some liberal commentators argue that Walmart is actually good for low-wage workers because they gain more as consumers from its "low, low prices" than they lose as workers from its low wages. But this static snapshot analysis fails to capture the full impact of globalization, past and future.

Globalization affects the economy unevenly, hitting some sectors first and others later. The process can be understood in terms of the hands of a clock. At one o'clock is the apparel sector; at two o'clock, the textile sector; at three, the steel sector; at six, the auto sector. Workers in the apparel sector are the first to have their jobs shifted to lower-wage venues; at the same time, though, all other workers get price reductions. Next, the process picks off textile sector workers at two o'clock. Meanwhile, workers from three o'clock onward get price cuts, as do the apparel workers at one o'clock. Each time the hands of the clock move, the workers taking the hit are isolated. In this fashion, globalization moves around the clock, with labor perennially divided.

Manufacturing was first to experience this process, but technological innovations associated with the internet are putting service and knowledge workers in the firing line as well. Online business models are making even retail workers vulnerable—consider Amazon, for example, which has opened a customer support center and two technology development centers in India. Public-sector wages are also in play, at least indirectly, since falling wages mean falling tax revenues. The problem is that each time the hands on the globalization clock move forward, workers are divided: The majority is made slightly better off while the few are made much worse off.

Globalization also alters the historical divisions within capital, creating a new split between bigger internationalized firms and smaller firms that remain nationally centered. This division has been brought into sharp focus with the debate over the trade deficit and the overvalued dollar. In previous decades, manufacturing as a whole opposed running trade deficits and maintaining an overvalued dollar because of the adverse impact of increased imports. The one major business sector with a different view was retail, which benefited from cheap imports.

However, the spread of multinational production and outsourcing has divided manufacturing in wealthy countries into two camps. In one camp are larger multinational corporations that have gone global and benefit from cheap imports; in the other are smaller businesses that remain nationally centered in terms of sales, production, and input sourcing. Multinational corporations tend to support an overvalued dollar since this makes imports produced in their foreign factories cheaper. Conversely, domestic manufacturers are hurt by an overvalued dollar, which advantages import competition.

This division opens the possibility of a new alliance between labor and those manufacturers and businesses that remain nationally based—potentially a potent one, since there are approximately 7 million enterprises with sales of less than $10 million in the United States, versus only 200,000 with sales greater than $10 million. However, such an alliance will always be unstable as the inherent labor-capital conflict over income distribution can always reassert itself. Indeed, this pattern is already evident in the internal politics of the National Association of Manufacturers, whose members have been significantly divided regarding the overvalued dollar. As one way to address this division, the group is promoting a domestic "competitiveness" agenda aimed at weakening regulation, reducing corporate legal liability, and lowering employee benefit costs—an agenda designed to appeal to both camps, but at the expense of workers.

Solidarity has always been key to the political and economic advancement of working families, and it is key to mastering the politics of globalization. Developing a coherent story about the economics of neoliberal globalization around which working families can coalesce is a key ingredient for solidarity. So, too, is understanding how globalization divides labor. These narratives and analyses can help counter deep cultural proclivities to individualism, as well as other historic divides such as racism. However, as if this were not difficult enough, globalization creates additional challenges. National political solutions that worked in the past are not adequate to the task of controlling international competition. That means the solidarity bar is further raised, calling for international solidarity that supports new forms of international economic regulation. ❏

DOES U.S. PROSPERITY *DEPEND* ON EXPLOITATION?

BY ARTHUR MacEWAN
March/April 2019

> Dear Dr. Dollar:
> *I regularly hear the claim that U.S. prosperity depends on exploiting poorer countries, but I have never once seen an actual argument for it. What is the support for this claim?*
> —Ryan Cooper, via Twitter

Let's start with the two congenital bloodstains on the cheek of U.S. economic development—slavery and the genocide/taking-of-lands of Native American peoples.

Certainly, the prosperity of the United States has depended to a substantial degree on the labor of slaves, based on stealing people from poor societies, disrupting the social order, and depleting the labor force of those societies. In the decade leading up to the Civil War, for example, the value of raw cotton exports accounted for over half of the value of all U.S. exports. Then there were the direct profits from the slave trade, which built the fortunes of several northern U.S. and European families. And the initial phase of U.S. industrialization, the cotton textile industry, was based on low-cost slave-produced cotton.

As to the economic role of lands taken from Native Americans, the value, though incalculable, was immense. Indeed, some historians have argued that a major pillar of U.S. economic success was the availability of "open land"—the so-called "frontier thesis." Not to mention that a large part of that "frontier" was the huge tract of land taken from Mexico after the Mexican-American War.

U.S. economic success—from slavery, "open land," and other aspects of exploiting people of low-income societies—meant different things for different groups. Clearly, for example, southern plantation owners, financiers of the slave trade, and owners of northern cotton mills reaped major gains. Yet, the economic growth that these activities generated seeped down to a broad spectrum of society, benefiting others less than elites, but benefiting many nonetheless—of course, not including the slaves themselves. Likewise, while large-scale ranchers and land speculators gained disproportionately from stealing the lands of Native Americans, many homesteaders also benefited from "opening" the West. The Native Americans themselves, like the slaves, did not share in the prosperity.

Dependence on Government Support

As with slavery and the decimation of the Native American nations, economic activity beyond the current boundaries of the United States depended on government support, importantly including military support. This was especially evident

---

U.S. Economic Interests and Military Action

Excerpt from a speech delivered in 1933 by retired Major General Smedley Butler, USMC.

"I spent 33 years and four months in active military service and during that period I spent most of my time as a high-class muscle man for Big Business, for Wall Street, and the bankers. In short, I was a racketeer, a gangster for capitalism. I helped make Mexico and especially Tampico safe for American oil interests in 1914. I helped make Haiti and Cuba a decent place for the National City Bank boys to collect revenues in. I helped in the raping of half a dozen Central American republics for the benefit of Wall Street. I helped purify Nicaragua for the International Banking House of Brown Brothers in 1902–1912. I brought light to the Dominican Republic for the American sugar interests in 1916. I helped make Honduras right for the American fruit companies in 1903. In China in 1927 I helped see to it that Standard Oil went on its way unmolested. Looking back on it, I might have given Al Capone a few hints. The best he could do was to operate his racket in three districts. I operated on three continents."

---

in the "Gunboat Diplomacy" era in the early decades of the 20th century, when military action abroad was explicitly tied to economic interests, as was famously described and denounced by retired U.S. Marine Corps (USMC) Major General Smedley Butler (see box).

As Butler's statement makes clear, the activities being protected were often those of particular U.S. firms, not the prosperity of the U.S. economy in general. Indeed, in many cases, though the firms benefited, the military costs of the actions outweighed the direct benefits to the U.S. economy. Yet, by protecting the activities of particular firms, the U.S. government was protecting the access of U.S. firms to global markets and resources—that is, protecting the firms' ability to exploit the people and resources in many parts of the world. This access was driven by U.S. firms' search for profits and the firms' owners were the primary beneficiaries. Access, however, also provided low-cost goods—everything from bananas to oil—and markets for U.S. products to the benefit of the U.S. population generally.

At the outset of World War II in late 1939, working with the private, elite Council on Foreign Relations, the U.S. government began planning for the postwar era. According to Laurence H. Shoup and William Minter, in their 1977 book *Imperial Brain Trust*:

> The main issue for consideration [in this planning] was whether America could be self-sufficient and do without the markets and raw materials of the British Empire, Western hemisphere, and Asia. The Council thought that the answer was no and that, therefore, the United States had to enter the war and organize a new world order satisfactory to the United States.

For the United States, the outcome of the war was successful, of course, not only in its immediate military goal of defeating the Axis Powers, but also in establishing U.S. dominance and relatively unfettered access to the markets and raw materials of what the U.S. government referred to as the "Grand Area."

Among the concerns of the planners' efforts to secure the "Grand Area" was Southeast Asia. In one of their memoranda, they wrote, "the Philippine Islands, the Dutch East Indies, and British Malaya are prime sources of raw materials very important to the United States in peace and war; control of these lands by a potentially hostile power would greatly limit our freedom of action." Vietnam would later become the focal point of securing this area from a "hostile power."

The Issue Is Access

The issue in all of this is not the value of some particular resource or raw material. The issue is always access—access that is unfettered by a hostile local government or by costly regulations designed to promote local economic expansion. Since early in the 20th century, access to oil has been a dominant factor in the foundation of U.S. prosperity, and access to oil has often meant the political-military dominance of lower-income countries. Access to oil, however, has not meant simply that the United States would be able to purchase the oil produced in other countries, but that U.S. oil companies would be able to play the central role in controlling that oil and reaping the associated profits. Whatever other motivations were involved in the U.S. invasion of Iraq and the more recent actions against Venezuela, oil was certainly a major factor.

The dominance by U.S. companies of the global oil industry certainly brought profits to the companies. Yet, as the economy became increasingly oil-dependent, oil was relatively inexpensive, providing a major element in the foundation of U.S. prosperity. And much of this oil came from low-income countries. The formation of the Organization of Petroleum Exporting Countries (OPEC) in 1960 did bring about some change, forcing up the price of oil.

Varied Impacts: Countries or Classes?

However, the major oil companies have been able to maintain a great deal of power through sharing more with the elites of some of the oil-source countries. This "sharing" experience with oil, which is common in much of the relationships between U.S. firms and the low-income countries in which they operated, underscores the point that it is not quite accurate to say that *countries* are exploited by U.S. operations. Different social groups—different classes—in the countries are affected quite differently by these operations, some are thoroughly exploited while others benefit.

In the 21st century, the focus of U.S. economic connections to poor countries has shifted somewhat. Markets and raw materials remain important, but low-cost labor and lax (or lack of) environmental regulations have become important as well. All along, financial activity has played a role (see the Smedley Butler box). Access to low-cost labor and avoidance of environmental regulations have often been obtained indirectly, through reliance on local contractors supplying goods to U.S. firms (subcontracting). Walmart is a prime example, but many other firms have also been able to provide U.S. consumers with inexpensive items produced by low-wage labor.

It is true that many of the workers supplying goods to the United States have better jobs than they had had prior to engagement with the U.S. market. And, on a broader level, some countries have attained economic growth (though its benefits often go disproportionally to elites) from their connection to the U.S. economy. Nonetheless, U.S. prosperity at least in part depends on those workers receiving low wages, often working in unsafe or unclean environments, and denied basic rights.

Moreover, in examining the impact of U.S. firms' operations in low-income countries, a distinction needs to be made between the immediate and direct impact and the longer run and more general impact. The former may carry benefits, as the trade and investment created by these operations can generate some economic expansion and much-needed jobs in the low-income countries. Over the longer run, however, U.S. engagement tends to support unequal social structures and a weakening of an internal foundation for long run prosperity in these countries. Furthermore, the U.S. government, in its role as a supporter of U.S. firms' operations around the world, has often intervened to prevent social change that might have led to real improvements in the lives of people in low-income countries. (The list of interventions that Smedley Butler gives only begins to tell the story.)

Pillars of Prosperity

In addition to the international economic relations between the United States and low-income countries, the United States also has extensive economic relations with high-income countries as well. Indeed, the majority of U.S. global trade and the majority of foreign investment by U.S. firms is with other high-income countries. This activity does not generally have the same exploitive characteristics as U.S. firms' penetration of low-income parts of the world. Both are pillars on which U.S. prosperity has depended.

There are other pillars as well. For example, the relatively high degree of education among the U.S. population and the skills that many immigrants brought with them to this country are also pillars of prosperity. But, surely, the exploitation of people in low-income countries has been an important pillar. ❏

Sources: Smedley D. Butler, *War is a Racket: The Antiwar Classic by America's Most Decorated Soldier* (Feral House, 2003); Walter Rodney, *How Europe Underdeveloped Africa* (Black Classic Press, 2011); Andre Gunder Frank, *The Development of Underdevelopment* (Monthly Review Press, 1966); Arthur MacEwan, "Capitalist Expansion, Ideology and Intervention," *Review of Radical Political Economics*, Vol. 4, No. 1, Winter 1972; John Miller, "After Horror, Apologetics: Sweatshop apologists cover for intransigent U.S. retail giants," *Dollars & Sense*, September/October 2013; Arthur MacEwan, "Is It Oil?" *Dollars & Sense*, May/June 2003; Arthur MacEwan, "Is It Oil?—The Issue Revisited," *Dollars & Sense,* March/April 2017.

Article 9.6

ESSENTIAL—AND EXPENDABLE—MEXICAN LABOR

On both sides of the border, Mexican workers are now essential—to U.S. corporations.

BY MATEO CROSSA AND JAMES C. CYPHER
July/August 2020

Lear Corporation—one of the world's largest auto parts manufacturers—rose to position 148 on *Fortune* magazine's famous list of the 500 largest firms in 2018. It operates with roughly 148,000 workers spread across 261 locations. Its largest presence is in Mexico, where approximately 40,000 low-paid workers make seats and labor-intensive electronic wiring systems to be used, primarily, by the U.S. auto giants in auto-assembly plants on both sides of the border. The largest share of these workers slog away in three huge Lear plants located in the notoriously dangerous border town of Ciudad Juárez in Mexico.

On April 10, 2020 a worker named Rigoberto Tafoya Maqueda died from Covid-19, which had swept in from the north. He had been diagnosed in Lear's clinic with a mild allergy and was forced to continue working without a face mask, gloves, or hand sanitizer. A short time later, he went to the government's Social Security hospital, on foot, where he died. Four days later, according to Lear, 13 more workers at the plant had died—but the workers' labor union claimed that the actual number of work-related deaths from the pandemic was 30. Lear claimed it was not responsible in the least, while offering hollow condolences to surviving family members.

As of late May, no investigation of the workplace had been conducted and no legal charges of negligence had been raised against Lear or any of the other 320 *maquiladoras*—also known as *maquilas*, or more recently, by outraged workers, as "*ma*KILL*adoras*"—that employ approximately 230,000 in Juárez where workers have been sickened. By early May, 104 of these workers had perished, by early June the estimated number of worker deaths was above 200. In all of Mexico, this city, with the largest concentration of low-wage assembly plants, had the highest incidence of pandemic deaths—a mortality rate 2.5 times the national average.

Tijuana is the city with the second largest number of *maquilas* in Mexico. There, one in four "formal" sector workers (workers with registered jobs and certain rights to health care) work as low-wage laborers producing components for automobiles and many other industries. Tijuana is located in the state of Baja California in Mexico, where the highest number of pandemic deaths—519—had been recorded as of May 15. Of those deceased, 432 were *maquila* workers. By June 4, Tijuana had the highest number of Covid-19 deaths, 671, of any city in Mexico.

U.S. Business, U.S. State Department Demand: The *Maquilas* Must Open

Ciudad Juárez and Tijuana are tangible symbols of the imposed power structures under which transnational corporations operate throughout the Global South, most particularly in Mexico. In these two border cities, 1,000 miles apart, we find nearly one-fifth of the *maquila* workforce—500,000 out of a total of 2.6 million workers. Here, in response to corporations' treatment of workers during the pandemic, the scene has included bitter strikes, social outrage, and numerous well-attended protests all aimed at imposing plant closures and paid leave. The plant owners have refused to assume any responsibility whatsoever for their negligence, insisting that the work must go on. Instead, they have pressured local and federal governmental agencies to ensure that, in spite of an unsanitary environment, no new safety and health regulations of the workplace will be imposed. After reopening in late May, the plants have taken some measures to reduce health risks among the workers, including the use of masks and plastic dividers at workstations and in company lunchrooms.

At the same time, plants have increased the pace of production exponentially. Even with the measures taken, there have continued to be outbreaks of Covid-19 at the assembly plants. Indeed, the long-powerful U.S. National Association of Manufacturers (NAM) has used every opportunity to ensure that no sustained period of plant closures be implemented—including sending an unprecedented letter to Mexico's president on April 22, signed by 327 corporate titans who enjoy the lucrative benefits of sweating Mexican workers. Signatories included the heads of 3M Corporation ($32 billion in sales in 2019), Arcelor/Mittal USA ($15 billion in sales 2019), and Caterpillar ($54 billion in sales 2019). Using a lot of imagination, and no small amount of chutzpah, these captains of industry demanded that President Andrés Manuel López Obrador (or AMLO, as he is known)—who had declared at the start of his presidency that the neoliberal era that had defined Mexico's economy since 1986 was over—declare that Mexican autoworkers were engaged in an "essential activity." The letter demanded that the president assure that "all interruptions in the North American manufacturing supply chain would be minimized in these critical moments." AMLO responded immediately by stating that Mexico and the United States would come to an agreement and that "there were exceptional questions" to resolve with the United States.

Has there ever been an occasion when a president of a sovereign nation has been told that its populace—beset by a vicious pandemic—would have to march into poisoned plants in order to maintain the profit margins of foreign-owned corporations?

If that was not enough, Christopher Landau, the U.S. ambassador to Mexico, gave himself a pat on the back in late April by declaring via Twitter, "I'm doing all I can to save supply chains between Mexico, the United States, and Canada." Immediately joining the fray, the employers' and manufacturers' "peak business organizations"—long the real rulers of Mexico—began to lobby and orchestrate political pressure to guarantee that *maquila* output would not be interrupted. The large owners associations included the *Consejo Coordinador Empresarial* (CCE), which is comprised of the largest Mexican firms, and the arch-conservative Mexican Employers Association (COPARMEX), which was formed in 1929 by the anti-union oligarchy based in industrial Monterrey, echoed the arguments presented by the NAM. Also joining in was the Association of the Mexican Auto Industry (which was founded in 1951 by Chrysler, Ford, General Motors, Nissan, and Volkswagen, and lists *no* Mexican-owned companies as members).

A National Security Issue?

At this point, an unexpected actor entered the scene: The Undersecretary of Defense of the United States, Ellen Lord, declared to reporters in late April, "I think one of the key things we have found out are some international dependencies..." adding that "Mexico right now is somewhat problematic for us." In her remarks, Lord said nothing about the Mexican workers who toil in the *maquilas* becoming ill or dying. (*Maquilas* are now located throughout the country, not just along the U.S.-Mexican border.) She also added the "national security" argument to her framing of the pandemic's impact on U.S.-Mexico supply chains: "these companies are especially important for our U.S. airframe production." And, indeed, over the past 20 years the United States has outsourced a modest amount of aerospace production: in Mexico this consists of labor-intensive components that are used by the U.S. civilian aviation firms, along with some Pentagon military contractors, and are typically manufactured in *maquilas*. One example of this minor sideline of *maquila* manufacturing—and the conditions that workers face at these factories—is a Honeywell plant in Juárez where, on April 22, workers engaged in a three-day wildcat strike after learning that Covid-19 had spread into the plant, killing at least one worker.

One protesting worker summarized the situation:

> They do not want to give us [sick] days, we are worried because of the pandemic, management does not listen to us, they only tell us [to keep working] and they will give us a bonus of $18-$31.50 [dollars per week] but they will not respond to our demands, we have been on strike three days but the truth is that they are paying no attention to us.

Inaugurating the USMCA

The U.S. pressure game got quick results: on May 12 the Mexican government declared that the aerospace *maquilas* (which, as of 2020, had only 57,000 direct employees) and the very large auto parts and auto assembly industry—which employs nearly 960,000 workers and is a mainstay of the "export-at-all-costs" neoliberal model—were "essential" industries. With this decree, the alarm bells ceased in the United States. Further, the Mexican government set June 1, 2020 as the date to return to full operation in the auto industry, which ensured that the beginning of the NAFTA-II agreement (officially the United States-Mexico-Canada Agreement, or the USMCA) was still on track for July 1, 2020. President Donald Trump will undoubtedly use the official launch of the USMCA to maximum effect as he hones his electoral strategy. AMLO supports this new agreement to "help stop the fall of the economy" and promote new foreign investments.

The list of transnational firms that are already in production—or will shortly resume—where Covid-19 has spread is a long one, and includes such companies as: Lear Corporation, Honeywell, Syncreon Borderland, Foxconn, Plantronics, Leoni, Rockwell, Mahle, Electrocomponentes de México, Electrolux, Hubbell, Commscope, Toro Company, Ethicon, Cordis, Syncreon, Flex, Keytronic, Optron, TPI, and APTIV. In April, shutdowns affected approximately 60% of all *maquiladora* workers in Juárez—a situation that was probably representative for the entire

industry—suggesting that as many as 3,000 of the 5,162 *maquiladora* firms operating in April temporarily closed. The companies that are reopening are doing so
without regard for the deaths of hundreds of their plant workers (some registered,
some not). These firms have been the most enthusiastic advocates of restarting production as they have sought to drown out the resistance of their workers. On May
10, the *maquila* association (Index) reported that 55% of the *maquilas* were in
operation. On May 19, as a great number of plants reopened, *maquila* workers in
Jauréz and Matamoros marched to demand the closure of many plants, including
those operated by Foxconn in Santa Teresa (where there were six Covid-19-related
deaths, according to the workers), Electrocomponentes de México (10 deaths), Lear
(30 deaths), Electrolux (seven deaths), Toro (two deaths), and Regal (13 deaths). The
workers asserted that none of these operations—which make a range of products,
from snow removal equipment to home appliances—were essential and that none
of them had met the sanitation requirements as mandated two months earlier. In
Juárez, 66 *maquilas* that make neither auto parts nor aviation parts (i.e., those never
categorized as "essential") have remained in operation throughout the health crisis.

All across the borderland, from Tijuana (with an estimated 1,000 *maquilas*)
through Mexicali in Baja California to Nogales, Sonora (with 70% of *maquilas* in
operation on May 18), and on to Juárez, Chihuahua, and then to Ciudad Acuña,
Cohauila (where 23,000 workers returned to their plants on May 20) and to the
other end of the border in Matamoros, Tamaulipas (where the hospitals were full of
dying workers), these states, and 269 municipal governments, had capitulated to the
pressure from the United States to reopen. Meanwhile, the Mexican federal government refused to impose its own hygienic measures.

NAFTA: Myth of Development, Reality of Deindustrialization

The destructive impact of the pandemic on Mexico reveals further the direct consequences of 26 years of neoliberalism under NAFTA, which exacerbated inequality and largely destroyed the nation's public health system, while imposing a new
regime of food precarity as once nationally produced grains sold at controlled prices
are now imported. This shift away from producing staple foods in Mexico has resulted in the displacement of millions of peasant cultivators—many of whom eventually migrated to the United States to work in the dirtiest, hardest, most unstable,
and unrewarded jobs available.

What's more, despite the increased prosperity that NAFTA promised, throughout the NAFTA era average workers' wages—measured in terms of their purchasing
power of basic goods—have generally declined. Over the past nearly three decades,
exports have surged (especially in auto and auto parts manufacturing), and Mexico
has been forced to de-industrialize as the domestic market has drowned in a sea of
cheap imports. As a result, the industrial share of the GDP fell from 36.2% in 1993
(the last year before NAFTA took effect) to only 29.6% in 2017 as manufacturing
ceased to be the driving force of the economy. In the period from 2003 to 2016, national content (with value originating in Mexico) across Mexico's broad manufacturing export sector averaged only 41%, while 59% of the value of manufacturing
exports does not originate in Mexico. Using cheap labor to process imported inputs

into goods that are largely exported to the United States now defines Mexico's ever-plodding economy. A large portion of the millions of manufacturing sector jobs that were lost in the United States after 1993 were transferred to Mexico where an enormous army of impoverished wage workers crowded into the *maquiladora* firms—which, as mentioned, now directly employ 2.6 million throughout Mexico.

As was the case in 1992–1993, when the business and political elites of Mexico opened the road to NAFTA—portraying the agreement as a much-needed lever to promote development—these same forces are now eagerly awaiting the USMCA. This delusionary enthusiasm found its way into an essay written by AMLO and published by the office of the president on May 16, 2020:

> To be the neighbor of the most powerful economy in the world under the current circumstances of global recession will help us to drive forward our productive activities and create new jobs. It is a fact that the agreement will attract more foreign investment to our industrial export sector.

But the rage of the *maquila* workers has further unmasked this myth of economic development, despite the fact that, after some attention received in April, the media has largely ceased coverage of labor strife on the border. On the first of May, International Workers Day, the streets of Ciudad Juárez woke up to graffiti proclaiming "STOP MAKILLAS." In this manner a diverse collective of workers began a campaign to raise awareness about perilous workplace conditions—announcing that "*el virus es la makilla*" (the virus is the *ma*KILL*a*) and that "*la makilla te aniquila*" (the *ma*KILL*a* will annihilate you)—and to demand new protections centered on *Salud, Trabajo y Dignidad* (Health, Work, and Dignity). Through these protests, they were able to communicate to the nation the completely arbitrary and unaccountable manner in which the transnational firms were operating along the border and throughout the country. The current policy is for these firms to force workers into the plants (lest they literally starve) on the pretext that they are involved in "essential" activities. Firms expect workers to continue doing their jobs without sanitary protections, given that distancing in these factories is impossible. Indignant workers have drawn attention to those who have been summarily fired, without justification as required by the labor law, when they resisted being forced into the deadly plants. These workers were then denied their indemnification for losing their jobs. (The labor law requires that employers pay workers fired without cause three months of salary plus 20 days of pay for every year of service, and a number of other smaller payments.)

"STOP MAKILLAS!" was also the cry heard on May 12, when the Mexican government declared that *maquila* workers in the aerospace and auto industries were "essential" (essential to the United States) and had to be forced to work, regardless of the utter absence of health and safety protections for workers. The workers responded by demanding they be put on leave at full pay (as well as that all necessary sanitary measures be taken).

But workers' concerns and their demands are clearly unimportant to the U.S. government and hundreds of U.S. companies operating in Mexico. U.S. Ambassador Landau was blunt in his advocacy of reopening in his widely circulated statement:

> We have to protect [people's] health without destroying the economy. It's not im-
> possible. … I'm here to look for win-win solutions. On both sides of the border,
> investment = employment = prosperity.

And so, only four weeks after shutting their doors, the *maquilas* were open without any clear information as to which, if any, measures had been taken to protect
the returning workers. Most workers were forced back onto the shop floor (although
some large export firms delayed until June 1). The agencies of the Mexican government (at all levels) and the company-controlled unions had fallen over backwards to
ensure that the profits would soon again be flowing, primarily to the United States.
In the border state of Chihuahua, for example, 93% of the 122 "essential" workplaces inspected were approved for operation by June 1. However, two weeks later,
additional plant inspections resulted in the closure of 44 out of 208 *maquiladoras*
for lack of compliance with sanitation requirements.

Drafted to Serve: Mexican Workers under the Defense Production Act

In March, the nationwide cries for more medical equipment evoked calls from
Washington, D.C. to essentially conscript medical supply firms under the Defense
Production Act. This Act was implemented in 1950 to force and enable the private
sector to prioritize production and delivery of strategic supplies in a time of national emergency. The president then demurred, while stating that such a policy would
amount to "nationalizing our businesses," then suggested that applying the act would
be similar to steps taken in Venezuela under President Hugo Chávez (1999–2013).

According to President Trump, running out of crucial medical supplies during an
unprecedented pandemic was not a sufficient reason to invoke the production authority of the state—failing market forces all along the medical supply chain could not be
tampered with lest the United States slip into Venezuelan-style economic paralysis.

On the other hand, as the pandemic predictably arrived at the nation's cramped
and fetid slaughterhouses, discomforting the Big Four meatpackers (JBS, with $39
billion in sales in 2017; Tyson, with $38 billion in sales; Cargill, the largest privately-
owned firm in the United States, with $20 billion in sales; and Smithfield, with $15
billion in sales) and disrupting shoppers, these meatpacking behemoths did nothing. At their plants, the meatpackers could not be bothered to protect workers; and
the spike of Covid-19 cases among meatpacking employees led to a slowdown in
the slaughtering of animals, which led to shortages of meat. The president quickly
swung 180° to apply the Act in late April. This mobilized a "critical infrastructure,"
especially the Big Four's infrastructure that very comfortably controls approximately 80% of the beef industry. (The top four in pork slaughterers controlled 64% of the
market in 2011, while the top four in poultry producers controlled 56% of the market in 2019.) Unlike meeting the demand for medical supplies during a pandemic,
slaughtering animals was, apparently, too "critical" to be left to the "free" market.

In 2017 the United States exported 13% of the cattle slaughtered, along with
27% of pigs, and 17% of chickens to other countries. While the Defense Production
Act's powers could control foreign markets (exports and/or imports), U.S. slaughterhouses were left free to sell to the highest bidder.

In effect, U.S. slaughterhouse workers and all others involved in the meatpacking supply chain had been drafted to ensure that the flow of profits for the Big Four continued. Implementing the Act meant that workers could no longer receive unemployment benefits. They were now "free to choose" between zero income and near-zero job prospects outside the meatpacking plants or work in one of the three most impacted job sectors (the other two being nursing homes, which mass deaths from Covid-19 have turned into veritable death camps, and prisons and jails, where infections have run rampant).

There's No Business Like Agribusiness

Right behind the arms-contracting corporations and aerospace firms that swarm the Pentagon stands the mollycoddled U.S. agribusiness interests. Just as the Pentagon was long ago "captured" by the arms contractors who weave in and out of top positions in the Department of Defense in order to return to the contracting firms through Washington's "revolving door," so, too, do the corporate chieftains of agribusiness rotate through the Department of Agriculture and the many other federal and state agencies that work hard to ensure that profits stay high in the agricultural sector.

In this sector government assistance at the local, state, and federal level has long been readily forthcoming to control the labor force and manage the surges in demand for seasonal tasks. Meatpacking, of course, can be undertaken without too much regard to the seasons. It is therefore rightly considered a manufacturing process that long ago adopted "continuous" production processes—often on a 24-hour basis. Like the seasonal-crop farm labor force, slaughterhouses long ago found that the best labor force is an immigrant labor force, documented or not. And, predictably enough, nearly 50% of this labor force consists of "Hispanics." Since nearly two-thirds of all Hispanics (according to the U.S. Census) are Mexican-born, we find that the use of the Defense Production Act to keep the slaughterhouses open is part of the larger process now taking place in both Mexico and the United States to force poor Mexicans to risk pandemic death, or long-term decrepitude, in order to make vehicles and auto parts for the U.S. populace and to ensure that its meat-centric diet is maintained. Embodied Mexican labor—workers who were expelled from Mexico during the long night of neoliberalism (1986–2018)—is the key component of the meatpacking supply chain in the United States. *Disembodied* Mexican labor is the key labor-intensive input of the U.S. auto/auto parts supply chain, as we have explained above.

Werner Sombart's "Free Lunch"

Famously, in *Why Is There No Socialism in the United States?*, Werner Sombart claimed (in 1906) that U.S. workers, unlike their counterparts in Europe, were loyal to "the promised land of capitalism" because it provided them with "reefs of roast beef." Indeed, before Prohibition (1920–1933) a typical saloon in the United States provided an overflowing sideboard "free lunch" for the "thirsty" patrons—roast beef being a mainstay. Sated, workers could then proceed to "bring home the bacon."

So, what would happen if "reefs" of roast beef disappeared from the food system, along with that defining metric, bacon? We have seen that exhausted health care workers have been made to wait for protective equipment until the "free market" got good and ready to sell them such equipment at whatever prices the market will bear. But could the general populace be made to wait for meat at prohibitive prices? Oh, no.

In a society where well-being has largely been defined by the ability to consume, it has long been taken as a given that meat, or any other food item, would be immediately available in any quantity desired, provided that the buyer had sufficient funds. When that turned out to not be the case, the Defense Production Act was immediately deployed to force an overwhelmingly immigrant labor force to make an ugly decision—go to the front and hope to dodge the pandemic's bullets or face deportation, hunger, or both. Suddenly, from the long valleys of California to the largely Midwest slaughterhouses, Mexican workers who had risked arrest and deportation to get to the United States were carrying letters or cards showing that they were "essential." The farmworkers were, as usual, forced to face a daily diet of poisonous pesticides and the risk of infection from the deadly pandemic. But slaughterhouse workers must spend their work shift in tight quarters, in a closed structure among hundreds of workers, usually with circulating air that will bring all possible viral pathogens right to them.

The Pandemic Behind the Pandemic: Neoliberalism

Behind the pandemic of 2020, which has left Latinos with nearly a six times higher infection rate than the average Iowan, lies a deeper pandemic which has spread despair across the United States for four decades. This pandemic—known well outside the United States as neoliberalism—transformed the once heavily unionized labor force in the meatpacking industry into low-wage, disposable drudges. Wages that were 15% above the national manufacturing average in the 1970s had, by the 1990s, fallen 20% below the median. Once subject to industry-wide bargaining agreements, plant unions now bargain weakly: in 2019 only 19% of the 292,000 meat processing workers were union members. In the 1980s and 1990s slaughterhouses were mostly shifted to "right-to-work" rural states to break the legacy of the large-city unions. These states allow workers a "free ride"—they can have the benefits of a union contract without paying dues—and this feature makes it almost impossible to maintain a union shop. Doubling up, employers began recruiting immigrants, particularly from Mexico. Today, the labor force has a turnover rate ranging from 60–100%, and the meatpackers union has been largely silent as the pandemic has spread.

Just prior to the decision to impose a military-style command system in the slaughterhouses, the Big Four dominating the supply chain (and the many small operations), facing massive pandemic outbreaks, demanded that the federal government impose labor rules that would exempt them from any workplace liability for death or illness arising from the pandemic. Corporations are maneuvering to use the Defense Production Act as a "liability shield" in order to stave off an expected wave of lawsuits alleging workplace negligence—such a wave would raise their liability insurance rates. Under the new arrangement, proven "negligence" may not trigger a court award—workers would have to prove "gross negligence, recklessness, or willful misconduct." Operating under the Defense Production Act, the meatpacking plants have become the spearhead of big U.S. capital—if they can weaken workers' rights to a demand a safe workplace, such new legal arrangements will be used by all sectors to weaken labor safety standards and drive down their operating costs.

Meanwhile, across the Midwest, the South, and the Rockies, where most plants are located, right-wing governors are working hand-in-glove with the meat barons, county health departments, and the Occupational Safety and Health Administration to hide any and all information with regard to infection rates and deaths from the pandemic. Only days after Trump invoked the Defense Production Act, data releases on the pandemic's spread at the slaughterhouses all but ceased. Still, county-wide data showed that in Finney County, Kan., home to a Tyson slaughterhouse, the infection rate on May 25, 2020 was one in every 26 people. This is nearly eight times the very high national average. The same results, as recorded by the *New York Times* map "Coronavirus in the United States," could be found over and over again: Cargill's plant in Ford County, Kan. produced an infection rate of one in every 21 people and Tyson's giant plant in Dakota City—operating with 4,300 workers—left nearby Woodbury County, Iowa with an infection rate of one in 39.

In Mexico and the United States, millions of "essential" Mexican workers— essential to the profits of U.S. super-corporations—are pressed to toil on: they must ensure that the U.S. populace face an even larger oversupply of motor vehicles and whatever "reefs of roast beef" remain after the lucrative export market has been supplied. ❑

Sources: De la Redacción, "Industriales de EU piden a México reabrir fábricas" *La Jornada*, April 23, (journada.com.mx); Manuel Fuentes, "Maquiladoras, a laborar por órdenes del Norte," *La Silla Rota*, May 20, 2020 (lasillarota.com); Joe Gould, "COVID closed Mexican factories that supply US defense industry. The Pentagon wants them opened" *Defense News*, April 21, 2020 (defensenews.com); Paola Gamboa, "Un bono de 700 pesos no vale más que mi vida" *El Heraldo de Juárez*, April 20 2020 (elheralddeJuárez.com.mx); Patricia Mayorga, "Indiferencia gubernamental y empresarial expone a obreros de maquilas al COVID-19," *La Verdad*, June 19, 2020 (laverdadJuárez.com); "Iztapalapa y Tijuana, cerca de los 700 muertos por COVID-19; ¿qué municipios registran más contagios?," *MedioTiempo*, June 6, 2020 (mediotiemp.com); "Piden cerrar maquiladoras en frontera mexicana por la pandemia de COVID" *INFOBE: México* , May 19, 2020 (infobae.com); Marco Antonio López, "Empleados acusan que los obligan a trabajar pese a muertes por COVID en maquiladoras de Chihuahua" *Animal Político,* May 18, 2020 (animalpolitico.com); René Villareal, "Comercio exterior y el desarrollo de capacidades" *Comercio Exterior*, Oct.-Dec. 2018; Andrés Manual López Obrador, "The New Political Economy in the time of the Corona Virus," Office of the President, May 16, 2020 (lopezobrador.org.mx); Alberto Morales, "AMLO comparte ensayo la nueva política económica en los tiempos del coronavirus" *El Universal*, May 16, 2020 (eluniversal.com.mx); Shawn Fremstad, Hye Jin Rho and Hayley Brown, "Meatpacking Workers are a Diverse Group," Center for Economic Policy Research, April 29, 2020 (cepr.net); Roger Horowitz, "The decline of unionism in America's meatpacking industry," *Social Policy* (32: 3, 2002); Union Stats, 2019 "Union Membership by Occupation: Standard Occupational Classification 7810—Butchers and Meat Processors," 2019 (unionstats.com); Michael Corkery, David Yaffe-Bellany and Drek Kravitz, "Meat Workers Left in the Dark Under Pressure" *New York Times*, May 25, 2020 (nytimes.com); "Coronavirus Map: Tracking the Global Outbreak" *New York Times*, May 25, 2020 (nytimes.com).

Article 9.7

STRINGENT, STINGY, AND SEVERE
The Covid-19 crisis in Modi's India.

BY SMRITI RAO
July/August 2020

Some months ago, *The Economist* magazine called the Indian government's response to the Covid-19 crisis one of the most "stringent" in the world. The two-month-long national lockdown imposed by the Indian central government from March 24 to May 30 involved a ban on all internal and international travel, including a complete suspension of all public transportation services, something no other country did. Most retail and production facilities were closed, with the list of "essential activities" exempted from this suspension being much narrower than in other countries.

But the economic pain and sacrifice of the Indian people throughout this lockdown seems to have been for nothing. Four months later, India is number three in the world when it comes to the country's number of Covid-19 cases—right behind the United States and Brazil. Daily new cases are still increasing exponentially. The official death count is low, at around 2.5% of confirmed cases, but only around 75% of deaths are ever officially registered in India, a problem compounded by testing shortages in the case of Covid-19 deaths. The relative youth of India's population might save it from the six-digit fatality rate of the United States, but the magnitude of the tragedy unfolding in the world's second most populous country is still immense.

How did India go from one of the world's most stringent lockdowns, to one of the world's most severe outbreaks? Based on the evidence thus far, one important explanation lies in what *The Economist* called the relative "stinginess" of the state's response. Whether we look at fiscal relief to Indian citizens during and after the initial lockdown, public investment in Covid-19 testing and treatment facilities, or federal assistance to the state governments trying to manage local Covid-19 outbreaks, the Indian government's response has been amongst the least generous in the world. This failure to appropriately use macroeconomic policy tools in a crisis is compounded by a more long-term failure of "social provisioning" in India. Successive Indian governments have failed to adequately invest in public programs that could ensure Indians' ability to fulfill their basic needs of health care, food security, water, and sanitation, all of which have become more vital in the wake of the Covid-19 crisis. The combination of "stringent and stingy" that characterizes the Indian government's response has contributed to its failure to control the spread of Covid-19.

Most importantly, this particular policy response was a choice, rather than something the government was pushed into. As the leader of a right-wing nationalist government that was just re-elected with an expanded electoral majority—and the backing of a very powerful right-wing grassroots movement—India's Prime Minister Narendra Modi had the political space to respond with much more spending on economic relief, which would have reduced the economic pressure to ease the lockdown. The much larger relief programs announced by other emerging-country governments, not to mention the United States and Europe, could have provided international cover for such a move, if such cover was needed. By the time India's lockdown was announced, the International Monetary Fund (IMF), the World Bank, and mainstream economists across the world were calling for the expansion of basic income guarantee programs, wage subsidies, large-scale deficit spending, and a host of other measures once considered far too radical. The fact that there were so few of these programs in India tells us something about the class bias of the government and about its understanding of its social contract with the Indian people.

India's "Stringent" Lockdown

India's first Covid-19 case was confirmed on January 30. Throughout early February clusters of infection were small, limited to international travelers, and managed by quarantines, public service announcements, and screening at international ports of entry. Unlike in the case of Brazil or the United States, the national leadership seemed to take the scientific evidence about Covid-19 seriously. In the Indian case, the inability to effectively manage the health and economic crises generated by Covid-19 stems from the ideological basis and design of the central government's response in light of that knowledge.

Evidence of limited community transmission in India emerged by early March as the United States and Europe began to go into lockdowns. However, Prime Minister Modi's own announcement of a nationwide lockdown was made without consulting state governments or relevant national authorities, and gave Indians barely four hours to prepare for a complete shutdown of all transportation and non-essential economic activity. No one outside of Modi's inner circle had an opportunity to plan for the economic impact of the lockdown. Modi's surprise announcement was drawing upon a colonial legacy of undemocratic law-and-order pronouncements from the Indian central government. His announcement was perhaps subconsciously reflecting the fact that the Indian state's coercive powers are still much greater than its ability to deliver welfare to its citizens. But the nature of the announcement also reflected Modi's own authoritarian instincts, something he shares with leaders like Donald Trump and Jair Bolsonaro of Brazil. Each has worked to cultivate the image of an "I-alone-can-fix-it" leader, and in Modi's case this has meant operating like a president despite being part of a parliamentary system.

Once the lockdown was announced, the coercive machinery of the state swung into action, unleashing the dreaded *lathi* charge (police hitting people with batons) to keep people off the streets. This was a tremendous hardship for the millions of Indians in rural and urban India who earn their living as small traders, street vendors, drivers of taxis or auto-rickshaws, and wage workers on construction sites and in factories. Farmers and home-based piece-rate workers were cut off from access to raw materials, supplies, and markets. But the defining images of the lockdown will be the heartbreaking pictures of millions of destitute migrants, children in tow, setting off on foot to walk hundreds of miles from cities like Delhi, Mumbai, or Chennai to their homes in distant states. They had never been able to access clean water, decent housing, or sanitation in the work-site camps they lived in. Now there was no income, either. If they were going to die, they told reporters across the country, whether of hunger or of the coronavirus, they would rather do so with their families, in their hometowns. As they set off on their journeys, did they encounter a government that was organizing transportation, rest stops, and food for them? Did they find well-stocked quarantine camps at their destinations where they could receive food and access to Covid-19 testing? "Darling, this is India," as the Bollywood movie title goes. They were on their own, well and truly "doubly free," as Marx famously called workers to whom capitalism grants a freedom to choose between work and starvation.

Why the Lockdown Didn't Work

Given that 90% of India's workforce consists of informal-sector workers with almost no benefits or savings, it was always obvious that a Covid-19 lockdown would be economically devastating for most Indian households. Furthermore, Covid-19 arrived as the Indian economy was already slowing down. This slowdown reflected an overall decrease in the growth of developing country economies after commodity price declines in 2015. But it was made worse by Prime Minister Modi's inexplicable decision to demonetize the Indian economy in 2016. India's GDP per capita growth had fallen even before the Covid-19 crisis, from an average of 7% in 2016 to below 5% in the last quarter of 2019.

And yet, the cumulative relief package announced by India during this period is among the least generous in the world. While the prime minister has claimed that government economic relief amounts to 10% of GDP, analysts ranging from investment bankers to public policy experts have concluded that actual new spending is closer to 1.5% of GDP. As the table on the next page indicates, of this new spending, a third consists of transfers targeted to formal-sector workers. The remaining expenditure, about 1% of GDP, consists primarily of an expansion in the entitlement of food provided through the country's Public Distribution System, and increased expenditures on the country's National Rural Employment Guarantee Scheme. These are much-needed expansions, but in accounting for barely 1% of GDP, they fall far short of the scale required to combat this crisis. For comparison, the United States has already spent 10% of its GDP on Covid-19 fiscal relief.

The Indian government is clearly aware of the need to sound like it is providing generous relief. It arrived at its (inflated) 10% of GDP Covid-19 relief package figure by 1) including welfare program adjustments that were already scheduled to go into effect this year and were merely advanced to count as Covid-19 relief, and 2) monetary easing and liquidity boosting measures. The latter are actions by India's Central Bank to lower interest rates and make it easier for banks to lend. While helpful for larger businesses and corporations who have existing relationships with banks in India, bank loans (and the burden of ultimately repaying those loans) are not what daily wage workers who cannot feed their families most immediately need.

There is the basic humanitarian imperative of trying to save lives through tangible transfers of the food, medical services, and cash that they need. There is also the economic case for such transfers: Macroeconomics teaches us that direct transfers to poorer consumers translate more directly into spending, and are thus a bigger

TABLE 1: THE COMPOSITION OF INDIA'S COVID-19 RELIEF: ACTUAL NEW SPENDING

	Expenditure (Billions of Rupees)	Expenditure (Millions of Dollars)	% of total
Investment in health care	₹ 1.5	$20	5%
Payroll tax cuts (primarily affecting formal-sector workers)	₹ 5.7	$76	21%
Other transfers to formal-sector workers	₹ 4	$53	14%
Expansion of the National Rural Employment Guarantee Scheme	₹ 4.4	$59	16%
Expansion of the public distribution system for food	₹ 4	$53	14%
Other yransfers to informal worker households	₹ 8	$107	29%
Total:	**₹ 27.6**	**$368**	**100%**

Source: Suhasish Dey and Anirban Kundu, "Atmanirbhar Bharat Abhiyan: Putting the Cart Before the Horse," Ideas for India, July 6, 2020 (ideasforindia.in).

boost for the economy, than changes to interest rates. This is something that even powerful central bankers, including the chairman of the U.S. Federal Reserve, have been pointing out since the beginning of the crisis, as they have urged legislators to provide direct fiscal relief.

The Indian government claims that concerns about a downgrading of its credit rating prevent it from spending more; that it worries about its ability to attract foreign investment. This is ironic, given that at the beginning of the lockdown capital outflows from India (and indeed the rest of the developing world) had already exceeded those after the Great Recession, as capitalists fled to the "safety" of advanced capitalist countries running historic levels of deficits. As with most attempts to placate financial capital, this one also failed. Credit rating agencies recently downgraded India's credit rating anyway—from stable to negative—citing the increased likelihood of an extended economic recession, which is of course compounded by insufficient economic stimulus.

In the end, the actual management of India's health and economic crises has been left to state governments, as have the bulk of test-and-trace efforts. India's federal system means that states have some leeway when it comes to health and social welfare policy, but the central government very firmly controls the purse strings. State governments in Indian states such as Kerala, which has a communist state government, have been much more responsive and responsible, but restrictions on their ability to borrow means that they are ultimately constrained by the central government's willingness to fund them.

A Failure of Social Provisioning

India's inability to effectively deal with the Covid-19 crisis is also the result of a more long-standing failure of social provisioning. That is, a failure to invest in the public provision of goods and services—such as water, housing, food security, and health care—that are essential to human well-being. When India began IMF- and World Bank-mandated programs of structural adjustment and financial liberalization in 1991, the country had a minimal social safety net. The main nationwide program with any systematic impact was the Public Distribution System (PDS), which was created in the 1940s to manage food scarcity, and currently provides 800 million people with subsidized grains through more than 500,000 fair price shops. Through the 1990s, the government was required to cut its already limited funding for such programs in order to address its balance-of-payments deficit.

However, as in other parts of the Global South, there was some expansion of the social safety net from 2004–2014 in response to grassroots struggles. As a result, the PDS became stronger in some states, and, at the national level, there was an expansion of mid-day meal programs for school children, pensions for the elderly, and, in particular, the institution of the National Rural Employment Guarantee Scheme in 2005, which guarantees 100 days of minimum wage employment every year to rural Indians. Interestingly, both programs have been particularly accessible to, and inclusive of, women. On the other hand, even after the expansion in the 2000s, social provisioning remained inadequate. Total spending by the Indian state on all social provisioning programs, including on public health, was around 3% of GDP in 2018, in comparison to 20% for the United States and Brazil, or 7% for China and Mexico.

The electoral win of the right-wing Bharatiya Janata Party (BJP) in 2014 had some elements of a backlash to these advances, and these social provisioning programs stagnated after the BJP took power. The government has attacked and attempted to weaken the grassroots movements that pushed for these programs. Since 2014, the BJP has also focused on so-called public-private partnerships as a means to expand basic social services. For example, right before the Covid-19 crisis hit, India's health care system, which was already almost fully privatized, was going to be pushed even further in that direction by a proposal to privatize district-level community health centers. The consequences of this push to privatize are being felt right now, as private hospitals turn away Covid-19 patients and charge exorbitant prices to those they allow in.

Power, Inequality, and Covid-19 in India

Sociologist Ananya Roy has written about informality as an idiom of state power in India. The fickleness of the state allows it the ability to create zones of exception and exclusion that operate to marginalize on the basis of class, caste, and gender. With the Covid-19 crisis, it is revealing to see how the absence of a substantive plan for governmental intervention has played out. The existence of around 100 million internal migrants living precariously on work sites across India is not a surprise to the Indian state or the Indian people—the urban boom of the last two decades has been built upon their labor. Yet during the lockdown, the state suspended all public transportation without organizing food, water, and health care for these migrants at their work sites. When it announced the first round of Covid-19 relief, it ignored the fact that eligibility for welfare programs in India is based upon your place of residence, and India's precarious migrants do not have proof of residence in the cities in which they live. And in its continuing refusal to extend sufficient support to state governments, it is disproportionately hurting the ability of poorer states—the home states of most internal migrants—to provide food and health care to their residents.

The state's failure to act has also accentuated the gendered character of the crisis. Inadequate access to non-market provisioning of basic food and health care hurts all Indians, but women are bearing the brunt of increases in the intensity of reproductive labor performed within the home during social distancing. Families are also sites of inter-generational and gendered violence—up to one in three Indian women are estimated to suffer from some form of domestic violence—and many women and children are now trapped inside abusive homes. Last, but not least, we know that during food and health care shortages in India, women are more likely to be excluded from access, as families concentrate their scarce resources upon feeding and caring for male breadwinners. Thus, the secondary health and economic effects of this crisis are likely to be worse for women, even as rates of mortality and job loss are currently higher for men.

While the actual relief delivered to Indian citizens has been inadequate, the central government has seized the opportunity to announce further pro-capital liberalization measures. Apart from cheaper credit, which disproportionately benefits larger capitalists, the government has approved the previously controversial privatization of state-owned enterprises and announced measures that would make it easier for corporations to expand into Indian agriculture. When some state governments went further and announced the rollback of labor laws such as those restricting the length of the work week, they did so with the support of the central government.

It is feeling increasingly like the state understands the class character of the pandemic all too well. The urban working class lives in crowded conditions with even less access to India's minimal safety net or public health systems than the rural poor. Urban daily wage workers tend to have high rates of tuberculosis, HIV/AIDs, and, in the case of women in particular, malnutrition, all of which make them more vulnerable to Covid-19. Many of the most destitute urban migrants are meanwhile drawn from the ranks of land-poor and landless families who live in rural India, who are in similarly poor health. If past pandemics are any guide, deaths are also likely to be concentrated among these groups—since they are at once the most marginalized and also, importantly, the most disposable subjects of a state that is much more concerned with representing the interests of economic elites.

Some Reasons for Hope

India's failure to provide food and housing to the majority of Indians in need increased the pressure to end the lockdown order. Those same failures now make prolonged social distancing economically unviable. The refusal to invest in a threadbare public health system, even in the midst of a crisis as severe as this one, makes it unlikely that the health care system will be able to save lives, a proposition that will be tested now that the virus is rapidly spreading. The sharp increase in cases in India is proof, if we needed it, that stringent lockdowns fail when they are also stingy.

The Indian government's response to this crisis appears to be of a piece with the backlash against the progress made by social movements in India in the 2000s. Apart from the pushback against programs expanding social provisioning in India, the government had also intensified attempts to marginalize Muslims and other religious minorities in India pre-Covid-19. These attempts included a draconian lockdown in the contested region of Kashmir, a change to citizenship laws that has the potential to exclude religious minorities, and a refusal to intervene to stop religious riots in the capital city of Delhi. Unsurprisingly, the Covid-19 crisis has also been communalized, with gatherings of Muslims singled out for blame when it came to spreading the virus. Efforts to censor the free press have also increased. The current Indian government does have the ability and inclination to seize even more coercive power under the cover of the crisis, and it will certainly try.

But there are at least three reasons for optimism. One is that the excellent performance of some state governments, such as Kerala, is bolstering the case for greater federalism and decentralization of state power. Second, the destitution of the urban poor has been exposed as never before. This may lead to greater mobilization of marginalized urban classes and castes to demand universal social provisioning. It may also imply more popular legitimacy for any such protest movement. Third, right before the Covid-19 crisis, we were seeing the emergence of popular resistance to Hindu nationalism from Muslim groups allied with other minority religious and lower-caste groups. The BJP's response to the coronavirus crisis has only further accentuated the insecurity felt by such groups. If this resistance reemerges, and it is able to ally with other marginalized urban groups, India may still see a popular movement that can push for better and more equally distributed social provisioning by the state as well as a retrenchment of the Hindu nationalist agenda. ❑

Sources: "Emerging-market lockdowns match rich-world ones. The handouts do not," *The Economist*, April 4, 2020 (economist.com); Blavatink School of Government and University of Oxford, "Coronavirus Government Response Tracker," (bsg.ox.ac.uk); Henrik Pettersson, Byron Manley, and Sergio Hernandez, "Tracking coronavirus' global spread," CNN, as of July 18, 2020 (cnn.com); Subhasish Dey and Anirban Kundu, "Atmanirbhar Bharat Abhiyan: Putting the cart before the horse," Ideas for India, July 6, 2020 (ideasforindia.in); William A. Galston, "Heed

Powell's Call for Fiscal Stimulus," *Wall Street Journal*, May 19, 2020 (wsj.com); International Labour Organization website (ilostat.ilo.org); Jagdish Rattanani, "Coronavirus: Time to commandeer private hospitals?," *Deacan Herald*, June 14, 2020 (deacanherald.com); Payal Mohta, "India's coronavirus lockdown is forcing women to do all the work," *South China Morning Post*, May 10, 2020 (scmp.com); Sheikh Saaliq, "Every Third Woman In India Suffers Sexual, Physical Violence at Home," News 18, Feb. 8, 2018 (news18.com); D. P. K. Pillay and T.K. Manoj Kumar, "Food Security in India: Evolution, Efforts and Problems," *Strategic Analysis*, Issue 6, 2018; Kabir Agarwal, "Six Charts Show That India Needs to (and Can Afford to) Universalise PDS," *The Wire*, April 18, 2020 (thewire.in).

Chapter 10

RESISTANCE AND ALTERNATIVES

INTRODUCTION

Many of the articles in this book are about problems in the U.S. and global economies. Both the dominant economic ideologies and the ruling institutions, many authors argue, favor the wealthy and powerful and are stacked against workers, poor people, developing countries, and other less-powerful actors in the domestic and international economies. That is not, however, the whole story. Those who are getting a raw deal under existing arrangements are not merely passive victims. Some are standing up and resisting poverty, inequality, and enforced powerlessness. Some are fighting for changes in policies and institutions that would help shift the existing balance of power—and improve conditions of life for those at the "bottom" —for a change. This chapter describes both resistance and alternatives to the current "neoliberal" economic orthodoxy, on both the domestic and international scenes.

Starting off the chapter, Francisco Pérez and Luis Feliz Leon (Article 10.1) propose that President Joe Biden's campaign promise to "build back better" should be based on truly participatory structures—not the restoration of the old political order. They argue that the pandemic has brought into focus the open class warfare of the billionaire class against everyone else, and that truly building back better calls for the creation of a solidarity economy.

Next, Arthur MacEwan points out that the burning problems in the U.S. economy—how to achieve sustainable growth and good jobs for all who want them—are not economic, but political (Article 10.2). That is, we have the resources we need to solve our problems, but they are not deployed correctly because powerful interests stand in the way.

Then, in Article 10.3, Luis Feliz Leon describes the efforts of The Drivers Cooperative (TDC) in New York City to establish a worker-owned app-based alternative to Uber, Lyft, and other ride-hailing companies. Leon describes TDC's struggle against the Silicon Valley titans and venture capitalists of Big Tech and how they're working to create a business model that is truly centered on workers' needs in an industry that's rigged against drivers.

Next, we have articles on why the United States needs to defund bloated and militarized police departments, why the right to form a union is a crucial step in improving workplace conditions in lower-income countries, and how to achieve sustainable economic development.

Sonali Kolhatkar (Article 10.4) describes how collective public rage over police violence and impunity has brought a long-standing activist call to defund the police into the spotlight. Kolhatkar further explains how protests against police brutality have a long history that predates the rallying cry of "Black Lives Matter" becoming a household phrase.

In Article 10.5, MacEwan takes on the thorny issue of how trade agreements can incorporate labor standards to improve conditions for workers in lower-income countries. MacEwan notes that barriers to exports from those countries, even those tied to labor standards, can harm workers by taking away employment opportunities. Activists pushing for international labor standards, in his view, should take their lead from the workers in the affected countries, and above all emphasize those workers' rights to organize for improved labor conditions.

Then, Jawed Nawabi (Article 10.6) focuses on land reform and its importance to economic development. Part of the case for land reform, he notes, is economic—for example, small farms actually produce more output per acre than large landholdings. However, the crux of the case is not narrowly economic, but sociopolitical. Land reform is so essential to economic development, Nawabi argues, because the power of large landlords stands in the way of needed development policies.

Next, Sirisha Naidu (Article 10.7) offers us a detailed overview of the massive protests in India by farmers resisting neoliberal reforms. These new laws concentrate power in the hands of corporations, increase monopolization, decrease farmers' income, and reduce food security. Protesters cut across traditional gender, class, caste, religious, and regional lines and call for India's government to put the needs of its citizens first.

Finally, closing out this chapter, in Article 10.8, Abdul Malik tells the story of the remarkable two-day wildcat strike by NBA players during the peak of the Covid-19 pandemic. He explains how Major League Baseball, Major League Soccer, the Women's NBA, and the National Hockey League also came to join the strike. The strike experience indicates the direction in which the players and their union are moving and what management power exists to hold them back.

Discussion Questions

1. (Article 10.1) What is the meaning of "nothing about us without us"? Provide examples of solidarity efforts in the areas of work, home, finance, and government. How might a solidarity economy overcome the existing class warfare between the billionaire class and everyone else?

2. (Article 10.2) According to MacEwan, in what ways are powerful vested interests standing in the way of needed reforms in the United States? How could this resistance ever be overcome?

3. (Article 10.3) How might a co-op help workers/drivers? What is the Big Tech independent contractor loophole? What is sectoral bargaining, and how does it relate to antitrust actions against tech behemoths like Amazon?

4. (Article 10.4) Kolhatkar mentions that Alex Vitale's work has taken on new urgency during the protests over George Floyd's killing. What does Vitale propose as a possible solution to addressing police brutality?

5. (Article 10.5) Opponents of international labor standards argue that workers in very low-income countries just need jobs, and will only be hurt by well-intentioned efforts to raise wages or improve working conditions. How does MacEwan propose to avoid such unintended negative consequences?

6. (Article 10.6) Nawabi argues that land reform is important mainly for "sociopolitical" reasons—that it is necessary to break landlords' stranglehold on political power in order to adopt needed economic development policies. What is the rationale of this argument? Are there analogous arguments to be made for societies that are mostly urban and industrial, rather than rural and agricultural?

7. (Article 10.7) Who are the protesters and what are they protesting? How do the new laws increase monopolization and corporatization of agriculture? How has neoliberalism contributed to India's agrarian crisis? How do the protests offer an alternative vision of the economy?

8. (Article 10.8) What is a wildcat strike? What precipitated the NBA players' two-day strike? How is the setting for this event like other potential strikes elsewhere in the economy?

Article 10.1

SOLIDARITY BEYOND THE CRISIS
How to Truly Build Back Better

BY FRANCISCO PÉREZ AND LUIS FELIZ LEON
November/December 2020

In the aftermath of the wreckage caused by the Covid-19 pandemic, Democratic presidential nominee Joe Biden's promise to "build back better" is more of an attempt to restore the old order than to create a fairer, sustainable, and resilient economy. Biden has refused to endorse proposals for a Green New Deal, defunding the police, and universal health care, making it clear that he is more committed to evading structural reforms than advocating for them. Despite the longest economic expansion in U.S. history and record-low unemployment rates leading up to the pandemic, the Covid-19 crisis has revealed that millions of American workers are just two or three missed paychecks away from the brink of starvation and homelessness. The miles-long lines snaking around blocks at food banks and perilous stays in motels without electricity are stark reminders that the foundations of the pre-pandemic economy were shaky. Biden's misplaced political calculation that people long for a return to the civility of the Obama presidency belies the reality that Obama's policies put vast swaths of the American public in the dire straits that the pandemic has only worsened.

In the spirit of building truly participatory structures that are grounded in a "nothing about us without us" approach to structural reforms, we asked leading movement organizers and thinkers across the United States: What does it truly mean to build back better? The answers we received shared a unifying set of demands requiring deep social and economic transformations of our existing society. In response to the multiplicity of crises we face, the best way to build back better is to build a solidarity economy—an economic system founded on collective ownership and direct democracy; one where workers control their workplaces, residents control their housing, and communities are truly in charge of their investments and governments.

Our Workplaces

The least powerful workers and businesses typically bear the brunt of any recession; someone must always take the hit. And it is workers who, while essential to the functioning of the economy in boom times, are sacrificed at the altar of capitalist accumulation in downturns. Six months after the beginning of the lockdowns, the affluent have recovered nearly all of the jobs they lost due to the pandemic, while 80% of the millions of jobs lost are concentrated in the bottom half of the income distribution. While the stocks of major corporations soar to new vertiginous heights, a majority of small businesses (58%) are worried that they will have to close permanently due to Covid-19. Statistics like this have prompted Joe Guinan, a senior fellow at The Democracy Collaborative, to warn of an "Amazon recovery," one in which, as small, locally based businesses die off, "big businesses and corporate behemoths hold an even greater share of the market, billionaires get richer (and more numerous), and inequality is supercharged."

To counter this takeover by corporate monopolies, activists have been encouraging states and municipalities to create local economy preservation funds. Inspired by the history of the Great Depression, progressive groups across the country are calling for a new version of the Reconstruction Finance Corporation (RFC), which existed from 1932 to 1957. The RFC purchased ownership stakes in thousands of corporations and used its position as a major shareholder to do things like limit executive pay. In a presentation to the National League of Cities, Marjorie Kelly, a senior fellow and the vice executive director of The Democracy Collaborative, explained that this reimagined version of the fund would invest in or outright buy out local companies in danger of failing because of the pandemic. The goal would be to relaunch these businesses when economic conditions will allow them to thrive. The fund would have a new mandate to support the local economy and, in some cases, create a more inclusive ownership structure that allows workers or the broader community to share the wealth that the business generates.

Take, for example, the Main Street Phoenix Project, a local economy preservation fund in Boulder, Colo. It was created by a group of business and community leaders who have committed to advancing employee ownership of the businesses they rescue. The group intends to raise $6 million that it can use to buy equity stakes in local restaurants and other small businesses, with the goal of building "a more equitable and resilient main street economy based on quality jobs, employee ownership, and vibrant neighborhoods." Local leaders in Broward County, Fla. and Asheville, N.C. have expressed interest in starting similar projects. In New York, a bill in the State Legislature proposes to raise funds for business investments through bonds sold to the Federal Reserve's Municipal Liquidity Facility, which shows one way such a fund could scale nationally. Similarly, in California, the Worker-Owned Recovery Coalition is advocating for the state government to provide financing, technical assistance, and outreach for transferring ownership of small businesses to their employees.

Our Homes

Samuel Stein, housing policy analyst for the Community Service Society of New York and author of *Capital City: Gentrification and the Real Estate State*, says that the converging crises of the moment demonstrate a number of key facts quite clearly: "good and stable housing is fundamental to personal and public health; wages have not kept up with rising housing costs; and speculation and over-leveraging put a lot of landlords in a precarious position."

Even billionaire real estate developer and Donald Trump booster Stephen Ross agrees, telling the *New York Times* in a meandering and contradictory interview: "In the city, we overbuilt like crazy and we had bad leadership. We were growing to the point where nobody could really afford to live here."

The outstanding $1.6 trillion in mortgages for multifamily residential real estate will become harder to service if a quarter of renters stop paying, reducing landlords' cash flow dramatically. Already in April, 20% of landlords feared being unable to pay their own mortgages. Despite sanguine hopes that the rental market would rebound in July and August, the number of empty apartments in Manhattan soared to 13,000 as New Yorkers fled the city and brokers were unable to find new tenants to fill vacancies.

Back in April, in anticipation of a wave of evictions, Representative Ilhan Omar of Minnesota proposed the Rent and Mortgage Cancellation Act, tasking the federal government with paying landlords and lenders on behalf of renters. Omar's bill would also provide funds for state and local governments, nonprofits, and community land trusts to purchase distressed properties.

Since Congress has been unwilling to provide renters with any assistance, and state and local government eviction moratoriums only postpone rent payments and delay evictions, this may be the end of housing as we know it, as activists are taking direct action to deal with the long-simmering housing crisis in this country.

Formed in response to a proposed rezoning of the Inwood neighborhood of New York City, the Northern Manhattan is Not for Sale Coalition argues that only community control of housing will deliver affordable and secure housing for low-income residents of color. Their counterproposal to the developers and city government aiming to gentrify their neighborhood is to create a community land trust (CLT), which promises to keep housing affordable by separating ownership of land and buildings, while creating wealth for working class families through the distribution of capital gains. With community representatives on its board of trustees, a CLT retains ownership of the land, which is the more speculative component of property values. Instead of traditional sales, a CLT typically offers "homeowners" a long-term lease. Homeowners can sell their house or apartment but never the land beneath and can only keep a predetermined portion of the profits if prices have increased. As Cheryl Pahaham, co-chair of Inwood Legal Action, a member of the coalition, explains, "community ownership and stewardship will create stable communities and enable people to move up the economic ladder, educate their children, support other family members, and will facilitate entrepreneurship."

Pahaham draws on the history of the tenant-led community housing movement in the 1970s that created models like the Tenant Interim Lease (TIL) program and Housing Development Fund Corporation (HDFC) cooperatives. These programs emerged in response to New Yorkers' activism against what Pahaham characterized as "systematic landlord abandonment and arson." The "Decade of Fire," as it came to be known, was epitomized by dystopian images of entire city blocks ablaze in the South Bronx, and these flames were fanned by racism, landlord neglect, and austerity. Landlords, viewing their housing stock solely as investments, chose to burn their buildings down to collect insurance payouts, sometimes with tenants inside, instead of paying the mortgage and maintaining livable conditions for low-income residents. Despite the origins of cooperative housing in the self-determination of New Yorkers to take back their neighborhoods and rebuild their torched homes, Pahaham questions whether the city's commitment was a genuine attempt to uphold the promise of affordable, cooperative housing. "If [New York City] was committed to this model of cooperative-owned housing, we would not have million-dollar HDFC apartments on the market, we would not have TILs disappearing inexplicably, and there would be a frank and fair and open discussion and planning and reckoning for those TILs and HDFCs that were struggling."

According to Jason Wu, housing attorney at the New York Legal Aid Society, "for the past decade, the city has removed numerous buildings from the TIL program and taken away the opportunity of cooperative homeownership from working class tenants of color. These buildings are then transferred to developers as rental properties, with little to no oversight."

Housing activists have learned from the failed policies of the past decades and are now advocating for more profound challenges to landlords' power. Wu argues that "when buildings are removed from the TIL program, they should be given the option of joining a CLT, instead of being transferred to developers that prioritize profits over people."

While much about the future of housing and urban development is uncertain, Pahaham emphasizes that "one thing is clear—we cannot go back to the rental market that routinely deprived tens of thousands of city residents of stable housing. That it was normal for city schools to educate 100,000 to 110,000 homeless kids every year is outrageous and incredibly offensive. Thanks to the Black Lives Matter movement, which is pushing for change and has politicians focused on the need to change, we have an opportunity to aggressively push for alternative models of housing, to demonstrate that housing justice is a racial justice."

Our Money

Difficulty accessing financing is the biggest barrier to converting businesses and housing to collective ownership, therefore, democratizing finance is essential for the solidarity economy sector to grow. Our current financial system does an awful job of meeting people's needs. The fact that we have a booming stock market while millions of people lose their jobs and homes demonstrates how little the fortunes of the financial sector are tied to ours. In response, solidarity economy activists have proposed community-controlled investment funds and public banks. The Seed Commons, a network of nearly 30 community-controlled funds in the United States, is small, but it demonstrates what is possible if small business owners and cooperatives could borrow from their neighbors instead of predatory banks.

State-owned public banks—like the Bank of North Dakota—could finance the conversion of failing small businesses and residential properties into worker and housing co-ops, or the creation of new co-ops, either directly or via community-controlled investment funds. In October 2019, activists in California pressured the state government to allow cities to form public banks. The following month, the governor of New Jersey, Phil Murphy, signed an executive order allowing cities in New Jersey to do the same. The Public Banking Institute wrote a letter to every state governor in April imploring them to set up public banks in each state to mitigate the upcoming financial collapse. Groups like the Philadelphia Public Banking Coalition are pushing their local government to heed this call. Federal Reserve support could, of course, turbocharge these efforts. Like private banks, public ones could lend to beleaguered small and medium businesses—including co-ops—through the emergency programs the Federal Reserve has set up for that purpose. Under the Paycheck Protection Program Liquidity and Main Street Lending Facilities, commercial banks originate the loans, but the Federal Reserve purchases 95% or 100% of the loans, respectively, from the banks, taking on nearly all risk that borrowers may not repay.

Our Governments

Our state and federal governments have failed to protect our lives and incomes. After passing the Coronavirus Aid, Relief, and Economic Security (CARES) Act, Congress has essentially sat on its hands. National governments in other rich countries have done more to prevent job losses and provide families with the money they need to allow everyone to stay home until it is safe to return to work, without the fear of losing their jobs and homes, or going hungry. For instance, in Germany the government pays up to 80% of workers' salaries if their employers agree not to lay them off, keeping unemployment rates below 5% throughout the pandemic. In contrast, in the United States, unemployment peaked at 15% in April, and the more generous unemployment benefits included in the CARES Act expired in late July. Since then Republican governors and legislators have blocked further relief, forcing workers to choose between risking their lives by returning to unsafe jobs or their livelihoods by staying home. In April, 70% of Americans supported a stay-at-home order, and by August, even after months of quarantine, 59% still did. So far, the federal and many state governments have failed to respond to the wishes of the majority. Instead of tax cuts for the rich and bailouts and protection from lawsuits for big corporations, grassroots democracy would prioritize public health, worker safety, and support to renters and small business owners.

"We know that no matter who wins this election, we'll still wake up on November 4 in a world where the people who bear the brutality of racial injustice, climate change, and Covid-19 are still excluded from the table when it comes to solving these emergencies," explained Elizabeth Crews, director of Democracy Beyond Elections, a campaign led by the Participatory Budgeting Project. "We have to reimagine how we relate to and participate in the decisions that affect our everyday lives. We have to rebuild democracy to focus on real community-led decision-making that is equitable, accessible, and significant. The voices of marginalized communities must be centered in directly deciding policies and budgets."

Participatory budgeting, a process where residents meet in neighborhood assemblies to discuss projects and directly vote on the items that will be included in the municipal budget, has attracted growing interest. It is currently being implemented to varying degrees by over 110 local governments in the United States and Canada, including in major cities like New York and Chicago. In 2016, the Phoenix Union High School District in Phoenix, Ariz. became the first school district in the United States to use participatory budgeting to allocate district-wide funds. Earlier this year, the district's students decided to not renew the schools' agreement with the city's school resource officers for the 2020–2021 school year. It demonstrates the potential for participatory budgeting to achieve racial justice when politicians fearful of police unions fail to tackle the issue head-on. Rahel

Mekdim Teka of the Participatory Budgeting Project says that the $1.2 million in now-available funds will be used to launch "a school participatory budgeting initiative that will center student, family, and community voices in redefining safety, and invest directly into that vision."

Not a Panacea

Co-ops, community land trusts, public banks, and participatory budgeting are not a panacea, especially if they continue to operate as islands of solidarity in a sea of capitalism. The vaunted Mondragón Corporation, the largest federation of worker co-ops in the world with over $13 billion in annual revenue, has been criticized for its lack of worker participation, use of temporary workers, and ownership of foreign subsidiaries. Still, the Mondragón Corporation has made the Basque economy more resilient, with unemployment 10% lower than in the rest of Spain after the country's housing bubble burst in 2010. Meanwhile, many of New York City's housing cooperatives have become unaffordable. Participatory budgeting projects tend to remain small, with politicians resisting attempts to give up control of public spending. Even in Porto Alegre, Brazil, where the Workers' Party created participatory budgeting to confront endemic corruption in municipal government, citizens were never able to control more than a relatively minor portion of the budget. Many public and development banks throughout the Global South in the 1970s and 1980s became vehicles for graft and nepotism until they were privatized as part of neoliberal structural adjustment reforms. Perhaps the major challenge for the growing solidarity economy movement is not simply to grow these institutions but to link them in ways where they reinforce one another and ensure they stay faithful to their missions.

How to *Really* Build Back Better

Not only has the pandemic economy thrown American society into open class warfare—it's now the billionaire class against everyone else. But in doing so it has also eroded people's confidence in elite brokerage. The powerful ruling class once entrusted with protecting the American people is now an unassailable institutional failure. In their absence, a new consensus has emerged: The only way to truly build back better is to build a solidarity economy. However the election results shake out, workers, organized and militant, are the solution to the struggles ahead. ❏

Sources: Center on Budget and Policy Priorities, "Chart Book: Tracking the Post-Great Recession Economy," Oct. 5, 2020 (cbpp.org); Josefa Velasquez, "Immigrant Corona Residents Lean on Relief Organizations—and Each Other," *The City*, Sept. 8, 2020 (thecity.nyc); Greg Jaffe, "A pandemic, a motel without power and a potentially terrifying glimpse of Orlando's future," *Washington Post*, Sept. 10, 2020 (washingtonpost.com); Emily Kawano and Julie Matthaei, "System Change: A Basic Primer to the Solidarity Economy," *Nonprofit Quarterly*, July 8, 2020 (nonprofitquarterly.org); Ben Stevernan, "Harvard's Chetty Finds Economic Carnage in Wealthiest ZIP Codes," Bloomberg Businessweek, Sept. 24, 2020 (bloomberg.com); Barbara Friedberg, "Why the Market Is Booming and the Economy Is Struggling," *U.S. News & World Report*, Sept. 15, 2020 (money.usnews.com); U.S. Chamber of Commerce, "July 2020 Small Business Coronavirus Impact Poll," July 29, 2020 (uschamber.com); Ted Howard, Ronnie Galvin, Joe Guinan, and Marjorie Kelly, "Owning Our Future After COVID-19,"

Democracy Collaborative, June 10, 2020 (democracycollaborative.org); Joe Guinan and Martin O'Neill, "Only bold state intervention will save us from a future owned by corporate giants," *The Guardian*, July 6, 2020 (theguardian.com); Marjorie Kelly, "How localities can save small businesses through economy preservation funds," The Next System Project, August 7, 2020 (thenextsystem.org); Marjorie Kelly, "Local Economy Preservation Funds: Keeping ownership local post-Covid," Democracy Collaborative presentation to the National League of Cities, June 24, 2020 (thenextsystem.org); The Main Street Phoenix Project (mainstreet.coop); New York State Assembly Bill No. A10362A (assembly.state.ny.us); Karen Kahn, "California Employee Ownership Alliance Proposes $10M Recovery Package," Fifty by Fifty, June 11, 2020 (fiftybyfifty.org); Samuel Stein, *Capital City: Gentrification and the Real Estate State* (Verso, 2019); David Gelles, "The Billionaire Behind Hudson Yards Thinks New York Is Too Expensive," *New York Times*, August 27, 2020 (nytimes.com); Federal Reserve Bank of St. Louis, "All Sectors; Multifamily Residential Mortgages; Asset, Level," Sept. 21, 2020 (fred.stlouisfed.org); American Apartment Owners Association, "1,000+ Landlords Respond to the American Apartment Owner's Association COVID-19 Survey: Here's what's on their minds," April 10, 2020 (american-apartment-owners-association.org); Robert Frank, "Empty apartments in Manhattan reach record high, topping 13,000," CNBC, August 13, 2020 (cnbc.com); Sophie Kasakove, "Ilhan Omar unveils bill to cancel rent and mortgage payments amid pandemic," *The Guardian*, April 17, 2020 (theguardian.com); Francisco Pérez and Luis Feliz León, "The End of Housing as We Know It," *The New Republic*, July 31, 2020 (newrepublic.com); NYU Furman Center, "Directory of NYC Housing Programs–Tenant Interim Lease Program," (furmancenter.org); Greg Olear, "A Look at HDFCs: Understanding Housing Development Fund Corporation Co-ops," The Cooperator New York, September 2017 (cooperator.com); Seed Commons (seedcommons.org); Stacy Mitchell, "Public Banks: Bank of North Dakota," Institute for Local Self-Reliance (ilsr.org); The California Public Banking Alliance (californiapublicbankingalliance.org); Emily Alpert Reyes, "Public bank is back on the table in L.A. after voters rejected the idea," *Los Angeles Times*, Oct. 11, 2019 (latimes.com); Public Banking Institute, "How State Officials Can Save Main Street in the Face of COVID-19: Three Urgent Actions," April 22, 2020 (publicbankinginstitute.org); David Dayden, "Unsanitized: Federal Reserve Policy Choices Maldistributed Recovery," *The American Prospect*, Sept. 18, 2020 (prospect.org); Quint Forgey, "Poll: Large majority of Americans think it's more important to stay home than return to work," Politico, April 23, 2020 (politico.com); Mallory Newall, "Most Americans support single, national strategy to combat COVID-19," Ipsos, August 4, 2020 (ipsos.com); Democracy Beyond Elections (articipatorybudgeting.org/our-work/dbe); New York City Council, "Participatory Budgeting," (council.nyc.gov); Participatory Budgeting Chicago (pbchicago.org); Jen Wahl, "Phoenix high school district to cut ties with law enforcement for 2020-2021 school year," 12 News, July 8, 2020 (12news.com); Noam Scheiber, Farah Stockman, and J. David Goodman, "How Police Unions Became Such Powerful Opponents to Reform Efforts," *New York Times*, June 6, 2020 (nytimes.com); Tom Burridge, "Basque co-operative Mondragon defies Spain slump," BBC News, August 14, 2021 (bbc.com); Valeria Ricciulli, "In the 1970s, the Bronx was burning, but some residents were rebuilding," Curbed, May 3, 2019 (ny.curbed.com); Heather Long and Andrew Van Dam, "As U.S. unemployment soared, Germany's barely budged. Is America's safety net enough?," *Washington Post*, Oct. 13, 2020 (washingtonpost.com); Participatory Budgeting Project, "Where is PB Happening?" (participatorybudgeting.org.); Michelle Higgins, "Bargains With a 'But,'" *New York Times*, June 27, 2014 (nytimes.com).

Article 10.2

WHAT WOULD FULL EMPLOYMENT COST?

BY ARTHUR MacEWAN
May/June 2015

> Dear Dr. Dollar:
> *What is the cost, the minimum budget the U.S. government could spend, to ensure everybody who wants a job can have one with decent pay and benefits? How could that be paid for?*
> —Brett O'Sullivan, Denver, Colo.

The barriers to a change of this magnitude—creating good jobs for everyone—are not so much economic as political. We can imagine arrangements by which the economy could function well and would achieve full employment, good jobs, and benefits. It is, however, hard in the present climate to think that steps in this direction would be politically possible (at least at the national level, though there are political possibilities in some states and localities).

There are things that could be done to move the economy in this direction without significant costs to society. Examples of steps that could improve pay and jobs without major government expenditures include raising the minimum wage and shortening the work week (e.g., requiring time-and-a-half pay for more than 30 hours of work per week). The former would improve workers' pay, and the latter would lead many employers to hire more workers to avoid the higher overtime rates. Also, the rules surrounding unionization could be improved; indeed, simple enforcement of existing rules (e.g., protecting workers trying to form a union) would be a significant step toward improving workers' opportunities.

Also, in terms of providing benefits, a major step forward would be the establishment of a single-payer ("Medicare for All") healthcare system, which would pay for itself by reducing the large overhead costs and profits of the private insurance companies while providing everyone with a prime benefit. Because a single-payer system would cost less than the current system, the payments (taxes) that the government would need would come from and be less than the current insurance premiums. The costs would go through the government, but there would be savings for society. Because this benefit would be for everyone, it would remove the problems that arise when healthcare is tied to employment.

Yet, full employment would also require government spending to stimulate job growth. While the economy operates as it has over the last several years, deficit spending is necessary to move us toward full employment. Especially in the current circumstances, with the economy far from full employment and with interest rates on U.S. government bonds extremely low, deficit spending would not impose large costs (i.e., the costs of paying the interest on the government borrowing to cover the deficit).

It is not hard to figure out what kinds of jobs should be created with government stimulus spending. Prime examples include environmental repair and preservation (including energy conservation), education and training, and infrastructure repair and extension (e.g., especially in public transportation).

Further, stimulus through deficit spending could be used for the government to directly create jobs. The quickest and most effective way to do this would be for the federal government to provide funds to the states to reverse the tens of thousands of layoffs of educational workers in the last few years. Also, there is an increasing need for workers in universal early childhood education, as has been instituted in New York City and a few states. Like expenditures on physical infrastructure, these expenditures on social infrastructure would have both short-run multiplier demand impacts and long-run impacts by raising productivity.

Such actions by the government would not require large tax increases, though higher taxes on people with very high incomes would help. Moreover, as the economy approached full employment, the bargaining power of workers would improve and unionization could be facilitated. As the economy moved back to full employment and incomes rose, taxes would increase without tax rate increases—thus preventing a continuing increase of the government debt.

There would certainly be objections to these sorts of changes. Defenders of the status quo would argue that stimulation of the economy would cause inflation and that raising the minimum wage and facilitating unionization would harm businesses' profits and lead them to cut back on investment (a "capital strike"). The inflation and cutbacks would, the argument goes, mean fewer jobs, and especially fewer good jobs.

With plenty of slack in the labor market, however, there is no reason to believe that government deficits would bring inflation, and as the economy approached full employment, deficit-based stimulus would no longer be needed. The real concerns of those opposed to stimulation of the economy are their opposition to the social programs that would probably grow with larger stimulation and their fear that the growth of those programs might ultimately lead to higher taxes on people with high incomes—prime defenders of the status quo.

As to the fear that business profits would suffer with the sorts of reforms proposed here, that would also be likely. Yet, weaker profits, while a real loss for those at the top, need not be bad for the rest of society. It is only necessary to look at the relatively recent period in our history when wages—including the minimum wage—were relatively higher, unions were stronger, and the distribution of income less unequal. Through the 1950s and into the early 1970s, these conditions were largely met, and the economy grew relatively strongly. There were many economic problems in those years (though not severe inflation) and many circumstances were different from today, but the experience of that period gives the lie to the claims that government stimulus, better working conditions, and greater economic equality would necessarily result in economic disaster.

These changes are blocked by the political power of business and the very wealthy—the infamous 1%—who employ specious arguments about inflation and the undermining of employment to protect their own interests. Changes that would move us toward more and better jobs would be good for most of us.

But they would impose costs on those at the top, who raise the fearful specter of "drastic change of the economic system."

Yet, these changes that would meet the goal of more well-paying jobs with good benefits could be accomplished without some drastic system change or some large increase in the costs to society through greater government expenditures and taxation. Could we get more substantial improvements with greater change? Perhaps. But let's first recognize that, even within the profit system, things do not have to be as they are today. ❑

Article 10.3

IN THE DRIVER'S SEAT

Can a cooperative in New York City point the way for reining in Big Tech?

LUIS FELIZ LEON
May/June 2021

A scrappy band of Uber drivers, a union organizer, and an Uber operations manager have joined forces to launch an experiment in cooperative economics in New York City, with the aim of siphoning business away from the dominant ride-hailing companies—Uber, Lyft, Via, and Juno. Seeding their experiment in one of the largest ride-hailing markets, they are underdogs in a sector flush with oodles of cash from venture capitalists. Despite the odds of taking on Silicon Valley titans, they've done their arithmetic and contend that the worker-owned ridesharing app they've created can provide drivers a deal that the dominant ride-hailing companies can't beat—worker control. By putting the needs of workers' first, The Drivers Cooperative (TDC) aims to give drivers the flexibility and higher wages that Uber and its ilk pay lip service to in marketing gambits.

Launched in December of last year, TDC's co-founders and member-leaders have disparate, but complementary, backgrounds: Erik Forman is a labor organizer who formerly worked as the education director of the Independent Drivers Guild (IDG), which represents thousands of for-hire vehicle drivers, including Uber drivers; Alissa Orlando was an Uber operations manager; Ken Lewis is a former Uber driver; and David Alexis is a former Uber driver and organizer. Forman, Lewis, and Alexis met through IDG, and Orlando joined them later when she learned about their experiment. As of February 2021, more than 2,500 cooperative worker-owners have joined TDC as active drivers, according to the cooperative's founders. As of last spring, Uber had 80,000 drivers in New York City.

In the wake of Proposition 22's passage in California last year, TDC serves up a model that offers a high-road alternative for drivers who depend on the ride-hailing industry to survive. Last November, the app-based companies Uber, DoorDash, and Instacart launched a $250 million ballot initiative campaign known as Prop 22 to roll back the state's Assembly Bill 5 (AB5). That bill was intended to resolve the problem of misclassifying drivers through a three-pronged ABC test to determine a worker's status as either an employee or an independent contractor. AB5 granted app-based drivers protections such as a minimum wage, overtime pay, and reimbursements for expenses. After the app-based companies notched a decisive victory, labor unions have begun to entertain capitulation, seeing the loss as a fait accompli. By contrast, TDC's model holds out a promise of eschewing capitulation in favor of imagining the alternative of workers' control in an environment rife with grueling work schedules, crippling debts, and dictatorial management by algorithms.

The Value (and Values) Proposition

While one of TDC's co-founders (Forman) and one of their member-leaders (Alexis) describe themselves as socialists, the group's aims are more modest and reform-minded, seeking to rein in an unfettered capitalism that has cast workers' dignity and protections to the wayside.

"It's a free-market economy. Drivers in their own organization have as much right as Uber to exist," Lewis told me while explaining the cooperative's vision.

In the case of TDC, Lewis said, "No one is really talking about any radical change" to the system as a whole. "We are talking about a radical change in how workers are treated."

Like Lewis, Orlando echoes a similar sentiment about creating a fairer economy. "I think that we're having this runaway capitalism, whereby you're having capital distort the market," Orlando said. The answer to that distortion is "reviving the normal rules that should apply to a capitalist economy."

TDC's main objective, says Orlando, is to "increase incomes for drivers, full stop. That is our mission," explaining that the cooperative is entering the marketplace to compete against Uber and Lyft in terms of who is providing a better deal to drivers. "What makes Uber unprofitable is [the] subsidization of prices to achieve a monopoly, pouring resources into fantasies like self-driving cars, and constantly battling drivers in court," Forman said.

In its bid to secure market share, Uber has offered driver incentives and customer discounts, pushing it into the red. "This is a monopoly practice," he added, noting it "won't be able to do this forever since shareholders are demanding profits."

Uber's profits tanked by 80% during the height of the pandemic. Despite the hit to its bottom line, the company has launched a $250 million incentive program to lure drivers back. Riders are becoming less hesitant about using the ride-hailing service due to increased vaccine availability and more state reopenings.

Despite the company's awareness that its incentives are unsustainable if it wants to become profitable, its spending on them increased from $259 million in the third quarter of 2019 to $316 million in the third quarter of 2020. In the first nine months of 2020, reports Edward Ongweso Jr. in the online magazine *Vice*, the company spent over $900 million on incentives. "Uber has needed to spend hundreds of millions on recruiting drivers because it burns through over 90% of its workforce each year," Ongweso wrote.

The cooperative understands these vulnerabilities. "If one outcome of our intervention is that Uber has to pay drivers more and charge customers less in order to maintain market share, this is still a win for us," said Forman.

TDC is charging drivers a commission of 15% for using the app, compared to the average 25–40% other app-based companies collect. The drivers earn between $35 to $50 an hour, significantly above the city's Taxi and Limousine Commission's (TLC) minimum wage of $27, according to Orlando. Part of the savings come from eliminating the incentives and marketing overhead that Uber and Lyft must spend to attract new drivers and customers. Instead, TDC is building partnerships with cooperatives such as Cooperative Home Care Associates in the Bronx, which employs nearly 2,000 African-American and Latina workers. They are also launching partnerships with progressive candidates in New York City to get voters to the polls during elections.

The cooperative's business model is solid: They have a class traitor like Orlando on their side. She left her job in Uber operations in East Africa to join the cooperative's team after the passage of California's Prop 22 granted app-based platforms exemptions to important labor laws and platform companies failed to provide paid leave and unemployment benefits to workers during a lethal pandemic.

Another factor in her departure was Uber "trapping people in a cycle of debt," she told me, referring to the company's Vehicle Solutions program, through which drivers can take out three- or five-year loans ranging from $15,000 to $20,000 even though there are cars eligible for the platform in a much cheaper price range. Workers take on these punishing loan terms for a variety of reasons, ranging from poor credit histories to a lack of financial literacy. But the "final straw," as Orlando put it, was Uber reducing prices by 20% in East Africa—putting downward pressure on wages while also further squeezing more labor out of drivers.

The experience of debt peonage is a common one. Alexis, another co-op member and a former Uber driver, describes logging into the Uber app in 2016 and seeing that his earnings on trips mostly went to paying a weekly $450 rental

---

AB5, Prop 22, and the PRO Act

In 2019, California's legislature introduced AB5 to close the independent contractor loophole and bolster ride-hailing drivers' worker protections. AB5 is modeled after the ruling in *Dynamex Operations W. v. Superior Court*, which required businesses to use an "ABC Test" to determine whether a worker was an employee, according to the following three criteria, the worker must: 1) be free from the company's control; 2) perform work outside of the company's core business; and 3) run an independent business. Uber and Lyft failed this test according to the 2020 court ruling in California.

In response to the California court's ruling, Uber's CEO Dara Khosrowshahi said: "If the court doesn't reconsider, then in California, it's hard to believe we'll be able to switch our model to full-time employment quickly, so I think Uber will shut down for a while." Khosrowshahi threatened a capital strike to shut down operations in the state until November, depending on the voters' decision on Proposition 22, a $250 million ballot referendum backed by Uber, Lyft, DoorDash and other gig economy companies to save their business model from paying worker benefits.

Prop 22 passed, exempting Uber and Lyft from classifying drivers as employees; Uber's capital strike was averted. In March 2021, members of Rideshare Drivers United (RDU), an independent organization of rideshare drivers in California, held rallies in one last-ditch effort to assert their employee status by championing the Protecting the Right to Organize (PRO) Act.

President Joe Biden has also come out in support of the PRO Act. The legislation is the most transformative labor reform since the anti-union Taft-Hartley Act of 1947, which banned secondary strikes, allowed states to pass right-to-work laws, prevented foremen from unionizing, and purged union ranks of their most militant and dedicated organizers. The PRO Act has passed the House. If enacted into law, among other benefits, it would ban many union-busting tactics and provide ride-hailing employees with the right to collectively bargain even if Uber or Lyft don't recognize them as employees.

fee on his 2015 Hyundai Sonata with one of the preferred leasing companies that contracts with Uber. Even though the fee was high, Alexis managed to service the debt. "When I was renting, no matter what was going on, you had to hit the road and work because if you didn't, you will see that charge hit your account. ... I would have to work to effectively pay off the balance before I could actually start making money," he explained.

"And the way that it was set up was 'lovely' because they are one of the preferred leasing companies with Uber, the money actually came directly out of my Uber account," he continued.

These experiences are what make the cooperative's experiment so attractive to drivers. Despite some cooperative members' stated reform aims, they are planting the seeds of something potentially different—public ownership, say, of the technologies running the apps—which could help create possibilities for change that actually feel within reach.

Seeding Alternative Models

The rideshare industry is rigged against drivers, so even valiant efforts at reforms like the Prop 22 fight in California or the minimum wage fight in New York City were easily overturned or deferred through legal maneuvering funded by the bottomless war chests of Uber and Lyft.

The solution is a new strategy. "Our approach is direct action—we are simply taking direct control of the means of production. Drivers already own the rest of the capital of this industry in the form of their vehicles; the app is the keystone. Once drivers own that, this will be the largest industrial sector under 100% worker ownership," said Forman.

Listening to Forman, it's easy to hear a prefigurative logic of what is possible if workers had control not only over one sector of the ride-hailing industry, but of the whole economy and society.

"[The goal of] our project is not only creating a better job within the industry as it exists today, it is also to aggregate workers together as a political force to transform the industry and society," he told me.

But as soon as the wings of that vision take flight, they are clipped by capitalist market realities—TDC will have to become a financially successful company in order to attract a broad group of workers.

Another related constraint has been getting access to capital. TDC has received funding from Shared Capital Cooperative and the Local Enterprise Assistance Fund, two cooperative loan funds. TDC has also raised money through grants and crowdfunding. But they are up against formidable foes with deep pockets.

To offset these challenges, TDC is also looking to build partnerships with natural allies like labor unions. "Labor organizing is a necessary complement to cooperative organizing because it raises the floor," he told me. If wages rise for app-based drivers, the wage enhancement increases the bargaining power of other low-wage workers.

The Dangers of the "Third Way"

If a cooperative can create a worker-owned app to compete with Uber's, can the U.S. government do something similar for public transit? Can the government nationalize the cloud computing of Amazon Web Services? Or at the very least break up the big tech companies using the existing antitrust laws on the books? These are the questions TDC's experiment provokes.

But other people have little inclination to imagine. They want to strike a deal fast.

The desperation is understandable. Labor unions have been battling Silicon Valley titans and losing for years. Rather than continue on that losing streak, unions have seized on the possibility of reaching a rapprochement with tech companies in exchange for sectoral bargaining.

Such deal-making with ride-hailing app companies is rotten to the core, and leads to compromises like the decision of the Machinists Union of New York City and Uber to create the IDG, which receives funding from Uber and Lyft and is, in effect, going national as a model.

Through multiemployer contracts, or sectoral bargaining, unions get to set standards for whole industries, instead of bargaining individually with each employer. Traditionally, labor unions have used the monopolies that sectoral bargaining can create as leverage to bring employers to the negotiating table.

Take, for instance, Amazon. It's too early to know if the countervailing power of unions and the regulatory state may come together to restrain the corporate behe-

---

From Uber's Guild to the Driver's Co-op

Many of TDC's members had previously been involved with the Independent Drivers' Guild (IDG), a company union partly funded by Uber and Lyft, where Forman worked as an organizer.

IDG was created after Uber drivers spent two years convincing the Machinists Union of New York City (a local of the AFL-CIO with a 20-year track record of representing livery car drivers) to represent them in negotiations with Uber, which began in 2015, and resulted in the formation of IDG in 2016.

"IDG was effectively a concession," Alexis told me, describing its relationship with Uber and Lyft. But he also acknowledges that IDG had installed portable toilets at the airport, giving the drivers' basic dignity on the job. IDG also won some major early victories for Uber drivers—such as successfully pushing the city to require a tipping option for all app companies. In addition to drivers' being automatically enrolled in IDG when they sign up to drive for Uber, the company union was wise to identify what workers cared about and then mobilize them on that basis.

Soon enough, however, the contradictions and limitations of IDG being in cahoots with the main ride-hailing companies became more apparent.

"I saw rank-and-file IDG members who were willing to do whatever it took to make real changes and whatnot, and a leadership that wasn't really quite responsive," Alexis admitted.

Alexis went in search of alternatives and settled on the idea germinating in the ranks and among organizers that a new organization was needed—one that would "allow drivers to have real power over their workspaces in a way that wasn't really available as an option through either the New York Taxi Workers Alliance or IDG."

moth. Senator Elizabeth Warren has proposed breaking up the company. President Joe Biden has selected Lina Khan, a prominent antitrust scholar and professor at Columbia Law School, for a vacancy at the Federal Trade Commission. (Khan wrote an influential paper on how Amazon violates existing antitrust law.)

But if unions are seeking a bargain, no better option exists than the threat of breaking up Amazon. The historian Nelson Lichtenstein argues that even the threat of breaking it up will force Amazon's hand and may bring it to the negotiating table with labor unions. That was the deal that was struck with a group of retail clerks in the 1930s, which later became the United Food and Commercial Workers International Union (UFCW).

Lichtenstein provides the example of the Great Atlantic & Pacific Tea Company, or better known as the supermarket chain A&P, which rivaled Walmart's and Amazon's market capture in its heyday in the 1930s. Explaining the union's position, Lichtenstein told me, "they said, 'Look, we will not support these anti-chain store laws, proliferating all over the place," in exchange for union recognition. "One reason we have more than a million grocery workers who are unionized today is partly a result of that kind of deal that was struck," he told me.

But the current compromise on offer isn't a sign of power but of acquiescence. Unlike the 1930s, workers today are not actors in a rank-and-file upsurge of militant strike actions. Instead, by entering into a compromise with the ride-hailing app companies, labor unions are admitting that they have no power and will make do with the scraps in order to collaborate with the bosses, figuratively squatting beside the legs of the table in case leftovers from the capitalists' plates spill to the floor.

"Whether you are a worker in Germany or in Alabama, the only way you win a decent life is by building enough power to create a crisis for the capitalist class," Jane McAlevey wrote in *The Nation* about the prospect of creating a third category of worker in exchange for sectoral bargaining with gig companies.

"That means the power to forge supermajority unity, striking, and causing profits to nosedive until the bosses remember that workers—whatever we call them—make the profits the 1 percent thrive on today, while everyone else suffers," McAlevey added.

As Forman puts it, "sectoral bargaining is a good idea—but can also cement a monopoly in place, which is part of why Uber and Lyft are open to it. They see it as a way to stabilize the regulatory environment for their exploitative business model."

A Race to the Bottom

The very existence of Uber and Lyft depends on a business model that is extractive and predatory. Uber's market-capture debut in 2011 was premised on a swift takeover of the taxi business by inundating New York City streets with cars, "with average monthly active vehicles increasing from 19,000 to more than 90,000" between 2015, when data first became available, and 2018, according to New York City's TLC. The traditional taxi services, which included both yellow taxis and livery cabs, operated within a highly regulated marketplace with licensing requirements that capped the number of cars on the street and guaranteed drivers a living wage. The yellow cab business, however, was predatory and riddled with problems long before Uber came along. For instance, drivers are required to purchase a permit, also known as a medallion, in order to drive a cab. Between 2004 and 2014, the cost for a single medallion rose to $1.3 million, and the cost is now back to under $200,000. Half a dozen drivers have committed suicide after they were unable to shoulder the burden of servicing debt loads of more than half a million dollars. The New York Taxi Workers Alliance has organized drivers to demand a restructuring of these onerous debts, but the plan New York City Mayor Bill de Blasio has put forward is inadequate, asking instead for a $125,000 ceiling on outstanding medallion debts.

"Stop with the suicide thing," Taxi and Limousine Commission Chairwoman Aloysee Heredia Jarmoszuk told the brother of a taxi driver who died by suicide when he mentioned the need for the city to put forward a more generous plan. "There's no better deal. This is it," Jarmoszuk said.

Undoubtedly, the market for medallions was already exploitative. But Uber took it over and the whole vibrant ecosystem of livery taxis, including a bustling array of cab companies serving New York City's diverse immigrant communities, came under threat. All of these companies were highly regulated.

Uber bucked the trend of regulation by initially setting up shop in cities illegally and using the piles of cash in its war chest to smear and intimidate anyone, including journalists, mayors, and former employees who stood in its way to unrestricted growth. In 2018, at the height of Uber's dizzying growth in New York City, there were 107,435 licensed for-hire vehicles, in TLC terminology, which included app-based black cars, liveries, and luxury limousines, with a total of 185,000 licensed drivers across all taxi types. The majority of drivers are immigrants, hailing from countries as diverse as Guinea, the Dominican Republic, Haiti, India, and China. To make up for depressed wages, these drivers logged brutal working hours into the app in hopes of approximating a living wage to feed their families and keep a roof over their heads in a city with staggering inequality.

But in the early days, Uber's appeal rested in the flexibility it provided to drivers. Lewis, one of the cooperative's co-founders, started driving for Uber in 2012 because as a graduate student he wanted a flexible schedule, and describes days even then when he had to sleep in his car to make sure he put in enough hours to make ends meet.

Alexis also began driving for Uber because the flexibility of the job allowed him to care for his wife, who has sickle cell anemia. Alexis also saw in Uber the opportunity to be present as a father and husband. He evokes pride in his identity as a "provider," as well as his commitment to not repeating the same pattern of long work hours and no family time that his father, as a Haitian immigrant and an economic and political refugee seeking a better life in a foreign land, had to endure when he came to the United States.

Six years into Uber's arrival in New York City, however, the appeal had begun to wear off. Early press reports that lent the company an aura of youthful inventiveness in a staid industry gave way to horror stories—a smattering of which ran the gamut from sexual assault, gender discrimination, and wage theft—which transformed then-CEO Travis Kalanick from boyish media darling to "entrant into the burgeoning pantheon of tech sociopaths," in the words of journalist Nikil Saval.

Crossing Lines

On January 28, 2017, as protesters gathered at airports to oppose former President Donald Trump's travel ban and taxi drivers organized through the New York Taxi Workers Alliance called a strike, stranding passengers at John F. Kennedy International airport, Uber decided to scab and #DeleteUber began to trend on social media. In the words of Uber investor and tech entrepreneur Hadi Partovi, "This is a company where there has been no line you wouldn't cross if it got in the way of success."

That same year, on Super Bowl Sunday, one of the many revelers out that night was Kalanick, who after some partying requested the company's high-end black car service, Uber-X, for himself and a couple of friends. In between Kalanick's corny repartee with his acquaintances about Uber's "hard year," the conversation turned serious when the driver complained to the CEO that drivers like him couldn't make a living with the company's new pricing structure.

To the plight of drivers, Kalanick then retorted: "Some people don't like to take responsibility for their own shit."

The Drivers' Cooperative is taking him up on that and defining their own working conditions and wages. And what's more, they may one day supersede their corporate overlords and a thousand new cooperatives will roar down the roads of America's cities, with drivers in control. ❏

Sources: Patrick Sisson, "Uber and Lyft drivers in NYC, concerned by coronavirus, say apps aren't helping enough," New York Curbed, March 13, 2020 (ny.curbed.com); Amir Efrati, "Uber's Bookings Now Down 80%," The Information, April 14, 2020 (theinformation.com); Edward Ongweso Jr., "Uber Spends $250M to Lure Drivers While Gutting Their Rights," Vice, April 9, 2021 (vice.com); "Uber Announces Results for Third Quarter 2020," Uber Investor, November 5, 2020 (investor.uber.com); Chantel McGee, "Only 4% of Uber drivers remain on the platform a year later, says report," CNBC, April 20, 2017 (cnbc.com); Editors, "How to Boost Unions' Power? Sectoral Bargaining," In These Times, October 22, 2020 (inthesetimes.com); Astead W. Herndon, "Elizabeth Warren Proposes Breaking Up Tech Giants Like Amazon and Facebook," New York Times, March 8, 2019 (nytimes.com); "BREAKING NEWS: President Biden Taps Lina Khan for Federal Trade Commission," The National Law Review, March 9, 2021 (natlawreview.com); Lina M. Khan, "Amazon's Antitrust Paradox," The Yale Law Journal, January 2017 (yalelawjournal.org); Nelson Lichtenstein, "Can a grand bargain empower Amazon's workers and limit corporate power?," Washington Post, March 25, 2021 (washingtonpost.com); Jane McAlevey, "Silicon Valley's Offer of Sectoral Bargaining Is a Trick," The Nation, March 3, 2021 (thenation.com); Hamilton Nolan, "New York City Drivers Cooperative Aims to Smash Uber's Exploitative Model," In These Times, December 10, 2020 (inthesetimes.com); Office of Policy & External Affairs, "2018 TLC Fact Book," NYC Taxi & Limousine Commission, 2018 (nyc.gov); Ben Smith, "Uber Executive Suggests Digging Up Dirt On Journalists," BuzzFeed News, November 17, 2014 (buzzfeednews.com); Fitz Tepper, "Uber Launches 'De Blasio's Uber' Feature In NYC With 25-Minute Wait Times," Tech Crunch, July 16, 2015 (techcrunch.com); Sarah Buhr, "Uber says it's 'absolutely not' behind a smear campaign against ex-employee Susan

Fowler Rigetti," February 24, 2017 (techcrunch.com); "An Economic Profile of Immigrants in New York City: First Results from NYC Opportunity Experimental Population Estimate," Mayor's Office for Economic Opportunity, 2018 (nyc.gov); Shannon Bond, "Uber Received Nearly 6,000 U.S. Sexual Assault Claims In Past 2 Years," National Public Radio, December 5, 2018 (npr.org); Tyler Sonnemaker, "Uber is paying $4.4 million to settle federal charges that workers experienced a 'culture of sexual harassment and retaliation,'" Business Insider, December 18, 2019 (businessinsider.com); "Press Release: Uber Agrees to Pay $20 Million to Settle FTC Charges That It Recruited Prospective Drivers with Exaggerated Earnings Claims," Federal Trade Commission, January 19, 2017 (ftc.gov); The Editors, "Disrupt the Citizen," *N+1*, Fall 2017 (nplusonemag. com); Eric Newcomer, "In Video, Uber CEO Argues With Driver Over Falling Fares," Bloomberg, February 28, 2017 (bloomberg.com).

Article 10.4

POLICE VIOLENCE IS ENABLED BY MASSIVE SPENDING

The Black Lives Matter movement shows again why America needs to defund bloated and militarized police departments.

BY SONALI KOLHATKAR
July/August 2020

Not since the mass protests that originated in Ferguson, Mo., in 2014 when a white police officer killed a black man named Michael Brown has the United States witnessed the current magnitude of the movement against police brutality. The brutal videotaped killing of George Floyd in Minneapolis on May 25, 2020, has pushed Americans to the limit of what they will tolerate from police.

Huge, multiracial protests have broken out in hundreds of cities demanding an end to racist policing. While many of the problems can be laid at the feet of President Donald Trump—whose administration has obliterated modest Obama-era police reforms, and who has delighted in openly encouraging police to be violent—the current status quo of accepting and encouraging racist and murderous policing has been a largely bipartisan project at the federal, state, and local level.

Protests against police brutality have a long history that predates the rallying cry of "Black Lives Matter" becoming a household phrase. Well before Trump was on the national scene, Democratic and Republican leaders have had many years to right the wrongs that black activists and community leaders were decrying. After Rodney King's brutal beating was caught on tape in Los Angeles and the acquittal of his abusers sparked a historic and violent uprising, there were years of reforms aimed at the Los Angeles Police Department (LAPD) that resulted in only the mildest changes. The liberal city, dominated by Democrats, continues to have the largest number of police killings nationwide, and to date, the city's first black female district attorney, Jackie Lacey, has refused to prosecute a single officer during her tenure.

When Eric Garner was choked to death by police in the borough of Staten Island in New York City, his horrific killing, captured on video, and his last words, "I can't breathe," sparked mass protests and deep discourse about reforming police protocols. But just as in Los Angeles, the core demand that activists have been making at least since the police murder of Amadou Diallo—that those who violate rights should be held legally accountable—has gone unmet. Daniel Pantaleo, the New York Police Department (NYPD) officer who put Garner in a chokehold, remained on the force for five years and was ultimately fired but never charged. Like the LAPD, the NYPD has enjoyed the protection of a largely liberal and Democratic political landscape.

During the presidency of Barack Obama, some modest reforms were enacted at the federal level, largely through executive orders as Congress remained unable to break through political gridlock. Obama's federal oversight of police departments through court-ordered consent decrees was a start, but in his last act as Trump's attorney general, Jeff Sessions signed a memorandum that undid the Obama-era consent decrees. Trump also resumed the flow of military equipment and weapons to local police departments.

Now, as mass protests are taking place all over the nation, the images of well-armed and flak-jacketed police facing off against protesters and violently subduing them while remaining encased in protective gear stands in stark contrast to our desperately under-equipped health care workers who have been vainly trying to save as many lives as possible during the coronavirus pandemic.

Police are clad head to toe in high-tech gear, face shields, and body armor, with no shortage of plastic handcuffs, rubber bullets, and tear gas canisters. The optics of these modern-day gestapo-like forces roaming city streets, bashing in heads, and firing tear gas into the faces of unarmed protesters are a reminder of just how many federal and state-level resources we have poured into law enforcement over the years at the expense of health care, education, and other public needs.

Even as the economic collapse triggered by the pandemic threatened to devastate public school systems, in the liberal havens of Los Angeles and New York City, law enforcement budgets remained unscathed. California's Democratic Governor Gavin Newsom proposed big cuts to schools to compensate for massive budget shortfalls at the same time that LAPD officers were receiving $41 million in bonuses. L.A.'s Democratic Mayor Eric Garcetti recently released this year's proposed city budget—typical of previous years—which sets aside a whopping one-third of all city spending for police.

Similarly, in New York City the Democratic Mayor Bill de Blasio's proposal to compensate for pandemic-related revenue losses is to make cuts to the school budget that are 27 times that of his city's police budget cuts. Alice Speri, writing in the Intercept, explains: "The United States spends some $100 billion annually on policing," and "[i]n cities across the country, policing alone can take up anything between a third and 60% of the entire annual budget."

And while the pandemic is forcing cities to make hard choices about which public services to slash, police department budgets have remained immune to cuts. Liberal cities like L.A., New York, and Minneapolis, in the words of one journalist in a recent article for *GQ*, "keep piling money on police departments."

Just as congressional Democrats for far too long have poured money into the U.S. military to fuel wars abroad—even outdoing Trump's thirst for military largesse—the Democratic Party's state and local leaders have poured money into our domestic armed forces—the police—to fuel a war on us, and especially those among us with black or brown skin.

Now, because the collective public rage over police violence and impunity has reached a fever pitch, something extraordinary is happening. A long-standing activist call to defund the police is receiving a mainstream platform. On May 30, the *New York Times* published an op-ed by Philip V. McHarris and Thenjiwe McHarris entitled "No More Money for the Police." Black Lives Matter has explicitly called for, "a national defunding of police," and is demanding, "investment in our communities and the resources to ensure Black people not only survive, but thrive."

Author Alex Vitale's 2018 book, *The End of Policing*, aptly articulated on its cover: "The problem is not police training, police diversity, or police methods. The problem is the dramatic and unprecedented expansion and intensity of policing in the last 40 years, a fundamental shift in the role of police in society. The problem is policing itself."

Vitale's work has taken on new urgency during the protests over George Floyd's killing. In a recent piece he wrote for the *Guardian*, he explained that the solution to ending police violence is for local authorities "to dramatically shrink their function." Vitale added, "We must demand that local politicians develop non-police solutions to the problems poor people face."

That means mayors and governors from all parts of the political spectrum need to stop subscribing to the notion that police can solve problems caused by poor education, health care, and jobs, and directly start diverting money from police into education, health care, and jobs. Liberal leaders in particular, who have paid mere lip service for years to social justice, need to put their money where their mouth is and wrest it out of the hands of police departments. ❏

Sources: Matt Zapotosky, Mark Berman and Erica Werner, "The Trump administration abandoned Obama-era police reform efforts. Now critics want them restored," *Washington Post*, June 1, 2020 (washingtonpost.com); Mark Berman, "Trump tells police not to worry about injuring suspects during arrests," *Washington Post*, July 28, 2017 (washingtonpost.com); Hanna Kozlowska, "Twenty five years after the Rodney King riots, American policing hasn't come far enough," Quartz, April 28, 2017 (quartz.com); Jessica Pishko, "How District Attorney Jackie Lacey Failed Los Angeles," The Appeal, Nov. 12, 2019 (appeal.org); Ese Olumhense, "20 Years After the NYPD Killing of Amadou Diallo, His Mom Asks: What's Changed?," The City, Feb. 1, 2019 (thecity.nyc); Yaseem Khan, "5 Years After Eric Garner's Death, Activists Continue Fight For 'Another Day To Live,'" Morning Edition, July 17, 2019 (npr.org); Jamiles Lartey, "Obama made progress on criminal justice reform. Will it survive the next president?," *Guardian*, Nov. 14, 2016 (theguardian.com); Katie Benner, "Sessions, in Last-Minute Act, Sharply Limits Use of Consent Decrees to Curb Police Abuses," *New York Times*, Nov. 8, 2018 (nytimes.com); Hank Johnson, "President Trump is giving police forces weapons of war. This is dangerous," *Guardian*, August 31, 2017 (theguardian.com); John Myers, "California's schools lose big in Newsom's budget," *L.A. Times*, May 18, 2020 (latimes.com); David Zahniser and Dakota Smith, "Despite a budget crisis, L.A. officials give new bonuses to officers with college degrees," L.A. Times, May 26, 2020 (latimes.com); Mayor Eric Garcetti, "FY 2020-21 Proposed Budget," the City of Los Angeles, April 2020 (cao.lacity.org); Caroline Lewis, "Coronavirus Takes $6 Billion Bite Out Of NYC's Budget," Gothamist, April 16, 2020 (gothamist.com); Alice Speri, "New York City and Los Angeles Slash Budgets—But Not for Police," The Intercept, May 22, 2020 (theintercept.com); Kristin Toussaint, "As cities make deep cuts because of COVID-19, police departments are keeping their funding," *Fast Company*, June 1, 2020 (fastcompany.com); Luke Darby, "This Is How Much Major Cities Prioritize Police Spending Versus Everything Else," *GQ*, June 1, 2020 (gq.com); John Haltiwanger, "House Democrats gave Trump 'everything he wanted' on a $738 billion defense bill while on the brink of impeaching him," *Business Insider*, Dec. 12, 2019 (businessinsider.com); Philip V. McHarris and Thenjiwe McHarris, "No More Money for the Police," *New York Times*, May 30, 2020 (nytimes.com); Black Lives Matter, "#DefundThePolice," May 30, 2020 (blacklivesmatter.com); "The End of Policing," Rising Up With Sonali, Dec. 11, 2018 (risingupwithsonali.com); Alex S. Vitale, *The End of Policing* (Verso, August 2018); Alex S. Vitale, "The answer to police violence is not 'reform'. It's defunding. Here's why," *Guardian*, May 31, 2020 (theguardian.com).

Article 10.5

INTERNATIONAL LABOR STANDARDS

BY ARTHUR MacEWAN
September/October 2008

> Dear Dr. Dollar:
>
> *U.S. activists have pushed to get foreign trade agreements to in-*
> *clude higher labor standards. But then you hear that developing coun-*
> *tries don't want that because cheaper labor without a lot of rules and*
> *regulations is what's helping them to bring industries in and build their*
> *economies. Is there a way to reconcile these views? Or are the activists just*
> *blind to the real needs of the countries they supposedly want to help?*
>
> —Philip Bereaud, Swampscott, Mass.

In 1971, General Emilio Medici, the then-military dictator of Brazil, comment-ed on economic conditions in his country with the infamous line: "The econo-my is doing fine, but the people aren't."

Like Medici, the government officials of many low-income countries today see the well-being of their economies in terms of overall output and the profits of firms—those profits that keep bringing in new investment and new industries that "build their economies." It is these officials who typically get to speak for their countries. When someone says that these countries "want" this or that—or "don't want" this or that—it is usually because the countries' officials have ex-pressed this position.

Do we know what the people in these countries want? The people who work in the new, rapidly growing industries, in the mines and fields, and in the small shops and market stalls of low-income countries? Certainly they want better con-ditions—more to eat, better housing, security for their children, improved health and safety. The officials claim that to obtain these better conditions, they must "build their economies." But just because "the economy is doing fine" does not mean that the people are doing fine.

In fact, in many low-income countries, economic expansion comes along with severe inequality. The people who do the work are not getting a reasonable share of the rising national income (and are sometimes worse off even in abso-lute terms). Brazil in the early 1970s was a prime example and, in spite of major political change, remains a highly unequal country. Today, in both India and China, as in several other countries, economic growth is coming with increas-ingly severe inequality.

Workers in these countries struggle to improve their positions. They form—or try to form—independent unions. They demand higher wages and better work-ing conditions. They struggle for political rights. It seems obvious that we should support those struggles, just as we support parallel struggles of workers in our own country. The first principle in supporting workers' struggles, here or anywhere else, is supporting their right to struggle—the right, in particular, to form independent unions without fear of reprisal. Indeed, in the ongoing controversy over the U.S.-Colombia Free Trade Agreement, the assassination of trade union leaders has rightly been a major issue.

Just how we offer our support—in particular, how we incorporate that support into trade agreements—is a complicated question. Pressure from abroad can help, but applying it is a complex process. A ban on goods produced with child labor, for example, could harm the most impoverished families that depend on children's earnings, or could force some children into worse forms of work (e.g., prostitution). On the other hand, using trade agreements to pressure governments to allow unhindered union organizing efforts by workers seems perfectly legitimate. When workers are denied the right to organize, their work is just one step up from slavery. Trade agreements can also be used to support a set of basic health and safety rights for workers. (Indeed, it might be useful if a few countries refused to enter into trade agreements with the United States until we improve workers' basic organizing rights and health and safety conditions in our own country!)

There is no doubt that the pressures that come through trade sanctions (restricting or banning commerce with another country) or simply from denying free access to the U.S. market can do immediate harm to workers and the general populace of low-income countries. Any struggle for change can generate short run costs, but the long-run gains—even the hope of those gains—can make those costs acceptable. Consider, for example, the apartheid-era trade sanctions against South Africa. To the extent that those sanctions were effective, some South African workers were deprived of employment. Nonetheless, the sanctions were widely supported by mass organizations in South Africa. Or note that when workers in this country strike or advocate a boycott of their company in an effort to obtain better conditions, they both lose income and run the risk that their employer will close up shop.

Efforts by people in this country to use trade agreements to raise labor standards in other countries should, whenever possible, take their lead from workers in those countries. It is up to them to decide what costs are acceptable. There are times, however, when popular forces are denied even basic rights to struggle. The best thing we can do, then, is to push for those rights—particularly the right to organize independent unions—that help create the opportunity for workers in poor countries to choose what to fight for. ❏

Article 10.6

LAND REFORM

A Precondition for Sustainable Economic Development

BY JAWIED NAWABI
May/June 2015

> *It is in the agricultural sector that the battle for long-term economic development will be won or lost.*
>
> > —Gunnar Myrdal, economist and Nobel laureate

The phrase "land reform" often conjures up memories, for those leaning right, of frightening extreme-left ideologies. On the progressive left, meanwhile, land reform is often treated as a passé topic.

With the advent of rising inequality, climate change, weak government institutions, failed states, terrorism, corruption, and a whole slew of other socio-economic problems—sown or exacerbated by three decades of neoliberal policies in the "developing world" (Global South)—it is high time we revisit the issue of land reform. We need to bring it back to the center of the discussion on sustainable economic development. Land reform is not political extremism; rather, it is a critical policy mechanism for the world to address issues of poverty, hunger, urban slums, and good governance.

What is "land reform"? It is usually defined as the redistribution of large landholdings to smaller ones. Land is transferred from large landlords to those who have been working the land as tenants (such as sharecroppers) or paid agricultural workers, as well as dispossessed underemployed or unemployed urban workers who migrated from rural areas looking for employment and wound up living in urban slums. That is one model of land reform. Another model is redistribution in the form of rural communes or cooperative or collective farms. A combination of the two models is also possible.

Reemergence of Land Reform Movements

Despite the attempts by international institutions (like the International Monetary Fund and World Bank) and oligarchic political elites in the global South to suppress land reform policies, there have been growing social movements pushing for land reform in the last two decades. Neoliberal "free-trade" policies have exposed small farmers to devastating global competition (especially from giant mechanized industrial farms in the global North), leaving hundreds of millions of them dispossessed, and have forced them into the reserve army of impoverished, unemployed, or underemployed living in urban slums. From Brazil and Mexico to the Philippines and Zimbabwe, social movements for a more just and fair distribution of wealth—particularly land—are confronting these devastating consequences of neoliberalism.

Social protest has led even elite institutions such as the World Bank to acknowledge the issue. The Bank's *World Development Report 2008: Agriculture for*

Development, at least rhetorically put agriculture and the productivity of small farmers "at the heart of a global agenda to reduce poverty."

Agriculture as a Technical Problem?

The central tendency of mainstream economic development theory since the 1940s and 1950s has been to view agriculture as a mere stepping stone towards industrialization. Economist Arthur W. Lewis' "dualist" model was particularly influential in casting agricultural labor in developing countries as redundant—with a "surplus" of workers adding little or nothing to agricultural production. This surplus labor force, Lewis argued, should be moved out of the agricultural sector—this would supposedly not reduce output—and into the industrial, which he viewed as the key sector of the economy.

Besides moving inefficient peasants out of the rural sector, mainstream development economists proposed to boost agricultural yields by consolidating small farms into large ones—supposedly to take advantages of economies of scale. Thus, instead of reducing land concentration, this would increase it, essentially accomplishing a reverse land reform. Such an industrial model of agriculture would use expensive capital equipment (imported from the global North), petroleum-based fertilizers, herbicides, and pesticides. Today's version of the model increasingly pushes the adoption of genetically modified seeds controlled by corporations like Monsanto.

During the 1960s and 1970s, this frame of thought led many international institutions (such as the World Bank, Asian Development Bank, etc.) and governments in the global South to embrace the "Green Revolution." The Green Revolution was essentially a plan to use "science and technology" to increase crop production in developing countries. The use of fertilizers, pesticides, and high-yield crop varieties was supposed to boost agricultural productivity, reduce rural poverty, solve problems of hunger and malnutrition, and thus avoid peasant movements and rural political instability. This was, as economists James M. Cypher and James L. Dietz put it, a "strategy wherein it was hoped that seed technologies could be substituted for missing land reform and for more radical 'red revolutions' of the socialist variety threatening to sweep across the globe at the time."

Viewing agricultural productivity as a purely technical problem, advocates of the Green Revolution did not aim to transform the structure of land inequality and landlord power. To take the case of India, the Green Revolution boosted agricultural yields, making the country technically self-sufficient in food production. However, the changes primarily benefited medium and large-sized landowners who used capital-intensive technologies, high-yielding mono-crop seeds, and large inputs of fertilizers and pesticides. "Rural inequity worsened because of the growing prosperity of the large and medium

> ### *Land Reform and Colonization*
>
> If we broaden the concept of land reform, the whole process of colonial settlement in North America, Central and South America, Australia, and New Zealand was one big land reform, appropriating the lands of indigenous peoples and distributing it to the European settlers. So land reform can be understood as a much more common experience of the "developed" world than it is usually thought of in the economic literature.

farmers and the unchanged position of the landless and small farmers," concludes Indian scholar Siddharth Dube. "And because large farms use more capital and less labor per unit of produce than small farms, rural employment grew much less than it would have if land reform had taken place and the increase in production come from smaller farms."

The Economic and Sociopolitical Cases for Land Reform

There are two broad arguments for the importance of land reform. The first is based on the widely observed inverse relationship between farm size and output per unit of land area: smaller farms produce more per acre of land than larger farms. Smaller landholdings are more productive and ecologically sustainable for a number of reasons:

1) Higher labor intensity. Small farmers use more labor per unit of land, which helps generate more output and more employment per unit.

2) Higher multiple cropping. They grow more crops per year on a given piece of land.

3) Higher intensity of cultivation. Small farmers leave a lower proportion of land fallow or uncultivated. In addition, they cultivate crops that are higher value-added per unit of land.

4) Lower negative environmental impacts. Small farms use fertilizers, pesticides, and other agrochemicals more sparingly than large farms. This reduces negative impacts of harmful chemicals on workers and neighbors. Small farmers, overall, have a greater incentive to employ environmentally sustainable techniques than large industrial ones.

While the economic case for land reform can be construed as a narrow technical argument on how best to boost agricultural productivity—which land-reform opponents could argue is unnecessary due to the advent of the Green Revolution—the sociopolitical argument is aimed against this kind of narrow technical thinking.

The importance of land reform is in changing the hierarchical structure of agrarian class relations while increasing productivity. The idea is to break the power of landlords, who keep peasants as a captive labor force in rural areas and act as a conservative political force at the local and national levels of the state.

The central mechanism by which landlords wield their power is through patron-client networks that give them control over local and regional government institutions. Landlords keep the poor majority depen-

---

Good Governance

The "good-governance functions" of the state are policies beneficial to the large majority of the population. Good-governance states exercise control over a certain territory, depend on a broad part of their population for revenue, and in turn provide the population with a wide range of public goods: the rule of law, transportation infrastructure (paved roads, extensive and affordable public transportation, etc.), public utilities (electricity, clean water, sewage systems), human services (health, education systems), and job security or at least temporary unemployment insurance.

dent on them for jobs and access to land, while also using them as a captive power base for local elections (in countries where there are elections, such as India and Brazil). This way, they can block the development of state programs providing public goods—like public roads, clinics, schools, water systems, etc.—for everyone. Instead, they perpetuate a more narrowly targeted development relying on private goods—fertilizer, pesticides, expensive high-yield seeds, privately controlled water wells, loans that put peasants in ever-deeper debt, etc. They provide, also, a form of private insurance system for those clients who exhibit proper loyalty, in contrast to social support systems available to all—which would reduce the peasants' vulnerability and the landlord's power. The consequence is that the state's good-governance capacities are distorted and corrupted, favoring the narrow interests of the landlords and the political elite that is connected to them (often by kinship).

Transformative sociopolitical land reform for developing countries is aimed at diminishing wealth inequalities in the initial stages of development and breaking the grip on power of the upper-class elite (including not only landlords but also big industrial, financial, and commercial capitalists generally allied with them). This democratization of society would make it possible to orient the state towards long-term national development policies which can create more conducive socioeconomic and sociopolitical conditions serving the population as a whole, and not just the elite.

The socioeconomic conditions would include a more egalitarian class structure in the rural sector, greater incentives for farmers to increase their productivity due to owning the land they work, greater farmer incomes allowing the farmers to send their children to school, better nutrition due to higher caloric intake, and greater small-farmer purchasing power leading to greater demand for the products of labor-intensive manufacturing. The sociopolitical democratization would mean the breaking of landlord power, political stabilization resulting from the inclusion of the peasant masses in the political system, and democratization of decision-making now liberated from landlord control of local and national state bureaucracies.

Land Reform Is Not Enough

There have been many more failed land reforms than successful ones. Reforms have failed mainly because they have not been thorough enough in breaking the power of the landed elite, and in extending the role of the government in an inclusive development process. Across Latin America—in Mexico, Bolivia, Brazil, Chile, and Peru—land reforms have had partial success, but for the most part have not dislodged rural elites and their industrial counterparts from political dominance. This has contributed to an image of land reform, even among the progressive left, as a tried and failed policy. There are also examples of half-successful land reforms in South and East Asia—in India, the Philippines, Indonesia, and Thailand—where peasants did reap some benefits like reliable ownership titles, which allowed them to borrow on better terms, boost crop yields, and reduce malnutrition, though without fundamentally altering the class structure.

On the other hand, successful land reforms were thorough, extensive, and swift. Key examples in the 20th century include Japan, Taiwan, South Korea, and China. Land in the first three countries was distributed as family-sized farms. (China initially had a collectivized land reform.) Looking at the Japanese and South Korean cases: In Japan in 1945, 45% of the peasants were landless tenants. By 1955, only 9% were tenants and even they benefited from much-strengthened protective laws. In pre-reform South Korea in 1944, the top 3% of landholders owned about 64% of the land, with an average holding of 26 hectares. By 1956, the top 6% owned just 18% of the land, with an average of about 2.6 hectares. Meanwhile, 51% of family farmers owned about 65% of the land, with an average holding of 1.1 hectares.

Nowhere in Latin America or Africa, nor elsewhere in Asia (except Kerala, India), did land reforms come so close to such equalization and radical reshaping of traditional social structures. The East Asian land reforms succeeded in bringing about long-term national development policies by creating more conducive socio-economic and sociopolitical conditions—breaking the existing power structure, and allowing for the emergence of developmentally oriented states (as opposed to neoliberal models that saw state promotion of economic development as anachronistic and "inefficient"). Successful land reforms require follow-up—supportive policies investing in rural infrastructure development (irrigation, electricity, roads, health clinics, schools), plus providing services such as clear and legitimate land records, micro-credit at reasonable rates of interest, and training for farmers in the newest skills for sustainable farming. Japan, Taiwan, South Korea, and arguably even China's development paths serve as examples of transformative land reforms in the last 50 years. What these countries achieved was remarkable growth with equity. ❑

Article 10.7

INDIA'S FARMERS' PROTESTS
What's behind one of the largest protests in history?

SIRISHA NAIDU
May/June 2021

In November 2020, in the midst of the Covid-19 pandemic, landowning farmers, and mostly landless farmworkers—men and women, young and old—gathered outside the capital city of New Delhi for one of the biggest demonstrations in the world. The assembly of yellow and green scarves, turbans, and flags was met with water cannons, barricades, and a *lathi-* (baton-)wielding police force that prevented them from entering the city. They were, however, joined by industrial workers, students, and civil rights groups protesting regressive and authoritarian policies. There were more than 200 million protesters opposing the government's economic policies. The farmers have continued their protests. On January 26, 2021, the 74th anniversary of India's Republic Day, the ranks of protesters swelled as they were joined by more farmers and farmworkers, along with their tractor-trailers (also referred to as "trollies"), and trucks as they marched and drove in a rally demanding their right to a livelihood and the right to protest, as enshrined in the Constitution.

The protests were a reaction to a set of farm bills that were proposed in June 2020 and passed on September 28, 2020. These bills were not afforded the treatment of a truly democratic process, which would have involved the input of state governments and the people most impacted by the proposed legislation.

Farmers in the state of Punjab had been protesting against the then-bills since June 2020 at the state level and when that failed, they decided to take the fight to New Delhi. The protesters were initially drawn in large numbers from the northern states of Punjab and Haryana, and later from the western part of the state of Uttar Pradesh (UP); all three states are in close proximity to New Delhi. As the days rolled by, they were joined by protesters from far-flung states and were also supported by solidarity rallies and marches in other states.

Tens of thousands of protesters first set up camp in the biting November cold and are now preparing for the unrelenting New Delhi heat. They have been successful in occupying five different locations and partially or fully blocking the major highways near these sites that run into the city. What started out as a temporary blockade has turned into a semi-permanent encampment. Some of the protesters have been in attendance with up to three generations of family members; others are on rotating shifts with family members, friends, and neighbors from their villages. The protesters have proclaimed that they have arrived with enough provisions for six months and are willing to stay for as long as needed. They perceive these farm laws as a matter of life and death. The protests, which are farmer-led but include a wide variety of groups, have come to represent a struggle against an economy that prioritizes profits over life. They demand an economy that represents the needs of the people—an economy that recenters agrarian livelihoods, food security, and human dignity at the core of economic policymaking.

The Implications of the New Laws

The farmers' and farmworkers' unions that are protesting the recently passed federal legislation have critiqued the prior structure of agricultural markets, too. Before these new laws, government-regulated markets (*mandis*) were overseen by individual state governments. The intention was to license traders and middlemen and regulate their transactions with farmers. Most farmers in India have small landholdings, and the average farmland is less than 2.5 acres. Hence, state regulations were intended to reduce the risk of the exploitation of India's farmers by traders and middlemen. Instead, the license requirement created barriers to entry by limiting the number of traders and other intermediaries in the *mandis*. This inadvertently left farmers with little bargaining power and made them highly dependent on middlemen, who also played the role of financiers, information brokers, and traders. Farmers were often forced to accept lower prices as a result.

Farmers' unions have long called for changes to this flawed system. However, instead of leveling the playing field, the new farm laws appear to have been formulated specifically to benefit private corporations. While the federal government and media have portrayed the bills, and now laws, as benefiting the farmers, the changes that these laws usher in are far from the reforms that farmers' and farmworkers' unions demanded. They pave the way to displace middlemen and small traders without attending to the needs and long-held demands of farmers to create a more equitable system. The laws fulfill the federal government's mandate to create markets that are profitable for corporate players at the expense of the livelihood and food security of the country's citizens.

When it comes to these new laws, farmers and farmworkers have a range of concerns, from the erosion of government supports and food security to changes in how contract farming is carried out.

First, the issue of paramount concern—the trigger for the protest—is the minimum support price (MSP), which is a price floor that guarantees a minimum price for farm produce. This ensures that farmers are protected from some degree of price volatility in national and international markets and is a common policy measure in a number of countries, including the United States. The recent laws, however, do not clarify how the MSP, which acts as a price floor for 23 principal crops, will be impacted by the legislation. The government has made some assurances that the MSP will continue despite deregulation. However, farmers and farmworkers are concerned that under the new laws, the MSP is unenforceable since large private agribusinesses and corporate firms may refuse to purchase crops at the higher MSP rate.

While MSP has eroded in many states, it is still strong in the three states which have contributed the bulk of the protesters (Punjab, Haryana, and UP). Farmers and farmworkers from these states are worried that the farm laws would create two parallel markets: the government-run *mandi* with the requisite regulations and a "free" market. Private corporations may initially lure farmers away from *mandis* by offering prices greater than the MSP. If this starves the *mandis* of sellers and they are forced to close, it will mean that farmers can no longer count on a guaranteed price for their produce. It also means that private corporations can accumulate monopoly power over the supply chain, thus effectively giving them control of prices. Further, farmers are also apprehensive that the state may favor open markets over *mandis* in order to stock up on essential food grains for emergencies or for its food distribution program.

In sum, farmers are concerned that the relationship between the Indian state and farmers, wherein the state provides some degree of revenue guarantee, will change drastically. This revenue guarantee is particularly significant because agriculture is an increasingly unviable source of livelihood and yet the economy has not produced sufficient alternative employment opportunities. The Indian state did not help matters by foregoing a consultative process with farmers' and farmworkers' unions when crafting the new farm laws.

Second, protesters and their allies are fearful about the impact of the MSP on the Public Distribution System (PDS), which ensures the provisioning of a fixed quantity of staple foods for free or at government-regulated fixed prices for 75% of the rural population and 50% of the urban population, as mandated by the National Food Security Act of 2013. The Indian state acquires this food from *mandis* at the MSP rate. With the strengthening of corporate players, the concern is that farmers will be forced to sell at low prices to corporations who will then sell the produce at higher prices, which would increase the cost of government procurement. This would undermine

---

The New Farm Laws

The protesters are objecting to three new farm laws that were implemented in 2020 and open up the agricultural sector to free markets at the points of production (through contract farming) and sale (through the complete deregulation of wholesale markets and storage requirements) and consolidate fragmented agricultural markets into a "one nation-one market" system. There have been public discussions about liberalizing agricultural markets since 2003 as farmers' unions, as well as economic and political commentators across the political spectrum, recognized the flaws in the earlier system that allowed middlemen to accumulate market power. Since then, as many as 17 of India's 28 states have amended their state laws to deregulate agricultural markets in varying degrees with the stated aim of increasing benefits to farmers. So, the recent laws primarily impact the states that have continued to regulate markets. These happen to be the northern states of Haryana and Punjab, which also reaped the highest benefits of the Green Revolution. (The Green Revolution in India started in the mid-1960s and was a period in which an industrial system of high-yielding varieties of seeds, chemical fertilizers, tractors, and other technologies were adopted to improve agricultural productivity.)

The **Farmers' Produce Trade and Commerce (Promotion and Facilitation) Act** allows farmers to sell outside of government-regulated markets (*mandis*), creating the possibility for greater competition and allowing private players to deal directly with farmers.

The **Farmers (Empowerment and Protection) Agreement on Price Assurance and Farm Services Act** provides a national framework for contract farming without state intervention. All aspects of agribusiness, processing, and services, including wholesalers, exporters, and large retailers, fall under the purview of this Act.

The **Essential Commodities (Amendment) Act** removes cereals, pulses (including a range of beans, peas, and lentils), oil seeds, edible oils, onions, and potatoes, which are all food staples, from the list of "essential commodities" under government control. It also removes them from government oversight on stocking limits, thus allowing corporations to engage in unlimited stockpiling, except if the economy is facing exceptional circumstances.

the PDS system as a whole, thus affecting a large proportion of the Indian population that can't even afford to purchase food at current market prices.

Protesters are concerned that the farm laws will also further erode the minimal social protections afforded by the Indian state. Economic policies in the last two decades have reduced social benefits and investment in social infrastructure and have privatized profit-making public utilities to the detriment of workers and consumers. The pace of neoliberal policies has accelerated under the current ruling political party, BJP (Bharatiya Janata Party), which has been in power since 2014. A government committee, along with the Chief Economic Advisor to the federal government, Arvind Subramanian, recently called for direct cash transfers rather than the current "in-kind" delivery of staple foods, and a reduction in PDS coverage from the current 75–50% to 20–40% of the rural and urban population, respectively. These recommendations have been cited by protesters as evidence that the current government is interested in dismantling or weakening the PDS system, thus galvanizing rural farmworkers as well as urban industrial and service workers—those who would be most affected by changes in the PDS—to oppose the farm laws.

Farmers from all states are also worried about the provisions of the Empowerment and Protection Act, which specifies new rules on contract farming. While it ostensibly lays out the rules of the game for engaging in contract farming, there are no provisions to safeguard the interests of mostly small farmers against corporate interests with a higher degree of bargaining power. The monthly income for landholding farmers ranges from $7.80 (for marginal farmers with less than 2.5 acres of land) to $103 (for large farmers with more than five acres of land). (I used an exchange rate of U.S.$1 = Rs. 73. These low incomes are often supplemented with other livelihoods.) Farmers depend heavily on unpredictable monsoons that have become even more capricious on account of climate change, and they also lack access to adequate storage for crops.

While farmers are continuing to struggle to make ends meet, agribusiness startup investments in India's farm sector have increased significantly in the last couple of years. For example, in the first half of 2019, investments in such businesses totaled $248 million (a 300% increase from 2018) and have mostly been focused on improving the supply chain. These figures, however, do not account for the large corporate players desirous of expanding their presence in the farm sector in India. Farmers do not expect to benefit from these investments in the agricultural sector. On the contrary, by implementing the "one nation-one market" policy and infringing on individual states' ability to legislate on contract farming based on specific crops, regional economies, and geographies, protesters believe that the new farm laws codify an uneven playing field that's not in favor of farmers or farmworkers.

This perception is alarmingly reinforced by provisions in each of the new laws that explicitly prohibit legal challenges against the state or private corporations. This means that farmers cannot sue agribusiness players for any breach of contract. Small farmers typically do not have the financial wherewithal to engage in legal challenges, especially when it comes to challenging large entities. Nevertheless, these provisions, which are integral to these laws, reinforce the perception that the laws were meant to benefit private corporations and have far-reaching implications not just for the agricultural sector but for all denizens of the nation.

The changes wrought by these laws have been made against the backdrop of an acute agrarian crisis that has lasted for more than two decades. Since the mid-1990s, when India undertook economic liberalization, the agrarian crisis has resulted in more than 300,000 suicides by farmers and farmworkers, according to the National Crime Records Bureau. These have been primarily due to high levels of indebtedness and the inability of farmers to withstand market and natural shocks. Yet 42% of India's population of 1.3 billion continues to depend on agriculture, either as farmers or farmworkers. The other viable alternative is mostly low-wage informal employment that falls outside the ambit of government laws on minimum wage and workplace safety; more than 80% of those outside of the agrarian sector are informally employed. It is therefore unsurprising that India's ranking on the Global Hunger Index and the country's child nutrition levels are abysmally low. The benefits of high economic growth have been highly unequal; according to Oxfam, the top 1% of the country's population holds 77% of the nation's wealth. The pandemic has worsened inequality, as it has in other countries, like the United States. The wealth of India's billionaires increased by 35% during the pandemic, whereas 122 million people lost their jobs during the same period.

The federal government's imposition of the new farm laws during the pandemic reeks of its preoccupation with profits and markets—the laws are a grotesque attempt to concentrate power in the hands of big corporations. One of the demands of the farmers is to roll back the new laws and instead implement the recommendations of the National Commission on Farmers, which was formed in 2004 before the current political regime came to power. Under the direction of professor M.S. Swaminathan, who led India's Green Revolution, the Commission proposed structural changes that would address the decline in farm incomes and productivity, the high number of farmer and farmworker suicides, as well as indebtedness, access to credit, and landlessness. Unlike the recent laws, these recommendations would actually address the crisis that farmers and farmworkers are facing.

Men Are Cooking, Women Are Protesting, and Other Forms of Social Transformation

The farmer-led protests that began in November 2020 against the farm laws that would lower agrarian income and reduce food security are impressive, though their outcome is so far undetermined. Nevertheless, the protests have already garnered significant victories that are likely to reverberate throughout society and lead to political action.

First, the farmers' protests have not only forced the issue of monopolization and the increasing corporatization of agriculture into everyday conversation, but they have also extended the critique to neoliberal policies that have celebrated the monopolization and privatization of health care, education, and other public services.

Second, protesting farmers have also been joined by farmworkers, particularly from certain regions in the state of Punjab. This is surprising because of the conflictual class relationship between farmworkers and farmers. Farmers are landowners, even if they are small landholders, whereas farmworkers are mostly landless and are employed as daily or seasonal wage workers by farmers. Also, in the states that have contributed the most protesters, farmworkers tend to be Dalits, who are lowest in the caste hierarchy, whereas farmers typically belong to higher castes. Yet, some farmers' unions in Punjab have been working in conjunction with farmworkers' unions to improve wages, mitigate caste-related violence directed at landless Dalit farmworkers, and pressure the state for better living conditions. The farmers' unions hope that this will build a stronger coalition that demands better treatment for agrarian India. However, there are severe challenges to this class-caste unity against state and corporate interests. This alliance is, moreover, nonexistent or nascent in many regions. Yet, it represents a new mode of politics in India, which has typically been fractured along class-caste lines.

Third, women have taken on an incredibly important role in this struggle. This is especially notable because women in India have a very low status and are considered undesirable as shown by their low sex ratio at birth of 900 girls to 1,000 boys in 2015, as well as women's low labor force participation rate in both the formal and informal labor force, which was about 20% in 2020. Furthermore, women from North India, who are the majority of the protesters, typically experience lower mobility and hold few leadership positions or public roles. Yet, women from North India have been prominently visible among those organizing the protests. Many women, including Dalit women, have travelled to New Delhi to represent their sons, husbands, and brothers who have committed suicide due to the agrarian crisis. Women have taken on the role of organizing daily rallies and cultural performances on social issues and even editing the *Trolley Times*, a bilingual (Hindi and Punjabi) newspaper that is produced by the protesters, for the protesters. They are demanding the right to financial security as farmers and farmworkers and asserting their right to occupy public space as "protesters in their own right," according to Navkiran Natt, the quiet but tenacious dentist-turned-co-editor of *Trolley Times* (which was named after the trolleys, or tractor-trailers, that have become a symbol of the farmer-led protests). They have also organized an International Women's Day celebration to recognize and honor the contributions of women as farmers, farmworkers, and as those responsible for sustaining households and families.

Fourth, farmers, farmworkers, and representatives of farmers' and farmworkers' unions have travelled from across India to the protest site in New Delhi. This cross-regional participation and solidarity is a historic moment in post-colonial India, which has maintained strong regional and subnational identities. More than 40 farmers' unions have come together under the banner of *Samyukt Kisan Morcha* (United Farmers' Front). Not only has this organization coordinated negotiations with the government as a collective entity, but it has also coordinated strategy and tactics, and issued media briefs, press conferences, and statements since November 2020. It is also in active discussion with more than 450 farmers' and farmworkers' unions across the country to coordinate actions in individual states for those who cannot travel long distances to the capital city during the ongoing pandemic. This is immensely significant because it represents a surge in solidarity between people who are subject to widely different economic and political histories while also subverting regional and subnational insularity.

Fifth, the protesters collectively model an alternative political vision. Tens of thousands of protesters have been camped along five highways leading to the capital city since November 2020, through one of the coldest winters the city has ever experienced. They sleep in trucks and tractor-trailers and makeshift tents. They eat collectively in *langars* (community kitchens that run on the principle of service, or *seva*, which is integral to the Sikh faith) run by local allies or the protesters themselves. Women are not necessarily relegated to kitchen work, and men are learning to cook for the *langars* in contravention of conventional gender norms. Protest sites have transformed into temporary mini townships with vendors and medical centers. There is a space for film screenings, and the social media accounts that have been set up by the protesters are deftly managed. More significantly, through the *Trolley Times*, protesters challenge the incorrect and negative portrayal of the struggle in the mainstream press and aim to keep all protesters (particularly the elderly, who form the bulk of the protesters and are not on social media) up to date on news across the five protest sites. The paper prints declarations made by the protest's leaders, engages in political education about the history of agrarian struggles in India, and provides space to issues of caste and gender that are typically ignored. They also have a very active Twitter account (@Kisanektamorcha) which allows them to reach youth, members of the Indian diaspora, and international allies with their messaging.

Lessons to Learn

The historic farmer-led protests are a clear response to decades of neglect of the agrarian economy, which until a few decades ago was the backbone of the Indian economy and, as noted earlier, still employs 42% of the workforce. The moral and policy stance of the federal government has been that of a benevolent patriarch that needs to be firm and sometimes stern (including activating the police, military, and paramilitary forces as needed), to support the growth of the economy, which allegedly benefits its denizens. The solution to the agrarian crisis, which is in no small measure a result of neoliberal policies, is sought in the implementation of yet more neoliberal reforms. The federal government is unwilling to learn from the failures of the individual states that have implemented similar policies.

A generous interpretation would be that the government is naïve, uninformed, or incompetent. A more realistic interpretation lies in the history of the state-market nexus that was strengthened since neoliberal reforms were first adopted in 1991 by the Congress Party. Since then, successive governments have attempted to mollify and woo Indian and multinational capital. None have been as strident in their efforts as the BJP. The current protests cement the identification of the BJP with corporate interests in the popular imagination.

The Indian state under both political parties—Congress and the BJP—has ignored or actively obscured lessons from the innumerable failures of neoliberal policies. Regular people finally appear to be waking up to the wretched conditions of their brothers and sisters who are toiling in the agrarian economy with little protection from the federal or state governments and who now find themselves pitted against corporate players. For example, recent revelations about the e-commerce giant Amazon's operations in India confirm what the protesting farmers have been saying all along, according to a recent post by the economist Rahul Varman at the Research Unit for Political Economy blog: "The Prime Minister and the Finance Minister have become the greatest cheerleaders for big capital," as the government looks the other way while Amazon evades regulations, or shapes policy to favor Amazon and other big corporations. According to Varman, the revelations about Amazon show that "the farmers are correct: recent policies and new laws will lead to their further marginalization and even decimation while corporates [sic] further consolidate their gains, with little actual oversight by the State."

The farm laws primarily serve the needs of profits and power. The farmers' protests constitute a challenge to such principles and offer a critique of the state and the economy. Even more importantly, in the course of protesting, farmers and farmworkers are developing and offering an alternative vision of the economy that prioritizes livelihood and food security for all; recognizes the deep divisions of caste, class, gender, religion, and regional differences; and makes an attempt to tackle them. The protests offer a vision of a collective that is challenging the defunct institutions of democracy and putting a better version of democracy into practice. ❑

Sources: "Indian Farmers Lead Historic Strike & Protests Against Narendra Modi, Neoliberalism & Inequality," *Democracy Now!*, December 3, 2020 (democracynow.org); Maria Aurelio, "India: Largest Strike in World History: Over 200 Million Workers and Farmers Protest against Poverty and Unemployment Triggered by Covid Lockdown," Left Voice, December 4, 2020 (leftvoice.org); "Parliament passes The Farmers' Produce Trade and Commerce (Promotion and Facilitation) Bill, 2020 and The Farmers (Empowerment and Protection) Agreement of Price Assurance and Farm Services Bill, 2020," Press release, Ministry of Agriculture & Farmers Welfare, September 20, 2020 (pib.gov.in); "Parliament passes the Essential Commodities (Amendment) Bill, 2020," Press release, Ministry of Counsumer Affairs, Food & Public Distribution, September 22, 2020 (pib.gov.in); Anna Priyadarshini, "'Misled,' 'brainwashed,' 'instigated': How primetime TV covered farmer protests," News Laundry, November 28, 2020 (newslaundry.com); "Minimum Support Prices," Farmers' Portal (farmer.gov.in); "Economic Survey Summary: Shanta Kumar Committee Report," Parivarthan, June 9, 2015 (iska.in); "Agritech In India—Emerging Trends in 2019," NASSCOM, July 2019 (nasscom. in); Shailender Kumar Hooda and Santosh Kumar Das, "A Policy Roadmap to End Farmers' Distress," The Wire, March 20, 2019 (thewire.in); "Farm Bills will Benefit Big Corporates, Not Farmers," An interview with P. Sainath, News Click India Youtube channel (Youtube. com); P. Sainath, "And you thought it's only about farmers?" People's Archive of Rural India, Dec. 10, 2020 (ruralindiaonline.org); Rahul Tripathi, "NCRB data shows 42,480 farmers and daily wagers committed suicide in 2019," *Economic Times*, September 1, 2020 (economictimes. indiatimes.com); Sirisha Naidu, "Why Not Pakodas? Part I: GDP and Employment" (aainanagar.com); Taniya Roy, "Child Nutrition Levels in India Worsened Over Last Five Years, Finds NHFS Survey," The Wire, December 10, 2020 (thewire.in); Oxfam International, "India: extreme inequality in numbers" (oxfam.org); Oxfam International, "The Inequality Virus: Davos India Supplement" 2021; Parth M.N., 'We will protest for as long as possible' People's Archive of Rural India, March 24, 2021 (ruralindiaonline.org); The Swaminathan Commission reports, People's Archive of Rural India, November 23, 2018 (ruralindiaonline. org); Shreya Sinha, "The Agrarian Crisis in Punjab and the Making of the Anti-Farm Law

Protests," The India Forum, Dec. 4. 2020 (theindiaforum.in); Ambedkar King Study Circle USA, "Agrarian Crisis Discussion #9: Farm Worker and Industrial Labor Solidarity," February 28, 2021 (Ambedkar King Study Circle YouTube channel); Ambedkar King Study Circle USA, "Agrarian Crisis Discussion #5: Contingent Solidarity & Kisan-Mazdoor Struggle," January 30, 2021 (Ambedkar King Study Circle YouTube channel); Priyanka Pulla, "What are the consequences of India's falling sex ratio?" The Hindu, March 3, 2018 (thehindu.com); Shinzani Jain, "The Alarming Drop in the Female Labour Force Participation in India," News Click India, December 3, 2020 (newsclick.in); Navsharan Singh, Bill Fletcher Jr., and Sonny Singh, Frontlines of Hope March 25, 2021 (IndiaCivilWatch ICW YouTube channel); "Women farmers hold protest marches, deliver speeches at Singhu, Tikri, Ghazipur borders," The Print, March 8, 2021 (theprint.in); Rina Chandran "'We are telling our story': Indian farmers record their protest in print," Reuters, February 4, 2021 (news.trust.org); Vedika Sud and Julia Hollingsworth, "Washing machines and libraries: What life is like in Indian farmers protest camps on Delhi's outskirts," CNN, February 5, 2021 (cnn.com); Seraj Ali and Prabhat Kumar "'Trolley Times,' a Newspaper of and by the Farmer's Protest," The Wire, January 9, 2021 (thewire.in); Rahul Varman, "Recent Amazon Revelations: What do they tell us about the ongoing farm protests?" Research Unit for Political Economy, March 2, 2021 (rupeindia.wordpress.com).

BUBBLE BREAKTHROUGH

The NBA work stoppage was a perfect model for a wildcat strike.

BY ABDUL MAILK
September/October 2020

Players in four major American sports leagues went on a wildcat strike in late August, with other leagues and sports watching closely.

This two-day strike began in the NBA on August 26. Players were responding to what they felt was the league's inaction around issues of racial justice, including in the wake of the police shooting of Jacob Blake in Kenosha, Wis. on August 23. Fred VanVleet of the Toronto Raptors noted in an extraordinary interview on ESPN that a stoppage of play would put owners' finances under threat, and force them to leverage their political capital to push authorities to prosecute the police who shot Blake.

VanVleet's analysis shows these workers understand the power they hold in the workplace. The strike was also the outcome of years of organizing on the shop floor, poor concessions from management, and worker frustration on the job.

Not the First NBA Wildcat Strike

Make no mistake: despite the #NBABoycott hashtag, this was a wildcat strike, arguably the most visible one in years.

To understand this wildcat strike, it's vital to know about the last one. The year of 1964 was a big moment for the NBA. The first-ever televised All-Star game was happening, and the flagging league needed it to be a success in order to secure ongoing television contracts.

Meanwhile, negotiations around a pension plan between the National Basketball Players' Association (NBPA) and the Board of Governors had broken down, with the Board stalling for months.

Hours before tip-off at the All-Star game, the players took an informal strike vote: 11-9 in favor. They told the owners they wouldn't play unless they got their pension plan. This was a do-or-die moment for the league, with its lucrative, near-guaranteed TV deal hanging in the balance.

Minutes before the game was supposed to start, the players' demand was met. It was the first pension plan in the history of professional sports. To this day, it remains the best one.

Covid-19, the Bubble, and Worker Power

Fifty-six years after the 1964 strike, when the NBA made its plans to restart play after the Covid-19 shutdown, in a "bubble" system at Disneyland, it did so amidst the ongoing protests around police violence in the wake of George Floyd's murder.

In meetings prior to the bubble being codified, mass Zoom calls with players and the union, the National Basketball Players Association (NBPA), were a forum to voice thoughts openly. Many players in the NBA, a majority-Black league, understandably expressed discomfort around playing a game for entertainment while there were serious issues of social justice and anti-racism that needed to be addressed.

The majority of them still committed, with key outliers. In the WNBA, league superstar Maya Moore took off the entire season in order to support the case of Jonathan Irons, a Black man serving a 50-year sentence for assault and robbery, who is widely believed to have been wrongly convicted and imprisoned by an all-white jury.

Then Jacob Blake was shot in the back seven times, two protestors were murdered at the hands of white supremacist militia, and the officers who shot Blake were put on administrative leave. On August 26, the Toronto Raptors indicated that they were looking at withholding labor for their first semifinal game against the Boston Celtics, and they were in conversation with the Celtics about making it a mutual decision. Raptors' head coach Nick Nurse went as far as to say some players were considering leaving the bubble entirely.

A few hours later, the Orlando Magic took to the court to play the Milwaukee Bucks, who, without any warning, didn't show up. They had struck, staying in the locker room and requesting a conference call with the Wisconsin Attorney General, Josh Kaul. Unlike past actions around racial justice, this was not sanctioned by league management.

Immediately, this sparked a domino effect. All games for August 26 and August 27 were cancelled. Commentators of color walked away from their desks. Referees and coaches both issued statements in support.

Most importantly, three other major active North American sports leagues joined the strike: Major League Baseball (MLB), Major League Soccer (MLS), and the WNBA. The next day, under public pressure, the National Hockey League paused all games as well. Despite its brevity, this was the most prominent sector-wide wildcat strike in recent memory.

Steady Organizing to Get to This Point

Miraculously, the August 26 strike occurred four years to the day after Colin Kaepernick first took a knee during the national anthem at an NFL game; and it should be noted that it took four years of pressure, organizing, and state violence to reach this point.

Watching vlogs and reporting from the NBA bubble is fascinating. There are ongoing conversations about racial justice behind the scenes.

It's clear that many players are uneasy about being insulated from the world while so much is happening. Watching these videos, which are quite earnest, and hearing anecdotes about conversations that weren't filmed, suggests that players were pushing each other to confront the idea that taking action was more important than playing basketball. Constant conversations and informal one-on-ones, as well as a guiding hand from the union, provided an excellent opportunity for players to educate, agitate, and organize one another to challenge league management.

Compromises around racial justice fought for and won by the union after the killing of Floyd in June were considered inadequate by many players: the league would commit to Black Lives Matter messaging throughout the remainder of the season, and players could choose pre-selected messaging around social justice to put on their Nike jerseys. The outrage, while simmering, was present. Players who would have preferred to wear blank jerseys were told they wouldn't be allowed to play. Despite the league's efforts to be "woke," including allowing kneeling for the anthem, painting "Black Lives Matter" on the court, and vague racial justice messaging, it's clear that it wasn't enough. Many players continued to express stress and dissonance with what they were doing versus what was happening across the United States.

It would be foolish to assume that all of the players were in complete agreement about what was going on outside of the bubble, or the steps that should be taken to address it. There's already a large diversity of opinions on police violence, police abolition, and police reform, both throughout the country and within major American sports leagues.

However, players presented a united front against league management. In the Milwaukee Bucks' statement to the public about withholding their labor, all players were present. Throughout the bubble games, nearly every player kneeled.

Also key, however, were opportunity, pressure, and demand. The NBA was slated to take a staggering loss on the season's Covid-19 interruption, and the bubble presented a last-second, three-point play to recoup economic losses. Every game counts. By instituting a stoppage of play at that moment, with all eyes on Kenosha, the players put the ball in the owners' court. Without knowing for sure, one suspects the Bucks' owner tried desperately to reach the governor's office.

Things may have been different if the NBA had allowed players to express themselves the way they wanted. As it was, the league scrambled to figure out what was going on, blindsided by a wildcat strike and lagging a step behind worker action.

The multi-sector nature of the strike was also the outcome of a well-seized opportunity. As previously noted, three other major leagues stopped play the same day. The largest two leagues, MLB and MLS, have nothing close to the political culture of the NBA, a league dominated by Black athletes who have historically been told to "shut up and dribble." The NBA is also smaller in terms of revenue than the MLB, but the MLB fell in line. A successful strike is not just a numbers game, it's also based on who is best to lead in the moment. The MLS and WNBA could not have done this on their own and made an impact, but their presence is obviously deeply felt as they withheld their labor in solidarity.

It's worth reasserting the timeline: four years. Good organizing, a good strike, and most importantly, a good outcome, is a confluence of time, effort, and opportunity. The time part is largely where organizing falters. You can't rush good organizing, and no grueling hour spent organizing is ever wasted.

A single aggrieved worker, four years ago, eventually led to an environment in which players can organize a total shutdown of three of North America's five largest sports leagues (plus one of the smaller ones).

What Now?

The collective bargaining agreement (CBA) between the NBA and the NBPA explicitly forbids strikes, and labor relations after 1964 have instead been marked by several lockouts, the most notable of which (a 190-day lockout in the late 1990s that forced the league to make major collective bargaining concessions) was considered a major loss for the union.

When the Milwaukee Bucks players walked, they were in flagrant breach of their CBA. But they're protected because it was a cohesive effort—they can't all be fired—and because the optics around workers being punished for reasons of justice would be disastrous for NBA management.

This upends the relationship between athletes and owners in significant ways, with the players flexing power outside the boundaries of their union, their CBA, and their own upper management.

After the wildcat strike on August 26, the superstar L.A. Clippers and L.A. Lakers voted to boycott the season, which had the potential to cancel the entire remainder of play. Those two teams, led by LeBron James and Kawhi Leonard, perhaps the two most dominant players currently in the sport, are at a revenue and audience level all their own.

Following a meeting of the NBA board of governors, and James holding an informal conversation with former President Barack Obama (in which Obama encouraged a return to play), there was an agreement to return to play, with concessions from the league. These concessions included the creation of a players' organization for racial justice, the conversion of stadiums into polling places, and an even greater emphasis on racial justice throughout the league's messaging. It's easy to see this as a loss, but it's an indicator of where the needle is moving and what institutional power exists to hold it back. James is 35 years old—and this strike was led by young players. Many players are still unhappy with the paradigm, and the balance of power has shifted towards players even further. It's an opening salvo of a power struggle within the NBA that will only escalate, not end, with this strike.

It's easy to point to this and indicate the degree of privilege these players hold. They are some of the most well-compensated in pro sports (due in no small part to their extraordinarily powerful union), but comparing player salaries to owner revenue largely shows a scaled-up version of a typical worker-manager pay imbalance.

It's still a management-worker paradigm, and the fundamentals of what led to this moment—a problem, management's inability to address this problem, difficult conversations on the shop floor, and a flashpoint that led to a total work stoppage—are repeatable in every workplace and in every sector. ❏

Note: A version of this article was published at Organizing Work (organizing.work).

Sources: Darren Dregger, "Will NHL players make their own statement by boycotting games?," TSN, (tsn.ca); NBA on ESPN, "Fred VanVleet frustrated with lack of progress on police brutality," August 25, 2020 (youtube.com); Robert Rubino, "1964 stars threatened to boycott game," The Press Democrat, Feb. 15, 2014 (pressdemocrat.com); Mark Riddix, "Top Pro Athlete Pension Plans," Investopedia, Nov. 27, 2019 (Investopedia.com); Tadd Haislop, "NBA bubble, explained: A complete guide to the rules, teams, schedule & more for Orlando games," Sporting News, August 26, 2020 (sportingnews.com); Justin Hickey, "Kyrie Irving Set Up Player Zoom Call Regarding NBA Bubble Concerns," Basketball Forever, June 13, 2020 (basketballforever); Scott Davis, "Bradley Beal is the latest NBA player to opt out of the 'bubble.' Here's who else is sitting out," Insider, July 7, 2020 (insider.com); Kurt Streeter, "W.N.B.A.'s Maya Moore to Skip Another Season to Focus on Prisoner's Case," *New York Times*, Jan. 22, 2020 (nytimes. com); Josh Weinstein, "Nurse: Some Raptors have pondered leaving bubble following Jacob Blake shooting," The Score, August 26, 2020 (thescore.com); Ashish Mathur, "Report: Bucks host call with Wisconsin Attorney General and Lieutenant Governor following Jacob Blake shooting," Clutch Points, August 26, 2020 (clutchpoints.com); Adam Wells, "NBA to Discuss with Players Kneeling During Anthem amid Injustice Protests," Bleacher Report, June 16, 2020 (bleacherreport.com); Ohm Youngmisuk, "Kenny Smith walks off TNT 'Inside the NBA' set in solidarity with player protest," ESPN, August 26, 2020 (espn.com); Matisse Thybulle, "Welcome to the Bubble-Day One," YouTube, July 9, 2020 (youtube.com); Matisse Thybulle, "Welcome To The Bubble - Episode #05," YouTube, July 26, 2020 (youtube.com); Lori Ewing, "Raptors coach Nick Nurse says players, staff in 'constant discussion' about protests," CBC, June 9, 2020 (cbc.ca); Elias Schuster, "NBA Players Are Starting to Voice Serious Concerns on Restarting the Season in Orlando," Bleacher Nation, June 12, 2020 (bleachernation.com); Nik DeCosta-Klipa, "Kyrie Irving is reportedly urging players to sit out the NBA's restart plan to press for racial justice reform," Boston.com, June 13, 2020 (boston.com); Steve Loung, "Raptors' Norman Powell 'disappointed' with NBA's jersey message options," Sports Net, July 16, 2020 (sportsnet. ca); Jonathan Sherman, "Video: Jimmy Butler Gets Denied by NBA Officials as He Tries to Play With Blank Jersey," Heat Nation, August 1, 2020 (heatnation.com); Ricky O'Donnell, "Paul George opened up about his mental health struggles in the NBA bubble," SBNation, August 26, 2020 (sbnation.com); Ben Golliver, "Why not everyone was kneeling during the NBA anthem," *Washington Post*, August 3, 2020 (washingtonpost.com); Emily Sullivan, "Laura Ingraham Told LeBron James To Shut Up And Dribble; He Went To The Hoop," NPR, The Two-Way, Feb. 19, 2018 (npr.org); Phil Taylor, "To the Victor Belongs the Spoils," Sports Illustrated, Jan. 18, 1999 (vault.si.com); Scott Polacek, "Report: Lakers, Clippers Voted Not to Finish Season After Jacob Blake Shooting," Bleacher Report, August 26, 2020 (bleacherreport.com).

CONTRIBUTORS

Frank Ackerman was the principal economist at Synapse Energy Economics in Cambridge, Mass., and one of the founders of *Dollars & Sense*. He died in July 2019.

Nicole Aschoff is a writer, editor, and sociologist. She is the author of *The New Prophets of Capital* (Verso, 2015), an editor-at-large at *Jacobin*, and managing editor of the Boston Institute for nonprofit journalism.

Dean Baker is co-director of the Center for Economic and Policy Research.

Peter Barnes is co-founder of Working Assets and is a senior fellow at the Tomales Bay Institute.

John Bellamy Foster is editor of *Monthly Review* and a sociology professor at the University of Oregon.

Mateo Crossa is a Ph.D. candidate in the Doctoral Program in Development Studies at the Universidad Autónoma de Zacatecas (México).

James M. Cypher is a *Dollars & Sense* Associate and a professor of economics in the Doctoral Program in Development Studies, Universidad Autónoma de Zacatecas (México).

Gerald Epstein is a professor of economics and co-director of the Political Economy Research Institute (PERI) at the University of Massachusetts-Amherst.

Nancy Folbre is emeritus professor of economics at the University of Massachusetts-Amherst. She contributes regularly to the *New York Times* Economix blog.

Ed Ford (co-editor of this book) is a retired economics professor from the University of South Florida.

Gerald Friedman is a professor of economics at the University of Massachusetts-Amherst.

Jayati Ghosh is a professor of economics at the University of Massachusetts-Amherst.

Elizabeth T. Henderson (co-editor of this book) is co-editor of *Dollars & Sense*.

Michelle Holder is an associate professor of economics at John Jay College, part of the City University of New York.

Janelle Jones is chief labor economist at the U.S. Department of Labor.

Sonali Kolhatkar is the founder, host, and executive producer of "Rising Up With Sonali," a television and radio show that airs on Free Speech TV and Pacifica stations.

Luis Feliz Leon is an organizer, journalist, and independent scholar in social movement history making good trouble in New York City.

Arthur MacEwan is a *Dollars & Sense* Associate and professor emeritus of economics at the University of Massachusetts-Boston.

Abdul Malik is a writer and IWW member based in Edmonton in Alberta, Canada..

John Miller is a *Dollars & Sense* collective member and a professor of economics at Wheaton College.

Sirisha Naidu is an associate professor of economics at the University of Missouri-Kansas City.

Jawied Nawabi is a professor of economics and sociology at CUNY Bronx Community College and a member of the *Dollars & Sense* collective.

Yeva Nersisyan is an associate professor of economics at Franklin and Marshall College.

Doug Orr teaches economics at the City College of San Francisco.

Amanda Page Hoongrajok is an assistant professor in the department of economics and finance at Saint Peter's University.

Thomas Palley is an economist and the author of *Financialization: The Economics of Finance Capital Domination* (Palgrave Macmillan, 2013).

Mark Paul is an assistant professor of economics at New College of Florida and a Fellow at the Roosevelt Institute.

Francisco Pérez is the director of the Center for Popular Economics and a Ph.D. candidate in economics at the University of Massachusetts-Amherst.

Robert Pollin teaches economics and is co-director of the Political Economy Research Institute at the University of Massachusetts-Amherst.

Smriti Rao is a professor of economics and global studies at Assumption University and is a resident scholar at the Women's Studies Research Center at Brandeis University.

Alejandro Reuss is a historian, economist, and former co-editor of *Dollars & Sense*.

John Schmitt is the vice president of the Economic Policy Institute.

Zoe Sherman is an associate professor of economics at Merrimack College and a member of the *Dollars & Sense* collective.

Bryan Snyder (co-editor of this book) is a senior lecturer in economics at Bentley University.

Intan Suwandi is an assistant professor of sociology at Illinois State University and the author of *Value Chains: The New Economic Imperialism* (Monthly Review Press, 2019).

Chris Tilly is a *Dollars & Sense* Associate and is director of the Institute for Research on Labor and Employment and a professor of urban planning, both at UCLA.

Ramaa Vasudevan is an assistant professor of economics at Colorado State University and a former *Dollars & Sense* collective member.

Jeannette Wicks-Lim is an assistant research professor at the Political Economy Research Institute at University of Massachusetts-Amherst.

Valerie Wilson is the director of the Economic Policy Institute's Program on Race, Ethnicity, and the Economy.

Marty Wolfson teaches economics at the University of Notre Dame and is a former economist with the Federal Reserve Board in Washington, D.C.

L. Randall Wray is a professor of economics at Bard College and senior scholar at the Levy Economics Institute at Bard.